No one brews Koffee &
conversation like Karan

DIAMOND BOOKS
www.dpb.in

ISBN : 81-288-1802-3

Published by

Diamond Pocket Books (P) Ltd.
X-30, Okhla Industrial Area, Phase - II
New Delhi - 110 020
Phone : 011-41611861
Fax : 011-41611866
E-mail : sales@dpb.in
Website : www.dpb.in

Edition : 2008

Printed at : Adarsh Printers, Delhi-110032

When you are the son of one of India's finest movie producer directors, it shows. When you have grown up with some of today's hottest heroes and heroines in Bollywood, it shows. When your passion for movies is exceeded only by your genius for churning out one blockbuster after another, it shows. It shows in every breath you take, and every move you make. Karan Johar is no ordinary movie director. True, he has directed some of the most entertaining productions of our time, and has been behind some of the biggest casting coups in history. True, his list of 'friends' make for a veritable 'Who's Who' from the Mumbai movie industry and is the envy of many. But his magic goes well beyond that. Like all true performers, he comes to life when you're least expecting it. Like all true greats, he comes alive when the moment demands it most. Turn on the arclights, cue the drumroll, and you've turned Karan Johar on. That's a special moment, for you know that it's countdown time: For action. For thrills. For, yes, magic.

And that is what Koffee with Karan, television's pioneering celebrity talkshow, is all about.

The favorite haunt of movers and shakers from both within and without Bollywood's privileged circles, this is a show that has treaded many firsts. It has pried open stars notorious for their reticence, it has completely redefined chatshows with its refreshing candour, and most significantly, it has made for hours and hours of top-of-the-line and edge-of-the-seat entertainment. In a world where masala is the watchword, Koffee with Karan is the indisputable garam-masala. If you've seen it once, you'll vouch for the tang, the zing, and the sizzle.

For those who haven't (you've got to be a rare bird!) or would like to relive those moments from TV one more time, we present this unique compilation – of those ground-breaking instants and rare scenes that have gone to make Koffee with Karan what it is - absolutely and unquestionably awesome!

So. Are you ready to open the hamper?

CONTENTS

Welcome to Koffee with Karan

Good evening. I remember at one time, I used to weight around 102 kilos with a 42-inch waistline. One day, my mother walked into my room. She held me by my face and said, 'Has anybody told you how good looking you are? You should be an actor or a model.' I thought my poor mother was going through a temporary bout of dementia. Had she popped one or two sleeping pills? Then, I realised that she was just being a mother. All mothers love their children. So mum, now that I am in front of the camera today, this show is just for you.

Like every other talk show, I will have a host of celebrities who will come and chat with me. But, *Star World* and I wanted to make the show a little more candid. We have attempted to make it conversational. I hope the caffeine offer on my show will be addictive!

1

Shahrukh & Kajol
Powerhouse Performers

My first guest tonight is someone I have known since I was 18 years old. Contrary to belief, Kajol is not my childhood friend. I still remember I was invited for a party organised by a magazine. I had lost a little bit of weight. I was 18 years old. So, I wore my new suit. I thought I appeared rather dapper. So I walked into this party and thought everyone would say, 'My God! Who is this kid on the block?'.

I was introduced to Kajol. She looked at me. Then she burst laughing! I stared at her and asked what was so funny. She replied, "I don't know whether you are funny or not, but you look really funny!' She continued laughing throughout night. She does that even today.

How do I introduce Kajol? I do not know what to say. If I really had to, then perhaps I would say that she is the best actress this generation has ever witnessed. She is the proud mother of a baby Nysa – the baby is a year-and-a-half old. She is the wife of a superstar. I would like to call on Kajol with lots of love and loads of emotion.

KAJOL

Karan Johar: Ah! Someone is looking very nice. How did you manage that?

Kajol: Thank you, Karan, and Mickey Contractor.

Karan Johar: Great going! You were always somebody who broke the tradition at every stage. You were not like the conventional heroines. You have shunned glamour. You went ahead and got married at the peak of your career. You have a beautiful child. Did you always want to break rules? Or were you just this way, mad?

> **I'm just mad, stubborn and hotheaded!**
>
> *–Kajol*

Kajol: I am just mad, stubborn, and hot headed!

Karan Johar: Kajol! Get serious. Are you really this kind of a person? Did you really want to break the rules? Do you always do what is not the obvious thing?

Kajol: No. I do what is the obvious thing for me; I do what I feel like doing. I do what I feel is right, more than anything else. That is why I did such things at every stage. It has really worked well in my career.

KAJOL: MARRIAGE VS CAREER

Karan Johar: When you married Ajay, you were considered as the numero uno actress. You had given huge hits for the industry and the fans. You went ahead and got married and shocked everybody. Everyone thought, 'What a tremendous loss!' Do you ever look at the marriage that way?

Kajol: No.

Karan Johar: Have you had any regrets?

Kajol: Never.

Karan Johar: You just wanted to get married?

Kajol: I wanted to get married. It was the right time in my career. I believed it was the right decision to take.

> **I do not feel that I have quit my career. I do not think I have missed anything.**
>
> *–Kajol*

Karan Johar: You have a great marriage. You have a beautiful baby. You are happy today. You are content with your life. You would not look back and find that you had lost many years of cinema?

Kajol: Not at all. I do not feel that I have quit my career. I do not think I have missed anything.

Karan Johar: Meanwhile, where did you really go?

Kajol: I wanted to have a baby after I finished *K3G*. I wanted to take some time out. I did not know how long it was going to be. May be it was my indecisiveness.

> **I wanted to have a baby after I finished *K3G*.**
>
> *–Kajol*

Karan Johar: You are open to coming back.

Kajol: I do not think that I ever left. I have always been interested in the film industry. That interest will always remain – whether I do movies or not. I think I have too many friends here to leave films completely.

Karan Johar: Every one really looks forward to see you. I get e-mails and letters from fans saying, 'We want to see Kajol with Shahrukh Khan.' I see it as part of the team's success.

Kajol: Definitely.

Karan Johar: Do you know that Shahrukh will be our next guest tonight? He needs no introduction. The trade thinks of him as the *Badshah of Bollywood*. Audience call him the King Khan. His wife quite often believes him to have a dual personality. Do you think so, too?

Kajol: A little mad, a little demented.

SHAHRUKH KHAN

Karan Johar: OK. We shall call the demented Shahrukh right on *Koffee with Karan*. Long time no see!

Shahrukh Khan: Yeah. We have not met for the last 20 minutes.

Karan Johar: We were just discussing about you. We came across this word – comeback. Did you ever think she was not around?

Shahrukh Khan: Kajol cannot go anywhere. Kajol is absolutely in the hearts, in the minds, in the memories, and in celluloid forever. I think that she is a beautiful living legend. I think she is simply stunning.

Kajol: Oh! So sweet! Thank you.

Karan Johar: OK. We have already wasted ten minutes. Is that really too much time? What do you think, Kajol?

Kajol: Not really. I am enjoying it.

Shahrukh Khan: We can go on and talk on this episode about Kajol.

Karan Johar: Could we talk about Shahrukh now?

Kajol: Yes, please!

SHAHRUKH ON STARDOM

Karan Johar: I am sure everyone wants to know – what does it feel to be Shahrukh Khan?

Shahrukh Khan: Nothing at all. I have been so for 38 years. It is quite easy to live with the entity – myself.

Karan Johar: You may look at it like that. A whole world got -completely mesmerized by you.

Shahrukh Khan: I find it completely funny and very odd. Perhaps, I find it very lucky that people think about me. I never pondered that I would do this for posterity or how I do things. I just keep working. I wake up in the morning and I keep working for the whole day. I could say 'thank you' to those people who like me a lot.

Karan Johar: Why do they like you so much?

Shahrukh Khan: A lot of people working with me also wonder why they like me so much.

> I feel I'm very lucky that people think of me.
> —*Shahrukh Khan*

Karan Johar: We have chatted on several occasions what both of you feel about yourselves.

Shahrukh Khan: We are very sexy!

Karan Johar: Yeah! In other words-

Kajol: We are not very good looking!

Shahrukh Khan: Yeah, we are very odd!

Kajol: No, we are attractive. We have a strong nose.

Karan Johar: You are not a good-looking couple. And yet-

Shahrukh Khan: We have this Caribbean and Latin sort of thing.

Kajol: That is right! We rock!

Karan Johar: Is that where your sex appeal lies?

Shahrukh Khan: Yeah!

Karan Johar: Do either of you ever wonder, 'how did I become such a big star?' You always knew it?

Shahrukh Khan: No, I did not.

Kajol: Look, I always knew that I was a great human being from the beginning. It took me a little time to discover myself. That is the end of it.

Karan Johar: Being humane has nothing to do with star quality! Shahrukh, did you feel that wonder?

> The day actors and stars believe their image is conditioned by public response, believe it or not, they are screwed up!
> –Shahrukh Khan

Shahrukh Khan: Yeah, I did. I know it sounds very clichéd. The kind of work we do as actors when we come on screen is a very serious thing. I believe this tends to be the philosophy of super-duper stardom. We are loved by a section of people. What they think about us is not because of our innate personality but because of the reflection from the screen. How they feel when they look at us – whether they are awed? Whether some of them think that we are the specific boy/girl next door? Or are we the people they want to take home? It is left to their assessment. It has nothing to do with us personally. The day actors and stars believe their image is conditioned by public response, believe it or not, they are screwed up!

Karan Johar: Do you agree, Kajol, with Shahrukh's philosophy?

Kajol: Yes. I also believe it is the effect of our personalities. I am not over emphasizing the fact. What we show onscreen connects the people to the roles we play. Or the way we react onscreen.

Shahrukh Khan: We look very normal onscreen, just like the average people.

Kajol: The whole point is to look normal, but not otherwise.

Karan Johar: Kajol! We are back to you. You were extremely laid-back about your career – things just happened to you. I recollect them as happy accidents, as opposed to Shahrukh's. You wanted this big mansion, you wanted to be the biggest star, and you wanted to be the industry's best. What do you feel about that?

Shahrukh Khan: I think she has worked very hard. I believe that I have worked positively in her career.

Karan Johar: I know that.

Shahrukh Khan: She has worked really hard. She has more honesty than I have.

> We look very normal onscreen, just like the average people.
> –Shahrukh Khan

Kajol: No.

Shahrukh Khan: No?

Kajol: You have definitely 300 per cent more energy and honesty than I ever had.

Shahrukh Khan: No. She has only done what she felt like. Similarly, I have done things, which I thought....

Karan Johar: She followed her instincts.

Shahrukh Khan: She only did what she felt was right. I have done things I believed to be right. I seem to be driven more by my conscience. She seems more laid-back.

Kajol: Yeah. We are pretty much...

Shahrukh Khan: 10/10!

ON CHEMISTRY

Karan Johar: Definitely; I would say you came 10/10 on screen. I mean you were outstanding in your roles. Let us analyse your chemistry.

Shahrukh commented amazingly in an interview. He said that he could make love to a cow onscreen and make it look sexy! It was a fabulous comment.

Karan Johar: What do you say about Kajol?

Kajol: That I was a cow, you dog...!

Shahrukh Khan: No, I was talking about my director's......

Karan Johar: That we were cows?

> I can make love to a cow onscreen and make it look sexy!
> –Shahrukh Khan

Shahrukh Khan: No. It is over-simplification; people do so when they watch films. 'This picture has worked.' 'It was a social drama.' 'The clothes draped were nice.' 'NRIs would like it a lot.' 'Their chemistry was lovely.' No. That is not the only truth. They are just simplifying things. There is a lot more that has gone in the films we have acted in. The producers remained on good terms with us. The roles and scenes befitted our skills.

Kajol: Yeah!

Shahrukh Khan: We started our career together. We were comfortable from the days of *Baazigar*. I recall reaching the set quite late. It was the New Year's Day. Nobody had landed there except Kajol. She was a little earlier than the imprisoned cameraman Thomas...

Kajol: Often Thomas was in jail.

Shahrukh Khan: She yelled in Marathi, which I could not appreciate. She told Ravi dada how late the hero was. We were all foggy and tired. We had slept at 6 a.m. She told him that I did not even talk.

> We started our career together. We were comfortable from the days of *Baazigar.*
> –Shahrukh Khan

Kajol: You might have prayed for me to stop talking!

Shahrukh Khan: Stop talking! It has been so for some years. We started off like that. I had never seen her film and she had never seen mine. The word is not chemistry – there was a lot of comfort and that comfort exudes chemistry and hence, love or romance or closeness. A lot of fondness might go beyond.

SHAHRUKH ON KAJOL

Karan Johar: The comfort zone and chemistry go hand-in-hand. Yes, that's true. Let us revert to *Baazigar.* You told me during the sets that Aamir called you once saying he wanted to sign Kajol. This took place after you spoke to me. You said that I should not touch her even with a bargepole!

Shahrukh Khan: No. The event took place after a few days. She does things off the cuff. She enacts with ease when acting a scene out, which I dislike. I dislike people who act like they were not acting. I called up Aamir and left a message on his answering machine. Kajol's eyes and her face just light up the damn screen. I used to say like Naseerudin Shah – not that I am comparing both of them. I have worked with him. He seems so easy and yet when the camera is turned on, he does something – he seems a different personality.

> I do not think Kajol is aware of how easily she emotes.
> –Shahrukh Khan

Karan Johar: He lights up the screen?

Shahrukh Khan: Yes. It is same with her. That is the nicest part about Kajol. She does not know that she does it – I do not think she is aware of how easily she emotes.

Karan Johar: Aamir had already replaced her with someone else but your opinion of Kajol had changed.

Shahrukh Khan: It was good for me – I have always had Kajol to work with in the films!

Kajol: Shahrukh lied that he is honest. During *Baazigar,* he would tell me to lie. He used to say, 'Why you are being so honest? Do not be so honest or earnest. You do not need to cry in every scene!'

Shahrukh Khan: She really did!

Karan Johar: Did she really break down in every scene?

Shahrukh Khan: Yes, except for one shot. It was a very sensual part of the song. We were very new. She had to sing "My heart is alone.." She was unable to do it honestly.

> During *Baazigar,* he would tell me to lie. 'Do not be so honest – you do not need to cry in every scene!'
> –Kajol

Karan Johar: That was not how she would react in real life.

Kajol: It was really over the top. I just could not get it. Then the timing or something would go wrong.

Shahrukh Khan: It was a shot. Seeing that she was unable to give the shot, Saroj Ji asked me to pinch her. I remember the shot went – it was like "My heart is alone.." and pinched her! That is how the shot was filmed!

ON AJAY DEVGAN

Karan Johar: It is quite evident that both of you share a great chemistry. On the other hand, you and Ajay are a real life couple but your chemistry never sizzled onscreen. Is this because of the comfort zone you share with Shahrukh?

Kajol: I have known Shahrukh for a longer period. I was rather uncomfortable with him in the early part of our friendship.

> I have known Shahrukh for a longer period. I was rather uncomfortable with Ajay in the early part of our friendship.
> –Kajol

Karan Johar: Have you considered him to be your boyfriend? Do you think it was awkward at first?

Kajol: It was not really so but it might have been a little comfortable. I cannot explain it.

Shahrukh Khan: I will explain. They were honest because they were in love. Honesty cannot be captured on camera. You have to act it out for the camera.

Karan Johar: All right. Has this comfort zone brought any domestic repercussions?

Karan Johar: Did it bother your husband Ajay?

Kajol: No, it never did.

Karan Johar: Never? There were rumours afloat of him not allowing you to work with Shahrukh. Were these rumours untrue?

Kajol: Yes.

Karan Johar: Do you want to bury those rumours?

> Most people disbelieve that a famous couple can be happy. Everybody has some problem or they will create one.
>
> *–Kajol*

Kajol: I think people will believe the worst. Most people disbelieve a famous couple can be happy. Everybody has some problem or they will create one.

Karan Johar: People wrote about a rumour that Ajay had a problem with Shahrukh. Maybe it was due to your onscreen chemistry?

Kajol: No. He did not have any problem.

Shahrukh Khan: I did not have any problem with Ajay. I admit that whenever we met (which was very rare), he has been very cordial and very sweet. I am glad that I have recently met him after so many years. We hit it off very well. I would like to warn Ajay about the problems he will face when my son Aryan would want to take Nysa out for a date!

Kajol: Hey, right!

Shahrukh Khan: That will be the time when he will beat the hell out of me!

Kajol: Aryan is going to be a motorcycle dude!

Karan Johar: Will this be the case when Aryan woos Nysa?

Shahrukh Khan: I think when Ajay comes to know, he is going to jump on a trampoline and beat me!

Karan Johar: Let us revert to domestic repercussions. You have tried to maintain every relationship. Did you want to keep your friendships before marriage away from your married life? Ajay came from a different kind of friend-circle. Did you not want to blend the two?

Kajol: No, it was not really so. It was just the fact that he is a social with the people who know him. Otherwise, he is polite, but sometimes not. He does not make friends very easily. Neither has he

> Ajay does not make friends very easily.
>
> *–Kajol*

the time to do so or to cultivate a new social circle. I like to maintain a distance between different sets of friends. It is OK as long as I do not have to spend too much time with either set. So, I was fine too.

Karan Johar: He is Kajol's husband. We have worked together. Shahrukh and I co-produced this film where he was in the lead role. I got to know him much later.

Kajol: I do not like the fact that you like him. You are my friends. You belong to me.

Shahrukh Khan: It shows what a lovely marriage they have – she can have her own circle without bothering that her husband is away from her and it is the same for him. It is evident how much mutual trust and love they have. I understand and appreciate that kind of relation.

Karan Johar: It is quite amazing. You know that you were a frequent visitor to Shahrukh-Gauri's house or mine. He never came with you. You have your friends and he has his own. You both are a couple; still, you can lead your separate lives.

Kajol: Ajay was very categorical. He told me to spend time with family and friends as and when I found the opportunity. He worked continuously even after our marriage.

Shahrukh Khan: Now you are exaggerating. You mean to say we sat idle when he worked continuously?

> **Ajay told me to spend time with family and friends as and when I found the opportunity.**
> *–Kajol*

Kajol: But seriously, he was!

Shahrukh Khan: Were we not doing work before? Say something else other than his work!

Karan Johar: We have set those things straight. Ajay has no problem with Shahrukh or me. He has loads of fun. And he is a good father. Shahrukh, you too are a tremendous father.

ON PARENTHOOD

Karan Johar: Shahrukh and Kajol, how does it feel after Nysa, Aryan and Suhaana – a decade of association and now with three children between you? How does it feel being a parent?

Shahrukh Khan: I know I am going to repeat what she will say. Either of us would give the same answer.

Kajol: I think it is the best feeling in the world – nothing can be

> **It is the best feeling in the world – nothing can be compared to it!**
> *–Kajol*

compared to it! Everything you say or think in your life will be touched by one person in your life.

Karan Johar: Shahrukh, I was there when Aryan was born. I saw you weeping when Gauri developed some medical complications. You were not bothered about the child – you just wanted to save Gauri. Today, when I see you, it is just Aryan.

Shahrukh Khan: You know the decision to have a child is to let a piece of your heart walk outside your body. Heart is something we are very close to. It is a wonderful feeling to allow that.

Kajol: Nobody knows – nobody tells about your feeling towards your child until you have one.

Karan Johar: It was like that when Aryan was born.

Shahrukh Khan: But it would be very wrong to interpret that they saved the child and let the wife go – you cannot do that.

Karan Johar: Today, Aryan and Suhaana dominate your life. Do you think Gauri has taken a back seat?

> **The decision to have a child is to let a piece of your heart walk outside your body.**
> *–Shahrukh Khan*

Shahrukh Khan: I think everybody and everything – even work – took a back seat in life, as far as the kids were concerned.

Kajol: Nothing could replace them other than parents.

Shahrukh Khan: Absolutely; nothing compares to it! Even with my body, I would not mind going around in tight jeans just for Aryan.

On 'Devdas'

Karan Johar: Shahrukh, I read what Sanjay Leela said about you two years back, 'Shahrukh has sorrowful eyes. He looks like a loner. He craves for love.' It sounded a bit sad.

Shahrukh Khan: And you sound like Simi!

Karan Johar: Do you agree with Sanjay Leela Bhansali?

Kajol: That you are craving for love? Please let me know!

> **Sanjay did say that I had perfect Devdas eyes!**
> *–Shahrukh Khan*

Shahrukh Khan: You should know about this, Kajol, when I crave for love! I think people perceive it when someone is longing for love. Some people think there must be something more between the actor and actress than just singing and dancing – and fluffy hair!

Kajol: And now it stands up!

Shahrukh Khan: I need to gel my hair. I do not know how or why, but people ascribe that I am lonely and I am craving for love and stuff like that.

Kajol: No, I do not think you are lonely or you crave for love. There are many people around you 24×7. It will be difficult for you to feel so.

Karan Johar: You belong to the kind of *"Bheed Mein Tanhayi..."* You know, so many people, yet...

Shahrukh Khan: Like 'those who smile are sad'. It is nice to romanticize so. Sanjay did say that I do remind him a lot of Devdas. He did say that my eyes..

Karan Johar: That you were the perfect Devdas!

Shahrukh Khan: Yeah!

Kajol: He said you were a perfect alcoholic. Are you?

Shahrukh Khan: No.

ON EACH OTHER

Karan Johar: I can vouch for you. Kajol, how do you think of Shahrukh as a person? If you had to say something about him, how do you react? How do you perceive him?

Kajol: He is super-intelligent. He is a very warm human being. He creates so much warmth, energy, light and fun. I believe him as someone who could be depended upon.

> Shahrukh is super-intelligent and a very warm human being. He creates much warmth, energy, light and fun!
>
> *–Kajol*

Karan Johar: Do you agree with the result of the recent poll, which described him as the sexiest person?

Kajol: Second only to my husband!

Shahrukh Khan: That's because he works harder!

Karan Johar: Do you think she is sexy?

Shahrukh Khan: I believe so – amazingly! She is very good looking and she is unaware of this trait – that makes it nice. It will be so.

When you perceive heroines in general, they are attractive, good looking and possess wonderful qualities. And that's why they are there. Most of the actors have wonderful qualities. I think Kajol's rawness has not diminished over the years. She is attractive, pretty, nice and good-looking.

Kajol: I still have not acquired those traits that I should have.

Karan Johar: She is clumsy. She keeps falling all the time.

Shahrukh Khan: She met with an accident when she fell in *Kuch Kuch Hota Hai.* She lost her memory!

Karan Johar: Had she lost her memory? She might have thought herself to be someone else.

Kajol: I did not think I was somebody else. You are lying – do not lie!

Shahrukh Khan: She was like 'Who are you?'

> **She is very good looking and she is unaware of this trait – that makes it nice.**
> *–Shahrukh Khan*

Karan Johar: She asked, 'What am I doing here? Who am I?' She fell off the bicycle while shooting a college song.

Shahrukh Khan: We were worried that we would have to re-shoot everything and that we would have had to re-teach her what she had done in the film. We took her to a hotel room so that she could be alright. She woke up to say 'What happened? Who am I? What is this? Where are we?'

Karan Johar: We told her that she was a dancer.

Shahrukh Khan: It was a sort of true love that came out when we made her speak.

Karan Johar: Yeah, she kept asking for Ajay. She remembered him and forgot everybody else. Do you remember?

Kajol: No, I don't.

Rapid Fire

Karan Johar: I have what I call the rapid fire round. A volley of questions will be thrown at you. Now there's a time limit. You cannot think too long.

Kajol: OK.

Karan Johar: I am the judge. Whoever answers very well will win the *Koffee hamper.*

Shahrukh Khan: I would give my life to get that hamper. What a lovely gift you are giving us!

Karan Johar: I will ask Kajol first. A quality you hate about Ajay?

Kajol: Unsocial.

Karan Johar: A quality you hate about Shahrukh?

Kajol: Nothing really.

Karan Johar: A quality Ajay hates about Shahrukh?

Kajol: Nothing really.

Karan Johar: **Do you think any actress is better than you in this generation?**
Kajol: **No.**

Karan Johar: Do you think any actress is better than you in this generation?

Kajol: In this generation? No.

Karan Johar: Do you think Rani Mukherjee is a good actress?

Kajol: Yes.

Karan Johar: Which actor would make the worst Prime Minister of India?

Kajol: Govinda.

Karan Johar: Which actor do you think will make the best prime minister?

Kajol: None.

Karan Johar: Should an actor be a Prime Minister?

Kajol: No. Actually, I should say, yes.

Karan Johar: But you said so just now when I asked about the Prime Minister!

Kajol: .He/she should be an actor. I did not say that he should belong to the film industry!

Karan Johar: So you think he needs to be a good actor?

Kajol: Yes.

Karan Johar: One word you would use for a critic?

Kajol: Sharp.

Karan Johar: A film in recent times that you wish you had done?

Karan Johar: **Which actor would make the worst Prime Minister of India?**
Kajol: **Govinda.**

Kajol: Nothing really.

Karan Johar: If you were in *Kal Ho Na Ho,* the film would be.. Complete the sentence.

Shahrukh Khan: Can I? *Kal Ho Na Ho, lekin parson to hoga!*

Karan Johar: If you were in *Kal Ho Na Ho,* the film would be...

Kajol: *Kuch Kuch Hota Hai.*

Karan Johar: What do you mean by that?

Kajol: The character in *Kal Ho Na Ho* was very much like my character in *Kuch Kuch Hota Hai.*

Karan Johar: Who do you believe to be an overrated actress?

Kajol: Myself.

Karan Johar: According to you, who is the most overrated actor?

Kajol: I think most of the new guys.

> *Karan Johar:* **If you were in** *Kal Ho Na Ho*, **Kajol, the film would be...**
> *Shahrukh Khan: Kal Ho Na Ho, lekin parson to hoga!*

Karan Johar: The best book you have ever read?

Kajol: There are too many to count.

Karan Johar: The sexiest man alive in India.

Shahrukh Khan: I will give you the Koffee hamper.

Kajol: It is my husband, hands down!

Karan Johar: Madhuri Dixit or Sridevi?

Kajol: Sridevi.

Karan Johar: Preity Zinta or Kareena Kapoor?

Kajol: Kareena Kapoor.

Karan Johar: Sanjay Bhansali or Farhan Akhtar?

Kajol: Farhan Akhtar.

Karan Johar: Hrithik Roshan or Abhishek Bachchan?

Kajol: Abhishek.

Karan Johar: Karan Arjun or Karan Johar?

Shahrukh Khan: I think Karan Arjun.

Kajol: I like Karan Arjun definitely!

Karan Johar: Ajay Devgan or Shahrukh Khan?

Shahrukh Khan: You will not get the Koffee hamper, so say it!

Kajol: Ajay Devgan.

Karan Johar: OK. Kajol, I am very, very disappointed because your rapid fire was invalid. You just see how Shahrukh answers!

Kajol: Yes, I want to see how Shahrukh answers!

Shahrukh Khan: I will answer like

> *Karan Johar:* **The sexiest man alive in India.**
> *Kajol:* **It is my husband, hands down!**

Kajol. I have already won, sweetheart. I don't even have to answer.

Karan Johar: What nonsense?

Shahrukh Khan: I can have a heart attack, so better go easy on me.

Karan Johar: This is rapid fire! Describe an actor in one word.

Shahrukh Khan: Passionate.

Karan Johar: One word to describe Shahrukh Khan.

Shahrukh Khan: Immense. I cannot use the word 'passionate'.

Karan Johar: Is Shahrukh Khan the best actor in the country?

Shahrukh Khan: In the world.

Karan Johar: Describe an actor in one word.
Shahrukh Khan: Passionate.
Karan Johar: One word to describe Shahrukh Khan.
Shahrukh Khan: Immense. I cannot use the word 'passionate'.

Karan Johar: Is Kajol the best actress in the country?

Shahrukh Khan: In the universe.

Karan Johar: Then what would you say to Juhi, Aishwarya and Sushmita?

Shahrukh Khan: That there are more galaxies in the world!

Karan Johar: An Indian film you wish you were a part of?

Shahrukh Khan: *Sholay*.

Karan Johar: An Indian film you wish you weren't a part of?

Shahrukh Khan: *Kuch Kuch Hota Hai.*

Kajol: You take the hamper – I am gifting it to you!

Karan Johar: Is Gauri the sexiest woman alive in India?

Shahrukh Khan: No. It is Maharani Gayatri Devi.

Karan Johar: Is Shahrukh Khan the best actor in the country?
Shahrukh Khan: In the world!
Karan Johar: Is Kajol the best actress in the country?
Shahrukh Khan: In the universe!
Karan Johar: Then what would you say to Juhi, Aishwarya and Sushmita?
Shahrukh Khan: That there are more galaxies in the world!

Karan Johar: Women find Shahrukh Khan attractive and desirable because... Complete the sentence.

Shahrukh Khan: Of my lonely intense eyes which crave for love!

Karan Johar: Men find Shahrukh attractive and desirable because...

Shahrukh Khan: Of my lonely, passionate craving nose.

Karan Johar: So, do they find your nose sexy?

Shahrukh Khan: I think they do.

Karan Johar: What would you say to a die-hard Aamir Khan fan?

Shahrukh Khan: 'Guys, you got to find an icon you could look up to.'

Karan Johar: What would you say to a die-hard Salman fan?

Shahrukh Khan: I would say, 'God bless you!'

Karan Johar: A piece of advice to Karan Johar would be..

Shahrukh Khan: Start making some cool films, please, of which I am a part.

Kajol: That was low.

Shahrukh Khan: But I am supposed to be like that.

Karan Johar: The strange rumour about yourself?

Karan Johar: **The strange rumour about yourself?** *Shahrukh Khan:* **The strangest thing people wonder about me is whether I am a homosexual or bisexual! You know, I cannot have two kids by heavy petting!**

Shahrukh Khan: The strangest thing people wonder about me is whether I am a homosexual or bisexual!

Karan Johar: So, that is the strangest rumour you have heard about yourself?

Shahrukh Khan: Yeah. You know, I cannot have two kids by heavy petting!

Karan Johar: The year when you don't have the awards?

Shahrukh Khan: I'll always assert that awards don't deserve me.

Karan Johar: Aryan or Gauri?

Shahrukh Khan: Aryan.

Karan Johar: Aishwarya or Sushmita?

Shahrukh Khan: Both.

Karan Johar: Critics or politicians.

Shahrukh Khan: Critics.

Karan Johar: Ram Gopal Verma or Mani Ratnam?

Shahrukh Khan: Mani Ratnam.

Karan Johar: Juhi or Madhuri?

Shahrukh Khan: Juhi.

Karan Johar: That will be the end of my *Rapid Fire*. I am very pleased to announce that both of you to have lost.

Shahrukh Khan: But, why? I gave you all the answers. Just because said *Kuch Kuch Hota Hai*?

Kajol: Basically, you don't get the hamper. I don't get the award because I did not answer well.

Karan Johar: Nobody will get that hamper. I am sorry.

Kajol: Is it such a great hamper that you want to keep it to yourself?

Shahrukh Khan: No. I am not going without this hamper.

Karan Johar: Nobody wins this hamper.

Kajol: We were bitchy to Karan. So, we have not won the hamper. We have to ask some questions.

Karan Johar: Yes. That is what the whole round is about.

Kajol: OK, Karan! I would like to talk about your wardrobe. The day you first met me with a three-piece suit in a disco party, you were often told to have looked quite handsome. But you looked completely out of place in it. Everyone else was so casual and Karan arrived in a three-piece suit, complete with a vest – You asserted that you looked so cool.

> **I am not going without this hamper!**
> –*Shahrukh Khan*

Karan Johar: I thought I was looking wonderful. My mother told me so; she said I was looking great.

Kajol: She is your mother. Obviously, she thought you often looked great.

Karan Johar: Your turn now, Shahrukh.

Shahrukh Khan: My questions are simple. Rank the following directors in order that you like.

Kajol: Oh! I love this. That is very nice Shahrukh. Go for it.

Karan Johar: Oh God!

Shahrukh Khan: Mr. Yash Chopra, Mr Sanjay Leela Bhansali, Mr. Farhan Akhtar, Mr. Ashutosh Gowariker....

Kajol: Aditya Chopra.

Shahrukh Khan: And Aditya Chopra.

Karan Johar: No, that is not fair.

Kajol: Why?

Karan Johar: You cannot include Aditya Chopra.

Kajol: Karan Johar?

Shahrukh Khan: Farah Khan?

Karan Johar: That is too big. There are eight of them. That is quite a big list. I cannot really be a part.

Kajol: Why?

Shahrukh Khan: Choose any five of them.

Karan Johar: How can I be a part of this?

Kajol: Choose any five.

Karan Johar: How can I?

Kajol: What do you mean? This is your rapid fire round. You have to answer!

Shahrukh Khan: You asked many things about actresses and Salman.

Kajol: About Ajay.

Shahrukh Khan: About babies. You do not get the hamper – give it here!

Karan Johar: Yash Chopra, Sanjay Leela Bhansali, Farah, Karan Johar. I included Farah because she is a dear friend and senior to me by one film.

Shahrukh Khan: See, you are sweating a little. You are not giving any answer.

Karan Johar: OK. My list is Yash Chopra is number one. That is it. A little bit of request, though. It was wonderful to have spent appreciable time with you.

Shahrukh Khan: No, I am not taking off my clothes on this show!

Karan Johar: I know Kajol cannot do it and neither can you. I know you do a better job. I want you to sing a song to Kajol. Preferably, you should sing one of your romantic songs in a beautiful baritone voice.

Shahrukh Khan: I can sing it. 'Don't leave me yet because my heart is not full yet.' More?

Karan Johar: Yes.

Shahrukh Khan: 'You have just come. You are just like paradise.'

Karan Johar: It sounds really strange. I feel really very emotional after the show. I really feel I am sitting in this chair because of you both. I mean that with all my heart.

Kajol: You mean to say that if we were not here....

Karan Johar: No. I mean to say that we are doing *Koffee with Karan*. I am Karan, because of the two films I have directed. You are the reason behind the success of *Kuch Kuch Hota Hai* and *Kabhi Khushi Kabhi Gham*.

Shahrukh Khan: I would like to say what Kajol and I feel at this time. The success is all yours. We thank you from the bottom of our hearts. This show is very funny and nice. It will surely do well. We reciprocate with the love you gave us onscreen. Thank you for the role played by Karan.

Karan Johar: Thank you. I think I am going to die on this show.

Kajol: No. You have done a lot for us, Karan. You are talking about a body of work you brought us together to work for.

Shahrukh Khan: Do you remember the shot in *Kuch Kuch Hota Hai*, Karan, when Rani comes in draped in a white sari at the end? If we continue talking like this, Simi....

Kajol: She will come! No. Thank you. Do a quick favour – you will find a little mug next to you. It is a memento from the show *Koffee with Karan*. Please remember – this personally autographed mug could be yours only if you answer these questions. Thank you very much. Thank you for being on *Koffee with Karan*. This is our first episode. This heralds a new season. Thank you. Now, we will walk towards what I call the koffee wall.

● ● ●

2

Rani and Kareena
Sailing in the Same Boat

We started our careers around the same time. My first guest tonight is Rani Mukherjee. I still remember – Shahrukh and Kajol were on board when I cast *Kuch Kuch Hota Hai*. Only the role of Tina was not cast. I approached every film heroine I could think of – Tabu, Twinkle Khanna, Aishwarya Rai, Raveena Tandon, Urmila Matondkar, et al. They heard my narration of shots, story, action, romance, etc. They loved to hear me, but refused to participate. Rani Mukherjee replied yes. I had one look at her and said, 'Oh my God! How is she going to pull off as the college bomb? She neither has the best physique nor the requisite height. How am I going to manage this film?' She accepted the challenge. You have seen *Kuch Kuch Hota Hai*. She is a brilliant actress now and continues to be my dear friend – Rani Mukherjee!

RANI MUKHERJEE

Karan Johar: Hello darling! Welcome to my show! How do you feel to be interviewed by me?

Rani Mukherjee: It is awkward.

Karan Johar: Yes – because you are a phone call away.

Rani Mukherjee: We chat all the time on the phone. It is quite strange – the scene of sitting on that formal sofa and…

Karan Johar: Looking really glamorous..

Rani Mukherjee: Yes!

THE LULL

Karan Johar: So, I will ask what *Star World* wants to know from you. You have been through this whimsical career where it was interrupted by a sudden lull. You know, there was what I call the B-Brigade – there was a *Badal*, a *Bichchoo* - none of the films did really well. Suddenly, there was a talk – 'where's Rani Mukherjee?' How did you feel around that time?

Rani Mukherjee: I have learnt a lot while working in those films. It is very important for an actress to act in such films. So I guess I have gone through an elevated phase, where I had comfortable roles befitting my skills. I wondered whether I could do a variety of roles. I was rather lucky to have worked with wonderful stars and directors. I came to know artistes like Salman, Anil Kapoor and Bobby during this phase. I shared a great rapport and time working with them. People found my potential during that time. I have enjoyed all their acclaim and criticism.

Karan Johar: Would you now look back and label them as mistakes or interpret them as a commercial move?

Rani Mukherjee: They might be so, because they did not fare as well as they were supposed to. It was an acid test when you work in such films and professionals like judge them. So I guess I have enjoyed them and I will never regret such decisions because I feel they are a part of my career or a part of my journey. These were the films that made me grow. I have made mistakes and learnt quite well through those films.

> **The people found my potential during the time when I was doing so called B-grade films!**
> –Rani Mukherjee

Karan Johar: So then, they are mistakes!

Rani Mukherjee: No! The mistakes that I have made – as in my performance or clothes.

Karan Johar: So, do you feel that you have learnt a lot from those mistakes?

> *Films like Bichchoo and Badal made me grow as an actress.*
> *–Rani Mukherjee*

Rani Mukherjee: Yes. I believe we were not really quality-conscious. You want to work because you have just joined the industry. What really makes the image of an artist? It is acting in a lot of films around the clock. I would sit back and think that I would do one film a year, or may be two. That is what the monster time permits. I just wanted to work. I think that was a trial-and-error period. I think I have enjoyed it. Today, I want to be selective.

KAREENA KAPOOR

Karan Johar: Yes. The next guest tonight is a superstar. She is not really very selective! I am talking about Kareena Kapoor. She knew that she is a stunner – glamorous and beautiful. I met her in *Kabhi Khushi Kabhi Ghum* during the Bombay Times Party many years ago. She was standing, just looking like a super star. I told her she is my 'Poo'. And nothing has changed even today. What you cannot deny that Kareena Kapoor is that she is a superstar in every possible mode. Rani! Do you agree?

> **Kareena Kapoor is a star – you cannot take that away from her!**
> *–Rani Mukherjee*

Rani Mukherjee: Absolutely! She is a star. You cannot take that away from Kareena Kapoor.

Karan Johar: Let us attribute her as the most glamorous heroine of the film fraternity today – Kareena Kapoor! Welcome to my show, darling!

Kareena Kapoor: Thank you!

THE MIXED BAG

Karan Johar: We were just chatting. Rani was articulating how she is selective today. Do you think you will become so, too? You told me in the negative. Correct me if I am wrong.

Kareena Kapoor: Yes, you are absolutely right. I do not want to bank on one film a year. I have followed the policy (very sincerely) of Sridevi, Madhuri Dixit and Karishma Kapoor. They have done some fifty films at a time. A few have worked leaving others to flop. I believe in that strategy. I will proceed with that concept.

Karan Johar: So, you disagree with Rani's theory of banking on a couple of films?

Kareena Kapoor: Well, the films that she has are bankable. I mean she has been working with stalwarts like Yash-ji and Sanjay Leela Bhansali, Karan Johar. She has the right set of films. I have been doing a mixed bag.

Karan Johar: Do you think that works fair enough for you because you are a superstar today?

Kareena Kapoor: I do not know!

Karan Johar: Don't you think that you are a star today? I have heard of the fees you charge that only superstars charge and the fact that you get it – that means you deserve it.

> **Flops are a part of one's career graph except for Karan (Johar)– he is the lucky one!**
> –Kareena Kapoor

Kareena Kapoor: That is what I believe. You know I had only a few success. I make no bones about saying that. Later, twelve films flopped. Well, flops are a part of one's career graph and Rani; even you have had them. Karan, you have not got any. Then you are the lucky one!

Karan Johar: Well, I am a director, so that is fine.

Kareena Kapoor: I wish you made twelve films. It would have been possible for me to star in atleast two of them!

On Friendship

Karan Johar: Are you both friends?

Rani Mukherjee: Yes, we are!

Kareena Kapoor: Of course, we are!

Karan Johar: I have a lie-o-meter. I use it whenever I feel someone is lying.

Kareena Kapoor: I would like to correct that we are not the best of friends. We might not talk for five or six months. She might get pissed off with me. I might get pissed off with her. Rani has been there at times where she has seen me crying, which I will never forget. So, she plays an important part in my life. She will always be in my memory.

Karan Johar: So, let us put this way that there is a comfort zone. Are Kareena Kapoor and Rani Mukherjee friends? So let us find how the two entangled together.

Kareena Kapoor: Oh God!

Rani Mukherjee: Kareena and I are friends. Kareena is real. That is what I love about her.

> *Kareena Kapoor:* **We are not the best of friends.**
> *Rani Mukherjee:* **Kareena is real – that is what I love about her.**

Karan Johar: That she is. She is honest. Do you believe two actresses can be really good friends?

Rani Mukherjee: Not all the time.

Karan Johar: Let me go back to you, Kareena. You had a friendship with Esha Deol. It does not exist today.

Kareena Kapoor: Of course, it does!

> **I would rather not be close friends with an actress!**
> *–Kareena Kapoor*

Karan Johar: Oh! I just spoke to her the day before her flight from Canada.

Kareena Kapoor: She was shooting for *Dus*.

Karan Johar: You speak to a lot of people – are they all your friends?

Kareena Kapoor: Not all are my friends. Esha is a friend. We do not have time to really keep in touch.

Karan Johar: Would you rather not be close friends with an actress?

Kareena Kapoor: Yes. Not really close.

Karan Johar: That is what I ought to hear. Bravo! Well done! Do you agree, Rani?

Rani Mukherjee: No, not really.

Karan Johar: You and Aishwarya had a friendship. I believe that it exists?

Rani Mukherjee: You know the reasons. I have no problems with anybody. I do not have any personal problem with Ash. I think maybe Ash might be having some. We have stopped talking over the phone. I have not really met her at

> **I guess that when Ash and I meet, we shall quarrel with each other!**
> *– Rani Mukherjee*

any social party. I guess that when we meet, we shall quarrel with each other. If the actresses (like us) could be friends, we could be so. It is not as if they could not. You have to be clear in your mind. You should not be insecure. You could go on like that.

Karan Johar: Sure, I understand that.

THE GREEN-EYED MONSTER

Karan Johar: Let us take both of you. Rani, clearly, has been successful in the recent past. There had been *Chalte Chalte* followed by *Hum Tum. Saathiya* was a commercial success. You, Kareena, were very good in *Yuva*, but very honestly when you see Rani you say. 'Oh! My God! She is suddenly emerging' – does that bother you?

Kareena Kapoor: I do not think so. I have survived through the worst.

Rani Mukherjee: I do not think hits and flops will matter other than friendship. I think it is strange. Every actress has her own career graph. The way I have started my career graph will end up at a certain point. Kareena's career graph is different. So we cannot have similar career graphs. I might do certain kind of films; she will do different films. It does not connote that something wrong has happened with me if she gives a hit and vice-versa. We can be friends and survive in the industry. There is so much of work for everybody.

> **My genre of films? Bad films! Saying no to good films and saying yes to the bad ones!**
> *–Kareena Kapoor*

Karan Johar: That sounds very theoretical. Does it really apply? I mean, when you have a Kareena Kapoor success in your phase, don't you say 'Oh my God! Is that success taking me away from my position?' Isn't everyone very competitive? I know I am. I will get very much affected when I see the film of another director – and not in a very negative way; it is just in a competitive way.

Rani Mukherjee: It is like when you see a certain film you have liked the actress. If you watch a very great film, you just feel like. 'Wow! I wish I were in that.' But it does not mean that I want that. I have my share of good things happening and so does other actresses.

Kareena Kapoor: I feel that both Rani and I come from different genres altogether.

Karan Johar: What is your genre? I would like to know.

Kareena Kapoor: Bad films! Saying no to good films and saying yes to the bad ones! Rani signs the right films while doing so.

Karan Johar: Do you think you have the kind of space and place in the industry?

Kareena Kapoor: I have started three to four years late.

Karan Johar: So, you are saying that Rani is a senior?

Kareena Kapoor: No, she is not. I mean..

Karan Johar: She's older.

Kareena Kapoor: No! We are of the same age, I think, isn't it, Rani?

Rani Mukherjee: May be, more or less.

Karan Johar: Would you like to address heroines as senior actresses?

Kareena Kapoor: Oh God!

Karan Johar: OK. When you see a great performance of Rani Mukherjee and the success of the film, does it not affect you? Both of you were pitted against each other in *Yuva*. Did you want to check each other out when you watched the film? Did you believe you were better than Rani Mukherjee and Esha Deol? Or did you just want to see your individual performance? Be honest! I have my lie-o-meter!

Kareena Kapoor: I just wanted to see what kind of film Mani Ratnam has made.

Karan Johar: You went to check out Mani Ratnam?

Kareena Kapoor: No. I went to

> **When I went to see *Yuva*, I had reached that stage where I had just wanted the film to run – nothing else!**
> *–Kareena Kapoor*

see the movie. I am a big fan and admirer. I wanted to see what kind of film he has made.

Karan Johar: So you did not want to see whether you were better than Rani or vice-versa?

Kareena Kapoor: I have reached that stage where I have just wanted the film to run. I wanted to go and see it on that count. I had no interest in who was in the movie! Indeed, I am honest!

Karan Johar: OK. Well done! And you, Rani – did you get to see your individual performance? Did you think you were the best heroine in the film?

Rani Mukherjee: I am self-obsessed. So, I guess I went to see how I had done. Also, I went to see how the film was with three stories blended together. I did not have any clue about such concept. I knew what Abhishek and I had done because I had just shot for that.

Karan Johar: OK. *Mujhse Dosti Karoge* was clearly the other film you did together. Perhaps that was where your bonding might have commenced?

> **Karan and I will finally get married some day!**
> *–Rani Mukherjee*

Rani Mukherjee: Actually, I met Bebo much before at a *Filmfare* party, where she came along with Lolo. She had not even joined the films.

Karan Johar: Was she junior to you?

Rani Mukherjee: No. I loved Kareena from the beginning.

Karan Johar: I know that there was a genuine affection.

GRAPEVINE

Karan Johar: The alleged romantic link-ups concerning both of you haven't really affected you. For example, Rani, you and I have been rumoured to have married (if you remember).

Rani Mukherjee: We will finally get married some day.

Karan Johar: My God! Is that a proposal? What do I do? Go down on your knees, darling! No, but there have been rumours. There has been Aamir, Govinda and similar kind of rumours. Does that make you feel awkward with those actors when you come across them? Govinda is a married man. How does that affect you?

Rani Mukherjee: It does not make me feel awkward. I guess the press should be more responsible.

Karan Johar: You mean they report without getting the facts. Yes. I think actresses are always pitted against these kinds of rumours. I think what we need to

> **If somebody asks you about a rumour, just look through them!**
> *–Kareena Kapoor*

do is just to ignore them. You have to come home and find out the results. You have to be answerable to our parents. You should do our work and get back to the reality. So, it doesn't affect you?

Rani Mukherjee: No.

Karan Johar: What about you, Kareena?

Kareena Kapoor: I think that one had to learn to switch off after sometime. You have to get accustomed to the state

> **Shahid brings a smile to my face and a twinkle to my eyes!**
> –Kareena Kapoor

of developments. If somebody asks, you just look through them. You have to be cruel. That's the only way.

Karan Johar: Do you believe that no one should intrude into personal life?

Kareena Kapoor: Absolutely.

Karan Johar: OK. I am sorry I am intervening today – that is the vibe of the show. We are here to have fun. So nothing is too serious. So, rumours galore! I do not know the reality behind the current rumour. Please correct me – are you seeing Shahid Kapoor?

Kareena Kapoor: Yes. He is someone who plays a very special role in my life. He brings a smile to my face and a twinkle to my eyes. So he is that someone special.

Karan Johar: OK. Are you seeing someone, Rani?

Rani Mukherjee: No.

FRIENDSHIP VS ARTISTIC FREEDOM

Karan Johar: Rani, there is an accusation that is always thrown at me – 'Why is not Rani Mukherjee the lead player in your film?' Do you ever feel that?

Rani Mukherjee: No. Personally, I do not think about it. It has never bothered me because my father was a director. I understand that

> **When I did not hear from you regarding _Kal Ho Na Ho_, it hurt me!**
> –Rani Mukherjee

when a director makes a film, he always wants to cast somebody who he feels is right for the role. I might not necessarily be the right choice. I do not think that is a problem. You are such a close friend of mine that

I love you beyond your films. I will always wish you well. So I do not think it as disturbing.

Karan Johar: Well, it is good to hear that – I am glad. Did you ever think 'Why Karan has not come to offer me the role in _Kal Ho Naa Ho?_'

Rani Mukherjee: When I did not hear from you, it rather hurt me. I felt whether you take me or somebody else in your film, you ought to have informed me. I share that comfort level with you. I heard it from somebody else. I wondered why Karan failed to do so. Neither of us thought that we had such worsening relationship.

Karan Johar: I know it is my fault. I do apologize.

Rani Mukherjee: I remember when I cried in front of Aamir, about which you don't know.

Karan Johar: I did not even know that Aamir was the next shoulder to cry on!

Rani Mukherjee: Yes. It was not a cry for 'Oh God! Preity got the role!' or anything of that sort. I was very happy, but I felt bad when I had the news from somebody else. Maybe I was a bit sensitive at that time. I was going through a lull in my career.

Karan Johar: You have emerged without my help. Now *Kal Ho Naa Ho* – we have been through this before. Kareena, I want to say that I have never held it against you. We know that we have gone through bitterness in our personal relations. What was your thought process at that point of time when you did not do *Kal Ho Naa Ho*?

Kareena Kapoor: I do not know what I went through. I do not know whether it was greed. Definitely, it was something that went wrong, which I have

> **When I saw *Kal Ho Na Ho*, I thought I had missed out the role of a lifetime!**
> –Kareena Kapoor

realized. The film achieved huge success. I knew I had done something wrong to a friend. Whatever it may be, I have really missed you, which made me upset; I have ignored your calls. I know things went wrong, because I lost a friend for more than a year-and-a-half. I did not care about the role or the film. I know I did something wrong which hurt me when I was shooting in New Zealand for Suraj-ji. I wondered whether I had lost Karan completely?

Karan Johar: Did you feel like calling me up at some point of time and say, 'OK, now I want to be a part of the film'?

Kareena Kapoor: Yes.

Karan Johar: Why did not you call me?

Kareena Kapoor: I knew Preity was in. And I knew you were already shooting.

Karan Johar: What thought came to you when you saw the film?

Kareena Kapoor: That I had missed out the role of a lifetime.

Karan Johar: No. I do not mean that way. Did you feel, 'Oh my God! I could have done this role better.'

Kareena Kapoor: No. She was wonderful in the film. The credit goes to you. Of course, it also goes to the director, Nikhil, who changed her overnight.

Karan Johar: Well, it is behind us. I want to say that I should apologize for not having confided in you. I just felt really guilty. We were somewhere linked to the film in a certain way. I had even asked you to do just that one shot. I just felt that your presence would bring luck to the film.

Kareena Kapoor: Why you did not ask me for a shot in the end?

Karan Johar: I asked you for 365 shots, darling! When I did not, I settled eventually for that one.

Kareena Kapoor: OK. We became friends after one shot!

BUBBLE TROUBLE – PREITY ZINTA

Karan Johar: OK. Preity Zinta – clearly, there was a friendship that went sour with her, Rani.

> **There was never a friendship between Preity and me.**
> *–Rani Mukherjee*

Rani Mukherjee: No; there was never a friendship, Karan, to be very honest. We shared a great working relationship. Preity and I gelled well when we worked together. It was especially so when we did *Chori Chori Chupke Chupke* and *Har Dil Jo Pyaar Karega*. It was like Preity and Rani always put together.

Karan Johar: You did one *Piya Piya! Oh Piya Piya!* number. It was like the sisters' sledge song.

Rani Mukherjee: Yes. I guess Preity and me were physically OK. We looked similar. We have similar body language. We look great together on screen. People saw Preity and me with each other. This was blown out of proportion in the magazines, where they called us twins. Preity and I were rather shocked. We tried to justify that we were not really the best of friends. The fact now remains that Preity and I are working.

Karan Johar: So, status is not the best of friends but comfortable working equation?

Rani Mukherjee: Yes.

Karan Johar: Kareena, Preity and you are certainly not the best of friends – I know that.

Kareena Kapoor: No, but I do not know her. I had a very brief association many years ago.

> **Preity and I look great together on screen – this was blown out of proportion to us being 'twins'!**
> *–Rani Mukherjee*

She was very friendly with one of my friends during my boarding school days. There has never been an interaction. I would love to work with her. I think she has really done well in *Kal Ho Naa Ho*.

Karan Johar: I am trying to understand the status, the equation, the tension right now between Preity Zinta and you.

Kareena Kapoor: We are not friends. We continue to be wonderful actresses.

Karan Johar: Two actresses do not have to be friends, Bebo; you know that.

Kareena Kapoor: Yes, that's fine. I still feel that she has done a really nice job in *Kal Ho Naa Ho*. She deserved the awards that she has got, because it was a beautiful role. I do not really know her so I won't comment because it is not right.

Karan Johar: It is so strange. I just feel Bebo has grown older, more mature – and not just age wise – while watching you. I just feel that she was somebody else just two years back – she would have said something. Today, things are so different. Don't you think, Rani?

Rani Mukherjee: Yes.

Karan Johar: I know what Bebo would have said even on camera, two years ago. Today, she is sounding quite wise.

> **Preity and I are not friends. We continue to be wonderful actresses!**
> *–Kareena Kapoor*

Kareena Kapoor: It is not right to comment on somebody I do not know. That is what I believe.

Karan Johar: Would you like to see what Preity Zinta has to say about both of you?

Preity Zinta: Should I be honest? Or should I be good? Rani, I think you and I get along. However, the media has portrayed us to be the best of friends – we are not so. It has been a pleasure to work with you. We have a great chemistry. I hope we do good and great films together. I do not think there is any discomfort between Rani and me. She is pretty cordial and says, 'Hello!'

We do not have to be like 'I love you baby' types as long as two actors maintain their decorum and protocol and say hello to each other and remain nice. We do not really hang out, talk or gossip whatever. But it is cool. I think Rani is a very good actress. I have always liked her performances. I have always liked the way she works. You want to do better obviously when there are good actors around you. If there is quality, then it gives you a chance to do things better. So I think, yes, her work affects me in a very positive way. Of all the actors I have worked with of my generation or any of the contemporaries, I think she is the best actor we have.

> **Kareena says 'Hi!' to me whenever Karan is around!**
> *–Preity Zinta*

Kareena, thank you for *Kal Ho Na Ho*! I would assert that she always helped me for it! I do not have any problem with her unless she ignores me. Kareena says 'Hi!' to me whenever Karan is around! I think Kareena and I are both actresses of the Indian film industry and we should just take a chill pill! I think Rani, Kareena and I could share a creative space together – the industry is big enough. Lots of films are being made. We can co-exist happily in this industry. I wish we could.

Karan Johar: So, is it true that you wish her only when I am around?

Kareena Kapoor: I will let her think what she wants. I believe she does say 'Hi!' to me as she is my senior. Next time, I will definitely meet and say 'Hi!' to her. I like her, so it is fine!

Karan Johar: She is a changed person! Bebo, you have disappointed me. What happened to you?

Kareena Kapoor: I am just honest! There is no difference.

Karan Johar: You are happy in your world. You look it because you are in love! Rani! What do you have to say about Preity's comment? You agree with that statement? You have said practically the same thing. Say something!

Rani Mukherjee: I think Preity talks too much. She should talk less. I want to tell her that through your show.

> **I think Preity talks too much. She should talk less.**
> *–Rani Mukherjee*

Rapid Fire

Karan Johar: I have this *rapid fire round.* I throw a volley of questions at you. You do not take too long to think. Whoever I think is good in this round wins what I call the *Koffee with Karan hamper.*

Kareena Kapoor: Can we get one film each if we are really good in the rapid fire round?

Karan Johar: I think that was the line of the show! I am going to start with Rani Mukherjee. Your rapid fire starts now. 2005 is going to be your year, because.... complete the sentence.

Rani Mukherjee: I am doing great films, I am working with great directors and my roles are great in the films!

Karan Johar: Bravo! One thing you have that Kareena does not?

Kareena Kapoor: I can answer that! Yash Chopra!

Karan Johar: One thing Kareena has that you don't have?

Rani Mukherjee: Shahid!

Karan Johar: One thing Kareena has that you don't have?

Rani Mukherjee: Shahid!

Karan Johar: OK. Wonderful! The thing that comes in your mind when you think of Vivek Oberoi?

Rani Mukherjee: No comments.

Karan Johar: A film you wish you had done?

Rani Mukherjee: *Devdas.*

Karan Johar: If Ash had done *Chalte Chalte*, the film would be.... complete the sentence.

Rani Mukherjee: It would have fared the same.

Karan Johar: OK. If you were the perfect *Tum,* was Saif the perfect *Hum?*

Rani Mukherjee: Yes, he was. Maybe he was more perfect than me.

Karan Johar: If you were offered *Julie,* you would say?

Rani Mukherjee: No.

Karan Johar: The strangest rumour you heard about yourself?

Rani Mukherjee: That I am getting married to you.

Karan Johar: Oh! You found that strange, Rani? Don't break my heart! Whom would you marry – an N.R.I doctor, a millionaire, an industrialist or a handsome hero?

> *Karan Johar: Bravo! One thing you have that Kareena does not?*
> *Kareena Kapoor: I can answer that! Yash Chopra!*

Rani Mukherjee: Handsome hero.

Karan Johar: What would you say if Abhishek Bachchan proposes to you?

Rani Mukherjee: I want to skip that one.

Karan Johar: OK. One actor you have been attracted to?

Rani Mukherjee: Shahrukh.

Karan Johar: Wonderful! The actor you think you make the best on-screen pair with?

Rani Mukherjee: Aamir.

Karan Johar: Aamir with moustache or Aamir clean-shaven?

Rani Mukherjee: Clean-shaven.

Karan Johar: OK. Great! Aamir or Shahrukh?

Rani Mukherjee: Both!

Karan Johar: That was fast. Both meaning? OK. Sanjay Leela Bhansali or Karan Johar?

Rani Mukherjee: Both. What is this?

Karan Johar: Hrithik or Abhishek?

Rani Mukherjee: Both.

Karan Johar: Not cool, Rani! OK. I know you will answer this one – Preity or Kareena?

Rani Mukherjee: Kareena.

Karan Johar: All right. You performed rather miserably towards the end!

Kareena Kapoor: That hamper is mine, Rani!

Karan Johar: Yes, that rapid fire was not rocking. Some of those answers were brilliant while you fell short in others. I am going to Kareena Kapoor.

> *Karan Johar: One actor you have been attracted to?*
> *Rani Mukherjee: Shahrukh.*

Let me see how she fares in my rapid fire round. The Year 2005 is going to be your year because....

Kareena Kapoor: Let us see! I do not know!

Karan Johar: One thing Rani has that you do not have?

Kareena Kapoor: I have said that – Yash Chopra!

Karan Johar: OK. One thing you have that Rani does not have?

Kareena Kapoor: May be the price I will get.

Karan Johar: Wonderful! One word that comes to your mind when I say Preity Zinta?

Kareena Kapoor: *Kal Ho Na Ho.*

Karan Johar: OK. The sexiest actor in India?

Karan Johar: OK. One thing you have that Rani does not have?
Kareena Kapoor: May be the price I will get.

Kareena Kapoor: Shahrukh Khan.

Karan Johar: OK. Aamir, Salman, Shahrukh, Saif – rank the Khans in order of your preference.

Kareena Kapoor: Shahrukh, Salman, Aamir, Saif.

Karan Johar: OK. Aishwarya, Preity, Rani, Kareena – rank in order of your preference.

Kareena Kapoor: Kareena, Rani, Preity, Aishwarya.

Karan Johar: Rahul Gandhi is... complete the sentence.

Kareena Kapoor: Too cute!

Karan Johar: What would you say if Shahid Kapoor proposed?
Kareena Kapoor: Wait for 8-10 years!

Karan Johar: What would you say if Shahid Kapoor proposed?

Kareena Kapoor: I will wait for 8-10 years.

Karan Johar: The thing that you have learned from your sister?

Kareena Kapoor: Dedication and sincerity.

Karan Johar: If you were offered the role in *Murder*, what you would say?

Kareena Kapoor: I would demand Rs. 5 crore.

Karan Johar: If you were stranded in a lift with Amisha Patel and Bipasha Basu?

Kareena Kapoor: I would say, 'Let us go to the show *Koffee with Karan.*' That would be fun!

Karan Johar: That does not sound very convincing. OK. Neha Dhupia says two things sell – Shahrukh Khan and sex. Your comments?

Kareena Kapoor: Only Shahrukh Khan.

Karan Johar: If you were offered the role in *Murder*?
Kareena Kapoor: I would demand Rs. 5 crore!

Karan Johar: What would you say to Mallika Sherawat if you meet her?

Kareena Kapoor: Probably I would not say anything to her.

Karan Johar: Fame or fortune?

Kareena Kapoor: Both.

Karan Johar: **Shahrukh Khan or Shahid Kapoor?**

Kareena Kapoor: **Shahid Kapoor.**

Karan Johar: Success or love?

Kareena Kapoor: Both.

Karan Johar: What both-both? You both..

Kareena Kapoor: I am greedy for good things in life!

Karan Johar: David Dhawan or Mani Ratnam?

Kareena Kapoor: Mani Ratnam.

Karan Johar: Well done! Yash Chopra or Sanjay Leela Bhansali?

Kareena Kapoor: Most definitely, Yash Chopra.

Karan Johar: Wonderful! Shahrukh Khan or Shahid Kapoor?

Rani Mukherjee: That was a good one!

Kareena Kapoor: Shahid Kapoor.

Karan Johar: Hrithik Roshan or Abhishek Bachchan?

Kareena Kapoor: Abhishek Bachchan – he was my first hero.

Karan Johar: Wonderful! Rani, I think she has performed a little better than you.

Kareena Kapoor: Rani, let us share this hamper! Come on!

Karan Johar: I think you have Yash Chopra and Kareena has the *Koffee hamper*.

Kareena Kapoor: How mean!

PUBLIC OPINION

Karan Johar: You do know that the next segment is going to be lots of fun. We chatted with lot of boys in the film fraternity. We wanted to check out two different aspects - (a) who is sexier – Rani or Kareena and (b) who was the better actress? We did this little survey – it is a fun type of survey. It should not be taken seriously.

Kareena Kapoor: How come we were not called for any survey to judge other people? Why are other people only judging us?

Karan Johar: Well, why not? You are beautiful women. The men have adjudged you. Both of you are my favorites – I mean that.

Who is sexier?

JI: I will just call you back. I am sitting with Karan Johar!

Uday Chopra: That is not a good question! I cannot say!

Male: This is a black mail!

JI: Ask me more questions.

Fardeen Khan: I wore my darker glasses.

> **How come other people are judging us and not vice-versa?**
> *–Kareena Kapoor*

Male: I am just joking! This man, Karan has killed me (right now). Please forgive me!

Fardeen Khan: Bebo! I think she is gorgeous.

Male: Rani Mukherjee - a fantastic actress!

Male: Kareena is a youth icon. She is very cool. She is very confident.

Kareena Kapoor: What is really nice about Rani is that she is very natural.

Zayed Khan: Kareena is full of glamour but I am a Rani fan. So, I find Rani everything that is nice and everything that is sexy.

Rani Mukherjee: I love you, Zayed!

Uday Chopra: Kareena is fire on screen.

Shahrukh Khan: Kareena is, blatantly, a star.

Male: Rani is, right now, a little ahead as an actress.

Uday Chopra: At times, Kareena does a little overacting. There might be another Rani, who is a great performer. But I do not know whether there will be another Kareena. I love the way Rani acts; I love the way she looks. I think Rani is definitely the better actress between the two.

> **Kareena has got a great, cute arse!**
> *–Fardeen Khan*

Shahrukh Khan: Rani is extremely photogenic.

Fardeen Khan: I find Kareena a lot sexier. She has got a great, cute arse. Rani has got an earthy kind of sex appeal.

Male: Kareena is much more sexy. I think Rani is good housewife material – she is the girl you would want to take home. Kareena is somebody you might try to hide.

RD: I think Kareena is sexier.

Male: I think Rani is sexier than Kareena.

Shahrukh Khan: My personal taste would be that Kareena is sexier.

Uday Chopra: Kareena is sexy. Because I think she has a great arse.

Male: Kareena, for me, is sexier. I think Rani is beautiful.

> Rani is the girl you would want to take home. Kareena is somebody you might try to hide!
>
> *–Male*

Fardeen Khan: Rani, you want to cuddle and take home, go meet mom.

Kareena Kapoor: So, what about me?

Fardeen Khan: Bebo, you will be taken to Maldives, overseas!

MARKS ON SEX APPEAL AND ACTING ABILITIES

ACTING SKILLS

Kareena Kapoor: Rani as an actress would get a score of 9 on 10 from me. Kareena definitely as an actress would get 8 or 8.5 on 10.

Male: Rani would be about 9 on 10 and Kareena would get about 7.5 or 8.

Shahrukh Khan: Rani is 9.5 and Kareena, from what I have seen, an 8.

RD: Rani would get 9 on 10 and Kareena – very close – 8.5.

Male: I would give Rani 9, and Kareena 6.5.

Male: Rani I would definitely give about 9 on 10 and Kareena I will give about 7.

Uday Chopra: Rani would get somewhere between 9 and 9.5 and Kareena – I would give her 8.

Male: Rani is 9. Kareena would be 8.5.

Zayed Khan: I give Rani 9; Kareena 8/10.

SEX APPEAL

Male: On a scale of 1-10, I would rate Kareena 7.5 and Rani 6.

Fardeen Khan: Kareena, 9 and Rani, 7.

JI: Kareena, probably 6 on 10 and I will give Rani a 6.5 on 10.

Uday Chopra: I would give Kareena about 9.5 and Rani definitely an 8.5.

SAK: 8 to Kareena and 7 to Rani.

Male: I would give Kareena 9.5. I would give Rani as an 8. Kareena Kapoor I will give about 8 on 10 and Rani about 6 on 10.

RD: Kareena, on sex appeal I would give 9 on 10 and Rani 8.5 on 10.

Male: On sex appeal, Rani 8.5 and Kareena 7.75 on 10.

SAK: I am just angling for a job, like most of you.

Fardeen Khan: Rani, you got a cute arse too, but I think Bebo's is cuter.

Rani Mukherjee: How sweet!

Kareena Kapoor: I think it was wonderful, Rani! They were all so sweet!

Karan Johar: So, let us clap!

Rani Mukherjee: It was very nice that the boys came and accomplished this. Thank you!

Karan Johar: So, clearly Kareena was the sexier and Rani was the better actress.

Kareena Kapoor: I have something to say which I genuinely want to say because I am really honest. I still do feel that John was a bit conscious because of his girlfriend. I thought he was a bit mean. But Uday, Fardeen – they were rock stars!

Rani Mukherjee: I did not think John was partial.

Kareena Kapoor: You are a Bengali and his girlfriend is too! He kept ripping me apart and giving me like a 6 and 6.5!

Rani Mukherjee: John is really sweet. I do not think John is like that.

CONCLUSION

Karan Johar: I think both of you are winners. You win the fact that you are the better actress. How does that make you feel?

Kareena Kapoor: Yash Chopra! I guess we should settle for it!

Karan Johar: Yash Chopra! There is victory everywhere! Well, I want to just say that I have had the best time chatting with you. It has been my most comfortable show. I have had a ball! I think the comfort zone I share with you, I shared with you right across this show. I do not know if you guys felt the same.

Rani Mukherjee: We are very happy to be on *Koffee with Karan*!

Karan Johar: All right.

Kareena Kapoor: Who knows, *Kal Ho Na Ho*?

Karan Johar: I have a small request before I let you go. There is a mug right next to you, Bebo. I want you to sign it. Please remember, this personally autographed mug can be yours if you participate in the *Koffee Quest contest*. Now, we will proceed to what I call the coffee wall. We will go and place that mug. Thank you.

● ● ●

3

Preity Zinta & Saif Ali
Hot Shots

Good Evening. Welcome to *Koffee with Karan*. My first guest tonight is Preity Zinta. She really should have a talk show of her own – she keeps talking. The best part of her personality is that she does not care if you are not listening to her. Everyone thinks she is cute. You know that. Everyone calls her the girl next door. God forbid, if she moves next door, please get your best pair of earplugs on. You will really need them. I am just kidding. She is quite adorable. She is vivacious. She is mint fresh. She is a superstar. I shall describe her in one word – bubbly, the word she hates. Let us call on the bubbly Preity Zinta right on.

PRETY ZINTA

Karan Johar: Hello Preity, you are looking pretty in pink.

Preity Zinta: Hello!

Karan Johar: So, Preity. Welcome to my show.

Preity Zinta: Thank you. I have heard what you said about me.

Karan Johar: It was tongue-in-cheek. But that is the vibe of this show, you know. I did say this one word – bubbly, which you hate. Why? What is the problem with this word?

Preity Zinta: I think there are other aspects of my personality also. I have just got stranded with bubbly, bubbly, bubbly.

> **I do not like the word 'bubbly'– I cannot be bubbly forever!**
>
> *–Preity Zinta*

Karan Johar: You do not like the word bubbly?

Preity Zinta: No.

Karan Johar: Everyone thinks you are bubbly. That is the first word, which came to everyone's mind, when your name was mentioned in a recent survey. People said, 'Preity Zinta is very bubbly.' They said she is a very bubbly character!

Preity Zinta: I too have my good days followed by bad days. There are times I get offensive. There are times I get serious. There are times I get thoughtful. I cannot be bubbly forever. But people think just that, because I played certain characters onscreen that had a lot of energy pep. I mean, even as a person, you know I have energy and pep, but not all the time.

THE GRAPEVINE

Karan Johar: OK. There is another aspect that really annoys you – rumours. Tell me what these rumours are. How do they bother you? Well, it was Saif some time ago. Then came Brett Lee in the IIFA awards in Singapore. Later, it was somebody called Brian (Cyrus – the veteran Bollywood piano artist), who was on the shoot of *Kal Ho Na Ho*. Then there was Abhishek Bachchan. So, do you want to say something about them?

Preity Zinta: All I want to say is, 'Oh! It is such a big problem!'

Karan Johar: Yes, single. But you cannot be so ready to mingle.

> **I am single but not ready to mingle!**
>
> *– Preity Zinta*

Preity Zinta: Exactly. I think it is a big munch. Folks! I am friends with people like Abhishek. Saif, obviously, we were doing *Kal Ho Na Ho*, and I am extremely fond of him. He is a very good friend of mine. Brian, as you know has worked on *Kal Ho Na Ho*, so obviously, I am not going to be snobbish with people. I am going to be friendly. Brett Lee, I have met him, because he wanted to meet me. He came for IIFA. So, just because you are talking to someone.... I would say if I see someone. I think it will be a big munch when people think now you are single.

Karan Johar: So, that is because Preity Zinta is single. Do these rumours really affect you? I mean does it become awkward when you meet the people with whom you are working?

Preity Zinta: Sometimes, it becomes awkward because some of them are married, but anyway, people are very chilled out. But it turns very awkward when my mother, who stays in Shimla, is called up. The local newspaper carries news items. When I am working, my phone is switched off, so she does not have any contact with me. They hound my family members.

Karan Johar: When you start seeing someone, will you announce it?

Preity Zinta: Yes. There will be a board. I will come on your show and say it.

Karan Johar: You were in a relation with Dane (a Danish man)- Lars, very sweet fellow. I mean, I know him.

Preity Zinta: That was a year ago. We broke up.

Karan Johar: Yes. I mean there was a fan who came to me one day and asked, 'You know, there are rumours about Brett Lee and Brian.' He asked me what was cooking between Preity and white men. He was a huge fan of Preity Zinta. He said 'I have heard that if you are non-white, then Preity will be uninterested.' I know you have made that impression. I said, 'OK. When I meet Preity the next time, I will ask her.' Is there a white fixation?

Preity Zinta: I do not think so. I think I have also seen somebody who is an Indian. So, it is ridiculous to say that there is a white fixation.

> **It is ridiculous to say that there is a white fixation!**
>
> – Preity Zinta

Karan Johar: There have been rumours all around.

Preity Zinta: Exactly.

Karan Johar: Good looking

foreign men! It is great! If you find them good looking, why not? I mean you are a young girl.

Preity Zinta: Sure, sure. But the thing is that I like a person, who is (a) somebody and (b) being white, black, grey, pink, or orange is not the criteria. It is the heart that counts, really.

> I am like one of the Mills and Boon girls- I want to be in love like every girl!
>
> *– Preity Zinta:*

Karan Johar: Yes. So you are like one of the *Mills and Boon* girls. You want to be in love, like every girl does.

Preity Zinta: Of course.

Karan Johar: Talking about these rumours, one of them was with Saif, who is our guest tonight. You know, it is so strange; every one considers him to fall under the westernized category of actors. People say he is not an Indian at all – he is too English. Someone even said that he has the eyes of his mother Sharmila Tagore. They also say that he cannot speak chaste Hindi.

Preity Zinta: I do not think it is true. I believe that he speaks very good Hindi.

Karan Johar: Of course. But all that has changed. Suddenly, he is westernizing his USP in Hindi. He is urbane and metrosexual and the girls think so.

Preity Zinta: Metrosexual!

Karan Johar: His mother's eyes are being replaced with bedroom eyes. They believe he is really hot. He is really sexy. Now, he is Nawab! He speaks perfect Urdu. You know that Hindi intonations are fine now. There is one word that has changed it all. I am sure you do know what that word would be.

Preity Zinta: *Hit*, Big *hit*, Super *hit*!

Karan Johar: So, what does *hit* translate to his success? That is what has completely changed the graph of Saif Ali Khan.

> If you are successful, then anything works!
>
> *–Preity Zinta*

Preity Zinta: Of course, I did know you are going there. But success? I mean if you are successful, then anything works. If my hair was like that then my film would be a big hit. And that hair would be in vogue.

SAIF ALI KHAN

Karan Johar: I think we should bring him on. I think we should welcome the new Khan in the Khan monopoly – Saif Ali Khan. Hello.

Preity Zinta: Hello, Saif!

Karan Johar: Good evening, Saif.

Saif Ali Khan: Good evening!

> **You deserve what you ought to – you are not looking at payback.**
>
> *–Saif Ali Khan*

Karan Johar: I must say you are looking rather glamorous together.

Preity Zinta: Thank you.

Karan Johar: Well Saif, we were just talking about how the perception towards you has changed in a year-and-a-half. I think ever since *Dil Chahta Hai*, really. I mean things have just changed. Your entire career has taken a huge upswing. What I really wanted to ask you personally more than professionally was – How do you feel like while reflecting upon those years when you were passing through the rough patches in your career? Today, do you feel like giving it back to your detractors? I mean, what is your feeling today?

Saif Ali Khan: No. I have stayed up nights. I have looked at the mirror and watched speeches made during award ceremony. I thought some nasty things have been told about me. I have found that whenever you get closer to things; you do not feel anymore about your antecedents. You deserve what you ought to. You are not looking at payback. Neither you remember the speech that talked of you highly. You just feel a little humble and responsible with some success. I think I have learned a lot of things. I have done loads of work. I think I am very lucky. Times have changed. Directors like you have cast me. That has made a huge difference in my personality.

Karan Johar: No. It has a lot to do with you Saif. I remember the day I saw *Dil Chahta Hai,* I thought he was out of work and out of the industry! And out of complete circulation. I said, 'God, he is so good!'

> **I was in la-la land and doing really bad films before *Dil Chahta Hai*!**
>
> *– Saif Ali Khan*

Saif Ali Khan: I was in la-la land.

Karan Johar: You were in la-la land. You were doing very bad films. Suddenly, Farhan Akhtar came with the super-duper hit *Dil Chahta Hai.* Your role was the best in the film. I mean better than Preity.

Saif Ali Khan: Which I said I did not want to do.

**I did not want to do
*Dil Chahta Hai!***

–Saif Ali Khan

Preity Zinta: Why then did you come on the show?

Saif Ali Khan: I said I did not want to do the movie.

Preity Zinta: Really, I wanted to do the part with him. I thought it was the mad part.

Karan Johar: *Dil Chahta Hai* was the film shot some three years ago. Let us forget *Dil Chahta Hai* now.

Preity Zinta: *Kal Ho Na Ho?*

Karan Johar: No, none of my movies – I dislike to do so. I told every one how much she talks about! Keep quiet. I cast you in *Kal Ho Na Ho* because you were so brilliant in *Dil Chahta Hai.* I thought you could stand your ground. I mean, in the front of Aamir Khan, Akshaye Khanna, Dimple – not Preity – but you know Aamir. You were really good. That is why I cast you.

Saif Ali Khan: We do not want to speak about *Dil Chahta Hai.* But I had asked him on the very first day. Aamir Khan told me that he thought I was doing something wrong. He sat with me and told me how I played it completely wrong – the character should have been portrayed differently. I went home rather confused, returned next day and replied, 'I am sorry. I am just going to do it my own way. Thank you.' I have realised that I should have never asked another actor. What should I do?

Karan Johar: Trust the director; trust me.

Saif Ali Khan: Absolutely.

Karan Johar: Well, I am going to talk about you, your onscreen and off-screen chemistry – rather, on rumours. Technically, Preity, Saif was your first hero. I mean officially, it was Shahrukh Khan in *Dil Se.*

Preity Zinta: Yeah.

Karan Johar: But technically, both of you started working in *Kya Kehna* where you were a— pregnant girl.

Aamir Khan told me that he thought I was doing Sameer's character all wrong in *Dil Chahta Hai!*

–Saif Ali Khan

Preity Zinta: Pregnant girl, yeah.

Karan Johar: Naughty girl.

Preity Zinta: We started *Kya Kehna*. The film got a bit delayed. I did *Dil Se.*

Saif Ali Khan: *Soldier* first?

Preity Zinta: No, first I did *Kya Kehna*. I signed *Soldier* later.

Karan Johar: So basically, my question was that he was your first hero. You had this feeling, I am sure, when you worked with your first hero – I mean, you know you had this—

Saif Ali Khan: What are you trying to say, friend?

Karan Johar: I am not saying anything.

Preity Zinta: We have done three films together, you know.

Karan Johar: I know; *Dil Chahta Hai, Kal Ho Na Ho* and *Kya Kehna*. How does it feel like working with Saif? How was it like initially?

Preity Zinta: Saif is very chilled. You know, he is very cool. The first time I saw him, he was rather nervous about my personality. I had never been to acting school. I was enacting for the first time, but he was OK; he was nice.

Karan Johar: He was a nice guy and fun-loving?

Preity Zinta: He was sweet.

Karan Johar: What happened with the accident? I have heard that it was like big bonding time.

Preity Zinta: I told Saif I am the only girl who knows what goes inside his head.

> I told Saif that I am the only girl who knows what goes inside his head!
>
> –*Preity Zinta*

Karan Johar: What happened? What was this accident?

Saif Ali Khan: We had rehearsed the motorcycle jump on Juhu beach with a little jump on a ramp. Of course, we went to Khandala to shoot this sequence. It was raining and muddy. It was not the same kind of ground. She was on the set. Just like a guy, I thought, 'Let me try and impress her.'

Preity Zinta: Shut up Saif! He is talking rubbish. Not to impress me – there was some other girl who said, 'I will give you one slap.'

Karan Johar: We will get back to that aspect about Saif later.

Saif Ali Khan: I did it OK for the first time. I said, 'Let me do it again with some excitement and stuff.' The bike skidded before I hit the ramp. I just went flying. There was a rock in the middle of the field. I tumbled over 30 times very quickly and smacked. Oh God! I hit that. I felt some kind of

> After the accident, Preity told me, 'You will probably look like Frankenstein at the end when they stitch you up!'
> –Saif Ali Khan

wetness that would have swollen. People went on taking photographs.

Preity Zinta: Yeah, I know. Exactly.

Saif Ali Khan: I was taken to the army hospital. She said, 'You will probably look like Frankenstein at the end when they stitch you up. Look, we can arrange for a plastic surgeon..' Later, we settled for a doctor.

Preity Zinta: Yeah, his wife was not in town.

Karan Johar: And you called his friend, Zaks.

Preity Zinta: Yes, I called his friend and said 'Hi, this is Preity. Saif has met with an accident.' He was rude to me over the phone. He replied, 'Don't you have a life?'

Saif Ali Khan: He said, 'Why did not you call me when his brain came out?' Zaks is like my godfather. He does not come to meet me very often. The only way to get him over is to cry wolf as kids. I tell him, 'Oh, I have had an accident; please come over' and he would come rushing.

> I called Saif's friend, Zaks, after the accident and he said, 'Don't you have a life?'
> –Preity Zinta

Preity Zinta: That is very silly, Saif.

Saif Ali Khan: Yeah, very silly.

Karan Johar: So Preity was at the receiving end. Apparently, he said some really nasty things.

Preity Zinta: Yeah, because everybody had left and it was just me.

Saif Ali Khan: Don't joke like this and similar kind of things.

Preity Zinta: Yeah, it was just him and me at the hospital because...

Karan Johar: He did believe you.

Preity Zinta: Our director got very ill; he got very hypertensive. So, the action director left.

Karan Johar: Oh God! So the action director was not around. The director was also in another hospital.

Preity Zinta: There were two people from production.

Karan Johar: You were in another hospital.

Saif Ali Khan: Breach Candy Hospital.

Preity Zinta: They were downstairs. They told me, 'Sign this form.' I replied, 'I am not signing any form or anything.' I got very upset.

Karan Johar: Oh God!

Preity Zinta: Saif had a big bump on his head. He looked like an alien. I thought he was a bit confused.

Karan Johar: What was it? Did he forget his wife and children?

Preity Zinta: No, he didn't forget anything. He was sitting and then he said, 'Can I smoke a cigarette?'

Saif Ali Khan: Yes, nobody lets me do it.

Preity Zinta: The doctor told me that he should remain conscious. He should not sleep and that there might be a problem. I was really scared. I wanted to keep him awake. I kept thinking, 'What if he dies?'

Saif Ali Khan: She spoke to me.

Preity Zinta: I was like, 'Saif, you are such a lovely guy!' I was so nervous. I was like.... I hope does not die.

Karan Johar: Oh God! You thought he was going to die?

Preity Zinta: Yeah. You know, he started looking very scary. His head went on swelling out. Because of the swelling, his eyes started drooping. I sat with him.

Karan Johar: It was quite an awful accident, Saif! So, Preity was a big help!

Saif Ali Khan: No, I mean it was the worst accident I ever had. I have not experienced death. There was a lot of blood. I was pretty scared. The point to be noted is that there was nobody around from home. My friends were not around. We did not even have the phone number of the doctors. I mean one does not carry such things around normally. So, it was Preity who organized the things at that stage. I mean the bonding and stuff was all right. But it is actually quite an experience to share. It is quite a vulnerable sort of thing to happen to somebody. I was really appreciative.

Karan Johar: Such incidents make two people come closer. I think these are very humane experiences.

Preity Zinta: You do not think you are actors. I think your human instincts emerge. I freak out virtually if I see blood., I just went, 'Oh my God! No, no, no!' You should know first aid. You can put on ice, which Saif dislikes. One guy suggested we take him to a doctor, that he should have some stitches. He was an actor. How many stitches you got?

Saif Ali Khan: 100 plus stitches.

Preity Zinta: 100 stitches!

> **I got 100 plus stitches!**
> *–Saif Ali Khan*

Karan Johar: My God! So, would you say something like this brought you guys closer as friends?

Saif Ali Khan: Yeah, definitely.

Preity Zinta: Of course.

Karan Johar: You think there was a friendship right after this? You were just co-stars before. Would you call this a friendship after knowing each other?

Preity Zinta: Definitely.

Karan Johar: OK, great. You know, what comes across onscreen is really terrific onscreen chemistry. Everyone who saw *Kal Ho Na Ho* and a little bit of, of course, *Dil Chahta Hai* before *Kya Kehna* said, 'Oh God! Preity and Saif in *Kal Ho Na Ho* – that pair's acting is superb! They were really comfortable with each other.' It came across successfully.

> **It is not necessary that real lovers will share any chemistry onscreen or vice-versa.**
> *–Saif Ali Khan*

Saif Ali Khan: The chemistry is quite crazy. If you look around, it is not necessary for lovers to share any of this chemistry.

Karan Johar: I am not calling you lovers. No, I am saying as per the story around.

Preity Zinta: No, but there are people who are couples. They do not come across so onscreen.

Saif Ali Khan: There are people who dislike each other.

> **Some people think you are a burden if you are not a big star!**
> –*Saif Ali Khan*

Preity Zinta: Who are these couples?

Saif Ali Khan: I do not know. You have said so.

Preity Zinta: I do not know anything.

Karan Johar: *Ho Gaya Na!* Let us move on. What I am trying to interpret is that you guys really came across close even onscreen. You did *Kal Ho Na Ho* later. You had a good time working on that film as well.

Preity Zinta: I think the roles were great together. It was especially so in the part I love – when the hot babe looks at him and I look at him and he says, 'Who is she?' I say, 'Leave her alone.' That section was very cute, whole wit integrating with main plot.

Karan Johar: You guys really had a superb time.

Saif Ali Khan: I do not know what it was. I have worked with lots of people. Most people have been really nice. Some people treat you differently if you are doing well. Others think you are a burden if you are not a big star. We share these vibes between us, Preity and me. We trust each other. I have never misbehaved with her or made her feel that I look at her in some other way. I am not interested in physical or any relation with her. It will lead to mistrusting me when I start pulling her leg. I can practically say anything to her.

Preity Zinta: Yeah.

Karan Johar: Really, that might be your feeling, but that wasn't the feeling you probably gave out because there were all these kind of rumours.

Saif Ali Khan: Right.

Karan Johar: We were in New York. You got a text from Fardeen, Saif.

> **I got a text from Fardeen saying, 'Be very careful, brother!' and that Preity and I had made it!**
> –*Saif Ali Khan*

Saif Ali Khan: Yes.

Karan Johar: What did the text say?

Saif Ali Khan: He said Preity and I made it. 'Be very careful, brother!'

Karan Johar: Oh God!

Preity Zinta: Guess what happened subsequently?

Saif Ali Khan: I replied to Amrita when she called up about what I have heard.

Karan Johar: Was everything held in gray clues?

Saif Ali Khan: They remained gray until the *Stardust* article blew up the relation between two random hearts in New York. The beautifully drafted piece had exposed the simmering relations.

Preity Zinta: Yeah. I like the way people just tolerated me because I called up Saif and asked him, 'Do you want to leave?' I never saw Saif again. Saif, however, ignored me without any reason.

Saif Ali Khan: No.

Preity Zinta: Keep quiet!

> **Saif ignored me after the article without any reason!**
> *–Preity Zinta*

Karan Johar: He did not ignored you. He was often caught in another frame of mind.

Preity Zinta: Do not lie!

Karan Johar: We will revert to the alleged romantic affair between Saif and Preity.

Preity Zinta: Not fair, no affair.

Karan Johar: No affair?

Preity Zinta: No affair.

Karan Johar: I mean I have not noticed any development, you know.

Saif Ali Khan: You did not notice means you did.

Preity Zinta: You are quite sharp to react.

Karan Johar: I swear I did not know. I was quite shocked when Fardeen sent the mail text.

Preity Zinta: I quipped with the incident when he showed me the message.

Saif Ali Khan: I was equally shocked.

Preity Zinta: So, he went on ignoring me.

Karan Johar: There have been clever people who hide everything really well.

Preity Zinta: Well, I do not know about anybody else. I think about myself. I am pretty cool. I will never hide while observing somebody.

Karan Johar: Yeah.

Preity Zinta: I have do's and don'ts. 'A' is that I will never involve myself with a married man. I believe he is my buddy.

> **I will never involved myself with a married man.**
> *–Preity Zinta*

Karan Johar: So, nothing took place on record?

Preity Zinta: No.

Saif Ali Khan: Absolutely not. I will not justify anything. I mean there are some hundred ways of looking at things. They are being overfriendly and candid.

Karan Johar: Yeah. It is all about the reverse psyche.

Saif Ali Khan: Right. I shall believe we get on well, because there is clarity between us; there is no confusion. Nobody is trying to take advantage.

> **I believe that I am extremely attractive!**
> –*Saif Ali Khan*

Preity Zinta: Yeah.

Saif Ali Khan: I believe that I am extremely attractive. I always try to keep away from unsavory things.

Karan Johar: How attractive do you think Preity is?

Preity Zinta: Say nice things about me.

Saif Ali Khan: Of course.

Karan Johar: Are you attracted to her as woman?

Saif Ali Khan: I had not really thought about that. Yeah, she is attractive.

Preity Zinta: Right, correct answer. Most actors are beautiful and attractive.

Karan Johar: She is pretty without makeup.

Saif Ali Khan: Some mornings, it's worrying.

Preity Zinta: Your nose is very long. You shut up!

Karan Johar: OK. Let us talk about the rumour. It had a unique buzz.

Preity Zinta: Karan, forget the rumour. It is over now.

Karan Johar: I recollect its feedback – a domestic one. Well, I mean, to a certain extent.

Saif Ali Khan: I am still uncomfortable. Our family is quite private about this.

Karan Johar: I understand.

Saif Ali Khan: Sure. You know my wife has been in the movies. Similar rumours made us insecure. We were in America for 40 days. It has overtaken every development.

> **Rumours make my wife and me insecure.**
> –*Saif Ali Khan*

Preity Zinta: I hope everything is fine thereafter.

Karan Johar: I am sure of it.

Saif Ali Khan: I believe that trust is very important. It helps clear such things. It is quite annoying when you do not deserve that.

Karan Johar:. Preity, you also faced that. Was it awkward for you, too?

Preity Zinta: I do not have a wife!

> I react crazily on the first day. I go hyper ballistic. I kill that journalist!
>
> –*Preity Zinta*

Karan Johar: No, but you had met his wife at some point of time. You are civilized in every sense. Will it not keep you in an awkward position? I believe the whole vibrations put us in an awkward position.

Preity Zinta: Not really, Karan. I believe it was clear. He told me about a party. The party was at Shahrukh's house.

Karan Johar: Yeah.

Preity Zinta: I saw Saif with Amrita when I got out of the car. I was like bingo! I am not that kind of person. If I am awkward, I will be so. Else, the situation will not arise.

Karan Johar: So, you were not awkward at all?

Preity Zinta: No.

Saif Ali Khan: Why should we be?

Preity Zinta: Exactly!

Karan Johar: How do you deal with rumours in general? I mean, he had a couple of such rumours. You have had many more. How do you deal with them?

Preity Zinta: I react crazily on the first day. I go hyper ballistic. I want to kill that journalist.

Karan Johar: One such rumour was that everyone thought you are marrying Abhishek. The rumours have evaporated now.

Preity Zinta: That is because what Jaya aunty told me – 'Preity, I loved playing your mother in *Kal Ho Na Ho*.'

Karan Johar: Yeah.

Preity Zinta: She was amazing to work with. I do not think that I have worked with a more selfless and amazing actress. I never felt the difference about the character role Jaya aunty played and what she is doing now. To

> I have never worked with a more selfless and amazing actress than Jaya aunty!
>
> –*Preity Zinta*

me, she was really a mom in that film. You know, she never interrupted like, 'No, this is my line and this is your line.' She never differentiated things like that.

Karan Johar: You think may be because you really felt so warmly towards her? You have said such amazing things. People thought, 'She is just trying to remain cordial. She will assume the role of the would-be mother-in-law.' People have crafted such vibes about you.

Preity Zinta: Poor Abhishek has got stuck in the whole game.

Karan Johar: I mean because every son indeed has to be nice to their mother.

Preity Zinta: You! You are the one who has started that rumour. Do you accept that?

Karan Johar: I did try very hard to do so.

Saif Ali Khan: What?!

Karan Johar: I thought something might happen. I do not know whether you are aware about that, Saif. Do I try when things will not work?

Preity Zinta: Keep quiet. The whole rumour has gone through the roof. 'He is the one, you are single and he is single. Why don't you get together?'

Karan Johar: Did you believe such rumours?

Saif Ali Khan: I have heard it.

> **Karan, you started the rumour about Abhishek and me!**
>
> *–Preity Zinta*

Preity Zinta: Shut up! You believed it and inquired about it. I asked you. Everybody believed it.

Saif Ali Khan: I have questioned it.

Karan Johar: I had started believing it. I was the one who had created it.

Saif Ali Khan: You see the problem? Generally, people who are in this line – like my family – my wife knows that there is hardly any smoke without fire. People can easily say rubbish in the magazines like *Stardust*. But, once in a while...

Preity Zinta: Here, the smoke machine installed is doing the job.

Saif Ali Khan: She calls me as the smoke machine?

Preity Zinta: Are you a smoke machine?

Karan Johar: Do not put that on me, darling. Come on.

Preity Zinta: It blew up as a joke. It ripped the roof later.

Saif Ali Khan: I was like, 'See, it is Abhishek!'

> The rumour about Abhishek and me blew up as a joke and ripped the roof later!
>
> *–Preity Zinta*

Karan Johar: That is what I was trying to get across! I mean, it is not me. It was like your ticketless position.

Saif Ali Khan: Yes.

Preity Zinta: I was like, Saif, Abhishek, Brett – Oh my God!

Karan Johar: Yeah, you were the *rumour queen* for the whole year.

Preity Zinta: Yeah. Abhishek is also very sweet.

Saif Ali Khan: You know, I got to know him now and..

Preity Zinta: ..we all hung out together.

Saif Ali Khan: Sweet!

Preity Zinta: No, he really is a great guy.

Karan Johar: He belongs to the *chilled out* variety. He is really adorable. I love him.

Preity Zinta: He is very well mannered. He is very cultured.

> I do not think the rumour about Abhishek and me bothered him from any angle!
>
> *– Preity Zinta*

Saif Ali Khan: I love him, too.

Preity Zinta: I do not think it has bothered him from any angle.

Saif Ali Khan: He is calm and cultured.

Karan Johar: He is because you guys know the truth, I am sure.

Preity Zinta: He looked at things written about us.

Saif Ali Khan: The only time it bothers you is when it affects or hurts your family, you know; that is all.

Karan Johar:. Has that occurred in the past? Has it cost you emotionally?

Saif Ali Khan: Yes, I would say so, in some ways. You have ascertained that if you behave in a certain manner, people will write.

Preity Zinta: Which manner, Saif?

> If you behave in a certain manner, people will write.
>
> *–Saif Ali Khan*

Saif Ali Khan: Are you running the show? What are you doing?

Karan Johar: No, she is not. She is just being herself, Saif. OK! We are done with rumours. We have denied it. Nothing of that sort has happened?

Saif Ali Khan: Nothing.

Karan Johar: Nothing took place between Abhishek and Preity. How boring is that? Did something else happen?

Preity Zinta: We had fun! We party, we rock!

Karan Johar: Anything else? Acknowledge yourself on the show – nobody is watching.

Saif Ali Khan: Yeah, just two of us.

Karan Johar: Just me and *Star World*. Nobody else. Do you want to make any confession, Preity?

Preity Zinta: Say something!

Saif Ali Khan: What?

Karan Johar: OK. I am going back to *Kal Ho Na Ho*. I think my equation with you really is *Kal Ho Na Ho*. I think it has been amazing. You all know that Saif had been working with Preity and me. Of course, I tried to work with him in *Kuch Kuch Hota Hain*. He did not participate in my film. We will not go there. His kind of threw me out of his house and said, 'Who are you? I do not want to act in your film. You are Karan Johar. You have never made a film before.' And that is a lie. But there were things. We have been through that before. I worked with you, Preity, for the first time. Of course, you were not my first choice – it was Kareena. You stepped in very beautifully. Today, you are a part of this family. It has been an amazing experience. You have worked with Shahrukh Khan in a mainstream film. You had not worked in between with Shahrukh for many years. Was there a problem, Preity?

Preity Zinta: Yes. I would not say there was a major problem. We never really talked to each other. There was a little communication gap; we never discussed it. We just went our own way. That is problematic.

Karan Johar: We worked it out. You were a part of *Kal Ho Na Ho*. You were working in the domain of Shahrukh Khan.

Saif Ali Khan: Yes. And with you.

> Initially, there was a communication gap between Shahrukh and me – we never discussed it.
>
> *–Priety Zinta*

Karan Johar: And with me.

Saif Ali Khan: Who wept when he performed! He told me to repeat again.

Karan Johar: Preity, you have worked with Shahrukh after five years.

> **I worked with Shahrukh in** *Kal Ho Na Ho* **after 5 years**
> *–Priety Zinta*

Preity Zinta: Yes.

Karan Johar: There was some problem after *Dil Se*. You have ignored that. Do you want to ignore it now?

Preity Zinta: Well, it was not a big problem. We just did things our own way. We did not really do films together quite often.

Karan Johar: OK. That is the right thing to say. What happened later? Probably, something happened. We do not want to get into that development. Now, Saif, you have worked with Shahrukh in my film. I have worked in two films with him before as well. I have a great equation with him. He is like part of the family, i.e. part of the Dharma family.

Saif Ali Khan: Yes.

Karan Johar: Did you have insecure moments as a co-actor?

Saif Ali Khan: Well, you know honestly, very briefly, yes I think, apart from anything else. Perhaps just likely envious of the kind of control he had over his craft. The kind of respect you had for him. The kind of bond you had. But the feeling was very fleeting because you made me very comfortable. But as an actor I am not very confident, but also the root of insecurity is not knowing your job that I felt.

Karan Johar: Yes.

Saif Ali Khan: So if you know him slightly, Shahrukh is the kind of actor – you look at each other in the eye. If you do not know what you are doing, you are dead. If you know what you are doing, then it starts going places and really good things happen. He is not at all selfish, I think, as a performer. He is very concerned about the big

> **Shahrukh is the kind of actor– if you do not know what you are doing, you are dead!**
> *–Saif Ali Khan*

picture. So it would be very infantile for me to feel insecure about his achievements, which I would myself like to achieve. He drove a shot many a times by saying, 'OK! Let us get together. We have got to move on.' So the security of a person is concerned with the outcome of being good because you are part of the same product. So, he helped us in many ways. His attitude was almost paternal towards the film unit. I think he presented that even on shows. He is concerned about what you are doing.

Karan used to cry when Shahrukh was about to die in *Kal Ho Na Ho!*

–Preity Zinta

Preity Zinta: Yeah, that way, he is very good. Even the few actors who are in the limelight will never give cues. He will stand and will give you a perfect cue. He will give ten options until you perform the assigned task with perfection. He needs to stand on what he targets. He will never feel rehearsing with the assistant or do it like that.

Saif Ali Khan: He just loves what he does.

Preity Zinta: Yeah. That is great about him.

Karan Johar: Yeah. There were those days when you were quite on the location.

Preity Zinta: I would like to hear this.

Karan Johar: You were really very quiet. You suddenly slipped into this kind of mood.

Saif Ali Khan: I was a little confused as a person because I had never enjoyed so much.

Preity Zinta: Because you used to cry when Shahrukh was about to die!

Karan Johar: I have never cried in any of the shots. You made me laugh.

Saif Ali Khan: I am basically confused. I do not enjoy any movie, especially a good one. I just think it was a nightmare – all the way through.

Karan Johar: Yeah.

Saif Ali Khan: I would notice Shahrukh many times looking thoughtful or angry at something. I would think, 'obviously, it has to be me.'

I suffer from persecution complex!

–Saif Ali Khan

Karan Johar: So you have this persecution complex.

Saif Ali Khan: Yes, completely so. I know it is really wrong.

Karan Johar: Oh God! Yes. I mean I have realized that subsequently. I have had many chats about this.

Saif Ali Khan: I spoke to Shahrukh. We sat down. He puffed the cigarette in between our conversation. We began to talk.

Karan Johar: You have cleared the air; that was not really conducive?

Saif Ali Khan: That was not clear; probably it was about something completely different. I mean, it had nothing to do with me anyway.

Karan Johar: It was not really so; suddenly, you felt like a lost child. I had noticed you sitting quietly in the corner of a set. You know, he felt like that as he had a remarkable role in the episode.

Saif Ali Khan: Yes, but I am like that. I just get confused.

Karan Johar: I do not know whether you are aware of this. We were shooting the proposal sequence. You know, Saif proposes to you in that picturesque lovely setting. Saif was really hysterical about the scene. He was just puzzled and cried, 'Why should I say this? Why am I asking you to marry me? Why this and why that? I hope I will not come across like a loser. Remember what I told you, Saif?

Saif Ali Khan: Yeah.

Karan Johar: I told Saif at that point in time that he was going to win every award for the film.

Preity Zinta: Yeah.

Karan Johar: Trust me; it is true Hindi film style.

Preity Zinta: Trust me, Saif, you were rocking in *Kal Ho Na Ho*.

Saif Ali Khan: Thank you.

Karan Johar: Did you think she had rocked as well in the film?

Saif Ali Khan: Yes, of course. You have brought something to the character that nobody else could.

> **Saif, you were rocking in *Kal Ho Na Ho!***
>
> –Preity Zinta

Karan Johar: I think we were chatting that Kareena was the first choice. How did you feel? You know, you stepped into Kareena Kapoor's shoes.

Preity Zinta: Someone else asked me the same question some time ago. I replied that you keep trying on pairs of jeans in a shopping spree and until it fits with your physique, you do not buy them. The next person comes in, tries it, and buys them. I remember when you called me, I replied, 'Can I hear the script?' Once I heard the script, I wondered why Kareena wanted me to do this film. It was all over the place – Kareena was the first choice; Preity is the second choice. So, I finally said, 'Thank you, Kareena!' It does not matter. Anyway, this film was my destiny.

Karan Johar: Now that you have seen the film, tell me who would have been the better Naina – Kareena or Preity?

Saif Ali Khan: I cannot imagine anyone else.

RAPID FIRE

Karan Johar: We shall move on to what I call the *rapid fire round*. I will throw a volley of questions at you. You have 90 seconds with you. Whoever answers more questions in those 90 seconds shall win what I call *the Koffee with Karan* hamper.

Preity Zinta: It is great to win the hamper.

Karan Johar: It is full of coffee goodies.

Preity Zinta: OK.

Saif Ali Khan: How are you going to do it? One at a time or together?

Karan Johar: No, it is not together. It commences with the lady.

Preity Zinta: Why me first? First him!

Karan Johar: Well, that's because you are a lady! Ladies, come first.

Preity Zinta: I do not mind.

Karan Johar: You are so bewitching, lady, so I think it is right to start with you!

Preity Zinta: OK. Shoot.

Karan Johar: So, this is my *rapid fire* to you. Do not take much time to ponder. And come on, be cool about it – you are generation X.

Preity Zinta: Yeah, yeah, yeah.

Karan Johar: So, here goes. The most hilarious rumour you heard or read about yourself?

Preity Zinta: Brett Lee.

Karan Johar: What habit you would like to break?

Preity Zinta: Early morning.

Karan Johar: On a scale of one to ten, rate yourself on your acting ability.

Preity Zinta: Ten.

Karan Johar: The sexiest man you know in India.

Preity Zinta: India? Sexiest man?

Karan Johar: Too long.

Preity Zinta: OK. I cannot.

Karan Johar: Say Saif.

Preity Zinta: Saif.

> *Karan Johar:* **The sexiest man you know in India?**
> *Priety Zinta :* **India? Sexiest man?!**

Karan Johar: Great! If you actually see a news reporter and someone asks you to say something about *Koffee with Karan*, what would you say?

Preity Zinta: It is witty and sharp.

Karan Johar: The best actor in India today.

Preity Zinta: Amitabh Bachchan.

Karan Johar: The best actress in India today.

Preity Zinta: Sridevi.

Karan Johar: Your 4 AM friend?

Preity Zinta: Phone.

Karan Johar: If you were someone else, you would be?

Preity Zinta: Madonna.

Karan Johar: Love or money?

Preity Zinta: Love.

> **If I were someone else, I would be Madonna!**
> —*Priety Zinta*

Karan Johar: Abhishek or Hrithik?

Preity Zinta: I like both.

Karan Johar: No, say one, commit.

Preity Zinta: Apple!

Karan Johar: Susan Roshan or Gauri Khan?

Preity Zinta: Susan is my best friend, Gauri is too!

Karan Johar: No. You are not being fun. OK. Next question, hair in *Armaan* or hair in *Lakshya*?

Preity Zinta: Hair in *Armaan*.

Karan Johar: OK, Rani or Kareena?

Preity Zinta: Rani.

Karan Johar: Kareena or anyone else?

> If someone asks me, I would say I was great in bed!
> —Saif Ali Khan

Preity Zinta: Anyone else.

Karan Johar: OK. I think we are done with 90 seconds. I think it was really wonderful. Preity, you were very brave. Congratulations! We move on to you, Saif Ali Khan, to *Rapid Fire*. You have 90 seconds, which we always exceed. The idea is to have lots of fun. This is your *rapid fire*. Here goes the question I will ask. If someone asks you how you were in bed, you would say?

Saif Ali Khan: Great!

Karan Johar: Three qualities you think you have that other stars do not.

Saif Ali Khan: Humility, honesty and a sense of self-depreciation.

Karan Johar: Great! The worst historical character you would choose!

Saif Ali Khan: Prithviraj Chauhan.

Karan Johar: OK. You have watched a really bad film. When you meet the producer and director, what would you say?

Saif Ali Khan: Thanks a lot for calling me on the show.

Karan Johar: When I say black-buck, the one word that comes to your mind..

Saif Ali Khan: Jail!

Karan Johar: You wish you were Salman Khan, because…

Saif Ali Khan: He makes lots of money.

Karan Johar: The sexiest woma you know in India?

> *Karan Johar:* When I say black-buck, the one word that comes to your mind..
> —Saif Ali Khan: Jail

Preity Zinta: See, even he thinking; you better take my name!

Saif Ali Khan: Preity Zinta.

Karan Johar: You say Preity Zinta, but you don't really mean it. We move on. If you had to advise Mallika Sherawat, what would you say?

Saif Ali Khan: I would say that she is fantastic. Keep it going, baby!

Karan Johar: OK. If a man made a pass at you, you would say....

Saif Ali Khan: It depends on the meaning.

Karan Johar: Glad to clarify that. The best Indian film you have seen in recent times?

Saif Ali Khan: *Sholay.*

Karan Johar: The worst Indian film you have seen in recent times?

Saif Ali Khan: *Aao Pyar Karein.*

Karan Johar: OK. For me, *LOC* was—

Saif Ali Khan: Long.

Karan Johar: If you have to change one thing about yourself, what would it be?

Saif Ali Khan: Six inches taller.

Karan Johar: Six inches what?

Saif Ali Khan: Taller.

Karan Johar: Taller! OK, height wise.

Saif Ali Khan: Yeah.

Karan Johar: The one person in the world who truly loves you?

Saif Ali Khan: My mom. How sweet!

Karan Johar: Barjatya or Ram Gopal Verma?

Saif Ali Khan: Ram Gopal Verma.

Karan Johar: Who is sexier – Preity or Kareena?

Saif Ali Khan: Preity.

Karan Johar: Aditya Chopra or Kunal Kohli?

Saif Ali Khan: Aditya Chopra.

Karan Johar: Tendulkar or Dravid?

Saif Ali Khan: Dravid.

Karan Johar: OK. For me, LOC was–
Saif Ali Khan: Long!

Karan Johar: Who is sexier – Preity or Kareena?
Saif Ali Khan: Preity!

Karan Johar: Aishwarya Rai or Sushmita Sen?

Saif Ali Khan: Aishwarya Rai.

Karan Johar: All right. Sushmita, you have lost out on Saif's sex appeal. Saif, you win this coffee hamper.

Saif Ali Khan: Sorry, ma'am.

Karan Johar: We have finished the *rapid fire* round with Preity Zinta and Saif Ali Khan. We shall proceed ahead.

Preity Zinta: Hello.

Karan Johar: Did you really do the show for the love of talk show or did you do it for me?

Preity Zinta: I really did it for you.

Saif Ali Khan: You.

> **Saif has got a long nose!**
> *—Female*

Karan Johar: Not for the spirit of a talk show?

Preity Zinta: You have brought a lot of things out. I would never talk forever. I have realised that you cannot be so fake.

POLING TIME

Karan Johar: OK. We had fun. You know what else? I had fun when we went on our little coffee trip. I took Preity and Saif to a little coffee house to do a survey. So, do you guys want to see what happened?

Saif Ali Khan: I am dying to see that.

Preity Zinta: Me too!

Karan Johar: You want to see it, so does everyone else. We had coffee with Preity Zinta and Saif Ali Khan, separately.

Preity Zinta: Yes.

Karan Johar: All right, we are going to watch that just now. Keep watching.

Preity Zinta: This is Preity. I am doing a bite on *Koffee with Karan* with Saif. I wanted to know about Saif. What do you think about Saif?

Female: He is cool, very cute.

Preity Zinta: Very cute!

Female: Very handsome.

Male: He is damn cute and a good actor.

Female: He is not that good – I mean he is OK. He has got a long nose.

Male: I think he is a pretty good actor.

> **Preity isn't smoldering and sexy–she is cute and very bubbly!**
> *—Male*

Male: He has turned around very graciously. He is really smart.

Female: I think he brings in a refreshing change.

Male: OK. He has a good jaw line. He is nice. He has good style.

Preity Zinta: Good style!

Female: He is my favorite actor.

Preity Zinta: OK. All the girls like Saif.

Saif Ali Khan: Hi, I am Saif Ali Khan. I am on the show *Koffee with Karan.* The hot topic for the day is none other than Preity Zinta. So sorry, Preity, if I am part of anything that leads to anything amiss. What things come to your mind when I say Preity Zinta?

Male: Pretty. Brilliant actress.

Female: Preity has a lot of life.

Male: She is damn cute, very bubbly and a good actress, indeed.

Saif Ali Khan: Smoldering and sexy?

Male: No, that is fine.

Female: Very smart.

Male: Her dimples are lovely. She is cute. She is one of the bubbly characters.

Preity Zinta: Given a choice between Aamir, Shahrukh and Saif; who would you go for?

Male: I will choose Aamir.

Male: Aamir – Shahrukh Khan.

Female: Saif – Saif Ali Khan.

Saif Ali Khan: Shahrukh Khan.

Female: Saif – Shahrukh.

> **Preity is just crazy, all the time!**
> *–Female*

Saif Ali Khan: Who is better? *Rani in Hum Tum* or Preity in *Kal Ho Na Ho*?

Male: I prefer Preity.

Saif Ali Khan: You prefer Preity?

Male: Rani.

Female: Rani is better in *Hum Tum* – she as an actress first and Preity second.

Preity Zinta: Who would you prefer with Saif – Rani and Saif in *Hum Tum* or Preity and Saif in *Kal Ho Na Ho*?

Male: Rani.

Female: You two!

Preity Zinta: I think that is so because I am in front of you. It is like, 'OK, good. I like you.'

Female: You! I like you guys.

Male: You, I guess.

Preity Zinta: I like him. Saif, I hope you have been watching.

Female: She is just crazy, all the time.

Saif Ali Khan: Awful.

Female: I think she is like the cutest actress onscreen. Personally, she is my favorite. I love her dimpled face.

Saif Ali Khan: OK. You just have to say something bad about her..

Female: I cannot.

Preity Zinta: Do you think he has a long nose?

Female: Yes, he does.

Preity Zinta: Yeah, it is cute.

Female: Yeah, it is.

Preity Zinta: I like it, Saif; I like it.

Saif Ali Khan: What about her legs?

Male: Yeah, she has pretty hot legs. She has great legs.

Saif Ali Khan: She had nice legs.

Male: Yeah, she does.

Saif Ali Khan: She has got a big bum, OK.

> **Preity has got a big bum!**
> *–Saif Ali Khan*

Preity Zinta: Me!

Saif Ali Khan: I keep saying where, you know, where is it?

Male: Yeah but, she is cute.

Saif Ali Khan: She is cute.

Male: She is hot.

Saif Ali Khan: She is a cute girl. I am sorry. Big bum!

Karan Johar: Did he really say that or you did?

Saif Ali Khan: He said so.

Karan Johar: No, I do not believe it!

Saif Ali Khan: Yes, he said it.

Preity Zinta: I do not think I have a big bum.

Karan Johar: Not at all – who was he talking about?

Preity Zinta: I don't think he was talking about me.

Karan Johar: He was talking about you.

Preity Zinta: I think he was talking about you!

Karan Johar: That was quite crazy, so clearly what we saw was this half divide. Every one thought Saif was superb and you were a bubbly character.

Preity Zinta: A bubbly character!

Karan Johar: You are very bubbly. I have said that the word will not leave you. That was fun! What did you think? What was the vibe you got when you went and asked the people?

Saif Ali Khan: I was heartened to see that a lot of people in the suburbs share the same opinion like we do. Obviously, they talked, discussed and shared the same vibe.

Karan Johar: So you believe you have a long nose as well?

Saif Ali Khan: I do, obviously. I believe you have noticed that. It is not that long. From a certain angle, it is quite sexy.

Karan Johar: I guess you are sensitive about your nose, aren't you, Saif?

Saif Ali Khan: No, I mean, I am self-depreciative. I would rather say it before anyone else. It might be stupid to wander around saying, 'You know, I have a great nose.' It has a certain character.

Karan Johar: I think I do not have a big bum. You have a big nose. She has the big bum. So, those were the issues.

Preity Zinta: I believe I have a big bum.

Karan Johar: I don't think we can go...

Preity Zinta: Further?

Karan Johar: ....deep into this topic; I think we should leave it right there. I had lots of fun with you guys. I hope you did too. We had a ball. I think it was a great fun.

Preity Zinta: Yeah.

Saif Ali Khan: It was fantastic.

CONCLUSION

Karan Johar: I have good chemistry with you two.

Saif Ali Khan: I am little worried.

Karan Johar: You are worried about what?

Saif Ali Khan: I was wondering what you said. I am worried about my nose.

Karan Johar: You are still worried about it? No darling, trust me.

Preity Zinta: Trust me!

Karan Johar: It's fine. Just trust me. I am saying you look hot – that's the way you are!

Saif Ali Khan: Thank you.

Karan Johar: All right. I want you to sign this mug right next to you. You are on *Koffee with Karan*, so you have to sign. Say something nice and write something really cool. This personally autographed mug could be yours only if you answer the questions correctly. Well, have you thought what to do with that mug?

Preity Zinta: It is full.

Karan Johar: Yes, it has lovely little things. Preity, did you do an MF Hussain on the mug?

Saif Ali Khan: I drew paste, she drew teeth. Why did you draw teeth? What is it about teeth?

Preity Zinta: It is to this mug.

Karan Johar: Thank you, Preity, for the input. Thank you, Saif, for being on the show. Thank you, Preity, it was wonderful chatting with you.

Preity Zinta: Yeah.

Karan Johar: I mean it was strange. We are really friends. We know we are phone calls away. It was quite fabulous to sit across on the lovely sofa and chat.

Preity Zinta: It was fun. I want to watch the episode.

Karan Johar: Yeah, it was fun. Thank you for everything. You are going to watch *Koffee with Karan*?

Preity Zinta: Yes.

Karan Johar: OK. I hope you and everyone else does.

Saif Ali Khan: Of course, I am sure they will.

Karan Johar: OK. What we are going to do with that mug? Can you take it to that *koffee wall?*

Saif Ali Khan: Great!

Karan Johar: Place it there. It will be there for eternity.

Saif Ali Khan: Lovely! And after that, whoever wins that mug.

Karan Johar: It is their lucky day and lucky chance!

Saif Ali Khan: Excellent!

Karan Johar: So, we will walk towards the *koffee wall,* come.

Preity Zinta: Yeah.

Karan Johar: That is Saif, the hamper boy!

● ● ●

Aishwarya & Sanjay Leela Bhansali
A Director and His Muse

One cannot help but say that she is the most beautiful woman on the planet earth. She has been the face of *Time* magazine besides that of the Indian cinema in the West, today. Probably, she is the only actor who is sought after by a host of international moviemakers. Her face, I believe, would lure many producers to launch a thousand films. So, let us call on the very fascinating, the glamorous, the beautiful *Miss World 1994*, Aishwarya Rai.

AISHWARYA RAI

Karan Johar: Welcome to my show!

Aishwarya Rai: Thank you.

Karan Johar: Do you feel strange to be in conversation with me like this?

Aishwarya Rai: I do not know. Let us see what will follow. It is always fun talking to you.

MS WORLD

Karan Johar: All right. How does it feel to be the most beautiful woman in the world? Silly question. I know you have been asked a lot of times

Aishwarya Rai: No. Sometimes, I feel they are just saying it because I have won the title, so I have to be welcomed with that note. I really don't know how to respond to it.

Karan Johar: Totally obsessed with hearing 'how beautiful'? Do you sometimes feel like hearing you seldom look nice?

> **My life is like anybody else's.**
> *–Aishwarya Rai*

Aishwarya Rai: I do. What makes you think I do not hear that?

Karan Johar: Who says those things? I want to know which person?

Aishwarya Rai: My life is like anybody else. I lead a life like anybody else.

Karan Johar: You are also Aishwarya, one Indian bride who always invites prejudice for no rhyme or reason. Sorry for the pun! How do you react? Sometimes, you are accused that you are not spontaneous. It is said that almost everything is rehearsed. Are you completely obsessed with hearing this?

Aishwarya Rai: It is a small world. You know who said it and why. Initially, it would definitely hurt a lot. I have not yet succeeded in developing a rhino hide. I am sensitive. It does hurt but the degree has changed with time. You also know why it is easier not to take it to heart.

Karan Johar: I want to set the records straight – your personal graces, the way you sit, the way you stand, the way you operate are part of your etiquette and the way you interact. So it is not that you are putting it on, are you?

Aishwarya Rai: What more validation is there than these titles? I was not trained. I am one actress without a formal training. I had that natural body language even in terms of a seasoned model – believe it or not! It has made my job somewhat easier. Sometimes, I feel shy, a little bit awkward in front of the camera. If I look at myself, it is just natural body language, natural grace that matters. I guess people will find it rather hard to assimilate or accept the attributes you practice or sustain.

> **Guess what! I have many detractors!**
>
> *–Aishwarya Rai*

Karan Johar: So, Aishwarya Rai has many detractors?

Aishwarya Rai: Guess what!

Karan Johar: Well, amongst those detractors, you have a great support system – friends. One of them, of course, has been Sanjay Leela Bhansali. He has been a pillar of support.

Aishwarya Rai: Yeah.

Karan Johar: You know he will be our next guest tonight.

SANJAY LEELA BHANSALI

Karan Johar: My next guest tonight is Sanjay Leela Bhansali. He is the most successful filmmaker in the country. His films are not films, but they are an oasis of experiences. The experiments of opulence, the beauty of sheer cinema are limitless. Every frame he does on the canvas is a painting on celluloid. Yet, it incorporates the personal note. I believe him to be my most favourite filmmaker. Let us call on Sanjay Leela Bhansali, the director Sanjay! How are you? Does it feel strange to be interviewed by me? I was just asking Aishwarya the same.

Sanjay Leela Bhansali: No, it feels good. I like talking to you. You are my only friend in the industry.

Karan Johar: How sweet! We are all friends today.

The Introvert

Karan Johar: Why are you like this, Sanjay? You are the country's most successful filmmaker – yet, one never sees nor hears about you much. You do not come out of the four walls of your home. You make films that are so open, so larger than life – yet, you do not go anywhere from your house to see those open spaces!

Sanjay Leela Bhansali: I like being with myself. I like thinking. I like dreaming and I suffer from social phobia. Because once you become a celebrity, you are always attacked. You are always laughed at. You are always talked about. It goes on unending. I would rather abstain from the glamour.

Karan Johar: So, is there somewhere a feeling of persecution at times?

> Once you become a celebrity, you are always attacked.
> – Sanjay Leela Bhansali

Sanjay Leela Bhansali: Yeah.

Karan Johar: Do you go out, meet those people – the people who love your cinema? Have you never enjoyed the feeling?

Sanjay Leela Bhansali: No, once I get down to a party, then I rock; I proceed nonstop.

Karan Johar: We have seen that. We have seen you dance and have a blast!

Sanjay Leela Bhansali: If I am in a good mood, then, I am all out there.

Aishwarya Rai: You are just selective.

Sanjay Leela Bhansali: Yes. I am very uncomfortable with people.

Karan Johar: And people from the fraternity, especially.

Sanjay Leela Bhansali: Not, at all! It is not a question of liking. It is that of being uncomfortable. I like people, but rather stay away.

Karan Johar: Do you feel there is a kind of comfort that I feel as a filmmaker? Or do you feel surrounded by the aura of negativity because you are immensely successful and feel humble?

> I am very uncomfortable with people.
> –Sanjay Leela Bhansali

Sanjay Leela Bhansali: No, I do not go out so much. I have not yet felt about it. I do not know about the negative aspect. However, I want to stay away from it. My world is beautiful. I dream. There is so much to do, and so much to think. I think it is always very difficult to execute what is in your mind. It takes a lot of your energy. I would rather save the energy and do what I want to rather than wasting the time in gossip.

Karan Johar: 'How are you, sweetie?' 'How are you darling?' 'How are you?' It is a waste of time. What does one say in a party? I always see photographs on Page 3 – standing and talking or laughing. What do they talk? I get completely confused. What is there to talk?

Aishwarya Rai: We meet a few connected people. That is when we really have conversations.

FRIENDSHIP VS RUMOURS

Sanjay Leela Bhansali: Aishwarya and I can talk for hours and hours and hours together.

Aishwarya and I can talk for hours and hours and hours together!

–Sanjay Leela Bhansali

Karan Johar: How do you perceive Sanjay, Ash – this part of his personality?

Aishwarya Rai: I accept him as he is. I mean I do not judge it. I do not question it. I can understand the way you guys perceive him. But for me, it is the person that I know. When we meet, we actually plan to keep the rest of the evening free. It will trail on until the wee hours if he comes late in the evening. We plan our menu, the snacks we devour and the works we discuss. We sit for hours.

Karan Johar: Clearly, there is a bonding; there is a rapport.

Aishwarya Rai: Certainly.

Karan Johar: There has been a bonding between Sanjay Bhansali and Aishwarya Rai. Then, there was a downswing. Who is going to answer this one? What happened to the friendship in between?

Aishwarya Rai: Nothing went wrong with it. You are talking about something that had appeared in a leading magazine, but I had never given the interview. I do not know how the media behaves. They probably have deadline bound articles. I am not the one who enjoys being regularly on the cover. I have never functioned like that. So, this particular magazine had to carry the article. I was keeping a very busy schedule. I was resuming my work after my accident. I could not have spared the time to give the interview. So, an article was carried in the magazine anyway with one or two or three intervening quotes. But I had never given that interview!

> **When Sanjay and I meet, the meeting trails on until the wee hours!**
>
> *– Aishwarya Rai*

Karan Johar: Is that the quote justifying Sanjay Leela Bhansali's survival in his life?

Aishwarya Rai: Not just him. It was not just exclusive to him. There was him and Shahrukh, where I said they are amazing professionals, but they have a long way to go as human beings!

Sanjay Leela Bhansali: I think in one way, she is right. Every human being has to constantly keep growing.

Aishwarya Rai: It applies to all of us, however I did not say that in the article, Sanjay! I clarified it – I made the journalist speak to you.

> **I am not the one who enjoys being regularly on the cover!**
> *–Aishwarya Rai*

Sanjay Leela Bhansali: It is very important to know that every relation goes through a change. If you are friends, you would have a different opinion. She did not want to work in my film for personal reasons, which I would endorse. And that would be fine. But the press has made it out to be a big reason for the rift.

Aishwarya Rai: That was the other odyssey. We have literally discussed it at our residence. This was prior to my accident, where we actually talked. He had been wonderful. He spoke to me about the film – his vision as a director. He did see us working as the ideal cast for the film. Unfortunately, I could not work with the kind of team he had anticipated. We were amicable about that. It was fine.

Karan Johar: What were the circumstances?

Sanjay Leela Bhansali: Well, she had to enact in the film *Bajirao Mastani.* It was well known probably on the national level. It was amicable with us. The media blew it out of proportion and cast it out as *'Aishwarya walks out of Bajirao Mastani'.* We had a communication gap. I was in the hospital for my amputated leg.

> **I could not work with the kind of team Sanjay had anticipated for *Bajirao Mastani!***
> *–Aishwarya Rai*

Karan Johar: Yes. Did you have an accident?

Aishwarya Rai: This was already out.

Karan Johar: Everything was happening simultaneously – your injury, this whole controversy.

Aishwarya Rai: I had been to the Cannes film festival. As soon as I returned, I went to the studio and resumed work. I was unaware of this article. Literally, my well wishers told me what the interview was all about. I never gave it.

Karan Johar: What were your sentiments?

Sanjay Leela Bhansali: I was extremely hurt by the fact that Aishwarya was not going to be *Mastani,* because she was really a central part of my work. A very important part of what I visualized or what I dreamt or what I wanted to make. And so is my friendship with Salman.

> **I was extremely hurt by the fact that Aishwarya was not going to be *Mastani!***
> –*Sanjay Leela Bhansali*

And I was in a dilemma, what should I do?

Karan Johar: You cannot make choices with friends.

Sanjay Leela Bhansali: True. And then, I wanted to stand by her and respect her wish – that she did not want to work. Yes, we did not meet in between for almost a year-and-a-half because she felt that I was not a good friend enough to be able to have gone and met her in the hospital, which any other friend would have felt the same way. I wanted her to go home and relax a little bit.

Karan Johar: So, there were small misunderstandings, which friends should demand of each other; I feel that is what friendship is all about.

Sanjay Leela Bhansali: The sad part is that the day I was about to go to her house, the day before the press revealed that she has walked out of *Mastani,* I was hurt that she could have picked up the phone and spoken to me directly before going to the press. I guess these are all the small misunderstandings.

Aishwarya Rai: Now, he had seen the headline.

> **There was a report that Aishwarya and I would go and take *sanyaas* together!**
> –*Sanjay Leela Bhansali*

Sanjay Leela Bhansali: I have often ignored the media. It became worse because there was a report about the kind of human being Aishwarya Rai wants me to become – that we would go and take *sanyaas* together!

Karan Johar: Quite funny, that comment!

Aishwarya Rai: He only told me when we met to see '*Joan of Arc'.* I must say how it happened. I was completing *Kyon, Ho Gaya Na.* We occupied two floors in Film City – we were literally one next to the other. He was shooting for *Black.* The media came to cover the shoot and we were wrapping *Kyon, Ho Gaya Na.* A journalist stayed back. It was really interesting to meet the scribe. His purpose was served – to stay to cover my yearning to meet him!

Karan Johar: To stay on and to clarify with Sanjay.

Aishwarya Rai: But the journalist had left. So I went there. He was not expecting me at all. I called the journalist and made him speak on the phone. I said nothing but about our friendship. 'That was an interview I never gave. It is an article you printed because you had to meet a deadline. I want you to actually say it to Sanjay.' He did say it to him and Sanjay said, 'I do not need any clarification!'

Karan Johar: Probably you chose not to believe it. You know that it hurts so much.

Sanjay Leela Bhansali: No, it is important to clarify. It was completely pointless! It was yesterday; it was over. She could have said something in anger. We have had our emotional outbursts. We restored our relation exactly as friends, where we had left.

Aishwarya Rai: Somebody wrote another piece.

Sanjay Leela Bhansali: The good part is that we have moved towards sainthood!

Karan Johar: You became glorified human beings!

Aishwarya Rai: That day when we met, we chatted for too long! I came there to clarify something and we sang four-five bhajans!

Karan Johar: You sang four-five bhajans! So we will sing the bhajans together?!

Aishwarya Rai: The film *Bajirao Mastani* is canned?

Sanjay Leela Bhansali: There is a lot of confusion. This *Mastani* is not only one – all *Mastanis* who come put me in trouble, I think!

Karan Johar: Kareena Kapoor was the *Mastani* but now is not.

> **When we met, we sang four-five bhajans!**
> *—Aishwarya Rai*

Sanjay Leela Bhansali: Yes, she has gone ahead and signed two films opposite Salman. I expected the duo to be reserved for my film. I wanted them together for the first time. So, they've done two films together without waiting for me.

DIRECTOR VS FRIEND

Karan Johar: All right. Pointless distance between Bhansali and Aishwarya Rai! There is no *Bajirao Mastani* being made. Sanjay! How do you see Aishwarya on screen? The way you have presented her – the world will say that she appears best in movies *Hum Dil De Chuke Sanam* and *Devdas*. So how do rate Aishwarya in the film as filmmaker?

Sanjay Leela Bhansali: I disbelieve that the directors will understand the aura of Aishwarya Rai. Neither have they understood the hype she generates nor her aesthetics or talent. Aishwarya has excelled in most of the films. She gropes to find something unique from the director. She had not succeeded in her bid to put the weight on directors. The rapport between Aishwarya and me has enhanced our relationship.

Karan Johar: Looking back to those ups and downs, did she dislike working with you?

Sanjay Leela Bhansali: You know, Karan, we fought amongst ourselves during the production of two films. I often love to hate Aishwarya.

> **I often love to hate Aishwarya!**
> *–Sanjay Leela Bhansali*

Aishwarya Rai: He always said like that and I always wondered why it was so?

Sanjay Leela Bhansali: We had umpteen fights on our schedules. Our studio aides wondered what the hell happened. We were found shouting and screaming quite frequently.

Karan Johar: Almost like a husband and wife from what I see– the celluloid husband and wife!

Sanjay Leela Bhansali: So, I forgive those fights. What misunderstanding has crept in? What was the distinct factor? It did not really bother me.

Aishwarya Rai: People do not understand our relationship. Sometimes, we both are just so passionate. Because both of us are very.......

> **You two are almost like the celluloid husband and wife!**
> *–Karan Johar*

Sanjay Leela Bhansali: Strong headed, passionate...

Aishwarya Rai: ..and honest.

Sanjay Leela Bhansali: And we love what we do, so it is crazy.

Karan Johar: No, but there is an immaculate bond – there is this affinity.

Aishwarya Rai: Madness – that's what he loves.

Karan Johar: What happens when you have to choose? Isn't that difficult? Like you said you had a problem with the male lead of *Bajirao Mastani*. If the situation has to be repeated today, because too much time has passed. What would you do again, if the crisis recurs? Would you sacrifice....?

Aishwarya Rai: Working with him? Yes! Because my reasons are still the same. There is no confusion in my reasons and it is crystal clear.

Karan Johar: It is a clear thought process.

Aishwarya Rai: I am not being stubborn. The reasoning had multiple ripples but it is not uni-dimensional. I have upheld it because we are adults to sort out the differences. It is not 'Will you?' and 'No, I will not.' We have discussed it and reasoned it out.

Karan Johar: Sanjay, do you abide by that reason? Do you feel that she is justified in not working with him?

Sanjay Leela Bhansali: It is something very personal. I do not justify it but assert whether it was right. It is her personal feeling. Yeah! And when it came to *Bajirao,* I was very clear that Salman was indispensable.

Karan Johar: For *Bajirao Mastani?*

Sanjay Leela Bhansali: For *Bajirao.* I felt that I need to befriend him. I was in a dilemma because on one side, I love Aishwarya and on the other, I love Salman. I was extremely torn between

> **When it came to *Bajirao,* I was very clear that Salman was indispensable.**
> *–Sanjay Leela Bhansali*

them. I think this film seldom could have been made minus Aishwarya Rai. If she agreed to enact the role, it would have to be opposite Salman. So, I abandoned the idea to make the film without them.

Karan Johar: So you went ahead and made *Black.*

Aishwarya Rai: Yes.

Karan Johar: And *Black* with Rani Mukherjee. How different was working with Rani? Aishwarya is all set to hear the answer of this question.

Aishwarya Rai: Oh, no! Now, you are going to read into everything.

Sanjay Leela Bhansali: Aishwarya is a star. Aishwarya has got an aura. She has the attitude and aptitude, but not Rani. Rani is the girl-next-door. She is completely

> **Rani is completely mad and a fantastic performer!**
> *–Sanjay Leela Bhansali*

mad! I had a wonderful working relation with her. She does not have the aura of a star, but is no less fantastic in performance. They were completely different in respect to performance.

Karan Johar: Did it break your heart, Aishwarya?

Aishwarya: That there is another leading lady on Sanjay Leela Bhansali's sets? No, because I had already taken the decision not do *Bajirao Mastani*. It's not that I had prepared myself I was not going to work with him. There is a kind of possessive streak – but not so much that I can't see him working him with anybody else.

Karan Johar: But particularly with Rani, with whom you also have had a kind of a problem, haven't you?

Aishwarya Rai: No. I keep saying that it is of absolutely no consequence.

Karan Johar: Is it a media hype issue?

Aishwarya Rai: It is of no consequence whatsoever. It really does not matter.

UNPLUGGING AISHWARYA

Karan Johar: What happens, Sanjay, when you pick up the newspaper in the morning and you read that there has been a *Bride and Prejudice*? There was criticism about that film and about Aishwarya's wardrobe. Ash, I do not know why they were after your clothes. Do you silently feel that I am the only one who makes her look stunning?

Sanjay Leela Bhansali: No. I feel a little proud of myself on how much I understand her. Even if she goes to the best director in the country besides me in terms of wanting to work with anybody else, I do not think they will understand her. I will never want another director to understand her.

> **I will never want another director to understand Aishwarya!**
> *–Sanjay Leela Bhansali*

Aishwarya Rai: So sweet!

Sanjay Leela Bhansali: It is a selfish feeling, though.

Karan Johar: Selfish feeling! What happens when you read Aishwarya badly dressed at Cannes or at a premiere?

Sanjay Leela Bhansali: I personally feel Aishwarya has been subjected to a lot of criticism, which she has to understand.

Karan Johar: She has been representing the country, she is doing so many things that go beyond looking a certain way or what she is wearing or not. That is completely stupid. I feel that Aishwarya has to understand one thing that whatever she is doing, she is going to be ripped apart by people. She has to stop

> **Aishwarya has to stop answering, stop justifying and stop caring about what people say!**
> –*Karan Johar*

answering. She has to stop justifying. She has to stop caring about what people say.

Aishwarya Rai: That is what we were chatting about earlier on today.

Karan Johar: This is the most amazing part – coming from someone like him.

Aishwarya Rai: Now that is his personality, which is incredibly contained. There is a confidence in being contained – so even the little bit that I speak he feels. He has known me for so long and says that I should not give up. He believes that you transcend this level. 'You do not even need to do this. Why don't you speak your mind?'

THE CANNES CONTROVERSY

Karan Johar: I want you to say something right now to those people who comment on your clothes on a daily basis.

Aishwarya Rai: I am completely off that topic. What I am there for is definitely more credible. It will account for why I am for these events or functions. People do not want to throw light on being a member of the jury of the prestigious Cannes festival. They would rather talk about...

Karan Johar: What you wore?

Aishwarya Rai: It is just easier to skirt it with such a short-lived memory of two days before the media sees you on crutches and two days later, see you on slippers. I mean when people say, 'what you are doing in slippers and not in stilettos?' do I have to justify that? It is ridiculous.

Karan Johar: When other designers, members of fashion fraternity speak out loud?

> **Do you think that the fashion designers in our country don't understand *Armani?***
> –*Aishwarya Rai*

Aishwarya Rai: They repeat themselves. Because like I said, truth is superior. So, do you think that the fashion designers in our country don't understand Armani?

Karan Johar: You said it. It is a statement in itself.

Aishwarya Rai: One thing I would like to say, which is not justification – it is just to throw light on – if the designers are clueless. For the normal people, the people out here who do not know that it functions a bit differently abroad. I do not really walk into a store and choose my outfits. The designer has their stylist sent to you to choose your entire look from top to bottom, literally just for the event.

Karan Johar: They have their stylist to choose from the outfit from a group of clothes. It is because it is that designer's statement on the red carpet.

Aishwarya Rai: It is really the statement of Armani. It is not me walking into the store and having made appropriate choices. I think that says everything.

THE OFFICE

Karan Johar: OK. Aamir Khan – *The Rising*. Shahrukh Khan – something went wrong in *Chalte Chalte*. Salman Khan, of course, is the past. Is that settled now or is there still a crisis?

> **There will not be any crisis anymore regarding Salman Khan.**
>
> *–Aishwarya Rai*

Aishwarya Rai: There will not be any crisis.

Sanjay Leela Bhansali: Of course! Shahrukh Khan was the common factor. He was in *Devdas*, but was not a part of *Bajirao Mastani*. You had a working rapport with him. You worked with Salman. I have always done my casting depending on the script. If I have to make *Devdas* with Shahrukh, it has to be Shahrukh. A good friendship does not mean that you have to make a film for the same person. The friendship does not need that. If it comes to *Bajirao*, then Salman suits absolutely bang on. It does not mean that Shahrukh and I seldom talk or there is a problem.

Karan Johar: You have a good rapport?

Sanjay Leela Bhansali: I just love Shahrukh. I think that he has given me such a wonderful

> **A good friendship does not mean that you have to make a film for the same person.**
>
> *--Sanjay Leela Bhansali*

performance in *Devdas* and is so wonderful to work with. I have no problem at all.

THE CHINESE-WHISPER SYNDROME

Karan Johar: You have been silent about your personal life. Neither do you speak about your alleged link with Vivek Oberoi, nor do you admit of having such relations with anybody.

Aishwarya Rai: I have never spoken about my personal life. I do not see any difference either. There is no need because I am here for the virtue of my work. That is how you know me. Of course, you have asked my opinion about 10,000 things on similar grounds. I have never done that nor do I wish to see any reason for such a change. Lest that be judged that, 'Oh, now she talks!' or 'Why did she adopt this manner?' or 'Why did not she do that before?' I just never did it nor see any reason for such change.

Karan Johar: What was that statement?

Aishwarya Rai: I had to make that kind of wihich statement generated a lot... it was almost like the ripple effect. It seemed like I had announced

> **I would not desire for any words ever misrepresented about people who are close to me.**
> *–Aishwarya Rai*

that I walked out of *Bajirao*, which was not what I did. I had to make a statement. A lot was being bandied and played about in the media regarding my personal life before, too. Everybody knows about the dirty stories that went on circulating. I had to make one statement. I wrote that from the hospital and I have released one standard statement to the media because the personal life is exactly that – it is personal. It concerns the people who are an intimate part of your life – your family, their emotions. It is very, very precious. It has to be respected. I would never let that fall victim to the Chinese-Whisper Syndrome where it just gets blown out of proportion. I would not desire for any words ever misrepresented about people who are close to me – my family, who are just so important to me, so important in life. So it was that one statement.

Karan Johar: But you are not denying Vivek Oberoi also.

Aishwarya Rai: Neither is this the *rapid-fire*!

Rapid Fire

Karan Johar: I am heading towards my *rapid fire round*. I expect rapid answers with a lot of fire from you. Do you think that is possible? I am commencing with the lady. The one whom I think is better at my rapid fire wins the *Koffee with Karan koffee-hamper*. I do not think the National Award meant that much to you, Sanjay, as much as this. OK. To the beautiful lady then; I am sure, you would find it difficult to answer. I think you are perfect in balancing the situations. One thing you would like to change about your physical appearance if you have to change something?

Aishwarya Rai: I do not believe in plastic surgery. I am content with the way I am.

Karan Johar: The hottest hunk in Hindi cinema today is?

Aishwarya Rai: Let us say Karan and Sanjay.

Karan Johar: An Indian film in recent times that you wish you had done?

Sanjay Leela Bhansali: *Murder.*

Aishwarya Rai: I have not seen the movie.

> *Karan Johar:* **An Indian film you wish you hadn't done?** *Aishwarya Rai: Aur Pyar Ho Gaya.*

Karan Johar: Tell me one movie which you wish you would have been part of in the last five or seven years.

Aishwarya Rai: *Khamoshi.*

Karan Johar: An Indian film you wish you hadn't done?

Aishwarya Rai: *Aur Pyar Ho Gaya.*

Karan Johar: The weirdest rumour you have heard about yourself?

Aishwarya Rai: That I was in Pakistan over a weekend staying at a certain politician's house – I was in London! The foreign press blew it all over the media. That was the ugliest thing they did.

Karan Johar: An alleged link-up that was not true.

Aishwarya Rai: There was one for which I did not have time at the beginning of my career. Obviously, I turned furious and took the *Star & Style* publisher to the court of law because they had carried an article where the world knew who it was and not me. It was projected that I was allegedly caught with Akshay Kumar and Raveena blew the siren. It was absolutely untrue.

Karan Johar: Well done, Aishwarya! That was the best piece of dope I have got out of you tonight. OK. The worst criticism you got about yourself?

Aishwarya Rai: When I went to the Cannes Film Festival, it was such a prestigious venue – yet they were questioning about a slipper when they knew that I had an injured foot!

> **I was allegedly caught with Akshay Kumar and Raveena blew the siren!**
> *–Aishwarya Rai*

Karan Johar: All right! What kind of a man would Aishwarya like to marry? Who fits the bill?

Aishwarya Rai: You guys will know when it happens.

Karan Johar: Give me a prototype, even if he is married to someone.

Aishwarya Rai: I cannot think about the prototype, considering the kind of experiences I have had. I would just like to take it as it comes.

Karan Johar: All right. The person that comes to your mind when I say is the *4 am friend?*

Aishwarya Rai: Zirak, my best friend from college.

Karan Johar: A woman of substance?

Aishwarya Rai: Me.

Karan Johar: God of Acting.

Aishwarya Rai: There are so many icons but the one that I have encountered is Amitji who is just incredible.

Karan Johar: The promising newcomer – Vivek, Shahid, Zayed, John.

Aishwarya Rai: Vivek is brilliant at his work.

Karan Johar: Cinematic genius? Karan, Sanjay..

Aishwarya Rai: I am amidst the presence of two.

> **A woman of substance?**
> **Aishwarya Rai: Me!**
> *– Karan Johar*

Karan Johar: All right. What comes to your mind when I say the following names? Shahrukh Khan.

Aishwarya Rai: Sharp! Brilliant! Media had a lot of fun with this name in my life.

Karan Johar: Salman Khan.

Aishwarya Rai: Next question!

Karan Johar: Vivek Oberoi!

Aishwarya Rai: The wonderful, wonderful friend.

Karan Johar: Very quickly then, these are the choices – Sanjay Bhansali on the sets or Sanjay Bhansali off the sets?

Aishwarya Rai: Both.

Karan Johar: Shahrukh, Aamir or Salman – who happens to be the most rocking Khan?

Aishwarya Rai: Shahrukh has been an incredible artiste to work with. I have not had the opportunity to work with Aamir – I really love his work.

Karan Johar: I saw you would not go the third way. Salman in *Hum Dil..* or Shahrukh in *Devdas*?

Aishwarya Rai: Both have done their jobs brilliantly.

Karan Johar: Rani or Kareena?

Aishwarya Rai: They were a part of *Mujhse Dosti Karoge*.

Karan Johar: That is what you have to say, Aishwarya? I am very disappointed with your *Rapid-Fire round*. You were neither rapid nor there was any fire. I think you are not going to win my *koffee-hamper*. Sanjay, your turn. The most exciting film you have witnessed in the last decade?

Sanjay Leela Bhansali: *Khamosh Pani*.

Karan Johar: OK. The basic thought that comes about the remix music videos.

Karan Johar: Remix music videos?
Sanjay Leela Bhansali: Rubbish!

Sanjay Leela Bhansali: Rubbish!

Karan Johar: David Dhawan comedy?

Sanjay Leela Bhansali: Over the top!

Karan Johar: Super hit sex film?

Sanjay Leela Bhansali: *Murder*.

Karan Johar: Crossover cinema?

Sanjay Leela Bhansali: Devdas.

Karan Johar: The worst criticism that you have heard about yourself?

Sanjay Leela Bhansali: I do not know how to make a film.

Karan Johar: Who said that?

Sanjay Leela Bhansali: Kareena.

Karan Johar: OK. The most under-rated actor in Hindi cinema today is?

Sanjay Leela Bhansali: Akshaye Khanna.

Karan Johar: The most over-rated actor in the Hindi cinema today is?

Sanjay Leela Bhansali: Vivek Oberoi.

Karan Johar: The sexiest actress in Hindi cinema is?

Sanjay Leela Bhansali: Mallika Sherawat.

Karan Johar: Rank the Khans in the order of preference – Shahrukh, Aamir, Salman.

Sanjay Leela Bhansali: Salman is my favourite. Then, Shahrukh, Aamir.

Karan Johar: The newcomer whom you think will be rocking in 2010 will be?

Sanjay Leela Bhansali: Mallika Sherawat.

Karan Johar: One unique quality that Aishwarya has?

Sanjay Leela Bhansali: Giggles!

Karan Johar: Rank the directors in the order of preference – Aditya Chopra, Ashutosh Gowarikar, Farhan Akhtar and Karan Johar.

Sanjay Leela Bhansali: Aditya Chopra, Karan Johar, Ashutosh Gowarikar, Farhan Akhtar.

Karan Johar: A recent Hindi film that you wish had directed?

Sanjay Leela Bhansali: *Dilwale Dulhaniya Le Jayenge.*

Karan Johar: Wonderful – I think the same. A piece of advice that you would like to give to Aishwarya?

Sanjay Leela Bhansali: Come back to Hindi cinema.

Karan Johar: Aishwarya Rai or Rani Mukherjee?

Sanjay Leela Bhansali: Both.

Karan Johar: Critical acclaim or commercial success.

Sanjay Leela Bhansali: Commercial success.

Karan Johar: Kajol or Madhuri Dixit?

Sanjay Leela Bhansali: Madhuri Dixit.

Karan Johar: *Devdas* or *Hum Dil De Chuke Sanam*?

Karan Johar: One unique quality that Aishwarya has?
Sanjay Leela Bhansali: Giggles!

Sanjay Leela Bhansali: *Hum Dil De Chuke Sanam.*

Karan Johar: *Filmfare* Award or *National* Award.

Karan Johar: A piece of advice for Aishwarya?

Sanjay Leela Bhansali: Come back to Hindi cinema!

Sanjay Leela Bhansali: *Filmfare* Award.

Karan Johar: Well done, Sanjay. Very well done. You get the hamper. You have won my *Koffee with Karan Koffee-hamper.* Here you go.

Sanjay Leela Bhansali: Thank you.

Karan Johar: Sanjay Leela Bhansali performed extremely well and won my *koffee-hamper.* All right. Sanjay, are you happy to win the rapid-fire round?

Sanjay Leela Bhansali: Oh, yes! Absolutely!

Karan Johar: Filmfare Award or National Award.

Sanjay Leela Bhansali: Filmfare Award!

PUBLIC OPINION

Karan Johar: All right, my last segment is going to be a lot of fun. We have asked people about questions. (i) Do you think Aishwarya will make it in Hollywood? (ii) What they think of Sanjay Bhansali as a filmmaker?

Do you think Aishwarya will make it in Hollywood?

Abhishek Bachchan: Yes.

Karan Johar: Sure.

Zayed: Yeah, for sure.

Hrithik Roshan: Make what in Hollywood?

Fardeen: She has the fair chance.

Sanjay Dutt: I hope she does, but I do not think so.

Sushmita Sen: I hope so, too.

Shobha De: I would seriously doubt it.

Bobby Deol: I wish she did.

Bipasha Basu: I think she has already taken a step towards it.

Abhishek Bachchan: Very talented, a wonderful professional and a great person to work with.

Zayed: I think she has got universal appeal.

Aishwarya making it in Hollywood? I would seriously doubt it!

–Shobha De

Fardeen Khan: She is talented and is stunning.

Ekta Kapoor: I do not know if she will – I hope so. My first assignment as a flunky was with her. She was awesome!

Shabana Azmi: I think she has got everything. She ought to decide whether she wants to go or feel secure here. She has what it takes.

Sushmita Sen: She is being put up there as someone who will take Bollywood into Hollywood. I really hope so for the sake of everyone.

Amitabh Bachchan: She will go for a certain distance and then there will be a glass ceiling.

Shobha De: Hollywood is full of light-eyed, pale-skinned girls with great figures and perhaps more talent.

Fardeen Khan: It takes a lot to make it there. It is not as easy as it seems. I mean the right break.

Bipasha Basu: It is great. None of the talented actors in Bollywood have done it. She is doing it, especially being a woman – I endorse her for that.

Farhan Akhtar: If anything goes wrong, it will arise from her side.

Hrithik Roshan: Why not? She will make it.

Karan Johar: Your onus on Sanjay Leela Bhansali as a director...

Amitabh Bachchan: I think he is a genius.

> **My first assignment as a flunky was with Aishwarya – she was awesome!**
> –Ekta Kapoor

Abhishek Bachchan: Wonderful!

Sunita Menon: Brilliant!

Fardeen Khan: I think he is meticulous.

Sushmita Sen: Fabulous!

Sunny Deol: I think he is a talented guy.

Sanjay Dutt: A great filmmaker.

Shobha De: He is hugely talented and neurotic.

Amitabh Bachchan: He is very aesthetic!

Zayed: He is very magnanimous.

Shobha De: He has a lot of potential.

Hrithik Roshan: He is the best.

Amitabh Bachchan: He is quite passionate about his work.

Bobby Deol: He is a great filmmaker.

Sunita Menon: I like his style.

Farhan Akhtar: He has been endowed with different style of filmmaking, what I normally appreciate.

Shobha De: *Devdas* was just the tip of the iceberg.

Sanjay Dutt: Let us see what he does in *Black*.

Sushmita Sen: Sanjay Leela Bhansali is capable of making very beautiful movies. He continues to be an Indian as far as his sensibilities are concerned.

Ekta Kapoor: He is definitely good – I could copy his skills of *Devdas* in the television soap serials!

Sunita Menon: He is intense; he is brooding.

I could copy his skills of *Devdas* in the television soap serials!
—*Ekta Kapoor*

Fardeen Khan: His attention to detail is fantastic!

Bobby Deol: Maybe because he thinks so beautifully.

Zayed Khan: He thinks about the things on a large scale and he goes through the pain of research to bring that alive.

Fardeen Khan: I love his senses, the colours.

Sunita Menon: He is very artistic.

Fardeen Khan: The way he exploits emotion.

Farhan Akhtar: I can understand how it works and I can understand how and why people like him.

Lots of stuff in his movies says a lot what he has not said.
—*Fardeen Khan*

Bipasha Basu: The essence of Indian personalities relies on their emotion. I think he portrays them very beautifully.

Fardeen Khan: Lots of stuff in his movies says a lot what he has not said. He really brings out that well. I think he's got an eye for that.

Farhan Akhtar: Credit to him for doing it.

Shabana Azmi: Interesting, I would love to work with him.

CONCLUSION

Karan Johar: What do you have to say about it, Sanjay?

Sanjay Leela Bhansali: I feel good about it. And I thank them all.

Karan Johar: Aishwarya! You were voted in by everyone to reach Hollywood. You possess the requisite talent as the most beautiful actress ever.

Aishwarya Rai: I do not know – this is just going on and on – about Hollywood.

Karan Johar: The fact is that they have expressed their belief in you.

Aishwarya Rai: That's wonderful. I thank them all – truly, I really do.

Karan Johar: Save a few comments by Shobha De.

Aishwarya Rai: Everybody is entitled to cast their opinion. I always reiterate this whole thing of working in the west. What you have sweetly said is, 'come back to Hindi films.' I mean I belong to here, I always mean to. You have seen me shine through Sanjay's cinema. I absolutely love what we do. Of course, I have probably done more roles befitting a typical Indian woman.

Sanjay Leela Bhansali: What excites me about Aishwarya is *Choker Bali, Raincoat* rather than a crossover film. She has got everything – success, name, fame, awards. *Choker Bali* was an outstanding performance.

Aishwarya Rai: I did enjoy doing that.

Karan Johar: Does this ever alarm you that people thought you might take a flight and never come back?

Aishwarya Rai: I am not doing any such thing. I will participate if anything interests me As an actor, it is not Hollywood but Bollywood. Yeah, it's not any kind of stardom or movie I am looking to make whatsoever. I guess Sanjay understands how I shall function. That is the way I have worked here. I am sure everybody knows that I have not made any moves here. I just work in the movies to remain happy and remain a part of this industry. It will hardly change in the future.

Karan Johar: Thank you very much, for being a part of my show and on *Koffee with Karan.* I had a very interesting time. I chatted with my most favourite moviemaker. And I believe Aishwarya is very talented and quite beautiful. Thank you for being on my show. But before I let you go, there is something I need you to do. There is a mug right next to you with a silver pen. Lift it up and sign on the mug outside. Remember, this personally autographed mug could be yours if you participate in the *Koffee Quest contest.* Thank you again.

Aishwarya Rai: Thank you.

Karan Johar: It really meant a lot. We shall walk with that mug towards that *Koffee wall* and place it there.

● ● ●

5

Fardeen Khan and Zayed Khan
The Handsome Devils

He is a star – stylish, sophisticated and suave. My first guest tonight does not have clout at box office, but has the support of women. His female fan following is undeniable. He is arguably one of the best looking boys in the fraternity. He is the son of veteran director and actor, Feroz Khan. Fardeen Khan indeed has the women going gaga. We are going to find tonight exactly how he makes them so. Let us call upon the man himself.

FARDEEN KHAN

Karan Johar: Hello, Fardeen! Welcome to *Koffee with Karan.*

Fardeen Khan: Hello!

Karan Johar: So Fardeen, I hope you shall keep the women going!

Fardeen Khan: This is what I have been told! I do not quite know why it so, neither do I consciously do anything.

THE WONDER YEARS

Karan Johar: I have found out a very interesting piece of information about you – when you were a student abroad.

Fardeen Khan: I had to adopt austerity measures when I was in the University. My father used to give me $100 every month. I blew it up in the first couple of weeks and remained broke the last couple of weeks! I had to work for a few days for more money.

> My father used to give me $100 every month – I remained broke in the last couple of weeks!
> –Fardeen Khan

Karan Johar: So, how was the experience?

Fardeen Khan: I could not get along with the chef. I was buzzing tables and taking orders behind the counter, so that was my first experience. I did not know what kind of life chefs faced in the kitchen for over eight hours every day under arduous circumstances. I was relatively new in America. Moreover, while taking people's orders one needs to know about the lingo of the customers for the toppings they have sought. Every time, I used to say, 'I beg your pardon' to the person placing the order (– I used to pretend that I did not understand. I used to write it down,) the chef would come out yelling – but it was fun. Everything was okay. The really bad experience was about the drug incident.

TROUBLED WATERS

Karan Johar: That kind of put you in the headlines. I was quite surprised about the attention it brought. Do you feel strange about that?

Fardeen Khan: The attention pushed me to stardom in a strange way. People really appreciated the way I dealt with the situation. My family and I were honest about the whole situation.

Karan Johar: Was it difficult to be so honest about something that could have been detrimental to your career?

Fardeen Khan: Absolutely! We never thought of dealing with it in any other way than the way we did. The important thing was that I had my family behind me. My dad always taught me to face the consequences coolly. He and the family did a good job to give me the appropriate support. Otherwise, it would have been a harrowing experience with the media blowing things out of proportion. Many things were inaccurate with prominent people attributing to the developments.

Karan Johar: Like what?

Fardeen Khan: There was this lady – I won't name her – she said that I should go to jail for 10 years because I pose a bad influence for the society.

Karan Johar: Have you ever met her when everything went back to normal?

Fardeen Khan: No – although I have been wanting to.

Karan Johar: Alright. Your family brings me to the next guest tonight.

Zayed Khan

Karan Johar: He is the new addition to the Khan monopoly in the film fraternity. He made an impression despite the presence of Shahrukh Khan in his blockbuster *Main Hoon Na*. Let us call in the very cool Zayed Khan right on. Welcome to *Koffee with Karan*.

Zayed Khan: Thanks!

Karan Johar: We were chatting with Fardeen. He has narrated about the support he had during the drug incident. Where were you at that time?

Zayed Khan: I think I was in Bangalore. Of course, I knew about the incident.

Karan Johar: Has he set a poor precedent for you?

Zayed Khan: No, he is a good brother!

Karan Johar: Zayed, its not that you are completely a good boy.

From what I have read and heard, you were doing naughty things in nightclubs, bashing a few people out!

Zayed Khan: Bashing? No! Actually, I am a very mellow person. Of course, there is the time when somebody is aggressive or just rubs me wrongly.

> **Fardeen just knows how to cover his tracks well!**
> *–Zayed Khan*

Karan Johar: Ah! That is something my older brother would have told me to develop!

Zayed Khan: You know I have got the whole training from Fardeen! He just knows how to cover his tracks well!

Karan Johar: I like that!

Fardeen Khan: I was always known to be totally mellow.

Zayed Khan: Yeah! You could see his body language. I still have to learn from him!

THE PAST AND THE FURIOUS

Fardeen Khan: You have to admit, Zayed, that you had beaten up a few boys.

Zayed Khan: It was a pure self-defense trick. I do not like to get into anything until it is forced upon me.

Fardeen Khan: Let us hear the truth.

Karan Johar: What was the truth? Two incidents have happened in *Olive* and *Athena* – the nightclubs of Bombay.

Zayed Khan: I do not think anything should have happened at *Olive*. Some obstinate guys broke a champagne bottle on my head. Of course, I went mad! I got seven stitches on my head. I refused the anesthesia available in the government hospitals because of its poor quality.

Fardeen Khan: Without any anesthesia? You should have broken a bottle on his head!

> **Some obstinate guys broke a champagne bottle on my head in *Olive*!**
> *–Zayed Khan*

Zayed Khan: Dude! I was in rush at that time!

Karan Johar: Zayed Khan and Fardeen Khan – you really are the bad boys.

Zayed Khan: I amuse myself with the fact that he has been a great brother and that he is stuck with me! He has been very supportive when I came across hurdles. I believe he used to help with his own experiences about what to and what not to do.

THE SUCCESSFUL ELUSIVENESS OF SUCCESS

Karan Johar: Fardeen, you have been five to six years in the industry. You have emerged as a star though box office success has eluded you. You still emerged! Have you ever analyzed yourself?

Fardeen Khan: I have tried to, but I do not know. Somewhere down the line, I seem to strike a chord. Sometimes, I watch my work and think 'why the hell do they like me?'

Karan Johar: Does it upset you when critics really run down on your performances? Does it take a toll on you?

Fardeen Khan: Initially, it did. I would berate 99 per cent of the critics – they are not really qualified to do what they do. A few could give constructive opinion, but most of them really do not know what the hell they are saying. I am my biggest critic. If I have not done well, I will be the first person to say that I have done a dirty job.

> I am my biggest critic. If I have not done well, I will be the first person to say that I have done a dirty job.
>
> –*Fardeen Khan*

Karan Johar: Tell me two to three films in which you think you could have done a better job?

Fardeen Khan: *Kitne Door Kitne Paas.* There are quite a few others.

Karan Johar: Zayed, what do you think about the way Fardeen performs on celluloid?

Zayed Khan: I think he is a very charismatic personality. He has the mood, attitude and the charisma. He is a lady killer with his looks. I do not care what people think about him. I know why people like him.

Karan Johar: You have this westernized image. You are from the film fraternity, and continue to be in the films. Sometimes, it seems you are being choosy when it comes to signing your films.

Zayed Khan: To be honest with you, the whole movie business has changed so dramatically over the last six years. One has to gauge the position of Indian movies in the international arena. The movies that are being made now are focusing on the international market as well. This makes people like me in some way feasible or appealing and hence I have been offered quite a number of roles. I believe people find me to be really 'cool'.

Karan Johar: You do not think that you are alien to the Indian mass?

> I believe myself to have been projected to be that cool so as to cater to the international market as well.
> —Zayed Khan

Zayed Khan: No, not at all. I was very Indian when studying abroad.

Karan Johar: You had that stigma attached to your personality. What do you think?

Fardeen Khan: Actors are restricted to some degree by their physiology, looks, demeanor and whole attitude. I will not try to play the role of a rustic, which could be ridiculous. I would look like a *Jadoo* man if I do. That's why I have been choosy about certain roles.

Karan Johar: So as an actor, you should know your USP, your strengths, your weaknesses, your limitations and should be ready to cash in on them.

Fardeen Khan: I have typically done contemporary roles in terms of my character being modern or Gen-X, thus

> I would look like *Jadoo* if I played the role of a rustic!
> —Fardeen Khan

appealing to non-resident Indians and the city audiences.

Karan Johar: Are you happy with the roles that come your way?

Fardeen Khan: I have enjoyed most of the work, although I do not want to get stuck in any mould.

ON SHAHID KAPUR

Karan Johar: You attempted a negative role in *Fida* recently and got the laurels. And *Fida* brings me to Shahid Kapur and the controversy attached to what had happened there.

Fardeen Khan: Sticky subjects! I would love to talk about it openly, but Bebo is a good friend of mine and for the sake of my friendship with Bebo, I should not say anything about the whole situation.

Karan Johar: I read an article where you said that Shahid has an attitude problem.

Fardeen Khan: It was an off the record conversation that was turned into an interview! There was a problem on the sets of *Fida*. I have worked with Abhishek, Anil and others. We have worked in a certain mode without being critical. This was a little different.

Karan Johar: Zayed, why do you think Fardeen is being so nice about the crisis?

Zayed Khan: Well, it is the better option! That is a lot said without saying anything!

Fardeen Khan: I believe if you have nothing to say, you better keep your mouth shut!

Karan Johar: How do you suppress yourself at this juncture? You really want to go out and say really bad things about Shahid – you don't like Shahid!

> There was a problem on the sets of *Fida*. I have worked with other actors before, but this was a little different.
> –*Fardeen Khan*

Fardeen Khan: Well, he is not my best buddy.

Karan Johar: OK, so we are going to stick to this – Shahid Kapur is no friend of Fardeen Khan. Brothers in arms are Zayed Khan and Fardeen Khan; we have closed the topic of Shahid Kapoor!

Zayed Khan: Wow!

DOSTI AND PYAAR

Karan Johar: Are you in a relationship, Zayed?

Zayed Khan: Yes; her name is Mallika.

Karan Johar: I have met her. She is a very sweet girl without any controversy. Rumours are afloat about Esha and you. How did those start because there is no smoke without fire?!

Zayed Khan: Well, I do not know. Esha and I are great friends. We have a great rapport. She is my buddy. Of course, there is a thin line from the public point of view. Somebody putting arm around your shoulder – it is like they are going out; they see each other; he is cheating on her.

Karan Johar: Do you deny such relation?

Zayed Khan: Absolutely. Nothing happened.

Karan Johar: OK! We have Esha Deol on record saying something. Would you like to hear it?

Zayed Khan: Sure!

Esha: It is safe to relate me to Zayed. My mom knows him since he was a kid. It is strange that people link us. We are good friends; he is one of my best friends. He treats me like the other guys. We hang out together in a group. His girlfriend is part of the scene. I dote over the guy – he is a sweetheart. He is always going to be a good friend of mine. People can link us as much as they want. I am sure he thinks of me as a good friend. I knew his girlfriend before I knew him. I am really not interested in getting involved with a guy attached to

> Zayed treats me like the other guys!
> –*Esha Deol*

someone; it is too much of headache for me! Find me someone good! Zayed! Hope you have a good time. Always be yourself and remain cool on the show.

Zayed Khan: I just used to do that when we mimicked certain people on the sets! Esha is like my buddy. She is the part of the troupe with whom I go and party with and have fun!

> It is safe to relate me to Zayed – my mom knows him since he was a kid.
> –Esha Deol

Karan Johar: Turning left now – Fardeen, Kareena Kapoor – the alleged romance and affair that could not happen?

Fardeen Khan: We never had an affair.

Karan Johar: OK! We have heard about the development – you told her that she has a cute....

Fardeen Khan: A cute, almost perfect heart-shaped butt!

Karan Johar: Do you feel that Shahid had a problem with you? He thinks something might have happened. You would understand that about an insecure boyfriend.

> Kareena has a cute, almost perfect heart-shaped butt!
> –Fardeen Khan

Fardeen Khan: Yeah!

Karan Johar: She has a very comfortable equation with you and adores you.

Fardeen Khan: We behave on the sets as if we were in the field. We are not trying to be someone else.....

Karan Johar: We have her on the record – Kareena Kapoor unplugged...

Kareena Kapoor: I know Fardeen since I was a kid. We are like family friends because our families have been close. I know about the 'Fardeen and Kareena together' story but we are just really good friends. We have done many films together. We have a great relationship. Fardeen is my buddy. He is a wonderful man. Whatever rumour has persisted for two or three years, it has seldom affected us. I want to give a message to Fardeen and Zayed. I know them both since they were kids. I am more friendly with Fardeen. I have bonded with him and I wanted to tell Fardeen that no matter what, he will always be a good friend. I would like to thank him for what he said about me on *Koffee with Karan*. I think he was really cool. Zayed rocks all the way. He is a great guy. He is a great looker and he has a great body. He will stay there. Fardeen, you got me into

> **Fardeen, I am going to praise you later; right now, I want to kick your ass!**
> *–Kareena Kapoor*

trouble for what you said on Karan's show. I am going to praise you later; right now, I want to kick your ass!

Fardeen Khan: I find Kareena hot; she is sexy. She has got a cute ass.

Zayed Khan: Kareena is like a full glam woman. I do not think there would be another Kareena, except Rani.

Karan Johar: What we have observed are two people about whom you two care about – Kareena and Esha. I think it is wonderful. You can have the platonic relationship in the fraternity. You have a girlfriend, who is OK with things from what I have heard, Zayed.

Zayed Khan: It is just a professional way about maintaining friendships. You can easily get uncomfortable. You might as well keep it straight, be as calm as possible and just enjoy everything.

Karan Johar: So there is nothing between Zayed and Esha or between Fardeen and Kareena. Do you see yourself settled down forever?

Fardeen Khan: Absolutely! When the time is right, I am ready to make that kind of commitment – it is a life-long commitment. Marriage comes

> **I come from a broken home so I know what it takes for a successful marriage.**
> *–Fardeen Khan*

with a lot of responsibility. It is not just about getting married. I come from a broken home so I know what it takes. You know you have to make it work.

Karan Johar: You were in a long relationship and then you thought that it would not have worked out in the long run.

Fardeen Khan: I screwed it up!

Karan Johar: It takes a lot of heart, to say that!

Fardeen Khan: You have to be honest to yourself, man!

Karan Johar: Any plans of marriage, Zayed?

Zayed Khan: Yeah! Sometime soon – just working something out before that. I have to secure my career.

Karan Johar: Well, I wish you the best whenever it happens!

Zayed Khan: Cheers!

Rapid Fire

Karan Johar: That was just to lighten up before we head towards my *Rapid Fire Round*.. I shall decide which of you is better at my *rapid fire round*. You will win the *Koffee with Karan Koffee hamper*. I am sure you are dying to win this, Fardeen – this is the one thing you just want! I am going to start with you, Zayed.

Zayed Khan: Then shoot!

Karan Johar: The sexiest woman in Hindi cinema today is?

Zayed Khan: Aishwarya Rai.

Karan Johar: What would you say to Sushmita Sen then?

Zayed Khan: Amazingly sexy, second to know.

Karan Johar: Three words to describe SRK.

Zayed Khan: Unbelievable, amazing and a friend.

Karan Johar: Three words to describe Farah Khan.

Karan Johar: If you had a teacher like Sushmita in Main Hoon Na? What would you do?
Zayed Khan: I would take private tuitions in a house!

Zayed Khan: Very focused, very determined and very bombastic...

Karan Johar: If you had a teacher like Sushmita in *Main Hoon Na*, what would you do?

Zayed Khan: I would take private tuitions in a house!

Karan Johar: One thing Fardeen has that you don't?

Zayed Khan: Great gadgets!

Karan Johar: What do those gadgets do?

Zayed Khan: That's brother talk!

Karan Johar: If Fardeen and you are equally crazy about a girl, what would you do?

Zayed Khan: I would blackmail him emotionally!

Karan Johar: Oh! What would you do on meeting Mallika Sherawat?

Karan Johar: If Fardeen and you are equally crazy about a girl what would you do?
Zayed Khan: I would blackmail him emotionally!

Zayed Khan: Say, 'You are hot!'

Karan Johar: OK. A recent worst Hindi movie you have watched?

Zayed Khan: I think *Shakk*.

Karan Johar: *Shakk*? What *Shakk*?? What are you watching, Zayed?

Zayed Khan: Ok, I have not watched it – I just saw the poster!

Karan Johar: OK. A recent very good Hindi movie you have watched?

Zayed Khan: I think *Munna Bhai*..

Karan Johar: Which person comes to your mind when I say the following – an overrated actor.

Zayed Khan: Pass.

Karan Johar: Underrated actor

Zayed Khan: I think Arshad Warsi.

Karan Johar: God's gift to man?

Zayed Khan: Woman!

Karan Johar: Style icon?

Karan Johar: God's gift to man?
Zayed Khan: Woman!

Zayed Khan: I think it will be between Sanju, Saif and Fardeen.

Karan Johar: If you were playing the role of a teenager boy in love with the teenaged girl and an older woman, who would you like your older woman to be?

Zayed Khan: I am actually playing one movie like that and the older woman is Aishwarya Rai. I would like her to be exactly the same.

Karan Johar: You are calling her an older woman?! Very quickly then – SRK or Hrithik Roshan?

Zayed Khan: Oh God! SRK, yaar!

Karan Johar: Sush or Ash?

Zayed Khan: Guys! This is a crazy man – Ash!

Karan Johar: Farah the choreographer or the director!

Karan Johar: Farah on or off the sets?
Zayed Khan: Farah off the sets for sure!

Zayed Khan: Farah the director – that was easy, man! Thank you!

Karan Johar: Farah on or off the sets?

Zayed Khan: Farah off the sets for sure!

Karan Johar: Esha Deol or Kareena Kapoor?

Zayed Khan: Esha.

Karan Johar: Alright! Thank you, Zayed! You did well!

Zayed Khan: You got me on one or two bad questions.

Karan Johar: Fardeen! If you are having a dream about Aishwarya, Kareena and Rani fighting over you for marriage, how would you like it to end?

Karan Johar: If Aishwarya, Kareena, and Rani fight over you for marriage?
Fardeen Khan: I shall propose to all three – I am allowed legally!

Fardeen Khan: I shall propose to all three; I am allowed legally! I will say, 'No need to fight, girls!'

Karan Johar: One thing in a woman, which drives you really wild, is?

Karan Johar: One thing you have but Zayed does not?
Fardeen Khan: Ten inches!

Fardeen Khan: Her eyes.

Karan Johar: If you were offered *Fida 2*, you would say?

Fardeen Khan: Yeah, sure!

Karan Johar: A newcomer that will come close to copy SRK is?

Fardeen Khan: Zayed Khan – I love you too, brother!

Karan Johar: An actress when she says she is a virgin is – complete the sentence.

Fardeen Khan: She is a liar!

Karan Johar: A Hollywood actress you would like to play strip poker with?

Fardeen Khan: Angelina Jolie.

Karan Johar: An Indian actress you would like to play strip poker with?

Fardeen Khan: Sush.

Karan Johar: The best-dressed woman in Hindi films today?

Fardeen Khan: I think it goes to Sush. She has an amazing sense. There are no two ways about it.

Karan Johar: What Zayed has, but you do not?

Fardeen Khan: A fantastic body!

Karan Johar: One thing you have but Zayed does not?

Fardeen Khan: I told you – ten inches!

Karan Johar: Oh! My God! One thing you have liked about Zayed's performance in *Main Hoon Na*?

Fardeen Khan: I think he was extremely endearing and confident. In a lot of scenes, I think he stood up and matched SRK's talent. They worked really well together, which I think is great for an actor just starting his career.

Karan Johar: Cinematic genius?
Fardeen Khan: Raj Kapoor!

Karan Johar: One thing you have disliked about his performance?

Fardeen Khan: I have told him. Sometimes, he has rushed through his scenes.

Karan Johar: Which person comes to your mind when I say the following words – Sex Goddess?

Fardeen Khan: Angelina Jolie!

Karan Johar: Cool dude with an attitude?

Fardeen Khan: Sanju Baba!

Karan Johar: God of acting?

Fardeen Khan: AB!

Karan Johar: Cinematic genius?

Fardeen Khan: Raj Kapoor!

Karan Johar: **Shahid Kapur or Viveik Oberoi?**
Fardeen Khan: **None!**

Karan Johar: Great answer. If you have to choose between a woman with brains and a great sense of humour and lots of money, whom will you go for?

Fardeen Khan: A sense of humour.

Karan Johar: Alright! Very quickly – Shahid Kapur or Viveik Oberoi?

Fardeen Khan: None!

Karan Johar: Urmila or Kareena?

Fardeen Khan: Urmila.

Karan Johar: Feroz Khan as an actor or Feroz Khan as a director?

Fardeen Khan: Director.

Karan Johar: Hrithik Roshan or Abhishek Bachchan?

Fardeen Khan: AB junior – he is my buddy.

Karan Johar: SRK or Aamir Khan?

Fardeen Khan: Aamir Khan.

Karan Johar: Salman Khan or Sanjay Dutt?

Fardeen Khan: Sanju.

Karan Johar: All right! Well done, Fardeen! I think, Zayed, I am going to give my hamper to Fardeen. I think he did better there, so congrats! This is your *koffee hamper*. We give it to you like a *Filmfare* Award. So, Fardeen won, though Zayed performed very well. Zayed, I have heard this strange thing about you lying on Juhu road! Is that true?

Zayed Khan: My girlfriend and I had a tiff. She was not talking to me. It was very late. So I lay down on the road and told her on the phone that I would not get up until she came down!

Karan Johar: In the middle of the road in Bombay?!

> **My girlfriend and I had a tiff, so I lay down on the road and got up only when she started talking to me!**
>
> *–Zayed Khan*

Zayed Khan: It is pretty residential area. It did not have too many cars. I finally spoke to my girlfriend!

Karan Johar: Have you done anything like this crazy, Fardeen?

Fardeen Khan: I have broken a few things here and there when I was angry, but never really lay flat on the road!

PUBLIC OPINION

Karan Johar: Well, we went to a host of women actually. We have some funny things. Would you like to see what happened?

Zayed Khan: Sure, do we have a choice?

Karan: Hi! This is Karan. I am at Olive and it is Thursday night. It is really rocking. I am here to find out how sexy Fardeen and Zayed are. So, Fardeen and Zayed, this one is for you. What do you say about Fardeen?

Female: I think he is really cute.

Female: His eyes have a sex appeal.

Female: Fardeen is very sexy.

Female: He is very hot.

Female: Honestly, I would say he is mediocre.

Female: He is cute and hot.

Male: He is extremely cool. He should always be like that.

Female: I think he's got a hot body!

Female: Not bad.

Female: I loved him in *Fida*.

Female: He is hot.

Female: He is sexy.

Karan: What would you do if you got naughty with him?

Female: I would have a glass of wine first!

Karan: What do you think about Zayed in *Main Hoon Na*?

Female: Cute.

Female: Zayed is well dressed.

Female: He is very good looking and has a very good body.

Male: Do you like him shirtless?

Female: I like shirtless Fardeen more than shirtless Zayed.

Female: Zayed is hotter than Fardeen and got a cute face.

Male: What do you like about Fardeen Khan – do you feel he is cute?

Female: He is Feroz Khan's son!

Karan: Do you feel Feroz Khan is better than his son?

Female/Male: Yeah, definitely.

Female/Male: I think Zayed is a good dancer. He is interesting to look at.

Female/Male: Zayed has something special about him – very sexy, very cute.

Female/Male: He has this boyish thing about him. A lot of sex appeal.

> *Fardeen Khan:* **Run that back again – I remember some faces....**
>
> *Karan Johar:* **You can catch those gals later!**

Female/Male: I love him in his short haircut that he has done.

Male: Zayed is cute, but Fardeen is cuter. Keep the good looks up! Keep attracting more women! Way to go, Fardeen and Zayed!

Zayed Khan: That was a marathon!

Fardeen Khan: It was a good fun! Run that back again – I remember some faces....

Karan Johar: You can catch those gals later!

FATHER FIGURE

Karan Johar: I want to talk about your fathers. who were both actors or directors; people who have been in the industry over the years; veterans. How has your father influenced your life?

> **My father has a huge influence on me – not in what I am, but the way I think.**
>
> *–Fardeen Khan*

Fardeen Khan: Where do I start? He has been the greatest influence in my life in so many ways – as a person, as an actor, as an achiever. He has really worked hard and is one who is responsible for his family. He is really the one who lives life on his own terms without having to explain himself or make apologies – it is fantastic! It comes with a lot controversy, a lot of conflict.

Karan Johar: He does his own set of things.

Fardeen Khan: I really respect him for that.

Karan Johar: Of course, he comes from yesteryears, so to say, but he is cool – the way he walks in award functions, the way he is dressed, the way he is on stage – people applaud him. Would you like to see yourself like that one day?

Fardeen Khan: I have never tried to emulate him in any way – I really do not think I could. He has his own persona, is cultivated. I want to be known for my own trips, but he definitely has had a huge influence on me – not in what I am, but the way I think.

Karan Johar: Zayed, is your father like Fardeen's? Do you have a different kind of equation with your father? Is there more formality, strictness, seriousness?

Zayed Khan: I think Fardeen and me arrive from the same spot. Our fathers have similar lives in respect of their whole career and they also have

> I can finally have a glass of wine in front of my father and it feels good!
> *–Zayed Khan*

similar relations. They are like Fardeen and me. My father is not flamboyant like Feroz chacha. He is little more reserved about his opinions and stuff. I take examples from his life. It is virtually impossible to completely emulate a life. He has set the precedent for my life. I do not think I will emulate him completely; if I can come anywhere close, I will be happy. I do consult my father for issues. He realizes that we are grown up. We had drifted apart for a very long time – for ten years. We have lost a lot of time, as far as bonding of father and son was concerned. It is a start again in the right direction. We know each other better. I can finally have a glass of wine in front of him and it feels good!

CONCLUSION

Karan Johar: Well, any last thoughts on being here?

Fardeen Khan: It was great being here Karan!

Karan Johar: There is a mug next there to you Zayed – the one with the silver pen in it.

Fardeen Khan: I am hosting a show next year - *Chai* with Fardeen! You are my first guest, Karan, and I will do five episodes with you!

Karan Johar: I have had it then! Please remember – this personally autographed mug could be yours only, if you take part in the *koffee quest contest.* Thank you, Fardeen. Thank you, Zayed. Thank you for being on *Koffee with Karan.* We are going to walk towards koffee wall and place that mug. It is going to lie there until someone wins it. Thank you.

● ● ●

6

Gurinder Chadha & Farah Khan
Desi Tadka

She is one Indian we are really proud of. She has had huge successes at an international level in the recent years. The Indian elements in her movies have put Punjab into almost every home in Manhattan. *Bhaji on the Beach, What's Cooking, Bend It Like Beckham, Bride and Prejudice* are cross-cultural in theme. These represent a brand of humour, typical of Gurinder. She is my first guest tonight – Gurinder Chadha. Let us welcome her.

GURINDER CHADHA

Karan Johar: Hello, my darling! Welcome to my show!

Gurinder Chadha: Thank you! Looking very dashing!

Karan Johar: You are looking lovely.

Gurinder Chadha: Are you going to be horrible with me?

Karan Johar: No, I promise, I won't be. Do you think that I am capable of being horrible?

Gurinder Chadha: No, but that is the reputation which precedes this show.

ALOO GOBHI AND $75 MN

Karan Johar: Oh! My God! Do I have a terrible reputation? No, I am not going to be horrible to you. I am going to ask you very nice questions. Congratulations for your successes on an international level. *Bend It Like Beckham* grossed $75 mn worldwide. My God! Indeed, a huge achievement for a small film like that.

> **I had not expected the success I received in America and India!**
> —Gurinder Chadha

Gurinder Chadha: Yes, I guess. It just appealed to the people across the world. I knew it would do well in England. I had made it for the English audience. I had not expected the success I received in America and India. I think that people tend to forget the world where we once lived in. In the West, a lot of cities are inhabited by people who come from a grandparent of one country or parents from another country. They are born and brought up in this country. So, you have an international community inheritance. The heritage in immigration accounts for it. My films appeal to those people as much as they appeal to Indians in Britain, like Chinese, Australians or Mexicans or Americans of any sort.

Karan Johar: You have a similar family background.

Gurinder Chadha: Yeah! It is all about the identity. The people who have a problem with my work are cultural purists. They feel that culture should remain pure in one

> **The people who have a problem with my work are cultural purists.**
> —Gurinder Chadha

shape or form. That is never going to happen. It has to evolve and change. I can take David Beckham as much as I can take a character like my mother or sister. I can learn how to make *Aloo Gobhi*, cook subji. These things are a part of the 'who am I' concept. I think it saddens me often when people do not appreciate the scale and scope of those thinking outside India in terms of fame.

ZARA HAT KE

Karan Johar: The general vibe in India remained that you were selling India to the west. It is that a criticism a filmmaker like you should receive? How do you interpret it?

Gurinder Chadha: In Britain, I am a British filmmaker. I sell Britain to the world. The Britons perceive me so. My husband is an American. I inhabit many places. I have been adopted by the Hollywood community, which is altogether a different experience. I experience three continents, three worlds. Indian politicians applaude me for making India feel proud. Tony Blair, the former British premier said, 'Wow! I love that your films fly the British flag.' So, I mean I am in a very unique position – I bridge my films with international etiquettes and the British Indian sensibility. That is my sense of Indian nationality from Southhall (a part of London populated by Asians). West London is very different from the people of Punjab.

Karan Johar: Yeah, of course.

Gurinder Chadha: I mean we are very different.

Karan Johar: What do you sense from the intellectual Indian audience or those who criticize you for selling India abroad? It is economically beneficial to the studios in terms of monetary gains because you pick up the variety of cultures Indian and Western and put it on the international platform. Are you aware what one reads about you in India?

> Tony Blair, the former British premier, said, 'Wow! I love that your films fly the British flag!'
> —*Gurinder Chadha*

Gurinder Chadha: No. You see, I make it clear that I would sell my culture at home as well. My films are always British in content and appreciation – how the British have gauged the Indian culture without mingling into the Indian population.

Karan Johar: Because you have been born and brought up there, you do not know about the Indian ethos.

Gurinder Chadha: Yeah, absolutely! I have never lived in India. My family had mixed parentage. My father was from Kenya, while my mother was an Indian. I have never lived in India. I had never been to any part of the Indian peninsula. I project myself to be a part of Indian heritage, but belonging to the British soil. I resemble non-resident Punjabis settled in Britain like Rishi Rich, Bally Sagoo, etc. You know, these very Punjabi–identified guys from London create the wonderful music by blending Indian beats to western rhythms.

> **My films are all about affirmation of the new identity.**
> – *Gurinder Chadha*

Karan Johar: Do you feel the loss of identity at times?

Gurinder Chadha: Not at all. It is an affirmation of the new identity. That is what my films are all about. I feel the people who are monocultural and monolingual have a hard time gauging the problem. Most people in the cities create a unique culture by blending together different cultures.

Karan Johar: Well, no matter what anyone says to you, I would like to say that you have done us proud. You have really produced such films for wholesale entertainment, putting the Indian state of Punjab in every Manhattan home. I believe it as a great achievement for a lady like you.

FARAH KHAN

We have another guest tonight who represents the womanpower in another way altogether. We are going to introduce her now. My next guest tonight is a leading choreographer in India. She is also a director to watch out from her very first film. She killed the myth that a woman director makes films only about women. She has an alternate cinema edge. When you look for sincerity, dedication and talent and probably the best sense of humour in the town, you have Farah Khan. She is yelling, *Main Hoon Na*. Let us welcome Farah Khan.

Gurinder Chadha: Farah wrote her own introduction.

Farah Khan: Hi, Gurinder! How are you? Hello Karan! You are looking good as usual.

Karan Johar: You are still not getting married to me, Farah.

Farah Khan: Oh God!

Karan Johar: OK. You stopped chasing me long time ago.

> This show is a very low-key affair, so I just want to pep it up a bit.
> –*Farah Khan*

Farah Khan: We have a list of women that we would like you to approve of.

Karan Johar: Well, we will get to that later. I am here to chat with both of you; this is my show.

Farah Khan: It is a very low-key affair; so I just want to pep it up a bit.

Main Hoon Na!

Karan Johar: I have congratulated Gurinder on her international

> I always knew that *Main Hoon Na* would be a big success.
> – *Farah Khan*

success. Same to you for *Main Hoon Na.*

Farah Khan: Thank you.

Karan Johar: Did you ever think that this would happen to you some day?

Farah Khan: Karan! You know me too well. I have always believed in it. Everybody has asked me, 'Did you think you would be such a big hit?' I have to say modestly, 'Yes, I did.'

Karan Johar: You always knew that the film would rock at the box office?

Farah Khan: Yeah.

Karan Johar: I did not think it would have made it.

Farah Khan: I totally believe in commercial cinema and Bollywood films. So I made this film with all my heart and knew that it would be a commercial success.

Karan Johar: Clearly, it came across right through in the film that you owed or paid rich

> I totally believe in commercial cinema and Bollywood films.
> – *Farah Khan*

tributes to those filmmakers you have watched.

Farah Khan: All the films that I love involved the likes of Naseer Hussian, RD Burman's music, and Ramesh Sippy.

Karan Johar: A lot of me in that. You had fun in making the film. It has worked very well.

Farah Khan: I had great fun.

ON CRITICS

Karan Johar: *Main Hoon Na* was a big commercial success with box office returns. There was some critical analysis that initially did upset you.

> **Critics – who are they? They have never made a movie in their life!**
>
> *–Farah Khan*

Farah Khan: Well, I think, we are familiar with that. Yeah! It being my first movie, I really thought everybody was going to love it. Of course, everybody says it is a wonderful movie. Some people did not find it as wonderful as I thought it to be. Yeah! The first day did upset me a lot. I was like, 'Oh God!! I have worked so hard. What is this review?' Later, I realized that they do not know anything. Who are they? They have never made a movie in their life. They do not know what a camera looks like. I do not think that they took the film in the right spirit; it is supposed to be a wonderful movie.

Karan Johar: It was supposed to celebrate the Indian cinema.

Farah Khan: Yeah. It was not an intellectual film on *invitro fertilization*. Since it was not that kind of a movie, do not treat the film like that just because a woman director has made it.

Karan Johar: *Kuch To Log Kaheinge* – you had a front-page story in a leading newspaper.

Farah Khan: It was rather unfair. It was a front page before my show opened. It was Friday, 9 o' clock in the morning. It was not on the review page, which comes on Sunday. You give two to three points to the films. It was bang on and, luckily for me, the paper had to admit it as the biggest opening of the year. I think until the last week, the paper said it still the biggest hit of the year so far until *Veer Zara* came along.

Karan Johar: What do you say about the critics? Do you take on the critics across the world – on India and the West? Because *Bride and Prejudice* had met that kind of critical response, there was an article that said it was hotter than the double dose of Windaloo. The other one said that Bollywood goes flat. There were two kinds of contradictory opinions. What do you say about critics?

> **I believe when you make a film for the right reason, you have fun with it.**
>
> *–Gurinder Chadha*

Gurinder Chadha: I believe

when you make a film for the right reason to make sense, you have fun with it. You enjoy it. You have good friends around you. The problem arises with the

> I believe what is unforgivable is that the publishers glorify journalists.
> —Gurinder Chadha

media hype. Obviously, they have to sell papers and make their mark. 'Oh! It is a great movie but not a story.'

Farah Khan: I believe that is what happened to me when the front page killed it. Probably, the movie was big enough for them to carry on the front page and get the film reviewed. You know; you have been through it.

Gurinder Chadha: I love my criticism – criticism is good. I think that criticism is healthy. I do not have a problem with criticism, but I have to encounter shoddy journalism. I believe what is unforgivable is that the publishers glorify journalists. Initially, the journalists were taught to learn and check facts. For me, one of the most shocking aspects in the film *Bride and Prejudice* was the scene of many people crying, 'Oh! It doesn't work. It has not worked in the West. It is proscribed' without checking, because the amount of five and four-star reviews was incredible.

Farah Khan: You know that initially when I completed the film, nobody accepted me as a film director.

Karan Johar: No, because you were already established.

Farah Khan: I was already established, so they were not really kind to me.

Gurinder Chadha: I think it is about the success. The film was banned across the UK after we earned Rs.150 to 160 mn in three weeks. It earned more revenue than any Hindi movie had.

Karan Johar: Yeah. The Friday and Saturday figure was more than a million pounds. Indeed, it was a huge achievement. You feel that the Indian press did not report the right facts and figures? You hold that against them today?

Gurinder Chadha: I think they were determined to present the state of failure and non-acceptance by the Westerners. I think that it is really bad journalism. I have no problem with the people criticizing the

> *Bride and Prejudice* earned more revenue than any Hindi movie had – Rs. 150 to 160 mn in 3 weeks!

technical factors or casting their own opinions. Such versions could have been done better. I am dealing with Hindi cinema. More so, dealing with Jane Austin. Of course, I do not expect everybody from the fraternity watch it and say, 'Wow! That was great!' You know, because my job is to present a new vision to the world, most of the people have forgotten to look that I have made a British movie – one that is not US centric.

Farah Khan: I too had a similar response – 'Why did she make this movie?' Not only the critics I know, but the big directors, the big film makers with whom I have worked with in their films were also disdainful with preconceived notions.

Karan Johar: I do not like 'them'. I like the names.

Farah Khan: I cannot take names as they did not personally say anything to me. They were bitching behind my back.

Karan Johar: This is what makes my show. I want names.

Farah Khan: Well! I cannot really take names because they did not really mean it personally. I am repeating that they did not personally say anything to me. There were text messages going around. I knew they were bitching about me, so they know who they are. Everyone was saying, 'It will flop on Saturday or Sunday.' They came to me on Tuesday night. They congratulated me for the movie being a 'huge hit'. Then, I was relaxed.

> I knew the people I had worked with as a choreographer were bitching about me!
>
> –*Farah Khan*

Karan Johar: Do you feel that Shahrukh has invited that kind of bias?

Farah Khan: I think Shahrukh is successful because people like him. You know how it is. He is already successful as an actor. Now, he is a successful producer. So, he is treading on a lot of toes.

Karan Johar: Do you feel Aishwarya Rai's popularity at home has biased the state of things? We have already discussed it with Farah – such bias existed in the movie *Bride and Prejudice*.

Gurinder Chadha: What shocked me the most in recent weeks has been the amount of personal victory at the cost of maligning other people. I think Aishwarya, obviously, has got many enemies. She is upset, perhaps, about the past dealings. I must admit that I am quite shocked at the slanderous nature.

Farah Khan: The previews in India are based on the fact whether you were nice to the concerned person. 'Did I upset this person somewhere? Why has he written this?' It is hardly objectionable.

Gurinder Chadha: But that is not journalism, is it?

> I must admit that I am quite shocked at the slander nature for Aishwarya!
> –Gurinder Chadha

Karan Johar: Well! The ensuing debate about the division between the filmmakers and the media at home will benefit neither.

Gurinder Chadha: If your film is reviewed with majority of such reviews crying, 'Oh! Aishwarya was fat;' that is how it affected our movie and its crew.

Farah Khan: No, even we have criticized movies after watching them and bitched about them.

Karan Johar: Me? Never.

Farah Khan: You know I never leave the room because the moment I leave the room, Karan will say something about me.

Karan Johar: What are you saying? This is not good for my reputation.

Farah Khan: You always know when I slide back in the room and you speak about me.

Karan Johar: Farah! That is just the way I am. Don't say anything about that!

Farah Khan: No! I have reiterated that we criticize movies. I am quite sure that criticism is fine. What happened with *Main Hoon Na* was not done properly. It was not done on the review page or section. It was purposely meant to harm the film.

Gurinder Chadha: At the end of the day, it does not matter.

SUPERWOMEN

Karan Johar: At the end of the day, the audience watched the movie. I do not think that you should care about anything else.

Farah Khan: No, I do not. It was my first baby; I was little hysterical. I thought, 'Why did it happen to me? I thought everyone liked me!'

Gurinder Chadha: Don't worry baby. Can I tell you one thing? It is going to get worse.

Karan Johar: Let us hold a war between the media and a filmmaker.

Gurinder Chadha: I want to just add, Karan, that when I told Farah that it was going to get worse, what I meant to say was that I think one of the most scary things for people in the world is a confident, talented, assertive woman. It is very scary – because we were not supposed to be so.

One of the scariest things for people in the world is a confident, talented, assertive woman!
–Gurinder Chadha

Farah Khan: A confidant man is encouraged. An assertive woman is categorized as a bitch.

Karan Johar: That is the perception in reality.

Farah Khan: Yeah, I guess so. I believe the men directors scream and yell, so they think that he knows what he wants. When we do it, they think that we are psychos.

Gurinder Chadha: It is beyond directing. I also deal with such things as one who reached the top. People do not like this kind of women to be so successful. We should be open to criticism.

A confidant man is encouraged and an assertive woman is categorized as a bitch!
–Farah Khan

They have to realize that successful professionals have to deal with many personalities in life. I have a guffaw when I read things about me. It makes you realize how hypothetical the situation is and how untalented they are. Many people are there to make you realize that. Why do you want to pull some people down from the pinnacle of success? Obviously, it is one's envy per se. Bu I think it is very constructive and makes you stronger.

Karan Johar: It is probably more so in your case. You have found it rather difficult to be a woman and a filmmaker in the West.

Gurinder Chadha: Initially, yes. I thought of meeting people for finance, especially in the West. Often, they were not interested because I am a female. We present the world from a female's point of view, no matter what kind of movie. But with a female making it, there will be an element of doubt reflecting the vision of her world. I think that that for a lot of people is quite challenging. I never had a problem once I made my

If men directors scream and yell, they think that he knows what he wants. When we do it, they think we are psychos!
–Farah Khan

first film. I can make very small, art-based mini British films. I have no problem with that variety. What I am going for is a global audience. Mainstream England is not enough for me. I want the world, but what I do takes care of the characters who belong to different races, colours and background. I put them in one vase. This factor was hardly understood by people. Many were myopic. They seldom have worked on a global level.

Once I was attending a wedding ceremony. A Texan Sikh gentleman met me and narrated how my film had changed his life. This was *Bend It Like Beckham*. I told him that he was overdoing the moral values. He replied to me in the negative. He continued that he was an Arab terrorist for so many years! I put Sikh men (Sardars) on the map. People did not see them in movies. *Bend It Like Beckham* had characterized a Sardar for the first time. The film had three dimensions – the character, the audience and me. We got it! So I am the Indian who presented people in a three-dimensional mode. Such is the context I work in, and as a woman, that is quite threatening. When I am glorifying characters, I am re-writing the history and your perceptions.

> **Mainstream England is not enough for me – I want the world!**
> *–Gurinder Chadha*

Karan Johar: You, Farah, felt similarly with men from the fraternity threatening your film?

Farah Khan: I had never felt like that until my movie was released. Suddenly, the men with whom I had worked with, liked me. They were very supportive and said nice things about me as I helped their products, barring one or two. Karan, you are a secure director. There are others who were rather shocked. Their aspersions remained – 'Why did she make this action movie?' 'We thought you would make something that was not a chick flick.'

Karan Johar: But as a woman, otherwise, in your working environment, have you ever felt that?

Farah Khan: I have never felt the gender bias. In fact, I got away with a lot of things.

On the Sets

Karan Johar: Oh! I have her seen on the sets; she is scary!

Gurinder Chadha: Oh! My God!

Karan Johar: She is a tigress.. Sometimes, I felt you were doing more to justify that you were a woman.

Farah Khan: No, Karan; I was scary even when I was five years old!

Karan Johar: Oh! You have always been like that?

Farah Khan: No, I think I used to go hysterical earlier – probably if I could not get anything right or my shot broke down or I would clarify the state of developments.

Karan Johar: You are clearly a monster on the sets.

Farah Khan: Well, I have become quite sweet now.

Karan Johar: That is what you think of yourself. Are you the monster on your set, Gurinder?

Gurinder Chadha: Not at all. In fact, I am quite timid by nature. I am a good girl. I go home in the night. I used to make food for my husband. I spend my day doing household chores. I am actually that kind of person.

Farah Khan: Actually, I am also not a monster when I direct the films. I am a sombre, sane person that choreographed for somebody. I get a little hysterical when I meet a person like you. I feel somebody watches me like the *Big Brother*. I have to cope with the state of things.

Gurinder Chadha: Being a monster, I think all the directors have to fight for their vision. I have a team on one side saying something with the British financers insisting, 'Why so? Why does this person have to be an Indian? Why cannot they be a white person? Why this lot of things is happening to Beckham in *Bend It Like Beckham*? Why has this girl got to be an Indian?'

Karan Johar: Do you think there was any racial bias behind the episode?

Gurinder Chadha: I am at the forefront for challenging that. You could make commercial movies for the international audience with coloured characters. Before I made Beckham, everyone said that that was an impossible proposition. You could never make a film with an unknown Indian girl for the sake of commercial success.

Karan Johar: Parminder Nagra is now doing well for herself.

She was the lead actor of *Bend It like Beckham*. She is in the American show 'E.R'. She is doing very well.

Gurinder Chadha: I think all the actresses enacting in Pride were (not just Ashwere given an international profile, even Anupam. I think after *Beckham*, Anupam has enacted in four American movies. I know Sonali Kulkarani is making a film in Italy. Namrata Shirodkar has fetched great reviews from the press around the world.

Karan Johar: So, you put them on the map as well.

Gurinder Chadha: I mean they will do that themselves, I helped a bit.

DANGER ZONE

Karan Johar: Controversy associates with everyone in the film fraternity. You have been a victim. You started off with one of your problem with Sanjay Leela Bhansali. I am going to focus my next segment to controversy. You had a problem with him.

Farah Khan: The problem is 10-year old, Karan!

Karan Johar: But there was a problem.

Farah Khan: We were best friends. We have worked together on songs from '1,942-A Love Story'. I was surprised who got the credit for the songs after the release of the movie. The perspective, indeed, had changed altogether. I did not expect a friend to do that. I expected him to pick the phone and tell me that I am commenting to the press; I am telling the people that I have done the songs. I would have been all right. I think I am quite generous that way. I became a bit paranoid about the credits, you know. You have resolved your differences because of your definite dealings. I do not care because everybody knows my work. I am much more secure. I know that. If they cannot figure out that it was my work, then....

> **Sanjay Bhansali and I were best friends – I did not expect a friend to do what he did.**
> *–Farah Khan*

Karan Johar: And now, the equation is civil with Sanjay Leela Bhansali?

Farah Khan: Yeah, absolutely! Life is too short. It takes too much time and effort to ignore somebody. It is much easier to go and say hello and get over with it.

Karan Johar: OK! You hold that thought. We are going to get to Gurinder Chadha's controversy. Many people know about this or they may have forgotten. Gurinder Chadha is going to spill the beans on Sunny Deol.

> **Life is too short. It takes too much time and effort to ignore somebody!**
>
> *–Farah Khan*

Farah Khan: Oh! Lady! Spill it, spill it, spill it!

Gurinder Chadha: What beans? *Koffee with Karan!* You will have to spill the beans. Well, he approached and asked me to make a Hindi movie with his brother in the lead character. I said to him, 'I cannot make a Hindi movie. I can make a British style Hindi movie. I am happy to do that.' He said, 'Great!' He gave me some money. My husband wrote the script. We spent a lot of time in Khandala with Dharamji, which was really fabulous.

Karan Johar: He is a wonderful man.

Gurinder Chadha: He is lovely. It was great – we had a lovely time. It became very clear when we started making the film that Sunny wanted to remain indifferent to my anticipation. I had a bound script with a story. I had sufficient number of characters. I wanted to make him a very romantic and sensitive hero. Practically, he should not be a yelling guy. Moreover, he should not feel insecure. I wanted to add some fighting scenes.

Karan Johar: The kit was eventually *Dillagi*.

Gurinder Chadha: No. It was totally a different film. What he made was totally a different film. My film had quite clear approach with Karishma enacting the role of a flamboyant girl.

Karan Johar: Karishma is one of the Farah's favourites.

Gurinder Chadha: I thought that at the end of the day, what Sunny wanted was a pure pop boy kind of thing. I had not anticipated that. You know what he did? He carried on his own things. I thought he needed the credit from the person who had approached me to make a film.

Karan Johar: No doubt, it worked very well finally for Gurinder. She made *Bend It Like Beckham,* while he

> **Sunny Deol wanted to remain indifferent to my anticipation.**
>
> *–Gurinder Chadha*

made *Gadar*. Both of them were apart. What I found interesting was that he was one of the few people who had this vision, which we discuss today.

Farah Khan: Obviously, he did not want the crossover.

Gurinder Chadha: He wanted to produce a Hindi movie. He wanted to adapt a style rather than the other way around.

> Sunny Deol made *Gadar* and Gurinder made *Bend It Like Beckham* both were very different yet successful.
>
> –*Karan Johar*

Karan Johar: Speaking about Karishma in London, she was probably the only actor with whom you disliked to dance!

Farah Khan: Such an old story, Karan! It happened during the party you hosted after *Kuch Kuch Hota Hai* got the *Filmfare* awards.

Karan Johar: I do not remember.

Farah Khan: Those were the silly differences between Karishma and her mother. Her sister lost control and spoke something nasty about me in the hotel lobby. I did not take kindly to her vitriolic remarks. So I decided it would be good if I never worked with her.

Karan Johar: And you stuck to that!

Farah Khan: I stuck to that. I speak to her now.

Karan Johar: I have every reason to bring it up because it has been such a long time.

Farah Khan: Now, why did you bring it up during our meeting?

Karan Johar: We should patch up with Sunny Deol, Gurinder, Karishma and Farah Khan!

Farah Khan: Oh! *Hum Tum Saath Saath!* Will that be coming on the show?

> I decided it would be good if I never worked with Karishma again.
>
> – *Farah Khan*

Karan Johar: I want Sunny and Gurinder to have a good equation, as well as Lolo and you.

Farah Khan: Lolo and I have a good equation. When we meet, we are quite civilized. We talk to each other. She is not working in the films anymore. She has worked out well.

MATCHMAKING FOR KARAN

Gurinder Chadha: Karan! You said that Farah and myself are very concerned for you as our brother.

Karan Johar: OK, as your brother.

Gurinder Chadha: We are your *didis*.

Farah Khan: I am not his *didi*.

> **Farah and I have been looking out for a girl for Karan!**
> *–Gurinder Chadha*

Karan Johar: You cannot get into that relation. I have a *Rapid Fire Round*. You have to do that later.

Gurinder Chadha: We have made a *rapid fire* for you. You have to answer it very quickly. We are very concerned – we would like you to settle down. We took it upon ourselves to visit some girls and told them whether they would make a good wife for you.

Farah Khan: And rate them one to ten. First is Rani Mukherjee.

Karan Johar: Rani Mukherjee would make an amazing wife to anyone. I am sure she is a wonderful girl.

Farah Khan: We are talking about you.

Karan Johar: Rani is like a sister. She is like you to me.

Farah Khan: I am your sister?

Karan Johar: Yeah! You are my two *didis*!

Farah Khan: Preity Zinta – I have ruled her out. I know she talks more than Karan. He likes a girl who would listen to him.

Gurinder Chadha: Sushmita Sen..

Farah Khan: You think she is the only classy one.

Karan Johar: She is wonderful. She is classy.

Farah Khan: You will get her diamonds!

Karan Johar: I would be intimidated with her. So, no. I love her. She is a lovely girl.

> **I have ruled Preity Zinta out – she talks more than Karan!**
> *– Farah Khan*

Gurinder Chadha: Can't she make aloo gobhi?

Karan Johar: I am sure she can!

Farah Khan: He does not eat cabbage!

Farah Khan: Aishwarya Rai.

Karan Johar: Aishwarya Rai is too perfect to be my wife.

Gurinder Chadha: Eligible?

Farah Khan: He is more eligible than Vivek. Come on!

Karan Johar: Oh, God! You are like matchmaking morons.

Farah Khan: Now my personal favourite in this list. Mallika Sherawat.

> *Karan Johar:* **Aishwarya Rai is too perfect to be my wife!**
> *Farah Khan:* **He is more eligible than Vivek!**

Karan Johar: Aaaaaa. No.

Farah Khan: I really think you should.

Karan Johar: I would commit '*murder*'.

Farah Khan: I think she is lovely.

Karan Johar: She is lovely. I love her, but no.

Gurinder Chadha: And then, obviously you cannot have Kajol. We all know you are in love with her.

Karan Johar: She is hooked, booked and cooked!

Gurinder Chadha: I love her onscreen, and as a person, know about Kajol's sister – as the seeker.

Karan Johar: Tanisha? No. She is somebody I have known since she was two years old.

Farah Khan: No, no! Not at all! Tanisha is poor. She is Kajol's younger sister. So, baby! We are running out of people.

Karan Johar: I think I have run out of time. We have *Rapid Fire Round*. You have delayed this sequence.

Farah Khan: This is more fun than your *rapid fire*.

Karan Johar: I do not want to marry any of the women on your list.

Farah Khan: Shall we go international and carry a list?

Gurinder Chadha: Yeah! Keira Knightly, Jennifer Lopez.... We do not need her. We forgot to mention Kareena Kapoor.

Farah Khan: Yeah! I knowingly took her out.

Karan Johar: You forgot Kareena Kapoor? I love Kareena and I love Lolo. I love the family. Kareena and I had a downswing in our personal equation, but here we are!

> **We forgot to mention Kareena Kapoor!**
> – *Gurinder Chadha*

Farah Khan: Tell us about that.

Karan Johar: No, we are not going to get into that. We are friends. We have forgotten everything.

Farah Khan: So, everybody is 'friends.'

Karan Johar: We are all okay now, static in our life. We have no problems with anyone.

Farah Khan: How sad!

> Everybody is 'friends'– how sad!
> – *Farah Khan*

RAPID FIRE

Karan Johar: We are happy people. I am really happy to announce my new round – the *rapid fire round*.

Farah Khan: Oh! God!

Karan Johar: I throw these questions at you and I expect very rapid answers. I am really bad at this approach. I am sure you will be very good.

Gurinder Chadha: Can I speak in Hindi?

Karan Johar: You can speak in whichever language you want to. I will decide the winner. Whosoever is better in my *rapid fire round* will win the *Koffee with Karan* koffee hamper.

Farah Khan: Very good.

Karan Johar: I will start with you, Farah. All the best. Have you ever wanted to kill a critic?

Farah Khan: Yes.

Karan Johar: Who?

Farah Khan: The *Mid Day* critic.

Karan Johar: Only two things will sell in *Bollywood* today – sex and Shahrukh Khan. Comment.

Farah Khan: I think just Shahrukh sells.

Karan Johar: One Hindi film you could remake?

> I think just Shahrukh sells, not sex!
> –*Farah Khan*

Farah Khan: *Deewaar!*

Karan Johar: Take on Sanjay Bhansali as a filmmaker.

Farah Khan: Overrated.

Karan Johar: Do you think Aishwarya will make it in Hollywood?

Farah Khan: Yes. Gurinder is answering for me.

Karan Johar: Your answer?

Farah Khan: I do not know. I will ask mummy and tell you!

Karan Johar: Wow! OK! One thing you love about Gurinder Chaddha's films.

Farah Khan: I love her sense of humour.

Karan Johar: One thing you dislike about Gurinder Chadha's films.

Farah Khan: I have not seen the *Bride and Prejudice*. I believe I would not like the songs as I have not done them.

> **Sanjay Bhansali is overrated as a filmmaker.**
> –Farah Khan

Karan Johar: Ah! Good! A piece of advice to other woman would-be-directors.

Farah Khan: Oh! I really don't want to give them any advice. Let them just go and do their own thing.

Karan Johar: All right! The worst dancer you have ever worked with?

Farah Khan: Anil Kapoor.

Karan Johar: OK! Any recent film you fell asleep while watching it?

> **Anil Kapoor was the worst dancer I have ever worked him.**
> – Farah Khan

Farah Khan: I fall asleep in every film, you know. That should not be counted.

Karan Johar: OK! An Indian film in recent times?

Farah Khan: The film I did not sleep in was *Kyon, Ho Gaya Na*? I wondered why I did not fall asleep. I kept on waiting for the sleep to overpower me.

Karan Johar: OK! An Indian film in recent times you wished you had made.

Farah Khan: None of them.

Karan Johar: OK! The film with dancers Sri Devi or Madhuri?

Farah Khan: Madhuri.

Karan Johar: Rani or Preity?

Farah Khan: Rani.

Karan Johar: Kareena or Aishwarya?

Farah Khan: Aishwarya.

Karan Johar: Farah Khan or Shiamak Dawar?

Farah Khan: Oh! Please! Farah Khan..

> **I kept on waiting for sleep to overpower me while watching *Kyon, Ho Gaya Na*!**
> –Farah Khan

Karan Johar: SRK or Salman Khan as dancers?

Farah Khan: As *dancers*??!

Karan Johar: Aditya Chopra or Sanjay Leela Bhansali as filmmakers?

Farah Khan: Aditya Chopra.

Karan Johar: Gurinder Chadha or Meera Nair?

Farah Khan: Oh, that is a tough one. Both.

Karan Johar: OK! Very good, Farah! Bravo! I turn to you, Gurinder.

Farah Khan: I better get the koffee. I am going to get too much into trouble.

Karan Johar: At least you deserve the koffee. Gurinder, the sexiest man in India?

Farah Khan: Too much time... the koffee is mine. .

Karan Johar: The best Indian actor on celluloid?

Gurinder Chadha: Balraj Sahni. Safe now!

Karan Johar: Your least favourite Indian actor on celluloid?

Gurinder Chadha: Too many to mention.

Karan Johar: Your least favourite Indian actor?
Gurinder Chadha: Too many to mention!

Farah Khan: Please mention some! Get into trouble, Gurinder!

Karan Johar: No. She is being polite. The worst criticism you had from whom?

Gurinder Chadha: You know any criticism, it comes and it goes out. It will not be good if you harbor that negativity.

Farah Khan: OK! I am definitely getting the hamper!

Gurinder Chadha: You know how it is like – what goes, comes around – I believe so.

Karan Johar: All right!

Gurinder Chadha: It was due to Karma. If anybody wants to peddle with negativity, the negativity is on them, not me.

Karan Johar: What would you say if you were stuck in an elevator with Meera Nair and Deepa Mehta?

Farah Khan: 'Get me out, quick!'

Gurinder Chadha: 'Shall we lunch together? What do you fancy? What is your menu?' We will not talk about anything else. You will just eat your way through that.

Karan Johar: A piece of advice to Aishwarya Rai would be?

Gurinder Chadha: Screw your critics – go for it!

Karan Johar: OK! The best Indian film you have seen? I know the answer to that. .

Gurinder Chadha: Well, it was my father's favourite, which is *Baijoo Bawra*. I love *Baijoo Bawra*.

Karan Johar: OK! A Hollywood actor you wish to get naughty with? Martin Anderson?

Gurinder Chadha: No! Well, I liked him when he was young – a lot. Tom Berry John; I think he is extremely sexy.

Karan Johar: Farah! Walk through her *rapid fire*. I will never ask you.

Farah Khan: No, I like Tom Barry John.

Karan Johar: OK! A quick round. Choose between Aishwarya Rai or Kajol as actresses?

Gurinder Chadha: Oh! They were extremely good in very different things.

Karan Johar: *Bend It Like Beckham* or *Bride and Prejudice?*

Gurinder Chadha: *Bend It Like Beckham.*

Karan Johar: SRK, AB or Dilip Kumar?

Gurinder Chadha: Dilip Kumar.

Karan Johar: Farah Khan or Saroj Khan?

Gurinder Chadha: They are safe!

Karan Johar: Critics in India or those in the west?

Gurinder Chadha: Who gives a damn?

Karan Johar: Keira Knightly or Aishwarya Rai?

Gurinder Chadha: Aishwarya Rai.

Karan Johar: OK. Well! Gurinder! Too much time – too clumsy there! You lose the *koffee hamper.* Unfortunately. The proud winner of my koffee hamper is the

extremely brave, the very strong – and I do not think she should walk out of the studio as she does not know what she is in for – Farah Khan!

CONCLUSION

Farah Khan: Can I take back everything I have said?

Karan Johar: Not at all. Everything you said is on record. We never told you what to say. Thank you, Gurinder. Thank you, Farah. You women have been absolutely amazing – entertaining personified.

Farah Khan: We will see you in a couple of years. I have to lie low.

Gurinder Chadha: Are you leaving the town, Farah?

> I will see you in a couple of years – I have to lie low after this!
>
> *–Farah Khan*

Karan Johar: I have to run the show. Thank you for being on *Koffee with Karan*. Congratulations! I have something for you to do, Farah! A little mug is waiting for you there.

Farah Khan: Yes.

Karan Johar: Just sign that, please. Autograph that for me. Please remember this personally autographed mug could be yours if you participate in the *koffee quest contest.* Thank you, Farah! Thank you, Gurinder!

• • •

7

Amitabh & Abhishek
The Big B's of Bollywood

Amitabh Bachchan, perhaps, has changed Indian cinema. He is my first guest tonight. Over the years, he has given impeccable performances and left an indelible impression on my life. When he was hospitalized after an accident I wrote a letter to him. He replied with a letter addressed to me and I was stunned!

I told my best friend, 'Guess what? Amitabh Bachchan has written me a letter!' And he looked at me and said, 'Guess what? Mahatma Gandhi has written me a letter.' Later when I was eighteen we met at a social gathering. I had just lost my puppy fat. He looked at me and said, My God, Karan, you have become half your size!' Of course, I thought I had achieved *Nirvana* when I heard that.

I went on to direct him at 28. I fainted on the very first day when we had to film. That was the kind of impact Mr. Bachchan had on my life. Today, I get to interview him. Let us call the one man the entire nation looks up to in every way – Amitabh Bachchan.

AMITABH BACHCHAN

Amitabh Bachchan: Hi, Karan!

Karan Johar: Good evening!

Amitabh Bachchan: Good evening, Karan! How do you feel here?

Karan Johar: Well, I am feeling very strange and awkward doing this interview with you.

Amitabh Bachchan: Why? You look OK.

Karan Johar: I do not know – well, something is happening to me.

Amitabh Bachchan: You are fine. Just open up your buckles.

THE INSPIRATION FOR PERSPIRATION

Karan Johar: Yes, I think I should just unbuckle myself. Well, I am going to ask you what everybody wants to know. How do you do it at this age? I mean you did *Shava Shava* at the age of 60. I will probably be living under an MRI scanner when I am 60. So, where do you get all that energy from?

Amitabh Bachchan: Sometimes, circumstances make you do strange things!

> **Sometimes, circumstances make you do strange things!**
> *–Amitabh Bachchan*

Karan Johar: I had to keep working – that was my compelling circumstance.

Amitabh Bachchan: I have to wake up in the morning, address a lot of issues. I really do enjoy working in cinemas or enacting in movies. So, it was great fun doing stuff like *shava shava*!

Karan Johar: What is that one thing that keeps Amitabh Bachchan going?

Amitabh Bachchan: People like you keep offering me wonderful roles, which I enjoy enacting. God bless those products and the people who want me to endorse them. It helps me to keep my company. Regarding our company, we have gone through a rough period. Our company had fallen in debt. The only way we could revive it was for me to earn for the company. So, endorsements....

> **The only way we could revive our company from debts was for me to earn for the company.**
> *–Amitabh Bachchan*

Karan Johar: You enjoy doing everything?

Amitabh Bachchan: Absolutely!

Karan Johar: It always appeared like you had a ball.

Amitabh Bachchan: Yes. That was the only way to do it.

A PROUD FATHER

Karan Johar: Great! How do you feel when you face the camera with Abhishek? What was your impression otherwise when you saw him off screen and later on the celluloid for the first time?

> **Abhishek was competent enough to stand on his own feet and proceed ahead.**
>
> *–Amitabh Bachchan*

Amitabh Bachchan: Well, just like any other father, I guess. It is an unbelievable phenomenon to watch your own children grow up and act in films during your lifetime. Nothing could be more fascinating for a father. Abhishek – a young man joining the same fraternity and gradually working his way up was extremely rewarding for us. There were accusations galore towards Jaya and me for backing him out like most star parents. Jaya and I had decided deliberately or unconsciously not to really go ahead in either promoting or pushing or creating an atmosphere for him, or trying to relaunch him in a particular manner, which happened to be the norm in the industry. We are very happy with his career. Abhishek took upon himself to work out independently and face the challenges per se. He was competent enough to stand on his own feet and proceed ahead. I think, God willing in the years ahead, he will touch wood and say, 'I have come up on my own strength.' That is really important for any young man.

> **There were accusations galore towards Jaya and me for backing Abhishek like most star parents.**
>
> *–Amitabh Bachchan*

Karan Johar: Indeed, that is wonderful! Congratulations on the overall success of Abhishek!

Amitabh Bachchan: Thank you.

Karan Johar: Abhishek is my next guest tonight.

Amitabh Bachchan: Oh, really!

ABHISHEK BACHCHAN

Karan Johar: Abhishek Bachchan is a childhood friend of mine. He is someone I have known since childhood. He has bullied me throughout my life. He will always bully me even now, though he is younger by four years. He claims to repeat the same tonight on my show. Let us summon Abhishek Bachchan.

Abhishek Bachchan: Hello!

Karan Johar: Hello, Abhishek! How are you? You can say hello to your father. Are you that close to him? You had an unconventional launch in *Refugee*. You subsequently did not have any success, so to say.

Abhishek Bachchan: Flop films!

BRICKBATS AND BOUQUETS

> I am glad I went through the flop films phase.
> –*Abhishek Bachchan*

Karan Johar: Well, I am not saying the word. That is a bad word in cinema. We do not say '*flop films.*' We call them films that have failed to reach the masses.

Abhishek Bachchan: OK. Good.

Karan Johar: Or have you missed the point?

Abhishek Bachchan: No; that is good.

Karan Johar: You had *Dhoom*. There is a lot of reason to celebrate. It was your first success. How does it feel? Have you ever traversed the journey of those films that failed miserably leading to *Dhoom*?

Abhishek Bachchan: Like you said, Karan, it is a journey. I think every actor has to take it head-on. You learn from your mistakes! Although, I do not think they were mistakes – I am very happy that I did those films. I stand by each and every one of them. They have taught me things, which I am pretty sure many other films might have failed to do. I am glad I went through it.

Karan Johar: Tell me what keeps you going and makes you learn from the experiences. That is the journey of life. Do you get elated when a movie of yours gets appreciation from the audience?

Abhishek Bachchan: It makes me euphoric. I cannot believe it. We still look at each other in the middle of the night and say, 'Oh, my God! The movie is doing well!'

> We look at each other in the middle of the night and say 'Oh, my God! Dhoom is doing well!'
> –*Abhishek Bachchan*

Karan Johar: You have a T-shirt that you never wore. You said you would wear it only when your film does really well. It is called **successful**. I have seen it. You want to tell us about it?

Abhishek Bachchan: That was just for fun.

Amitabh Bachchan: You had T-shirt called **successful?**

Abhishek Bachchan: Yes, I will present it to you.

Amitabh Bachchan: Yes, I really need it badly.

Abhishek Bachchan: I could not put *super* logo atop, Sir.

> *Abhishek Bachchan:* I have a T-shirt with the logo 'successful!'
> *Amitabh Bachchan:* Yes, I really need it

Amitabh Bachchan: A mere success will do. I really need it badly.

Abhishek Bachchan: OK. .

Karan Johar: Uncle Amit! You were there when Abhishek went through these films, which failed to perform well at the box office. Was there any moments of anxiety? Did you wonder about the career of your son?

Amitabh Bachchan: I had no doubts. I felt that Abhishek was on the correct path. I say that I feel that he has taken a step forward with each of his films, be it a small one. He was not moving back. I felt that it would not be long before something would come across.

A FATHER AND SON ON EACH OTHER

Karan Johar: I went through an interview of Abhishek during my research. He said that he always wanted to know – What does my father think of me as an actor?' Like the four options you give in the KBC for the contestant – OK, good, bad, or mind blowing. What kind of an actor do you think is he?

Amitabh Bachchan: Mind blowing is still a long way off.

Karan Johar: All right, so we will rule that one out.

Amitabh Bachchan: I would say he has been skimming over the other three options – sometimes OK, sometimes good, sometimes not so good.

> **Saying Abhishek's performance was 'mind blowing' is still a long way off.**
> *–Amitabh Bachchan*

Karan Johar: Do you think your father is over-critical of you, Abhishek?

Abhishek Bachchan: No, not at all.

Karan Johar: No?

Abhishek Bachchan: Actually, Pa has been possibly the only member or any person in my life who is anything but critical. I think first as parents when they see my films, they will react as parents. I think Ma cannot still get over the fact that I am acting and that too in front of the camera. So, she thinks that I am making a nice home video. Oh! I think she still reacts as an affectionate mother. Pa reacts more as, if I may say so, a colleague or a friend and he has never been critical. He makes me sit down and tells me what he feels about me. He tells me how to improve or what he thinks would be good. He has been the person who is extremely encouraging. He has been the stable factor who is always, like he puts it, 'Give it to me.' He tells very honestly with appreciable love and understanding. I think that is so because he understands what an actor goes through. Dad knows how to word something perfectly when the verdict befalls on any film. The reviews emerge on Fridays or Saturdays. He is the person who gives me the strength to keep going or keep trying. You know, he has given me the hunger to improve and learn.

> **Ma watches my films as watching home videos!**
> *–Abhishek Bachchan*

Amitabh Bachchan: OK, Abhishek! You have won an award now. You have praised your father long enough.

Karan Johar: Yes, I do agree. I remember we have watched your work together. Everyone went through Abhishek's completely ballistic performance. I remember Abhishek and me facing some points of criticism. Do you think he needed to improve in a performance like *Yuva*?

Amitabh Bachchan: I believe the style and body language were fine. But at a couple of places, the language style being used was also good and correct, whereas its portrayal was faulty – the outcome of which would reflect on an actor who was attempting to intonate like a Bihari.

Karan Johar: You felt the effort was evident?

Amitabh Bachchan: Yes, in some places – not in all, but in some places.

Karan Johar: All right.

Amitabh Bachchan: It is important that every aspect or every line or every moment is just correct; otherwise, it will stand out like a sore thumb. I felt that at places, some of the body language perhaps

> **Dad has given me the hunger to improve and learn.**
>
> *–Abhishek Bachchan*

was a little exaggerated. It wasn't needed. When you do that overtly, it will get noticed. If it is done wrong, then the wrong alone would get noticed.

Karan Johar: I see. Do you agree, Abhishek, of this constructive criticism?

Abhishek Bachchan: Yes, completely.

Karan Johar: You seem to be quite in agreement with everything said that is not so good about you.

Abhishek Bachchan: I am not self-depreciating. When you got somebody like Pa telling you what he feels about certain things, I think just as an actor you should politely listen. I consider him to be an experienced actor. With what all he has achieved, I think it would be stupid not to listen and think, 'Oh! He doesn't know anything purely as an actor.' Secondly, he is my father. He will not say anything to me when things go wrong. Sure, we have a relationship – brutally honest with each other.

Boom!!

Karan Johar: Has it ever happened that you have disliked his performance?

> **We have a relationship – brutally honest with each other.**
>
> *–Abhishek Bachchan*

Abhishek Bachchan: Yes.

Karan Johar: Can you give me an instance?

Abhishek Bachchan: Well, it is very wrong to interpret. I really did not like the movie *Boom*.

Karan Johar: All right.

Abhishek Bachchan: I thought it was fairly a universal opinion. With due respect to the makers and the co-actors, I think it was a wonderful effort. I did not want to see my hero or the person I have idolised as an actor to be relegated to such a role, which seldom was the case. I disliked it, so I told him.

Karan Johar: And you think that was valid for a film like *Boom* or other films that he worked in?

Amitabh Bachchan: It is a sentiment no different from the opinions of the audience. It is not possible at my age. We look at the structure of the Indian film industry. There was a young lead man opposite a young lady. The few films made with character artists playing central roles are very minimal. I would love to play a central role.

> I really did not like the movie Boom.
> –Abhishek Bachchan

Karan Johar: One that would offer you more substance?

Abhishek Bachchan: Absolutely.

Amitabh Bachchan: It is not possible other than in commercial debuts that one could get something interesting. I thought the whole concept of *Boom* was very tongue-in-cheek. I wish that the producer, the directors, the makers and the publicity people had the gumption to bring it out. Perhaps, that would have prepared the audience - something tongue-in-cheek. You know, this was sarcastic. It would hold your nose the other way. Perhaps they would have understood the humour I was avoiding to do. Kaizad and Aisha Shroff insisted. The outcome of the shooting was flashed on the front page of the The Times of India reflecting three gorgeous looking women. I said, 'Hey! I got to be in this movie which they have started.'

Karan Johar: So, was it the gorgeous women that mobilized you to do the film? Amazing! The way father and son have mutually criticized the debut is amazing. How do you feel about being tagged as the eligible bachelor?

Abhishek Bachchan: He feels great, you know. I mean, fantastic!

Amitabh Bachchan: I am terribly excited about the whole business.

> I liked the idea of meeting a variety of young girls in Boom!
> –Amitabh Bachchan

Abhishek Bachchan: He looks great.

Amitabh Bachchan: It is really, really cool.

Karan Johar: It is cool.

Amitabh Bachchan: Yes, I used to meet a variety of young girls.

Karan Johar: OK. How wonderful was that?

Amitabh Bachchan: I suppose to see just one entering and other coming out.

Karan Johar: I see! You like the idea?

Amitabh Bachchan: Absolutely, it is wonderful.

Abhishek Bachchan: I did not meet any of them.

Karan Johar: You need not.

Abhishek Bachchan: No.

GOSSIP

Karan Johar: What happened when you read about the alleged links up and romances? What is your role?

Amitabh Bachchan: I know that they are incorrect.

Karan Johar: Are they?

Amitabh Bachchan: Yes. It is terribly exciting to read!

> **Dad is the first person I tell everything.**
> *–Abhishek Bachchan*

Abhishek Bachchan: It is very nice and flattering that you know people find me so...

Amitabh Bachchan: Desirable.

Abhishek Bachchan: No, adventurous. Yes, he knows everything about me. He is the first person I tell everything.

Karan Johar: You know that your son is being looked upon as a very sexy man. Do you like the tag being affixed?

Amitabh Bachchan: Yes, he is my son. Something needs to be rubbed on to him.

Karan Johar: Does he get his brawn from you?

Amitabh Bachchan: I hope so.

Karan Johar: OK. I am sure.

> **When they say, 'Oh! You are looking very nice,' I reply, 'I have good-looking parents!**
> *–Abhishek Bachchan*

Abhishek Bachchan: When they say, 'Oh! You are looking very nice,' I reply, 'I have good looking parents.'

Karan Johar: OK. That is great. Congratulations!

Amitabh Bachchan: Thank you; keep repeating the same.

Karan Johar: OK. Wonderful. There have been similar linkups - Preity Zinta, Rani Mukherjee, etc. Well, do you want to-

Amitabh Bachchan: Add a few names?

Karan Johar: Lara Dutta; you want me to continue?

Abhishek Bachchan: They will come and beat me up, so....

Karan Johar: Have they?

Abhishek Bachchan: No.

Karan Johar: It sounds very suspicious. Have you believed in any rumour?

Amitabh Bachchan: No.

Karan Johar: You disbelieve?

Amitabh Bachchan: If he heard such rumours, he would report them.

Karan Johar: OK.

> I am a very boring person.
> *–Abhishek Bachchan*

Amitabh Bachchan: It is difficult to believe such things, unless they have really happened..

Karan Johar: OK. These affairs do not happen. How boring was that, Abhishek?

Abhishek Bachchan: I am a very boring person.

Karan Johar: Are you?

Abhishek Bachchan: Yes.

MRS. ABHISHEK BACHCHAN

Karan Johar: Well, baby, that is not what I have heard. How do you feel about Mrs. Abhishek Bachchan?

Amitabh Bachchan: Do you have any set of notions? I do not.

Karan Johar: No.

Amitabh Bachchan: She should be someone he should like; someone he preferred to have in his company. That will be OK with me.

Karan Johar: The whole country had been glued to the television sets.

Amitabh Bachchan: Yes, whoever wants to align with him, you are free to do so. I have no problems.

DAD-SUN DUO

Karan Johar: OK. I sense the vibe of such a friendship with your father. You are like buddies with him, but not so with your mom and sisters as much as you are with him. Such development is quite unusual. It is always the mother who will prove to be the confidante in such an equation.

Abhishek Bachchan: I am equally close to my mother. She will always remain a mother. A mother occupies a special place in everybody's heart. I cannot look down upon

> Whoever wants to align with him (regarding marriage), you are free to do so. I have no problems.
> *–Amitabh Bachchan*

my elder sister. She always behaves well with me. She takes care of me, talks to me whenever I am in need. My father has essayed different roles. He has been my best friend apart from being a father. He has stood by me, unrelenting and supportive, regardless of what went around. He reminded me once what dadaji told him – about befriending his son the day he wears a pair of his father's shoes. I began wearing his shoes when I was eleven years of age. I believe that that was emotionally the turning point in my life.

Amitabh Bachchan: It was very distressing when he began to wear my shoes and clothes.

Karan Johar: So he stepped into your shoes literally, otherwise.

Amitabh Bachchan: Sometimes, it was unacceptable. We forgave him for such incidents.

JAYA BACHCHAN - THE STRONG ANCHOR

Karan Johar: How does Jaya aunty fall into the scheme of things? She watched you like watching a home video. How does she come into the bond between a responsible father and an obedient son? Does she face the brunt at all times?

> **No. Jaya would never bear the brunt of either of us.**
> *–Amitabh Bachchan*

Amitabh Bachchan: No. Jaya would never bear the brunt of either of us.

Karan Johar: She has her own opinions.

Amitabh Bachchan: Yes. She is strong with her own mind. She is rather nice. We are divided on different issues, though we live under the same roof.

Karan Johar: I observed at your house how you were divided when Jaya aunty said something. You sawed her literally in between when she said something.

Amitabh Bachchan: That was a little personal thing. We made you believe that we were against her. I was quite sure how Jaya and Abhishek felt about me. It was taken in good humour. There was nothing serious.

> **When Jaya and I give conflicting opinions, he goes to Shweta.**
> *–Amitabh Bachchan*

Karan Johar: Wonderful. What happens during conflicting opinions from parents, Abhishek, when Amit uncle and Jaya aunty say what they like and give advice that differs? What do you do?

Amitabh Bachchan: He goes to Shweta.

THE SIBLING - SHWETA BACHCHAN

Karan Johar: Oh, she is another adult in the house.

Abhishek Bachchan: Yes.

Karan Johar: OK. We spoke about Shweta. She will be the one who takes our call.

Abhishek Bachchan: Certainly, she runs the show all over the place.

Karan Johar: Oh, really?

Abhishek Bachchan: Yes.

Amitabh Bachchan: We went there when he was in trouble.

Karan Johar: OK.

Amitabh Bachchan: She advises.....

Karan Johar: Something, we never know about Shweta.....

Abhishek Bachchan: Well, it is very scholarly fashioned. If any big decision is to be taken and Pa wants to advise or ask the family for opinion, we sit and get them her online and resolve the conflict.

Karan Johar: When there is crisis or something?

Abhishek Bachchan: Anything. It could be a happy moment – the signing of my first film. I remember we sat down and inquired about their

> **Before any big decision, we go online with our family and resolve our conflicts.**
> *–Abhishek Bachchan*

opinion. Shweta's opinion was invaluable and important because she is a part of the family.

Karan Johar: Does she run the show sitting in Delhi?

Amitabh Bachchan: Almost.

Karan Johar: Well, wonderful. Well, probably this is the perfect method in an Indian family.

THE 'EX' FACTOR - KARISMA KAPOOR

Amitabh Bachchan: There are delicate moments in life which can make or break relationships. Such events can have big consequences. For example a disagreement It can absolutely disappoint a young man like Abhishek and his family members, leading to separation. Unless the situation is conducive, something unpleasant will happen.

Karan Johar: Oh really!

Amitabh Bachchan: Yes, particularly with me.

Karan Johar: What are your sentiments about Abhishek in that phase today, when you look back?

Abhishek Bachchan: We have to put everything into our treasure house of experience. I have been taught to look upon every unpleasant situation with a positive gaze. I am a positive person. I get wonderful support from family and friends alike. So, I am not bitter about anything.

Karan Johar: There was hardly any regret in the relation break.

Abhishek Bachchan: No.

Karan Johar: Ever?

Abhishek Bachchan: Never.

> **There was no regret in the relationship break. Ever.**
> *–Abhishek Bachchan*

Karan Johar: Well. You must have been proud the way Abhishek handled it and emerged successfully.

Amitabh Bachchan: Yes. I think such episodes will improve his personality to qualify as a good human being, teach him to face the world in a stronger manner. He may be brutally honest. It gives you an opportunity of learning in the profession you are in. The family has worshipped what my father taught us years ago – to emulate the dictates of the heart.

> **I believe I am as bad an actor as ever before!**
> *–Abhishek Bachchan*

Karan Johar: Wonderful!

Amitabh Bachchan: We will leave the rest to God, who will never think of bad for us.

Karan Johar: Do you perceive being a better actor for it, Abhishek? Do you think a broken relationship turned you into a superior actor?

Abhishek Bachchan: No. I believe I am as bad as before.

Karan Johar: You don't really believe that?

Abhishek Bachchan: I do.

ABHISHEK ON MATURING

Karan Johar: Do you feel you have grown up?

Abhishek Bachchan: Obviously, as I told you, life teaches you a lot. It shows you how to grow up and prosper. It makes you grow up in situations and circumstances when you are least prepared for it.

Karan Johar: Sure.

Abhishek Bachchan: I do not give it a lot of importance. It is a part of the growing process. I would rather concentrate on important things like my family and my work. I have always believed Pa to be the perfect standard, who taught me to pull through problems. He taught me how to ward off a crisis in the late 1980's when he met with an accident. We had a problem with the ABCL and when his films flopped. I do not think of sitting in your show when my family is through some crisis. I think about what is important at such a predicament.

Karan Johar: Of course.

Karan Johar: Yes. We have made a film.

Abhishek Bachchan: Yes.

Karan Johar: Wonderful!

Abhishek Bachchan: The man!

Rapid Fire

Karan Johar: Let us go through the *Rapid Fire Round*.

Abhishek Bachchan: Oh!

Karan Johar: They are fairly easy questions really.

Abhishek Bachchan: All right.

Karan Johar: You have to answer in a jiffy. I will decide who wins the round and gets the *koffee hamper.*

Abhishek Bachchan: He does not drink coffee, so I can sip win right now.

Karan Johar: Well, maybe that is the sequence.

Amitabh Bachchan: Are there a lot of chocolates in there?

Karan Johar: Yes, there is chocolate. OK. You can lick sip have the chocolates, because I do not love them.

Amitabh Bachchan: Thank you.

Karan Johar: I will decide the winner. .

Amitabh Bachchan: We will share it any way. Take that basket.

Abhishek Bachchan: Perhaps, it will suit me with my straw hat.

Amitabh Bachchan: Great!

Abhishek Bachchan: The new picnic hamper that Ma has brought me.

Karan Johar: OK.

Amitabh Bachchan: Give the ribbons to mom.

Abhishek Bachchan: Yes.

Karan Johar: OK. I will sound like your father doing in KBC. This will be my intonation. Do you like it?

Abhishek Bachchan: No.

Amitabh Bachchan: Is that the question?

Karan Johar: No offence.

Amitabh Bachchan: No, not at all. You are doing a good job, Karan.

Karan Johar: All right.

Abhishek Bachchan: Was that the question?

ABHISHEK BACHCHAN

Karan Johar: That wasn't the question. Rank in the order of preference your father's films - *Zanjeer, Sholay, Deewar, Baghban* and *Agneepath*.

Amitabh Bachchan: You have to give the order of films?

Karan Johar: You have to give just one.

Abhishek Bachchan: *Agneepath, Deewar, Sholay, Zanjeer, Baghban*.

Karan Johar: OK, *Baghban* is his least favourite performance.

Abhishek Bachchan: Not in the least; he has done 110 odd films.

> I like Ma's performance only in *Abhiman*.
>
> –*Abhishek Bachchan*

Karan Johar: OK. Ma in *Abhiman* or Pa in *Abhiman*?

Abhishek Bachchan: Ma in *Abhiman*. I like her in that film only.

Karan Johar: What?

Abhishek Bachchan: It was with Pa.

Karan Johar: OK. A Hollywood actress who you would like to get naughty with?

Abhishek Bachchan: You – *Salma Hayek*. Me? Say about twenty of them.

Karan Johar: No. You are not being alert. Say one amongst them.

Abhishek Bachchan: Jishale. She went on acting recently.

Karan Johar: Who is Jishale?

Abhishek Bachchan: A Brazilian model who became an actor. OK?

Karan Johar: So, Jishale is the Hollywood actress you wish to be naughty with?

Amitabh Bachchan: Who is Jishale? Oh! She is....

Karan Johar: OK. An Indian actress you wish to be naughty with?

Abhishek Bachchan: None.

Karan Johar: That's a safer answer. Have you received a marriage proposal?

> **Women find Abhishek Bachchan sexy because he is Amitabh Bachchan's son.**
> *–Abhishek Bachchan*

Abhishek Bachchan: Somebody sent a marriage proposal on DVD.

Karan Johar: And what was it like?

Abhishek Bachchan: It was like the CV of a young lady. God bless her soul! Is she dead? It was so real. I feel extremely sorry.

Karan Johar: Women find Abhishek Bachchan sexy because.. complete the sentence.

Abhishek Bachchan: He is Amitabh Bachchan's son. Now can I have the *koffee hamper*?

Karan Johar: The thing that turns you on in a woman is?

Abhishek Bachchan: Her eyes.

Karan Johar: You know that will be the safest thing. What do you mean by her eyes?

Amitabh Bachchan: Do you dare not to go below?

Abhishek Bachchan: Yes.

Karan Johar: A film you wish you never were a part of?

Abhishek Bachchan: None. I just love my films.

Karan Johar: A film you wish you were a part....

> **I call Preity Zinta 'Zee'. She is one of the guys.**
> *–Abhishek Bachchan*

Abhishek Bachchan: *Agneepath.*

Karan Johar: Justify your linkup with Preity Zinta.

Abhishek Bachchan: Who?

Karan Johar: Preity Zinta, who else?

Abhishek Bachchan: Zee, please.

Karan Johar: Zee is what? That is a television network, which..

Abhishek Bachchan: I call Preity Zinta 'Zee.' Zee is a peach. She is one of the guys.

Karan Johar: This isare s even more rapid questions coming now. Pa doing action or doing comedy?

Abhishek Bachchan: Action.

Karan Johar: Ram Gopal Verma or Mani Ratnam?

Karan Johar: Priety Zina or Rani Mukherjee?
Abhishek Bachchan: Shilpa Shetty!

Abhishek Bachchan: Oh God! Very tough. Both. Diplomatic!

Karan Johar: Preity Zinta or Rani Mukherjee?

Abhishek Bachchan: Neither.

Amitabh Bachchan: Hello! Rani.

Abhishek Bachchan: They are very strong, like I told you.

Karan Johar: Shahrukh Khan or Amir Khan?

Abhishek Bachchan: Shahrukh.

Karan Johar: Why not Preity or Rani? Finally, I will put the question again. Priety Zinta or Rani Mukherjee?

Abhishek Bachchan: Shilpa Shetty.

Karan Johar: OK. Good. Salman Khan or Sanjay Dutt?

Abhishek Bachchan: Sanju Sir.

Karan Johar: Aditya Chopra or Karan Johar?

Abhishek Bachchan: Uday Chopra.

Karan Johar: Arranged marriage or love marriage?

Abhishek Bachchan: Both.

Karan Johar: You want two wives?

Abhishek Bachchan: I would not mind.

Karan Johar: What are you saying?

> **I would not mind having two wives!**
> *–Abhishek Bachchan*

Abhishek Bachchan: It is *rapid fire*. I like to flow with the tide.

Karan Johar: OK. I will let you know about your performance. Now, it is your father's turn. Sir, are you ready?

Amitabh Bachchan: Yes. Behave yourself, Karan.

AMITABH BACHCHAN

Karan Johar: OK. Your best performance to date by your opinion?

Amitabh Bachchan: Yet to come.

Karan Johar: Your worst performance to date?

Amitabh Bachchan: Yet to come. OK. That hamper is mine.

Karan Johar: Abhishek's best performance to date?

Amitabh Bachchan: *Yuva*.

Karan Johar: OK. Great, we had an answer! Abhishek's worst performance to date?

Amitabh Bachchan: I really forgot the name of the movie.

Karan Johar: Thanks. The second one?

Amitabh Bachchan: *Tera Jadoo Chal Gaya, Dhai Akshar Prem Ke.*

Karan Johar: I thought you liked the film *Dhai Akshar Prem Ke.*

> I liked *Dhai Akshar Prem Ke* in parts!
>
> –*Amitabh Bachchan*

Amitabh Bachchan: Yes, in parts.

Karan Johar: I think you didn't like *Shararat.*

Amitabh Bachchan: No.

Karan Johar: OK. We will not talk about your movies. If you were making your debut in *Dhai Akshar Prem Ke,* which director you would have opted for?

Amitabh Bachchan: Sanjay Leela Bansali.

Karan Johar: Wonderful. What would you say to the gorgeous women who characterize you as sexy?

Amitabh Bachchan: I have a 28-year-old son, who is available. I would look at them with disbelief.

Karan Johar: The best compliment? You have received many. It could be from anybody or from anywhere around the world.

Amitabh Bachchan: 'you think you are the tall, handsome, good-looking great actor. Let me tell you something, you are not.'

Karan Johar: Is that the best compliment you have ever received?

Amitabh Bachchan: Yes.

Karan Johar: A rumour afloat about Abhishek that you almost believed.

Amitabh Bachchan: I have checked it out, but found it to be untrue.

Karan Johar: Great! An Indian film that you wish you had done?

Amitabh Bachchan: Guru Dutt's *Kagaz ke phool.*

Karan Johar: Wonderful. Shahrukh, Salman, Amir, Saif – who deserves the title *King Khan?*

Amitabh Bachchan: Obviously, Shahrukh.

Karan Johar: Aishwarya, Rani, Priety – the most desirable diva?

Amitabh Bachchan: We love the three ladies.

Karan Johar: Yes.

Amitabh Bachchan: I have chosen - Aishwarya.

Karan Johar: OK. Who deserves the successor to host KBC?

Amitabh Bachchan: Myself.

Karan Johar: OK, only you. If Jai and Veeru had to be cast, whom would you recommend?

Amitabh Bachchan: Abhishek could do well in my role.

Karan Johar: OK. Dharamji's role?

Amitabh Bachchan: Probably Sanjay Dutt.

Karan Johar: *Baghban* or *Kabhi Khushi Kabhi Gham*? Don't worry, I would not feel bad. One is about loving one's parents. The other is about deserting one's parents. Differentiate between them.

Amitabh Bachchan: Yes. *Kabhi Khushi Kabhi Gham*.

Karan Johar: Oh! I love you. Prakash Mehra or Manmohan Desai? We can find some differences in berating them.

Amitabh Bachchan: Now you will get me killed. I acknowledge my success to them.

> **Aishwarya is the most desirable lady!**
> *–Amitabh Bachchan*

Karan Johar: Salim or Javed?

Amitabh Bachchan: They were together with me. I ~~had~~ have to opt for one?

Karan Johar: OK. Ram Gopal Verma or Mani Ratnam?

Amitabh Bachchan: I have not worked with Mani Ratnam. So, it has to be Ram Gopal Verma.

Karan Johar: Kajol or Rani Mukherjee as actresses?

Amitabh Bachchan: Kajol.

Karan Johar: Yash Chopra of *Deewar* or Yash Chopra of *Kabhi Kabhi*?

Amitabh Bachchan: Yash Chopra of *Kabhi Kabhi*.

Karan Johar: Critics or politicians?

Amitabh Bachchan: Critics any day.

Karan Johar: Great. That's your *rapid fire*.

REPORT CARD

Karan Johar: Abhishek! Your father fared better than you.

Abhishek Bachchan: No! Come on, I answered half of his questions.

Amitabh Bachchan: Give me the basket!

Karan Johar: I think your father answered better.

Abhishek Bachchan: It is so unfair. No, I will walk out of the show. I will steal it.

Karan Johar: No, you cannot. Sorry, I shall give it to you after the show. Congratulations, Amit Uncle, on winning the *koffee hamper!* OK. You can take it.

Amitabh Bachchan: Thank you so much, Karan.

Karan Johar: It is all coffee, it is all chocolate. Well, I think, Amit uncle, you were rocking in the *rapid fire*. Sorry, Abhishek! Maybe you will do better next time on my show.

Abhishek Bachchan: I will not come.

Karan Johar: Are you sulking, Abhishek? I will leave him to sulk.

Amitabh Bachchan: Thank you Karan, I truly deserve it. I am sure winning that hamper means so much to you. My apologies to those who did not vote for me. I have ignored them in my answers.

Karan Johar: All right. Do not worry – everyone is a winner. The participation is more important. I am so sorry, Abhishek. You are sulking. Would you smile back to the lovely ladies who love you? I will speak to your lovely ladies.

Abhishek Bachchan: I have replied to them.

Karan Johar: No. You did not.

Abhishek Bachchan: Yes, I did.

Karan Johar: No. You have lost it, Abhishek!

Abhishek Bachchan: I have still answered.

Karan Johar: Let us end the topic.

Abhishek Bachchan: We will be sharing.

POLING TIME

Karan Johar: No. You cannot. Speaking of the lovely ladies, we went from the film fraternity to other sectors. We wanted to know how sexy are Amitabh Bachchan and Abhishek Bachchan. So, who will fit the bill?

Abhishek Bachchan: I will answer that immediately.

Amitabh Bachchan: Is that what you truly asked?

Abhishek Bachchan: Yes, I cannot believe this.

Karan Johar: Yes, I did. Would you like to hear their comments?

Amitabh Bachchan: Yes, sure. Are we going to see it now?

Karan Johar: Yes. Brace yourself ~~cool~~.

THE OOMPH METER AMITABH

Female: An amazing persona......really cool....an institution by himself....really husky voice....a phoenix.....larger than life.....a legend.... too cool....very sexy man.....it is wonderful. Hey! When Mr. Bachchan runs the show, he did it in slow motion.

Abhishek Bachchan: I love the way he runs.

Female: You cannot look away from his eyes. There is no personality like him on the earth - well dignified, cultured, and beyond sexy looks. I believe he is just cool. He is the man who makes you feel like a woman. I still remember his voice in *Coolie* when he got off in a black top and ran away – Oh! Women went mad; I was one of them. His sex appeal lies completely in his performances, mannerisms, and the ability to gauge you on merits. I think his persona, his walk, the way he talks, and the way he looks at his age is incredible. You cannot separate him from his sex appeal. He has the intrinsic appeal. The way people react, the amount of respect he commands makes him extremely sexy. He has got this sonorous tenor. He looks after himself quite well. I hope to see him in my forthcoming film. The film depicts him to run away with me slowly. He is more vulnerable to attractive features. He reflects the example, *'I came, I saw, and I conquered.'* He puts any man of his age (60) to shame. Look at him! He is someone who symbolises the whole sex symbol tag – *'Real hot!'* He is extremely sexy; very, very hot. I think he is very hot and sexy. Extremely sexy. Sexiest man ever.

ABHISHEK

- Tall, dark and handsome. Youth icon.
- Naughty smile. Cinema's first item boy.
- Naughty and notorious with capital N. Found in you a pinup poster.
- Cute. Great height.
- Rustic.
- He is so cute. There is something very innocently sexy about Abhishek's smile; it's something like that he has..
- Smile, smile. Something secretive, something very baby like, something very innocent; I think his smile is super sexy.

Female: He is one of the most attractive men onscreen. It is like a guy back home to mother. Abhishek can be a complete baby. He loves to be pampered and throws his tantrums. My boyfriend always teases me about Abhishek, as I am a little partial towards him. His eyes are really nice. He looks real. That is what makes him look sexy. He inherited the tenderness of his mother and the dynamism of his father. His charisma oscillates in between, keeping one quite confused.

- Abhishek is adorable. His ability to get hung with everyone and assimilate relations besides showing respect remains a remarkable feature. He looks cuter than ever in *Dhoom*.
- He is extremely cute, but vulnerable.
- He emulates his father very much, but stays in his own persona.
- I think Abhishek has a naughty smile. You will find glint in eyes whenever he smiles. It intensifies his naughtiness - that trait makes him to be the favored man for a woman.
- He has mysterious looks. He is a real dandy, which often qualifies him to be sexy. Something you cannot put a finger on. It is like a gun put to your head. Oh my God! Very tough.
- Oh my God! He is difficult to personify. I am still confused.
- I will be dead. No comments.

WHO IS SEXIER?

- I think Abhishek is sexier.
- Definitely, I will go for Mr. Amitabh Bachchan. Amitji, you are the hottest.
- Abhishek, definitely.
- Senior B, of course – much sexier. Bachchan definitely has more sex appeal.
- Abhishek.
- I think it is Abhishek.
- I will say Mr. Bachchan. Well, I have a fascination for older people. That is all I would like to say, nothing else.
- I like Abhishek.
- I think Mr. Amitabh Bachchan is sexier. I think Abhishek.
- I think Abhishek.
- I think I will say Amitabh.
- I will be at an advantage if I say Abhishek is sexier because I shall gain if he proceeds to have an affair. He might produce a film with me. I think Amitji, you are still sexier than your son.

Amitabh Bachchan: I need some fresh air. I cannot believe what these people have said.

Karan Johar: Yes, congratulations on winning the survey and the *koffee hamper*.

Amitabh Bachchan: I cannot believe this. I need to hear them again.

Karan Johar: Would you like to?

Amitabh Bachchan: I would love to.

Karan Johar: Well, I am sure they would love to meet you.

> I want to actually meet Mallika Sherawat. I think she is awesome!
> –Abhishek Bachchan

Abhishek Bachchan: I want to actually meet Mallika Sherawat. I want to run in front of her. I want to say, 'Look baby! I can also run, you know.' I think she is awesome.

Karan Johar: Yes. I love the way every time. She said, 'I like the way.'

Abhishek Bachchan: I like it too.

Amitabh Bachchan: I shall not interfere. Abhishek actually runs this way.

Karan Johar: In cinema? Yes. So, were you flattered, Amit uncle?

Amitabh Bachchan: Yes, unbelievably. I would like to work now.

Karan Johar: Sorry, Abhishek. You are not as sexy as your father.

Abhishek Bachchan: I know that.

Karan Johar: They gave you a lot of compliments.

Abhishek Bachchan: Yes. See, here is the thing! He is married. I am single...

Karan Johar: Yes. So, is that the message to those pretty girls?

Abhishek Bachchan: Yes.

Karan Johar: You were right.

Abhishek Bachchan: I reflect my father. I have inherited appreciable characteristics from my father.

Karan Johar: Yes, we have found that from your traits.

Abhishek Bachchan: I am the perfect substitute of my father.

Karan Johar: Well, please!

Amitabh Bachchan: I should quietly withdraw from the spot, shall I, please?

> All the pretty girls, I am the perfect substitute of my father.
> –Abhishek Bachchan

Karan Johar: All right. I have a big favour..

Abhishek Bachchan: Call me at 98 2036 5523

Karan Johar: And whose number is that? Is it yours? Shut up.

Abhishek Bachchan: He is my sugar daddy.

Conclusion

Karan Johar: Well, the big favour. There is a mug, on your right. Will you autograph that with the silver pen, please?

Amitabh Bachchan: You try first.

Abhishek Bachchan: Please.

Amitabh Bachchan: Age before beauty.

Abhishek Bachchan: How can you say that?

Amitabh Bachchan: Yes. I have rehearsed that before you.

Karan Johar: All right. Please sign that with anything. Remember, this personally autographed mug can be yours, only if you participate in the

> **Girls! Remember! If he (Amitabh) is not available, I will be!**
> *–Abhishek Bachchan*

Koffee quest contest. All the best. We have reached the end of our tête-à-tête. Thank you for being on the show.

Amitabh Bachchan: Thank you, Karan. Thank you for hosting us.

Karan Johar: Wish you all the best. Thank you very much for sparing the time.

Abhishek Bachchan: Girls! Remember! If he (Amitabh) is not available, I will be....

Karan Johar: All right. That will be a great message. We have to proceed towards the coffee wall.

● ● ●

8

Gauri Khan & Suzanne Roshan
Neighbour's Envy, Owner's Pride

My first guest tonight is probably the most envied woman in India – Mrs. Gauri Shahrukh Khan! She is cool, confident and extremely glamorous. She is a proud mother of two children, Aryan and Suhana. She is sometimes accused of being a little aloof. She desires to maintain a low profile. We have come extremely close over the last 10 years. She is still a simple Delhite whose values are intact. She is the most stable factor in Shahrukh's life. Let us invite Gauri Khan.

GAURI KHAN

Karan Johar: Gauri! How do you feel to be on my show?

Gauri Khan: Well, you have forced me to come.

Karan Johar: I might have twisted your arm – a little. You seldom make public appearances or interact with the media and neither have you faced the camera with Shahrukh.

Gauri Khan: I did it once or twice. It was a rather boring event because I have nothing new to say. Talking about the same thing again and again – I really felt bored!

THE LOVE STORY

Karan Johar: What you are tired speaking about is your big love story with Shahrukh Khan. We kept discussing it quite frequently. You probably met him when you were barely 14 years old?

> **I was 14-and-a-half years old when I met Shahrukh!**
> *–Gauri Khan*

Gauri Khan: Yes, 14-and-a-half!

Karan Johar: You've known him for 20 years! That is quite a long period. You nearly did not marry Shahrukh Khan – and then there was a time when you ran off! Did you break off with him? I think you were playing hard to get!

Gauri Khan: I was studying in college. I believed I was too young to proceed into an alliance. I had a break for some time, may be a year or so. I wanted to do my own thing. I wanted to stay with friends. He was too possessive – I could not handle it. I wanted to remain myself, meet people, go out, and hang out. He used to avoid such moments.

Karan Johar: Did he come running after you to Bombay? Did he find you at a beach?

Gauri Khan: Yeah!

Karan Johar: You were very rude. He told me about your cold response. He used to present himself wherever you used to go.

Gauri Khan: I could not bear him being like that.

Karan Johar: Was he well cast in *Darr*?

Gauri Khan: Yes, totally! He used to curb my style. He is now

> **Shahrukh was too possessive – I could not handle it so I ran off!**
> *–Gauri Khan*

more relaxed wherever I may be. He was hysterical at the initial stages.

Karan Johar: I suppose age and maturity bring about these changes?

Gauri Khan: Absolutely!

> **Shahrukh is now more relaxed wherever I may be – he was hysterical at the initial stages!**
> *–Gauri*

SUZANNE ROSHAN

Karan Johar: You will find another lady who happens to be the wife of a superstar – Suzanne Roshan. We were unfamiliar with the fact that both women happen to be very close and dear friends in real life. She will be my next guest tonight. Suzanne Roshan hails from a renowned film family. She is the daughter of actor and filmmaker Sanjay Khan, and the wife of Hrithik Roshan. Probably, she is the most affable and amiable woman in the film fraternity. Her beautiful smile and warmth compel anyone to love her. She appears tonight on television for the first time. Her husband is even more nervous than her. The awesome duo, Gauri Khan and Suzanne Roshan, make a fabulous pair. Hello, Suzanne! Welcome to *Koffee with Karan*.

Suzanne Roshan: Hi, Karan!

THE LOVE STORY

Karan Johar: I was chatting with Gauri about how the relationship developed with Shahrukh, how they met each other and made life ahead. It was rather interesting how they fell in love. Tell me something about yourself – purely personal. How did the flamboyant Hrithik propose to you?

Suzanne Roshan: I have never spoken about this incident! We met a year before he became an actor. We discussed things over

> **I found a studded gold ring under our table at a local café – and I said yes!**
> *–Suzanne Roshan*

a cup of coffee at a local cafe. Suddenly, I found a studded gold ring under the table. I wondered what it was? I reached it with a spoon. It was like the eternity band. I was quite shocked! He inquired whether I would spend the rest of my life with him? I replied, 'Yeah, I will!'

Karan Johar: Interesting – a koffee proposal on the *Koffee with Karan!* What more could I ask you for?

Love–The Universal Religion

Karan Johar: Gauri! You are a Punjabi girl married to a Khan. Suzanne! You were a Khan married to a Punjabi boy. Tell me Gauri! The differences in your faith – how does that bond play in your marriage?

Gauri Khan: Shahrukh, lost his parents. Had they been there, our marriage would not have taken place. Everyone follows rituals at home, even if one belongs to a different faith. I lead the role while celebrating Diwali or Holi or any other festival. It has influenced our kids to remain virtually Hindu. Shahrukh had to obey my dictates. Our roots still lie with Hinduism.

Karan Johar: Yeah! But Aryan emulates Shahrukh!

Gauri Khan: He will follow his faith. He utters that he is a Muslim. He tells the same to my mother. She tries to ignore his innocence!

Karan Johar: Does she get upset?

Gauri Khan: She had been with him. She knows the reality. My mother wants to equate us as peace loving human beings.

Karan Johar: Are you trying to achieve it?

Gauri Khan: There is a balance. I respect Shahrukh's faith. It does not mean that I would become a Muslim someday by conversion. I do not believe in caste conversion. I believe everybody is an individual who inherits the traits of his or her ancestors. Obviously, one should not disrespect the faith of another. Shahrukh would not disrespect my faith.

> I respect Shahrukh's faith – it does not mean that I would become a Muslim by conversion!
>
> *–Gauri Khan*

Karan Johar: Suzanne! What about you? You hail from a Muslim background of an illustrious family and you are married to a Punjabi. It is just the opposite scene of Gauri. How do you deal with the relation?

Suzanne Roshan: Her report was absolutely correct – you can marry the groom of your choice of another faith. You are born and brought up in your faith. You have to respect the faith of another companion. You should let your kids enjoy the best of your

> A peaceful coexistence will bring the miracle of harmony in a relation because both the faiths are peace loving.
>
> –Suzanne Roshan

faiths. You should imbibe in them the confidence to respect every faith on earth. You should impart the essence of peaceful coexistence, irrespective of the ups and downs in life. It will bring the miracle of harmony in a relation because both the faiths are peace loving. The faiths represent the majority of the countries across the globe.

Karan Johar: Does Hrithik endorse your opinion?

Suzanne Roshan: Yeah! He upholds my thinking. He is not strong and possessive about the factor. He does believe to proceed with certain rituals of both the faiths. I do believe and respect them under the circumstances. He seldom motivates the kids to follow one religion or the other. We have to bring them up in an atmosphere of harmony and confidence.

Karan Johar: Gauri, I have seen Aryan. He prays for a while at night before going to bed. Will you tell us about it?

> Aryan says, 'I will do mamma's prayer followed by papa's.'
>
> –Gauri Khan

Gauri Khan: He says, 'I will do mamma's prayer followed by papa's.'

Suzanne Roshan: So sweet!

Karan Johar: He has a little English prayer with international flavour. You try to achieve balance of faith beyond borders.

TRUST VS TEMPTATION

Karan Johar: The superstar husbands interact, shoot and enjoy photo sessions with the most beautiful women of feature films. Gauri! Do you feel insecure on such occasions?

Gauri Khan: I have an aversion to your questions! I pray to God everyday. A little off the track, I seek God to let me find somebody else, if he doubles up with someone else! I believe he is handsome. It is true that we have a super marriage. I pray to God for our poised marital life.

> I seek God to let me find somebody else if he doubles up with someone else!
>
> –Gauri Khan

Karan Johar: And Suzanne – your response?

Suzanne Roshan: I pray to

God. I hardly venture out to inquire where he had been when Hrithik is away. I am virtually attached to him. I cannot live without him.

Gauri Khan: I beg to differ on her note. If he desires to be with somebody, I feel to stay away from him without waiting for a subsequent promise!

> Hrithik promptly reports me if some woman gets attracted to him!
> *–Suzanne Roshan*

Karan Johar: You are quite proud of yourself!

Gauri Khan: Absolutely. I will say, 'Let me look out for somebody!'

Karan Johar: Did such rumours ever affect you, Suzanne? So much is written about it all the time. Don't they get to you? Don't you feel why you married an actor? When you watch Hrithik's beautiful face, do you think 'is he not worth me?'

Suzanne Roshan: No. It is very strange to be honest. He promptly reports me if some woman gets attracted to him and tries to involve herself with him.

Karan Johar: You would otherwise continue to remain as his friend.

Suzanne Roshan: I do not think at any point I have been insecure – we are so open about everything! Insecurity arises with a mutual communication gap between the spouses. I do not think we should agitate ourselves for such mishaps to happen. One should know the facts in true perspective and solve any misunderstandings.

Karan Johar: Don't you feel insecure at such moments?

Suzanne Roshan: No, I don't.

CRITICAL ABOUT QUALITY WORK

Karan Johar: So, Gauri, you're happy being Mrs. Shahrukh Khan and Suzanne, you're happy being Mrs. Hrithik Roshan. Of course, you have interpreted of dealing with a situation in your own way. You have different personalities with different temperaments. Let us begin with Gauri. You are quite forthright about your opinion when you see Shahrukh's film. You are quite critical about his films as opposed to Suzanne. Do you feel that you are overcritical at times?

Gauri Khan: I do not feel so. Whether he is in a bad film or his

I am an audience. I try to convince Shahrukh if he has overacted or remained mediocre or below par.

–Gauri Khan

performance was poor, I do not applaud him. He has to acknowledge his performance. I am an audience. I try to convince him if he has overacted or remained mediocre or below par.

Karan Johar: Have you reacted honestly about his recent performance?

Gauri Khan: His past few films have been good.

Karan Johar: Oh really? Which film was below the mark?

Gauri Khan: Many. I have not seen any of his bad films – *Guddu* and similar debuts - *English Babu Desi Mem*!

Karan Johar: I remember you called him when you walked out of *Shakti*.

Gauri Khan: That was totally unbearable. That was his worst performance in a long time! **Karan Johar:** He gets quite upset when you say it?

Gauri Khan: He does – but he needs to deal with it. I respect him a lot for his professional skill. No doubt, he's a great actor and accessible to everybody as King Khan. He gets great write-ups, which he is aware of. He should know what he could not gauge from the other audience. I persuade him quite often as nobody wishes to let him know about that side.

Karan Johar: And Suzanne, you're so sweet basically! That is your basic personality. You are affable, amiable and prompt to react.

Suzanne Roshan: I have never berated his performance. I have tried to keep mum about his good or the worst

I have never berated Hrithik's performance.

–Suzanne Roshan

performance. Now, I feel it is my right as the responsible spouse to rectify his weakness or anomalies in performances. I have tried to remain honest. It is important to give him the right feedback.

Karan Johar: If you ignore him, who else will?

Suzanne Roshan: Yeah!

Karan Johar: Any film you disliked but was appreciated?

Suzanne Roshan: There are a couple of them – I did not like *Yaadein*;

I did not like Hrithik in the film for his inconsistent role.

Karan Johar: What happens when each of your spouses act in mainstream films? Did you feel uncomfortable with *Kal Ho Na Ho* and *Koi Mil Gaya* released last year?

Gauri Khan: I believe it was Hrithik's splendid performance – unparalleled! It was something extremely different.

COLLEAGUES OR COMPETITORS?

Karan Johar: Your opinion, Suzanne, about Hrithik as junior to Shahrukh in the career?

Suzanne Roshan: He has high regards for Shahrukh. The sleazy periodicals make them fight. Such vitriolic attack has poisoned Hrithik's conscience. He wonders how could they have betrayed him.

Karan Johar: Considering how they had sympathized with him during his initial career. How difficult was that for the two spouses when you met each other?

Gauri Khan: Oh! It was not for us. We were not like that.

Suzanne Roshan: It depends to what extent the analysis holds good.

Gauri Khan: In fact, for Shahrukh, it was difficult in the sense that the sleazy periodicals make a mountain out of a molehill.

Karan Johar: Were there any awkward positions between Shahrukh and Hrithik?

Gauri Khan: Yes, there used to be. Initially, I would say that Shahrukh was very awkward. Then, Shahrukh began to chat with Hrithik. Now, he is fond of Hrithik.

Karan Johar: Suzanne! Do you want to tell Gauri about the recent conversation between the guys, which wounded Hrithik badly?

Suzanne Roshan: It was the day when he realized he had not won the national award. He was disappointed which I gauged

from his behaviour. Shahrukh said to Hrithik, 'Don't feel bad because in my books you would have gotten the award. I don't think anybody else deserved it more than you.' That compliment launched him to cloud nine!

Karan Johar: It might have resulted in the same amount of euphoria of him having won the national award. He told me, 'Shahrukh Khan called up and explained the position – I feel I won it!'

Suzanne Roshan: Yeah!

A SUPERSTAR WIFE

Karan Johar: How do you handle your position with such poise and dignity?

Suzanne Roshan: It is really difficult being the wife of a superstar. I come across two people; one of them is my mum. My mother is not the wife of a superstar, but has the motherly love and care.

Karan Johar: You respect her?

Suzanne Roshan: Yeah! She has always been my role model. And I always get the warmth of Jaya aunty.

Karan Johar: Mrs. Bachchan?

Suzanne Roshan: Yes. She is very lovely. We are very fond of her. She is an upright and very beautiful lady.

Karan Johar: She had something to say about you. It is on camera. Would you like to see it?

Suzanne Roshan: Yeah! Why not?

Jaya Bachchan: I am happy that you are doing a wonderful job. It is so nice that you have actually grown as star wives. I see them as friends, which is again wonderful. I would address them more being married to an artist than a star. You need to give an artist a lot of space. You should give them the opportunity to be creative in order to understand that a creative person undergoes the swings in life. Indeed, it is a tough job to remain on track. I believe these girls are doing exceptionally well. Gauri is very comfortable with her position and relation – she looks comfortable and secure. She knows that she is very important for him. You can see the wonderful chemistry when Shahrukh conveys it. I really don't know how Hrithik and Suzanne are at home. It is a little difficult

> **Gauri knows that she is very important for Shahrukh.**
> *–Jaya Bachchan*

because they are still young. She is a very sweet girl. I like to give her a hug whenever I see her. I tell my children that you have to work out solutions if you want your marriage to work – don't wait for the other person to initiate.

Karan Johar: Suzanne! How do you react to her statement?

Suzanne Roshan: It is really nice to know that she is so fond of me.

Karan Johar: What do you say, Gauri? Do you agree with her statement?

Gauri Khan: Absolutely. I would just like to say that I find her a comfortable person. You can chat with her. I admire her because of the way she has brought up her two kids. I would like to learn that from her.

RAPID FIRE

Karan Johar: We shall have the *Rapid Fire Round*. We want to gauge how well do you know your spouses. Your spouses Shahrukh and Hrithik have already answered about their favorite things. We shall see how well do you know them and coordinate with us. Then, the winner will win what I call the *coffee hamper*.

> **Karan Johar:** His favourite co-star?
> **Gauri Khan:** Kajol.
> **Shahrukh Khan:** Actually, Johnny Lever!

Gauri Khan: Wow!

Suzanne Roshan: So sweet!

Karan Johar: Whosoever replies and co-ordinates better wins this coffee hamper. Let me start with Gauri without imitating the style of KBC – your time starts right now! His favourite food?

Gauri Khan: Tandoori chicken.

Shahrukh Khan: Tandoori chicken or chicken tikka.

Karan Johar: That's what he said so you're correct. His favourite performance?

Gauri Khan: *Kabhi Haan Kabhi Na?*

Shahrukh Khan: Yes.

Karan Johar: OK. Seems you have memorized it. His favourite colour?

Gauri Khan: *Black.*

Shahrukh Khan: *Black.*

Karan Johar: His favourite co-star?

Gauri Khan: Kajol.

Shahrukh Khan: Actually, Johnny Lever.

Karan Johar: What is the one thing he is obsessed with?

Gauri Khan: His son.

Shahrukh Khan: Computers.

Karan Johar: Who will make up if you have a fight?

Gauri Khan: Him.

Shahrukh Khan: I make up.

Karan Johar: One of his habits you wish to change?

Gauri Khan: Spending hours in the loo.

Shahrukh Khan: May be smoking.

Karan Johar: OK. He misplaces most often in the house?

Gauri Khan: His spectacles.

Shahrukh Khan: Specs.

> *Karan Johar:* **One of his habits you wish to change?**
> *Gauri Khan:* **Spending hours in the loo!**
> *Shahrukh Khan:* **May be smoking!**

Karan Johar: One Hollywood actress he would love to get naughty with?

Gauri Khan: Catherine Zeta Jones.

Shahrukh Khan: Catherine Zeta Jones.

Karan Johar: Yes, sounding very rehearsed. The last thing he does before going to bed is?

Gauri Khan: Reading.

Shahrukh Khan: Reading.

Karan Johar: All right! You got three wrongs, but this appears very manipulated and very planned. We shall get to that later, Gauri. Hello, Suzanne! How well you know your spouse? Your time starts now. What is Hrithik's favourite food?

Suzanne Roshan: Eggs.

Hrithik Roshan: Eggs.

Karan Johar: His favourite performance?

Suzanne Roshan: *Koi Mil Gaya.*

Hrithik Roshan: *Koi Mil Gaya.*

Karan Johar: No guesses there. His favourite colour?

Suzanne Roshan: Black.

Hrithik Roshan: Black.

Karan Johar: Black seems to be the colour of the day. His favourite co-star?

Suzanne Roshan: Shahrukh.

Hrithik Roshan: Shahrukh!

Karan Johar: My God, too much praise! What thing is he obsessed with?

Suzanne Roshan: The mirror!

Hrithik Roshan: The gym!

Karan Johar: My God, too much praise! What thing is he obsessed with?

Suzanne Roshan: The mirror.

Hrithik Roshan: The gym.

Karan Johar: He should have been obsessed with you! You have a bone to pick with him later. If you have a fight, who makes up first?

Suzanne Roshan: I do.

Hrithik Roshan: She does more than me.

Karan Johar: One habit of Hrithik that you would like to change.

Suzanne Roshan: He can never say no.

Hrithik Roshan: I can never say no.

Karan Johar: The item he misplaces the most at home is?

Suzanne Roshan: His phone.

Hrithik Roshan: My phone.

Karan Johar: One actress he would like to get naughty with?

> The camera caught you talking to your spouses on your cells and asking them the answers!
>
> –Karan Johar

Suzanne Roshan: Kylie or Charlize Theron.

Hrithik Roshan: Charlize Theron.

Karan Johar: Very well done, Suzanne! You had just one wrong. And you had three, Gauri. Ideally, you should be winning my koffee hamper. Neither of you are qualified to win – we left you alone and know what you have been up to! The camera caught you talking to your spouses on your cells and asking them the answers! One thing we did not realize about you was that you could cheat as well. Why were you cheating?

Gauri Khan: He mucked up and told me something else!

Karan Johar: That means he forgot himself. Of course, Hrithik did not muck up because I was banging him on. We have heard about your respective spouses. We would like to chat and confer with your husbands.

MEET THE HUSBANDS

Karan Johar: Shahrukh Khan and Hrithik Roshan are here! Hi! Welcome to *Koffee with Karan*! – The two men that make a world of a difference to Suzanne Roshan and Gauri Khan – their husbands.

Shahrukh Khan: Thank you, Karan!

> **I would wish everybody could get a wife like Gauri if she was not my spouse!**
> *–Shahrukh Khan*

Karan Johar: OK. Let us revert to the marriage, that is what we have really discussed. Shahrukh! How would you sum up your 20 years of marital life with Gauri?

Shahrukh Khan: It had been a good life. I cannot really sum it up. There is lot more to come – loads of happiness because of the babies. She is just very nice. I would wish everybody could get a wife like Gauri if she was not my spouse! OK; that is a wrong interpretation.

Karan Johar: If you had to go down memory lane?

Shahrukh Khan: The most important aspect has been that we have invested a lot of time in understanding each other. We were kids when we started off. I was the initiator. I do not know much about Gauri. It has been a very comfortable journey. I thank the Almighty for doubling me with her.

Karan Johar: Have you assimilated the periodic successes and failures? Is life any different in terms of emotional bonding with Gauri today after you had children?

Shahrukh Khan: Surprisingly, I never thought that Gauri would be a good mother! She does not fall under the children-friendly lady category. I mean I'm being honest. She never comes under cooing. You see girls really liking kids. I was pleasantly surprised that she's an absolutely wonderful mother. She has been the kind of mother the children need to have.

> **I never thought that Gauri would be a good mother!**
> *–Shahrukh Khan*

Karan Johar: Do you mean she provides that stability at home?

Shahrukh Khan: Yeah! She makes it very sensible, simple and specifically very middle class.

Karan Johar: Were those her values that she has not left behind?

Shahrukh Khan: Yeah! She has not changed from what I have known from her persona. I may have slipped or changed a little for better or worse, but she has remained where she was. She has remained in the middle class etiquettes to remain very simple, upright and honest. She is very intelligent in her own way – her intelligence lies in the fact that she is a silent observer of things. I do feel I take advantage of them and do things, which she do not mind.

> **Gauri remains very simple, upright and honest.**
> *–Shahrukh Khan*

Karan Johar: It would be right to say that she is the most stable factor in your life?

Shahrukh Khan: She is the only factor in my life – I do not have anybody else!

Karan Johar: I believe Hrithik saw you, Suzanne, five years before marriage. How many years have you been married?

Suzanne Roshan: Say about four years this December – it seems like a lot more.

Karan Johar: Everyday is a lifetime for a woman, I suppose.

Hrithik Roshan: It feels really strange – it has been a lot more than that. We were destined to be with each other as soul mates.

Karan Johar: You really believe that?

Hrithik Roshan: The first time I ever had a crush on a girl, her name was Suzanne. I was 12 years old. I used to play within the compound of this building. I saw this girl who was Suzanne. My friend would tease with the number, *Oh! Suzanna! I am crazy loving you!* Time rolled out; I never really got to speak to her. I was about 16 at my sister's wedding. She walked in when I told my best friend Uday Chopra that I would marry her some day. I had not even spoken to her at that time! We exchanged looks near the traffic light. Our relation materialized through a mediator. We called each other up, which bonded us from there.

> **I was 12 years old when I had my first crush –Suzanne!**
> *–Hrithik Roshan*

Karan Johar: So, you were destined to be with each other. Do you have something to say Gauri which you could not say so far? Do you feel you could share it with her in our presence?

Shahrukh Khan: I must have said everything to her. I speak a lot and she admonished me to shut up. I do not think I will make the same error.

Karan Johar: Anything special that you want to say? Or may be just thank her, or whatever comes to your mind.

Shahrukh Khan: The other day, I sat with a few friends on the sets. I felt like saying 'thank you' so that she could acknowledge it – whatsoever may be the reason. I just went up to her and found her lying on the bed yawning.

Karan Johar: Was that her characteristic?

Shahrukh Khan: So our romance went on!

Karan Johar: Anything you have not shared with Suzanne? Sometimes, you refrain from commenting about the state of things by taking your spouse for granted. You may feel not to share and wait for the correct opportunity to do so. May be you could share it in our presence.

> **Hrithik, you could ask Suzanne out for a date at a traffic light again!**
> *–Shahrukh Khan*

Hrithik Roshan: I do not think there is anything to say other than repeating that I love her. I think she knows it. I think a mere 'thank you' should be appropriate, as Shahrukh has said. I do not think that I would not have become an actor if she had not come in my life – that is untrue. She entered my life at a time when I needed her companionship. I owe a lot to her.

Shahrukh Khan: You know you could ask her out for a date at a traffic light again!

Karan Johar: That would be romantic!

KEEPING THE ROMANCE ALIVE

Karan Johar: Shahrukh, I know that you are romantic. You do not like doing romantic films, but you are romantic at heart. How do you express your romance?

Shahrukh Khan: We have known and loved each other for so long. The romance has not faded out in our lives and marriage.

Karan Johar: How do you keep romance alive?

Shahrukh Khan: We know each other so well that such expressions do not have any place.

Gauri Khan: It became insipid.

> **We do not need to drink wine on a moon lit night to express romance.**
>
> *–Shahrukh Khan*

Shahrukh Khan: It is strange and meaningless. It does not corroborate insipidity in romance – we have surpassed that phase. We do not need to drink wine on a moon lit night to express romance. These guys are younger and should meet again at the traffic light.

Hrithik Roshan: We will be approaching that stage.

Shahrukh Khan: You do not really need to say the three words. You know what your sweetheart has said. 'When I saw you, I realised that love is crazy.' We have reached a phase in our relationship where such silly things are meaningless.

Karan Johar: Do you want to assert that insignificant things in life are romantic enough?

Shahrukh Khan: Romance is afloat in the air. It charges the atmosphere as we move on from bedroom to drawing room. By getting two kids, we have justified the romance. The whole day we come across wild, very loud and screaming romance!

Karan Johar: Hrithik! Do you get an opportunity to have some romance since you don't have any issues as yet? I believe you are preoccupied with a different routine.

Hrithik Roshan: Yes. May be. We are on our way. We will find inspiration to beget kids of our own. We are still deserted on an island!

Suzanne Roshan: We are into those mad things.

> **Do not worry about kids – you can tie, gag or shove them in a storeroom!**
>
> *–Shahrukh Khan*

Karan Johar: Do you make holidays?

Hrithik Roshan: Yeah!

Shahrukh Khan: Do not worry about kids. You can tie, gag or shove them in a storeroom!

Karan Johar: You can be mean to your children. What about kids? Are you planning a family soon?

Suzanne Roshan: Yes.

Hrithik Roshan: A little more growing up and then we will think of a family.

Karan Johar: I think you need to grow up a little more before you bring one to grow up together. Are you scared to bring them in your life?

Hrithik Roshan: Yeah. A certain part of me is concerned. I want to give my son or my daughter the world I have not enjoyed. I would want him or her to have a happy life – a world in which there is no fear and just happiness. Such a world seldom exists. That is why I am scared. I need to grow up.

Karan Johar: Suzanne! I want to hear a number from you. Gauri! You can sing a number!

Shahrukh Khan: I drafted a number, which I used to sing when I used to meet her. I forget the lines because of my age and disenchantment to do so. The number is '*Gori tera gaon bada pyara, main to gaya maara aake yahan re*' sung by playback singer Yesudas.

Karan Johar: Do you feel shy in singing to her?

Shahrukh Khan: Yes, I feel shy in doing so.

Karan Johar: I think Hrithik sings very well.

Hrithik Roshan: I once made that mistake on the national channel – it was a disaster! I will avoid making the same mistake here!

Karan Johar: We will sing together.

Hrithik Roshan: 'Suzanna, Suzanna! I'm crazy loving you. Koi Mil Gaya!' This was like a joke.

Karan Johar: This is a remix, not a song!

KARAN UNDER FIRE

Gauri Khan: OK. Let us start with questions.

Shahrukh Khan: It will be your rapid fire round! Let me start – followed by Hrithik, then Suzanne and then Gauri and me.

Hrithik Roshan: Karan! Have you shaved your chest for the show?

Karan Johar: Yes, I have.

Suzanne Roshan: Anne French or razor?

Hrithik Roshan: **Karan! Have you shaved your chest for the show?**
Karan Johar: **Yes, I have!**

Karan Johar: No, it is something Uday gave me – I have done a terrible job.

Hrithik Roshan: You have to show that!

Karan Johar: No – I do not want to. So sorry!

Gauri Khan: OK. Who is Raj Vardhan Rathod?

Karan Johar: He just won the silver medal at the Olympics for shooting.

Shahrukh Khan: Which is the other event that favoured India with another medal in the Olympics?

Karan Johar: Hockey.

Suzanne Roshan: It would have been closer to the result if you have said football.

Karan Johar: I did not know that India is good at hockey.

Shahrukh Khan: OK. We grant you that one. Who do you like dealing with better – Star TV or Sony TV?

Karan Johar: Pass. Next?

Gauri Khan: Whose chat show would be better – Manish Malhotra or Sunita Menon?

> *Shahrukh Khan:* **What would you like to have – Hrithik Roshan's body or Shahrukh Khan's brains.**
> *Karan Johar:* **I have a body complex – I think I will have Hrithik's body.**

Karan Johar: Manish's.

Shahrukh Khan: What would you like to have – Hrithik Roshan's body or Shahrukh Khan's brains.

Karan Johar: I have a body complex – I think I will have Hrithik's body.

Shahrukh Khan: Just you wait for my next question!

Hrithik Roshan: What would you rather have – a marriage or one nightstand?

Karan Johar: A marriage.

Suzanne Roshan: Your actual age is 33 or 35?

Karan Johar: I am 32! I was born in 1972. I would never lie about my age. Lot of people tells me that I do not look 32. In fact, I look much younger!

Shahrukh Khan: Give the name of a person who associate with fake eyelashes?

Karan Johar: Our actresses wear fake eyelashes. Yesterday I shot with Kajol – she wore fake eyelashes. Actresses like Kareena, et al.

Shahrukh Khan: Fake hair pieces?

Karan Johar: That would be Preity Zinta. Her hair did not really work in one of her recent films.

Shahrukh Khan: Fake bosoms?

Karan Johar: Again there are a lot of actresses. They have done something. We should not mention their names.

Hrithik Roshan: What does IMPA stand for?

Karan Johar: Indian Motion Pictures Producers Association.

Suzanne Roshan: Life without movies or life without sex?

Karan Johar: Life without sex. Making a movie will end up in beep, beep (heart failure).

Suzanne Roshan: OK. Whom do you prefer – Amitabh Bachchan or Hrithik Roshan?

Hrithik Roshan: I am here, Karan!

> *Suzanne Roshan:* **Whom do you prefer – Amitabh Bachchan or Hrithik Roshan?**
> *Hrithik Roshan:* **I am here, Karan!**
> **Karan Johar: Jaya Bachchan!**

Karan Johar: Jaya Bachchan.

Shahrukh Khan: Aditya Chopra or Yash Chopra?

Karan Johar: Yash Chopra.

Gauri Khan: Sridevi or Kajol?

Karan Johar: Kajol.

Gauri Khan: *Filmfare* or *National awards*?

Karan Johar: National awards.

Shahrukh Khan: Largest mammal in the world?

Karan Johar: Blue whale.

Gauri Khan: You have lost the hamper.

Shahrukh Khan: So, it is ours.

Karan Johar: You stole my koffee hamper! Unfair.

Suzanne Roshan: Fine, Gauri and I will share it.

CONCLUSION

Shahrukh Khan: What do you like more – asking questions or answering them?

Karan Johar: Of course, asking questions. Who would like to answer those questions?

Suzanne Roshan: Now, do you know how we feel?

Gauri Khan: Yes, exactly.

Karan Johar: Listen, I do not know about you guys but I had a great time in chatting with Suzanne and Gauri. I have learnt

> Of course I like asking questions – who would like to answer them?!
> –Karan Johar

those facts which the world wanted to know. Thank you, Shahrukh and Hrithik. Thank you for being here and sharing the world about what wonderful couple you are! Do me a favour – you have cups aside. You know the ritual. You have to affix signature with a love message. Suzanne has to sign with Hrithik and Gauri has to repeat the ritual with Shahrukh. Let us proceed to koffee wall.

● ● ●

9

Bipasha Basu & Lara Dutta
Power Puff Girls

The leading lady of Indian cinema has truly come a long way. She is no longer just coy, fluttering her eyelashes. Basically, she wanted to be a good girl - but not now. Our first guest, who has been the bad girl onscreen, is Bipasha Basu. You might think of her as hot. In fact, she is the ambassador of sensuality. She is an ex-model, a Bengali beauty and the love of John Abraham's life. Let us welcome the super sexy, the super hot Bipasha Basu.

BIPASHA BASU

Karan Johar: Hello! Good evening dear! Welcome to my show, Bipasha.

Bipasha Basu: Thank you, Karan.

Karan Johar: Thank you for being on my show, Bipasha.

Bipasha Basu: You are welcome Karan.

Karan Johar: You look super glamorous!

Bipasha Basu: Thank you.

Karan Johar: And you really are!

Bipasha Basu: Thank you. Where is my koffee?

Karan Johar: You do not get any. I had koffee for myself. No, I promise you will get your quota.

Bipasha Basu: Oh!

BIPASHA: THE PERFECT *JISM*

Karan Johar: I will pose a thorny question. I saw you on the net and got cracked up. 'What is the *Raaz* of your *Jism*?'

Bipasha Basu: Oh my God!

Karan Johar: I thought it was really strange. I have read it on the net. I wondered how people could ask such questions.

Bipasha Basu: Well, I believe there is a lot of Bengali food. It has made me quite healthy in the middle.

Karan Johar: Yes, I know you went through this whole process. Why did you let yourself go?

> I disliked watching myself on screen.
> —*Bipasha Basu*

Bipasha Basu: I did not know that I let myself go.

Karan Johar: OK.

Bipasha Basu: Initially, I was working back-to-back. I had signed a lot of films, without leaving any time for anything else. The variety on the menu combined with no exersice makes for a bad combination. There was no work out. The industry lacks proper discipline. It made me really a tubby girl.

Karan Johar: Oh God!

Bipasha Basu: Oh, my God! I disliked watching myself on screen.

Karan Johar: Yes. I have watched a couple of films. I had been observing you. I had wondered what happened to the sex symbol. Where did that figure go?

Bipasha Basu: Yeah! It is a good jolt. You know, you learn from your mistakes.

Karan Johar: Of course. You look fabulous here.

> **I have been obsessed with my workout.**
> *–Bipasha Basu*

Bipasha Basu: I have been into the fitness centre during past seven months. I work out regularly. I have been obsessed with my workout.

Karan Johar: Very well done!

Bipasha Basu: It has been really good. I do not fall sick. I feel great. Everything has been good. There have been good, healthy exercises. The credit goes to Diane, Leena Mogre, Gold Gym and everybody.

Karan Johar: And John Abraham.

Bipasha Basu: John Abraham?

Karan Johar: He has worked on you.

Bipasha Basu: Yes, I have to emphasize he was the main person responsible. He knew that I did not have the time to work out, so he gifted a treadmill on my birthday. He told me, 'Bipasha, you can just go to the other room and start working out.'

Karan Johar: It is great. We should attribute a lot of the sexy figure to John. Indeed, he has really worked on you, in *every possible manner*.

Bipasha Basu: Definitely. He has been very positive.

Karan Johar: Returning to *Jism*, I have a favourite dialogue. I loved the way you said it; I want you to just say it to me. I love that dialogue. I loved the way you used it in your film. Yes, I used it in *Kal Ho Na Ho*. I let Lillete Dubey do it, but I want to hear it from you.

Bipasha Basu: Do not ask me to sit like that.

Karan Johar: No. I do not think we should put our legs in that particular way! Just say it to me, please.

> **John gifted (me) a treadmill on my birthday.**
> *–Bipasha Basu*

Bipasha Basu: Well, I will say it, but I do not know how to say.

Karan Johar: No. Say it as sexily as you can.

Bipasha Basu: This body does not know love. It knows just hunger - the hunger for another body.

> **The dialogue in *Jism* was very different from what I would actually say.**
> *–Bipasha Basu*

Karan Johar: Ah! Wonderful. I just thought it was a super sexy dialogue. It was just fabulous!

Bipasha Basu: Yeah! It was quite a shocking dialogue. Yeah! It is very different from what I could actually say.

Karan Johar: No. It is not in keeping with your image.

Bipasha Basu: No, the image is something else. That is exactly what....

Karan Johar: ... I thought you would be saying in the film.

Bipasha Basu: Yeah.

BIPASHA: HEART-TO-HEART

Karan Johar: So, tell me - you have known John for how long, Bipasha?

Bipasha Basu: Well, almost two-and-a-half years.

Karan Johar: Yeah. So that is a long time. You had a long relationship with Dino Morea earlier. I presume that was a longer relationship than the one with John Abraham.

Bipasha Basu: Yes.

Karan Johar: How do you compare that relationship and the relationship with John today?

Bipasha Basu: I do not compare them. I am not the only person in my life who has a second boyfriend. It is a part of the growing up process. When I met Dino, I think I

> **I do not compare my relationships with John and Dino.**
> *–Bipasha Basu*

was experimenting like a kid, though I was 17. We grew up as different individuals. Our chemistry still permits us to have fun as and when we meet. We sustain our friendship with positive vibes. I am quite mature and wanted someone of John's stature to proceed. It is no longer childhood love. It is definitely much more stronger.

Karan Johar: Deeper!

Bipasha Basu: And deeper.

Karan Johar: It is easy to balance your act with your earlier boyfriend who continues to influence you.

Bipasha Basu: Well, it is something that I am not serious about. It is not like I am the only one to have an earlier boyfriend.

Karan Johar: No, of course not.

Bipasha Basu: It is quite strange that people talked about us more. They asked me how could I have friendship with my earlier

> **I cannot just move on after having sufficient attachment (to Dino Morea).**
> *–Bipasha Basu*

boyfriend? I cannot just move on after having sufficient attachment. It does not mean that I should dislike that person. I know many women like me were perplexed about the position. Why do people single me out? You can ask any girl whether she hates her earlier boyfriend.

Karan Johar: I beg to differ. It will be wonderful if you keep that equation with Dino. There are many women who are unhappy with their earlier partners. They do not want to see or meet them.

Bipasha Basu: No, but then you do have..

Karan Johar: No, you have an association with Dino even today onscreen and off-screen.

Bipasha Basu: Yeah, but they differ under the circumstances.

Karan Johar: Yeah.

Bipasha Basu: It is those circumstances which makes you bitter or sustains the friendship. We grew up as the different individuals. We were not the same people anymore.

Karan Johar: Yes, I understand.

> **I don't think that I can dine with Dino and John together.**
> *–Bipasha Basu*

Bipasha Basu: So definitely, it was very mutual.

Karan Johar: You have not yet reached that phase where you could dine with Dino and John together?

Bipasha Basu: No, I do not think that I could do so.

LARA DUTTA

Karan Johar: All right. We have another hottie on the set. She is stunning, she is glamorous, and she is beautiful. The universe thinks about her so. Let us have Lara Dutta, Miss Universe 2000, as our next guest. Another successful crossover from the world of modeling to the world of Indian cinema.

LARA: GO FIGURE!

Karan Johar: Thank you Lara.

Lara Dutta: Thank you, Karan.

Karan Johar: Thank you Lara for being on *Koffee with Karan*. Thank you for coming, despite a leg injury.

Lara Dutta: Despite muscle cramp, actually. So, I am as glamorous as I could be on crutches.

Karan Johar: No, you are looking lovely. What did you do? Put your foot in your mouth? You could say that.

Lara Dutta: Yes, it does happen to girls in the fraternity. This was a little gym accident.

Karan Johar: Oh! my dear. We were just talking about the gym. Why do girls run on the treadmill just to look hot and sexy?

> I prefer to go to the gym so that I can watch men working out.
>
> *–Lara Dutta*

Lara Dutta: I do not know. I prefer to go to the gym so that I can watch men working out. Indeed, it is different altogether...

Karan Johar: Way to go.

Bipasha Basu: I cannot say about the men at my old gym. I started going to gym with Lara now.

Karan Johar: Yeah.

Bipasha Basu: ..in Mauritius.

Karan Johar: ....that is where you started getting into....

Bipasha Basu: I saw Esha working out. She is a girl almost of my age. She works out so much but I don't. I said OK, I will commence from there. I found Lara and others.

Karan Johar: So it was a full-fledged..

Lara Dutta: Power Puff girls.

Karan Johar: Was it a full-fledged gym?

Bipasha Basu: Yeah! Girls have worked out more than boys.

Karan Johar: Who were the boys?

Lara Dutta: Salman Khan.

Bipasha Basu: Salman Khan was the only one there.

Karan Johar: Was he?

Bipasha Basu: He would just come and go.

Lara Dutta: He was influencing us.

Bipasha Basu: Yeah!

Lara Dutta: So, I went to the gym to observe good-looking men.

Karan Johar: Salman worked out, but was he not naughty?

Lara Dutta: He was quite helpful. He got proper weights.

Bipasha Basu: I focused on my figure.

CHADDI BUDDIES

Karan Johar: All right! So, you guys know each other. Yes?

Bipasha Basu: For quite some time.

> **We (Lara and Bipasha) knew each other through modeling before entering the film industry.**
> *–Lara Dutta*

Lara Dutta: We knew each other through modeling before entering the film industry.

Bipasha Basu: Yeah, since we were models. Very long.

Karan Johar: Do you like each other?

Bipasha Basu: Yes. Are you trying to influence us?

Lara Dutta: The lie-o-meter.

Karan Johar: OK. Let me introduce you to my friend - the lie-o-meter. I do this when I think you are lying. I do not think you know each other for some time. Do you like each other a lot?

Bipasha Basu: Well!

Lara Dutta: I do not know... Actually!

Bipasha Basu: You want to use that meter or not.

> **I have known Dino since I was 15 years old. I have known John ever since he got into modeling.**
> *–Lara Dutta*

Karan Johar: No, I was just kidding.

Bipasha Basu: Well, I have..

Karan Johar: You can answer that.

Lara Dutta: We did not get

much of an opportunity to hang out when we were busy. We were constantly on shows or modeling. You were doing ad campaigns together. Quite surprisingly, Bipasha and I knew each other's better halves.

Bipasha Basu: Yeah!

> **Bipasha and I knew each other's better halves.**
> *—Lara Dutta*

Lara Dutta: ...than we have gotten to know each other. Oh really! You know Kelly and you know John.

Bipasha Basu: Dino and Kelly have been..

Lara Dutta: I have known Dino and John for.. I have known Dino since Bangalore - since I was 15 years old. I have known John ever since he got into modeling.

Karan Johar: Ah, this is a happy four-some. A criss-cross happy four-some. You have known Kelly?

Bipasha Basu: Yes, I have known Kelli for a long time, he is Dino's best buddy. We ate, woke up together. I have known Lara through Kelly for longer period. We seldom interact, for we are busy with work. She is doing well.

Karan Johar: You have not been able to.

Bipasha Basu: No.

Lara Dutta: No.

FRATERNITY FRIENDSHIPS

Bipasha Basu: We have bonded with two more girls in the 'No Entry' zone. Yes, they are Esha and Celina. The four-some had a gala time.

Lara Dutta: The industry could not figure us out together.

Bipasha Basu: Yeah!

Lara Dutta: It actually worked together.

Karan Johar: You knew Kelly, and you done so with Dino and John.

Lara Dutta: Yes. I have been in discotheques as Dino's younger sister. He was hitting on other girls. Hello! That was before he met Bipasha.

Karan Johar: You can tell her. I do not think Bipasha minds the incident.

> **I have been un discotheques as Dino's younger sister. He was hitting on other girls.**
> *—Lara Dutta*

Bipasha Basu: No.

Masala Grapevine!

Karan Johar: All right. How does it make the equation? The grapevine claims that John and you move like husband and wife. Is this true Lara and does it affect you Bipasha?

Bipasha Basu: I think the fact that we are here together says a lot.

Lara Dutta: Exactly!

Bipasha Basu: None of us have bothered about it. Actually, I know Lara and I know Kelly very well. I am very happy for them. I trust my boyfriend. The most important thing is that we are here together.

> **When you do your first film or two films with an actor, you will hear from the public that you have slept with him.**
> *–Lara Dutta*

Lara Dutta: Exactly!

Karan Johar: OK. Does that bother you?

Lara Dutta: Take everything with a handful of salt. You have to live with such rumours afloat. When you do your first film or two films with an actor, you will hear from the public that you have slept with him. You will be bonded with him for repeating films subsequently.

Bipasha Basu: Yeah!

Lara Dutta: This is just you know...

Karan Johar: The norms of the film industry?

Lara Dutta: Yeah, just the norms.

Karan Johar: Does that bother you at all?

Lara Dutta: I work really well with John. I have done *Elaan* with him. We vibe very well onscreen. We have great chemistry. He is a really good co-star to work with. A very few co-stars will facilitate you to get a fabulous look onscreen. You can do something. I will not ruin. I will not allow silly rumour afloat like Bipasha.

Bipasha Basu: Exactly.

Lara Dutta: We are secur women in our relations.

Karan Johar: Yeah.

Lara Dutta: These things are just in a day's work.

Bipasha Basu: It is sad that the secure women and those who are extroverts get targeted. They are targeted more than the people who hide.

> **We are secure women in our relationships.**
> *–Lara Dutta*

Lara Dutta: Yes.

Karan Johar: Your open relationship has affected you. Yeah! I mean Bipasha we always knew about you and Dino and then now John and you. Lara, Kelly has been in your life.

Lara Dutta: Totally!

Karan Johar: Almost...

Lara Dutta: Almost for the longest time.

> **Tiger (Woods) showed me how to put a few rounds of golf. It made me big in three days.**
> –*Lara Dutta*

Karan Johar: We have heard about the alleged romance with Tiger Woods.

Lara Dutta: I had helped Tiger on his foundation *Tiger Jams*. I did a three-day golf-a-clinic with him. I have helped him with his media drive. The media men thought that I could help him to face the media.

Karan Johar: Ah!

Lara Dutta: Tiger showed me how to put a few rounds of golf. It made me big in three days.

Karan Johar: Was that all you did?

Lara Dutta: Yes. Three-days of golf in Las Vegas.

Karan Johar: No hysteria on Kelly's end?

Lara Dutta: No. I think Tiger is more into Blondes than brunettes. So..

Bipasha Basu: You have such a big rumour of three days' stint?

Karan Johar: Yeah! Lara had an affair with Tiger Woods and got Kelly hysterical, wherever he was.

Lara Dutta: Yeah!

BIPASHA: LOOKS VS PERFORMANCE

Karan Johar: So, well these things happen. They are part and parcel of the industry. Tell me, you are considered very beautiful and stunning women. Sometimes, there is a stereotype attached to this. Do you sometimes get affected when people talk more about your *Jism* than your performance?

> **I do not want to be a legend.**
> –*Bipasha Basu*

Bipasha Basu: No. I think from the time I did films, I have been called a sex symbol right from day one, whether it was *Ajanabee, Raaz,* or *Gunah.* I have played the role of a housewife in Raaz. I wear polo neck T-shirts till today to work with ease.

Karan Johar: Yes.

Bipasha Basu: It had never bothered me. Films like *Rakht* and *Madhoshi* could not work. The filmmakers come to me with the lead protagonist's role, where there is not much of a skin show, but acting.

Karan Johar: Yeah.

GOAL(S)

Bipasha Basu: I am very satisfied with the roles I used to get. The media perceives me as the sex symbol, whatever films I do. The stain still haunts me. I intend to work for a few years. I do not want to be a legend. I will be fine so long as it is comfortable for a few years.

Karan Johar: I have read about that comment.

Bipasha Basu: Yeah.

Karan Johar: You have uttered in a magazine that you want to remain as a professional artist. You dislike being a legend. You spelt out that you want to work and quit. Does Lara endorse your statement?

Lara Dutta: I have absolutely no problem if the people think me as an artist meant for glamour or sex. Mr. Yash Chopra had admired me. His heroines have remained glamorous, whether they sleep or cry, or dance in the rain. I am a heroine of a Hindi film. I have no problem in looking ultra glam. I believe that is what Indian cinema is about. You are supposed to look beautiful, ethereal, sexy and glamorous, as much as you can. I would like to leave the legacy of having been a good leading actress.

Karan Johar: So would you like to glorify yourself as a legend?

Lara Dutta: Totally!

> **I have no problem in looking ultra glam.**
> –*Lara Dutta*

Karan Johar: Would you like to influence the generation Y...Z...?

Lara Dutta: Definitely.

LARA: PROLOGUE

Karan Johar: You dreamt of becoming an actress for Hindi films. I recollect when I came to gather opinion of Miss India contestants—

Lara Dutta: Right. I was the one at the back.

Karan Johar: Yes. Often, you were least interested in what I spoke. I have wondered why you behaved so?

Lara Dutta: Where's my lie-o-meter?

Karan Johar: No, I have found you quite interesting when you had disliked to hear my principle. Did you think you would land up where you are today?

> I would like to influence the Y-Z generation.
>
> *–Lara Dutta*

Lara Dutta: I have always wanted to act. I just.. you know..

Karan Johar: You were just shy of the media.

Lara Dutta: I have come from Ghaziabad, a small town in western Uttar Pradesh. I never dreamt to land in Mumbai. I never expected to get a role amidst hectic competition. I definitely was not ready to beat the rough road. I never believed to kick below its paddock, on being given the gift horse.

Karan Johar: Yeah. So you know...

Lara Dutta: Exactly. I shall give the maximum return on being given an opportunity to exhibit my skills.

Karan Johar: Congratulations to Lara for achievements! You too Bipasha!

BIPASHA: HONESTY IS THE BEST POLICY

Karan Johar: You were in *Ajnabee* and you were in *Andaaz*. Let us see - how was your debut with costar Kareena Kapoor? Were you uncomfortable in your first debut?

Bipasha Basu: Honestly speaking, I did not have any preconceived notions about films when I entered. I reached Switzerland among the team of 80 odd people. I did not know

> I could not speak to Kareena and found that she disliked speaking to me.
>
> *–Bipasha Basu*

anyone, but heard the people commenting on me. They were helpful on an alien soil. I could not speak to Kareena. I found on the subsequent day that she disliked speaking to me. I have ignored the incident for I was honest and upright. If someone dislikes talking, it was for my good. I would rather have a person who is very straight in front of me. If he speaks to get into work professionally, it will be OK. There was no tantrum when we had scenes together. Nothing unpleasant took the fun, but the media hype has churned the rumour mills.

Karan Johar: You have just discovered one day that she doesn't like you.

Bipasha Basu: Yeah! I never attempt to speak to someone

> I honestly like people who are direct rather than the people who say goodie goodie things.
>
> *—Bipasha Basu*

not inclined to talk to me. I will never ask that person what is his/ her problem? I will never do that so long as it will not affect my relations. You cannot experiment with that meter for me.

Karan Johar: Yeah, I know; you told when I reached there.

Bipasha Basu: I honestly like people who are direct rather than the people who say goodie goodie things.

Karan Johar: Give me an example of such a person who had been so.....

Bipasha Basu: Well, there are lots of personalities in the industry. I believe some 90 per cent of them are so.

Karan Johar: OK. Give me two names.

Bipasha Basu: I cannot. I will give them to you back stage. I have to work with them. My professional image gets spoiled.

LARA DUTTA: *MISS WORLD Vs MISS UNIVERSE*

Karan Johar: Oh God! How was your working equation with Priyanka Chopra? Media hyped something mischievous. Headlines roared *Miss World and Miss Universe clashed* in a film called *Andaz*.

Lara Dutta: Exactly. Media did similar hypes when Sush and Aish entered the Bollywood. They repeated with me and Priyanka. You are working for the first time in the film. You have come from a different background. You never had a premonition about the industry or its lobbies. You have to show up through your

> She (Priyanka Chopra) is gutsy with a lot of gumption and focus.
>
> *—Lara Dutta*

performance and your work. Oh God! Let me show up to work. Give everything that I have got. We seldom had any conflict or disinterest towards our roles.

Karan Johar: I was yearning to enact.

Lara Dutta: No. I have known Priyanka ever since she won the Miss India title. The people in the industry have made us argue over the differences in personalities. The industry relies on backbiting; pinpricking, lying, spying and making professionals fight amongst themselves on somebody's hearsay.

Karan Johar: Will it not divide us?

Lara Dutta: It does create confusion. Phone lines are available to sort the differences. Neither do we have to meet or hang out, except calling each other once or twice a week.

Karan Johar: Was it sorted out?

Lara Dutta: It was sorted out since we came together in the industry. We had to meet or speak directly or indirectly. So it was important for us to sort the differences out.

Karan Johar: So you like Priyanka Chopra?

Lara Dutta: Just look at him, the way he is spelling things! I do like her. She had been gutsy with a lot of gumption and focus. You have to admire things in people who are great. She knows what she wants. I admire such woman persisting through ups and downs.

Karan Johar: OK! Great.

Bipasha Basu: He is a naughty guy.

Karan Johar: Am I?

Bipasha Basu: You are a naughty guy.

Karan Johar: Lara! You have answered very well. Only a Miss Universe could reply so. OK. Great!

Bipasha Basu: Where is the crown?

On Amisha Patel

Karan Johar: OK. I am coming to the favourite topic of the show: Amisha Patel. I went through her startling background. She went on record to say that your role in *Jism*..... And how she spelt that she could not do such a role for the fear of upsetting her grandma. How do you feel?

Bipasha Basu: Well, I believe Amisha does not have the requisite physical attributes to enact in a film like *Jism*.

> I believe Amisha does not have the requisite physical attributes to enact in a film like Jism.
> —*Bipasha Basu*

Karan Johar: OK.

Bipasha Basu: I remain honest. I would not cast Amisha in *Jism's* role. The person should be some woman with lot of package, not just the body traits.

Karan Johar: Yeah!

Bipasha Basu: You need to have a very strong personality. She is too petite and too small to carry the role. You know her whole frame is wrong.

Karan Johar: Yeah.

Bipasha Basu: She would not fit in *Jism*.

Karan Johar: Didn't she remark about your big hips?

Bipasha Basu: Yeah. They were big. I do not mind Amisha commenting. I thank her for the comment – my hips were now small and rocking.

Karan Johar: All right! Well, they are rocking.

Bipasha Basu: Yes, they are rocking now.

Karan Johar: There is another one of her quotes on the shoot of a film you did in *Elaan*. She reported of "insignificant John and Lara with whom I should not talk."

Lara Dutta: Yeah!

Karan Johar: That's a quote you must have read, of course. It came up in my research. Do you like being called inconsequential?

Lara Dutta: No. I am very happy that a girl is at least focussed enough on her own problems. She had realized that she deals more than her life. I always think it is good not to comment on other's concept.

Karan Johar: OK!

Lara Dutta: No, honestly on a more serious note, yes, Amisha has taken potshots at people you know, more than just the two of us. There have been a lot of people who have worked with her and reported about the problem.

Karan Johar: Yeah!

Lara Dutta: It is not very nice. Especially because you know that this person doesn't really figure much in your life. Going into the facts, you will find Rani, Preity and others where none of us had any problem. She is just another co-star. She was obsessed with whatever demerits she had faced in her own personal life.

Karan Johar: Her personal life!

Lara Dutta: You need some solution. Every dog has his day. Everyone has ups and downs in big deals. You had to gyrate between ups and downs.

Karan Johar: OK. Did that justify Amisha Patel?

THE (MISS) UNIVERSAL EFFECT

Karan Johar: Let us turn to *Rapid Fire Round*. I throw a volley of questions. You need to reply with a racy approach. I shall decide who shall win the *Rapid Fire Round*.

Lara Dutta: Ah!

Karan Johar: If you are better, you win *Koffee with Karan* koffee hamper.

Lara Dutta: Lovely. Chocolates and all.

Bipasha Basu: Lara is going to win, for she speaks better.

Lara Dutta: I win brownie points for a broken leg.

Bipasha Basu: I want to have her hamper, but half the share. I am booking it.

Karan Johar: Why do you think Lara will be better?

> I fell off the bed when she (Lara) won the Miss Universe Contest.
>
> *–Bipasha Basu*

Bipasha Basu: She is very trained. She had the best answers. I observed her in the Miss Universe contest. We were being called down for rehearsals with another model, Vivek. I fell off the bed when she won the Miss Universe contest. I was so happy and went euphoric!

Karan Johar: Yeah! Way to go India!

Bipasha Basu: I was fired by the choreographer for being late. I gave him the good news, when he told some 15 people kept waiting that "Lara's won the Miss Universe!"

Lara Dutta: So sweet!

Karan Johar: Wonderful! She is so sweet, even today.

LARA DUTTA

Here goes your *Rapid Fire*.... Lara, brace yourself ahead. Do not take long time. Give me spicy reply. The *koffee hamper* will go your way.

Lara Dutta: OK.

Karan Johar: All right! What sexy thing brews with Kelly?
Lara Dutta: His bald pate.

Karan Johar: What about John?

Lara Dutta: Bushy hairs.

Bipasha Basu: Good answer, Lara.

Karan Johar: All right. Would you become a super sex symbol?

Lara Dutta: Of course.

Karan Johar: OK. Good answer. Shahrukh Khan, Aamir Khan and. Salman Khan. Rank the Khans on the sex appeal.

Lara Dutta: Shahrukh Khan, Salman Khan, Aamir Khan.

Karan Johar: The strange pick up line ever used on you....

Lara Dutta: Would you like to go to Wimpy's? I swear to you.

Karan Johar: Like to go where?

Lara Dutta: Well, Wimpy's was the new burger joint opened in Bangalore. He was one of my fellow models. It was like, 'Would you like to go to Wimpy's?', i.e., without taking anybody's name. I did not go to Wimpy's.

Karan Johar: All right. A woman hits on you?

Lara Dutta: Not tonight darling, I have a headache.

Karan Johar: All right. Infidelity is..... complete the sentence.

Lara Dutta: Unacceptable.

Karan Johar: The woman you dislike to be with Kelly at all?

Lara Dutta: Oh! Amisha Patel.

Bipasha Basu: She is already popular on our show.

Karan Johar: Yes, she had been in the limelight. Your take on the question - does size matter?

Lara Dutta: Yes.

Karan Johar: All right. What do you think of an actress claiming to be a virgin?

Lara Dutta: Yeah, right.

Karan Johar: All right. Lara, I hope you will give me chocolates after winning the hamper.

Bipasha Basu: You can take them. I do not like them.

Karan Johar: Priyanka Chopra won the Miss World title because....

Lara Dutta: She believed in the spirit of Mother Teresa.

Karan Johar: The sexiest man in India?

Lara Dutta: Rahul Gandhi.

Karan Johar: The sexiest man in India?
Lara Dutta: Rahul Gandhi.

Karan Johar: Safe and politically correct. All right! Abhishek Bachchan or John Abraham?

Lara Dutta: Abhishek Bachchan. Sorry, I adore him. He is like a —

Bipasha Basu: Yes, even I do...

Karan Johar: He is like a brother, Oh! A baby....

Bipasha Basu: I would say Abhishek Bachchan too, if I were asked......

Karan Johar: No! Do not be hurry until your turn.

Bipasha Basu: Oh! I hope similar questions will be put to me.

Karan Johar: You never know. Sushmita Sen or Aishwarya Rai?

Lara Dutta: Sushmita Sen.

Karan Johar: Miss Universe or Best Actress?

Lara Dutta: Best Actress.

Karan Johar: All right. Kelly on the bed or Kelly on the sofa?

Lara Dutta: Kelly anywhere.

Karan Johar: Kelly on the bed or Kelly on the sofa?
Lara Dutta: Kelly anywhere!

Karan Johar: All right Bipasha Basu or Priyanka Chopra?

Lara Dutta: Bipasha Basu.

Karan Johar: Well done, Lara! I would rate you 10 on 10 if I were a professor.

Bipasha Basu: Yeah, even I would give her 11/10.

BIPASHA BASU

Karan Johar: OK! Bipasha! Brace yourself for the *Rapid Fire*. What's the sexiest thing about John?

Bipasha Basu: His madness.

Karan Johar: Whether he is half or total Parsi? So he is...

Bipasha Basu: He is.

Karan Johar: All right. John's madness is the sexiest thing, nothing else.

Bipasha Basu: *'Yeh Andaar Ki Baat Hai.'* She is helping me with answers.

Karan Johar: Yeah. Millions of men feel to be with you rather than vice-versa?

Bipasha Basu: Let them wait till my next birth.

Karan Johar: Don't you say, *'Janam, Janam Ka Saath'* with John?

Bipasha Basu: No.

Karan Johar: All right. John proposed to you in what manner?

Bipasha Basu: Well, he came to Hyderabad with a ring. He took me for a walk and told me to spend my life with him. I had gone to an outdoor shooting. He offered me the ring.

> *Karan Johar:* Millions of men want to be with you rather than vice-versa?
> *Bipasha Basu:* Let them wait till my next birth.

Karan Johar: Ah! Well done. What's the toughest part about being a sex symbol?

Bipasha Basu: Maintaining the perfect shape.

Karan Johar: Rank the Khans on the individual sex appeal - Shahrukh Khan, Aamir Khan and Salman Khan.

Bipasha Basu: Shahrukh Khan, Aamir Khan and Salman Khan.

Karan Johar: OK, Salman lost on your round. The stranges pick up line ever used on you?

Bipasha Basu: People do not find me easy, right from my teenage years. They write letters or send messages, but nothing else. Bloodied letters.

Lara Dutta: How lovely!

Karan Johar: No pick up lines.

Bipasha Basu: Unfortunate. I got letters, gifts....

Lara Dutta: Torn shirts.

> *Karan Johar:* The strangest pick up line ever used on you?
> *Bipasha Basu:* Unfortunately, no pick up lines (for me)!

Karan Johar: All right! Nobody came and said 'Your place or mine, baby?'

Bipasha Basu: No Wimpy's for me.

Karan Johar: No? How sad. All right! The successor sexiest to John in India.....

Bipasha Basu: Well, John is the sexiest.

Karan Johar: That is why I told, besides John?

Bipasha Basu: Abhishek.

Karan Johar: OK. Great! One international face you would cheat on John for?

Bipasha Basu: I will never.

> **I want Brad Pitt, if he remained single.**
> —Bipasha Basu

Karan Johar: OK, if he was not around!

Bipasha Basu: OK. I want Brad Pitt, if he remained single.

Karan Johar: Oh, God! Over-fidelity?

Bipasha Basu: No complications in relations.

Karan Johar: OK! What would you do if you were struck in an island with Kareena and Amisha?

Bipasha Basu: I would sit with Kareena and talk because....we've both grown. And four years have gone by.....we have matured.....

Karan Johar: What would you do with Amisha?

Bipasha Basu: We shall send her to look for food. 'Go and get some fruits for us while we sit and chat.'

Karan Johar: *Ajnabee* was on wife swapping. Your take on husband swapping?

Bipasha Basu: Absolutely NO.

Karan Johar: OK. Ex-boyfriends or contesting actresses?

Bipasha Basu: Ex-boyfriends.

Karan Johar: John with or minus shirt?

Bipasha Basu: John minus shirt.

Karan Johar: *Raaz* or *Jism?*

Bipasha Basu: *Jism.*

Karan Johar: Vikram Bhatt or Pooja Bhatt?

Bipasha Basu: Vikram Bhatt.

Karan Johar: Lara or Amisha?

Bipasha Basu: Lara

Karan Johar: Very easy.

Bipasha Basu: He is asking very easy questions.

> **Karan Johar: Ex-boyfriends or contesting actresses?**
> **Bipasha Basu: Ex-boyfriends.**

Karan Johar: Brawns or Brains?

Bipasha Basu: Brains.

Karan Johar: All right! We have the brawny John with a brain.

Bipasha Basu: Yes. He is an intelligent man.

Karan Johar: OK! Dino as a boyfriend or John as a boyfriend?

Bipasha Basu: John as a boyfriend.

Karan Johar: All right! Safe and secure. Very well done Bipasha. You did really well. I think it is a close call.

Bipasha Basu: Please give it to Lara. She gave the funny answers.

Karan Johar: Should I? Yeah!

Bipasha Basu: I had a good laugh.

> *Karan Johar:* OK! Dino as a boyfriend or John as a boyfriend?
> *Bipasha Basu:* John as a boyfriend.

Karan Johar: You too were 10/10, because there was no skipping the difficult ones. No . I did not....Everyone is the winner. All right! Congratulations.

Lara Dutta: Thank you.

Karan Johar: You win the koffee hamper.

Bipasha Basu: Half is mine.

Lara Dutta: I cannot get up.

Karan Johar: No, I will hand it over after the show. You have done very well. I must say that I have done many shows. I had this *Rapid* Fire everytime, but this was exceptional with both of you getting 10 on 10. Every contestant fell short of it. You have done exceptionally well.

Bipasha Basu: Thank you.

KAHIN PE NIGAHEN...

> **Men hit on me in their own sweet way.**
> –Bipasha Basu

Karan Johar: Your beauty calls for men to hit on you once in a blue moon. Come on! I have my lie-o-meter.

Bipasha Basu: Well, in their own sweet way.

Karan Johar: They do?

Bipasha Basu: You can just say it is mindless flirting. You are waiting for the shot. You have nothing to do. May be somebody says a sweet thing or something once in a while.

Karan Johar: You could mean something, better ignore....

Bipasha Basu: It could be. You can ignore it because it really does not matter. You have to work and have the relation. You need to have fun while doing so; else the job will be boring.

Karan Johar: Tell me.....an actor and an actor had to..... Do not give the names, because you have already won. What would he say?

Bipasha Basu: Oh! You have broken up. Some problem. I replied that I have not broken up. Are you sure?

Karan Johar: OK. Give me a name. No, you would not?

Bipasha Basu: No. It could be, I am not lying. I will have to use the lie-o-meter.

Karan Johar: All right. Lara! What is the strangest pick-up line you heard from a hero? 'Come on baby, tonight?'

Lara Dutta: Tonight. There were plenty of them. They were uttered not on a daily basis, but were from our own fraternity. I did not mind, as it was a

> **There were plenty of people from our own fraternity with strangest pickup lines.**
> –Lara Dutta

fun. Someone said, 'He cannot help it. It is like a disease, so do not be offensive.'

Karan Johar: I wonder who it was.....

Bipasha Basu: We need to know.

Karan Johar: Is it Abhishek, the brat?

Lara Dutta: No, he is on the other end of the spectrum, who takes a veil or whatsoever and ties it around you. He yells, 'What the hell do you do on the sets?' or pulls down your skirt?

Karan Johar: You had a hot smooching scene with him?

Lara Dutta: It was hardly a hot smooching scene. I think we were so psychic by the time we woke up - I do not remember or know about it.

Karan Johar: So sad! Poor Abhishek.... You have no memory of kissing him?

Lara Dutta: Exactly.

Karan Johar: Really, Bipasha should have been upset. He is your favourite.

> **I have no memory of kissing Abhishek (Dhoom 2)!**
> –Bipasha Basu

Lara Dutta: I have no idea.

Bipasha Basu: Yes, he is my favourite. I have to play with him all the time.

Karan Johar: You have told in an interview that you would kiss John, but not Abhishek.

Bipasha Basu: Well, it was nothing other than the script. Every film has a kissing scene.

> **I cannot kiss anybody. I am very self-conscious.**
> *–Bipasha Basu*

Karan Johar: Yeah.

Bipasha Basu: I cannot kiss anybody. I am very self-conscious.

Lara Dutta: Yeah.

Bipasha Basu: I have to do selective kissing. It depends on the script. I really don't know.

Karan Johar: OK. Abhishek! Find a script so that Bipasha could kiss you onscreen. What amazed me was that you were secure in your relation.

JOHN AND KELLY ON BIPASHA AND LARA

We went visiting John and Kelly to ascertain what they spoke about you. So it applies to *Bipasha with love* and *Lara with love*. Comment.

Bipasha Basu and Lara Dutta: Yes, of course.

Karan Johar: It is my pleasure to show this clip.

Kelly Dorji: Lara as a person, as a girl, as a woman is very sexy. She appeals to every man, and to me that is sexy.

Lara Dutta: Interesting!

> **Lara appeals to every man, and to me that is sexy.**
> *–Kelly Dorji*

Kelly Dorji: You know that somebody else might find her attractive or sexy. It is OK. It reiterates her to be so. I am not insecure. The more people admire her, the more it reinforces me to love her more. She is very strong, but not judgmental. She knows what will suit her. Something, which I have never revealed about, is that *'she is a devil in disguise'*. She is quite capable of doing little inane naughty things and turning around with puppy eyes.

Lara Dutta: Puppy eyes!

Kelly Dorji: You cannot help but forgive her. Oh! Angel! I have not told you how much you really mean to me. There has been so much going on in our lives. Little puppies have been coming in our lives.

Lara Dutta: Yeah!

Kelly Dorji: My brother is getting married. There is love

> **Lara is a devil in disguise!**
> *–Kelly Dorji*

on the air surrounding us. I just want to tell you that whatever happens, we are still here for each other. I am here for you. I love you very much. I shall reciprocate with the love you have extended.

Bipasha Basu: So sweet!

Karan Johar: Is not that sweet now?

Bipasha Basu: He is too cute.

Lara Dutta: That is true, Kelly.

John Abraham: Bipasha! You are on *Koffee with Karan*. Karan will nag you just like he is doing with me. He will catch me unawares.

> **On a scale of 1-10, Bipasha is a perfect 11.**
> *–John Abraham*

Take care, Bipasha! He is a very mischievous guy. You have arrived on the scene with *Ajnabee,* a picture I saw much before I started knowing you better. I was very much impressed with your performance. I thought you have performed splendid in *Raaz* and *Jism*. I was very much impressed when I saw *Jism* when you have emerged out of the water during intro. It remained the most beautiful and sensitive shot of a woman fully clothed emerging out of the water. I have tried to capture the scene with other women, but in vain. You stood where you were. Bipasha, people love you for the person you were. Leave the fact aside that you are very sensuous and beautiful.

Bipasha Basu: There goes with my boyfriend.

John Abraham: ..like I told Karan that on a scale of 1-10, I would offer you 11. You are a perfect 11. Wish you all the best. My love to you. I am on the camera and speaking to you quite formally.

Bipasha Basu: I know that baby.

John Abraham: Take care.

Bipasha Basu: Well, this is my Parsi boyfriend. You have put a camera on him and he will be formal.

Karan Johar: Oh!

Bipasha Basu: He has just said that.

Karan Johar: He is very formal. Kelly is very sweet.

Bipasha Basu: Kelly is a Capricornian like me. He is a born Capricornian. I know him. He speaks exactly what he feels. John is a born Sagittarian, who will remain guarded.

Karan Johar: Is there anything like you want to say to the boys?

Lara Dutta: I think with Kelly, what he comments is that both of us have grown through a lot in our lives. We saw through the one-room matchbox apartment. We have emptied our pockets to buy bread when we went hungry for days. Today, we tend to two lovely puppies and a mouse. What really counts is that we have really stuck to our heels. Material things were unaccountable. We have got something really good. We hang on to whatever we have got.

Karan Johar: So, Bipasha do you have anything to say to John?

Bipasha Basu: Well, my mad boyfriend is super sexy, but virtually whacked. I know why he said such things, because I was bedridden. I had put on weight with negative energy. People wondered what had

> **We (Kelly and I) had to empty our pockets to buy bread when we went hungry for days.**
>
> –Lara Dutta

happened to Bipasha? I have regained my figure in the past couple of months. He believed in me and went on applauding me.

Karan Johar: Of course, he does. Any marriage plans?

Bipasha Basu: Well, I think John is just starting off. He needs to move with his career. For me, it is a new beginning. I have performed in many small-scale commercial films. I have done important roles. I want to switch over to those dependable and box office-friendly products with giant producers, bigger heroes.

> **I want to switch over to those dependable and box office-friendly products with giant producers, bigger heroes.**
>
> –Bipasha Basu

I have made an effort with my conscience and see whether it works for five years ahead till I get doubled with someone of my choice.

CONCLUSION

Karan Johar: Well. Cheers for a new beginning. Cheers to Lara for your marriage plans. Eventually. All right, two puppies need to have two children. Thank you so much Bipasha. Thank you Lara for being on the show. I had a great time and hope you have spared your valuable time.

Bipasha Basu: I do not think one person will have a great time watching the show.

Karan Johar: I hope you did have a great time. I did too, because that is the most important thing - I had fun on my own show. Please sign those mugs before signing off. You have to sign it together. Remember, this personally autographed mug could be yours if you participate in the *koffee quest*. Thank you, Bipasha. Thank you, Lara. Thank you for being on my show and answering the *rapid fire* so well. Thank you for being the people you are.

Bipasha Basu: Thank you for not using the lie-o-meter.

Lara Dutta: No, but he did.

Karan Johar: Thank you once again.

● ● ●

10

Ekta Kapoor & Sunita Menon
Kosmic Konnections

She has changed the dynamics of television. She is truly the first lady of Indian television. She has made it quite clear to young India that it is not just the boys who can make the big bucks. This is truly a success story. My first guest tonight is none other than Ekta Kapoor. Actually, Ekta and I share a lot in common. We both swear by the alphabet 'K'. We both are extremely superstitious. We both are fellow Geminians. We both are scared of flying. My God! Maybe we should be married – but more about that later. For now, let us call on the television visionary, Ekta Kapoor.

EKTA KAPOOR

Karan Johar: Good evening!

Ekta Kapoor: Good evening! How are you?

> **I have never been interviewed!**
> –Ekta Kapoor

Karan Johar: Looking lovely!

Ekta Kapoor: Thank you so much.

Karan Johar: Alright Ekta, welcome to *Koffee with Karan*.

Ekta Kapoor: Oh, it is my pleasure to be here.

Karan Johar: Does it feel funny to be interviewed by me?

Ekta Kapoor: Actually, it does because I have never been interviewed. It will be more funny and friendly to get interviewed.

Karan Johar: What does it feel like to be a millionaire at 29? How does it feel?

Ekta Kapoor: Honestly, the people think about it as something invaluable. I am reporting something, which is secondary. What interests me is that you should keep company with new trends in a completely new industry – that is television.

Karan Johar: True.

Ekta Kapoor: It will be bumpy ride for me, you know.

Karan Johar: For you, that is what is exciting.

Ekta Kapoor: Yeah!

THE JOURNEY

Karan Johar: Friends have told me from my teenage years that she would float a company with annual turnover of Rs.5 bn or Rs 6 bn that would rock the Indian television industry. Apparently, you have always said it. Is that true?

Ekta Kapoor: You can say so. I have told you that I would float a software company. I was never sure that I would do so because I was not so ambitious. I dreamt to become a journalist or a designer quite often.

> **I dreamt to become a journalist or a designer quite often!**
> –Ekta Kapoor

Karan Johar: Yes, you did. You even hosted a countdown show on the television, which not many people know about. It was called *'Super hit Muqaabla'* on

Doordarshan. You were the host. So you did what I am doing just now.

Ekta Kapoor: Yes. I did a pretty bad job out of it.

Karan Johar: Did you?

Ekta Kapoor: I decided later that my place was not in front of the camera.

Karan Johar: It is behind it?

Ekta Kapoor: Yeah!

Karan Johar: Yeah, I mean that is something amazing. It came up in my research. I cried, 'My God! When did Ekta host *Super-hit Muquabla?*' I was completely shocked. When did this happen?

Ekta Kapoor: I just try to forget it. I got bouts of amnesia when it appeared on the screen.

Karan Johar: Well, you tried something out at that point of time.

> I got bouts of amnesia when *Superhit Muqabla*, which I anchored, appeared on Doordarshan!
>
> –Ekta Kapoor

Ekta Kapoor: Yeah!

Karan Johar: Did you think you looked good in front of the camera?

Ekta Kapoor: Well, all of a sudden, I did not come on the camera – not the whole of me, just the face.

Karan Johar: You made sure of that, didn't you?

Ekta Kapoor: Yeah!

Karan Johar: All right, I have declared to the audience that we have much in common.

Ekta Kapoor: Absolutely, Karan!

Karan Johar: The alphabet 'K'. I have said that I am hysterical. I am really scared of flying, which I believe so are you.

Ekta Kapoor: Big time!

Karan Johar: I have never flown with you. I don't think that should happen or we fly simultaneously on the same flight!

Ekta Kapoor: I think the pilot will have a tough time.

Karan Johar: Yeah! I think because both will be requesting to land the plane fast. And of course, there is the fact that we are superstitious.

Ekta Kapoor: Very!

Karan Johar: We both remain clairvoyants and justify ourselves to be tarot readers. We visit astrologers frequently. We are quite mad actually, to think about it

Ekta Kapoor: Very!

Karan Johar: We approached Sunita Menon – a common factor!

Ekta Kapoor: Absolutely, yeah!

Karan Johar: So, Sunita! Of course, we know her to be a tarot reader, a psychic, a clairvoyant and whatever you may call her. Do you swear by her totally?

Ekta Kapoor: I do. Sunita has proved to be that guide in my life that I did not have before. I had friends; I had family, but did not have a guru. I believe that I needed a guiding light at a point because many things happened in my life at a quick pace. I lost control over my assimilation power. I recollect that what she predicted during the year 2000 happened in the subsequent year. It has changed my life. She has helped me through my bad phase.

> **Sunita has helped me through my bad phase.**
>
> – *Ekta Kapoor*

Karan Johar: What was that incident, Ekta?

Ekta Kapoor: She told me that transit Saturn would become intense in my birth chart. It would keep me obsessed with people. Suddenly, I went on looking at them. I was shocked even when I looked down my own close friends. The TRP evaluation reflected that I had done a wonderful job.

Karan Johar: Yeah!

Ekta Kapoor: She had predicted such things to happen. I needed her support again following her accurate forecast.

Karan Johar: Well, do you know that Sunita Menon is our next guest tonight.

Ekta Kapoor: Yeah, I do!

Karan Johar: She is the spiritual, the psychic, the emotional adviser to the entire fraternity and members of Mumbai society. Ekta, you know that, of course.

Ekta Kapoor: Absolutely!

SUNITA MENON

Karan Johar: She is Mumbai's favourite clairvoyant. Let us welcome Sunita Menon! Hello, Sunita!

Sunita Menon: It is very nice to see you.

Karan Johar: Yes, very nice to see you. You are looking very glamorous!

> I call Ekta my little devil – whenever I see her, I see two little hooded horns!
>
> *– Sunita Menon*

Sunita Menon: Thank you.

Ekta Kapoor: How are you?

Sunita Menon: Good.

Karan Johar: I love that. You meet us as if we were in a social get-together an hour before.

Ekta Kapoor: We always meet like that, even if we meet five times a day. It reflects our mutual love and affection.

Karan Johar: Wonderful! We were just talking about the tremendous influence you have in our lives.

Sunita Menon: Yes, my little devil. That is what I call her. Whenever I see her, I see two little hooded horns!

Karan Johar: My God! That is something we have not heard of.

Sunita Menon: The way I speak to her is like, 'What have you done?' It is like that. I used to say 'Sonu,' etc. That's how it goes!

Karan Johar: Oh God!

Sunita Menon: Yeah!

BREAKING THE RULES

Karan Johar: Well, Sunita, you are an amazing personality. People have adjudged you as somebody who looks through a crystal about their future. You will forecast for them on their psychic restitution of the past and the future. They have endorsed you as water diviner, a tarot reader and a clairvoyant.. The whole perception is a lady sitting very peacefully in white, meditating and predicting your future – you have completely broken that myth. You have broken the conventional norm! It is wonderful! I always endorse that. What is your take on the common perception of Sunita Menon?

Sunita Menon: People normally expect an older woman with grey hair, really fat, bespectacled with a coin-sized bindi on the forehead.

Karan Johar: Oh dear!

Sunita Menon: I will be looking at something say, 'Saturn's transit in the 7th house from horizon will keep the professionals utterly disappointed'. I am in my jeans with matching shirt, lounging on and saying, 'Hi, good morning, how are you doing?' Someone shared with me about his utter disappointment. 'I really expected a lot of the occult wisdom like the smoke emanating from somewhere! What happened to this one?' I told him, 'Look, I can rig it; I can make you produce some film.'

Karan Johar: Yeah! Things submerged completely – eerie and smoky.

Sunita Menon: Totally! Dark glasses, et al.

> **People normally expect an older woman with grey hair, really fat, bespectacled, with a coin-sized bindi on the forehead!**
> –Sunita Menon

Ekta Kapoor: Special effects and all.

Sunita Menon: Red light, a bit of smoke.

Ekta Kapoor: Background?

Sunita Menon: Yeah! A bit of background music will create something eerie to finish the entire scene.

Karan Johar: Did not you achieve such special effects earlier? You wore white sari with lot of white and pastel shades earlier.

Sunita Menon: There is a very good reason for that. I am glad you have recollected that.

Karan Johar: You were like that during my first meeting, were not you?

Sunita Menon: A film portrayed me as the lady sitting with kohl pencil and pulling cards out, having tousled long hair.

Karan Johar: Well, I know two such documentaries have reflected your looks.

Ekta Kapoor: I am going to die!

Karan Johar: One of them was Ekta Kapoor's film, *Krishna cottage*. The other was Ram Gopal Varma's product *Bhooth*. There was *Rakht*, another product.

Sunita Menon: Yeah!

Karan Johar: Sunita Menon finds her clones in the film?

Sunita Menon: Yet another, *Milenge Milenge*, where they portray another character – Sunita Rao. Oh God! I have lost control. You cannot go on like this. What would happen if I got thronged by an appreciable crowd around the year? I am not supposed to influence their sense of humour. I am not supposed to know about fashion or art or music or whatsoever. I am supposed to be that person obsessed with astrology. I have my own life, thanks to Mr. Manish Malhotra! We have had long sessions. Truly! Thanks to him for my metamorphosis.

Karan Johar: Well done, Manish!

Sunita Menon: Truly! He told me that I am a beautiful woman. I have good longevity. I need not have to tender apology for the way I went through my life. I should stop hiding behind clothes. The garb does not make me what I am.

> I have been impersonated in *Krishna Cottage, Bhooth, Rakht,* and *Milenge Milenge.*
> *–Sunita Menon*

Karan Johar: Yeah!

Sunita Menon: He told it emphatically. He went ahead through my future.

Karan Johar: We saw a metamorphosed Sunita Menon one fine day.

Sunita Menon: Absolutely! And not one fine day – it happened gradually. It became a big hit with a lot of odd characters wearing white salwars and tousled hair, burning candles. I believe such developments have defied my persona, simultaneously challenging the sacrilege of our rituals. I have explained to them that I will go the other way with a new look. Indeed, that will personify me forever.

Karan Johar: Well, that is wonderful! Congratulations for your accomplishment!

Ekta Kapoor: Thank you!

Karan Johar: Ekta, what do you think of the new look? I think she is looking even better now. I think I have to keep my guys beyond her.

Sunita Menon: She, of course, has many in queue!

EKTA AND HER DESTINY

Karan Johar: Yes. Ekta is very religious-minded with a self-realization interest. She consults you at all levels and even otherwise. Oh! My cynics! What would happen if Ekta did not have any of the above traits? Whether her success would have sustained without having any of the above traits?

Sunita Menon: No. She would have been successful. She would have been rocking. Success will come to those who dare to act.

Karan Johar: OK.

> Success will come to those who dare to act.
> *—Sunita Menon*

Sunita Menon: She has got a very powerful natal chart.

Karan Johar: Do the planets favour her?

Sunita Menon: Absolutely. Completely!

Karan Johar: Would Ekta gyrate even if she does not visit any shrine, or pay obeisance to any preceptor or visit an astrologer?

Sunita Menon: She would still rock.

Karan Johar: Her cynics should rejoice?

Sunita Menon: Very happy!

Karan Johar: Whose believe all this? Do such developments bring happiness?

Ekta Kapoor: What about my happiness?

Karan Johar: Yes, that's what I need to know.

Ekta Kapoor: Success in the tangible world does not bring inner peace. You might concentrate on something insignificant, leaving other important things leading to self-realization. Unless you have a mentor, you cannot have the stable life for your personality development.

Karan Johar: Sure, I completely appreciate the whole mindset.

Ekta Kapoor: Absolutely.

Sunita Menon: Yeah!

Karan Johar: Sometimes, people comment, 'What will happen?' You and I think quite differently.

Ekta Kapoor: Absolutely.

Karan Johar: How often does Ekta visit you?

Ekta Kapoor: Once a month. She calls me up every alternate day.

Sunita Menon: Yeah!

Karan Johar: Hysterically?

Sunita Menon: Yes.

Karan Johar: Does she listen to what you advise?

> Unless you have a mentor, you cannot have a stable life for your personality development.
> *—Ekta Kapoor*

Sunita Menon: No. She ignores the prime facts. She goes on arguing and justifying her stance. She will commence her own track, disbelieving mine. She realizes later about my timely advice.

Karan Johar: Any particular advice which she has disregarded and things came to a pass?

Sunita Menon: I recollect several incidents.

> **Ekta calls me up every alternate day hysterically and then refuses to listen to my advice!**
> –*Sunita Menon*

Karan Johar: Narrate one such incident; I am interested.

Sunita Menon: Many of them were related to her career. I wanted her to start producing films after 31. Whatever she does earlier will end up in flames. She refused and attempted at her 25th birthday, which flopped. She attempted to rein over television but in vain until the planets favoured in their transit. So, things have brightened after her crossing her 31st year. Her obstinacy had led her experiments to sheer waste of money and wrong concepts.

Ekta Kapoor: I have to give some flops, right? It is good.

Karan Johar: This is good for what?

Sunita Menon: Obstinacy?

Ekta Kapoor: You have to balance. A couple of hit serials and couple of flop films.

Karan Johar: I even heard from someone who flew to Delhi to report to the authorities that she made the films to evade tax sleuths.

Ekta Kapoor: Is it? What about the role of me as a prompt payee?

Karan Johar: Yeah! I will justify that none of the film world professionals will promptly pay taxes. They are defaulters forever and the authorities or the public cannot uphold them.

Ekta Kapoor: Absolutely!

> **I have to give flops for balance – a couple of hit serials and a couple of flop films!**
> –*Ekta Kapoor*

Karan Johar: The public memory is not evanescent. '*Kuchh To Hai*' or '*Krishna Cottage*' or similar ones produced or in the pipeline might have been the medium for tax evasion.

Ekta Kapoor: It was nothing like that. Being the daughter of an evergreen hero, I wanted to produce films. She advised me to hold until I crossed my 31st birthday. I attempted to make small duration documentaries. How can I keep quiet and experiment with acquired skills?

Sunita Menon: See how she continues to argue! Do you believe miniature films will work?

> Ekta will continue to err. She continues to play with her slipshod behaviour.
>
> –Sunita Menon

Ekta Kapoor: Ouch!

Karan Johar: Ekta, she is telling you that your films will flop. I am extremely shocked.

Sunita Menon: She will continue to err. She continues to play with her slipshod behaviour.

Karan Johar: Oh God! I think of those poor distributors who evince special interest in your products.

Sunita Menon: I predicted she would rock after her 31st birthday. Have patience and do something else to glorify your talents. Space out the venture of making films!

Ekta Kapoor: Guruji told me so on the sets of 'Kuchh To Hai' for the first time. Tushar shot the scenes with Natasha and Esha Deol on the character roles. They have wondered what Sunita Guruji told us. I often cooled them against her forecast that we would rock, irrespective of the storm we have encountered.

Sunita Menon: And she lied in front of me! The artistes went euphoric. Yeah, we are going to rock! I walked away from the set. I told the kid every effort she made would end in bullshit. Oh God! I will see you later and that has ended the round.

THE EMPATHETIC FORTUNETELLER

Karan Johar: Do you feel you could lose the objectivity of a situation?

Sunita Menon: Yeah! I do.

Karan Johar: Do you, at times, get blinded?

Sunita Menon: No, not at all. I cannot bring myself into the picture to say bad things. I know something bad is inevitable.

Ekta Kapoor: She is too sweet.

Karan Johar: So you sugarcoat with things?

> I cannot say bad things to a person about his/ her future. So, I lie!
>
> –Sunita Menon

Sunita Menon: I have not told you a lot of stuff because I cannot bring in myself to do so.

Karan Johar: Oh, dear!

Sunita Menon: It hurts me. It will be wrong on my part. You have to be very clinical somewhere, like a shrink. I wish that thing to go away from your lives. I do not want to tell her about it.

Karan Johar: Did you lie to us, Sunita?

Sunita Menon: I do. I have lied.

Ekta Kapoor: I know. I know she does.

Karan Johar: Do these focus on personal or professional issues?

Sunita Menon: If I say good things to you, I want it to happen. I believe when I say good things, I mean it – then, somewhere the bad ones will drift apart. I believe there is logic to that.

Ekta Kapoor: When she told me that '*Kuchh To Hai*' would not do well, she told me that I had to work hard and try my level best. I wondered whether it would be a hit? It is a learning process. I am here and have found my friend Karan is doing pretty well. Why cannot I give a hit?

Karan Johar: I would not do so well for the television. We were cut out for different reasons.

Sunita Menon: True, for different things. I am persuading her to understand that.

THE YOUNG AND THE IMPATIENT KAPOOR

Karan Johar: I will never attempt to produce something for the television. I knew that a 29-year-old is sitting on my head. I want to stay away. But Ekta never listens to you. Aren't you over-emphasizing the fact?

Sunita Menon: Yeah! She will come back every time when we discuss these matters. She will justify her stance. I will say, 'OK.' Because she knows that she is my weakness in many ways. I am very soft on her. I have tried to protect her from predicaments. I do not know what I will do for the rest of my life. I have plans, but somewhere she will always remain a little baby for me. The image I have carved out will be whether this kid in her dirty track will emerge successful. She lied about herself to me. She came to meet me and narrated the whole story of how she would be surgically operated. **She met** me to inquire about this medical treatment.

Karan Johar: My God! Is she a liar, a pathological liar?

Ekta Kapoor: Big time!

> **Ekta is a pathological liar – big time.**
> *–Sunita Menon*

Sunita Menon: I was so much concerned and inquired what was she doing?

Ekta Kapoor: She has asserted that I have told her lies and could not get an appointment. So, I had to bullshit my way through. I have a lot of virtues, but patience is not one of them.

Karan Johar: Oh, God! Way to go, darling! That is the way to be. You know, Ekta was this one girl who was very friendly with a lot of heroines and the heroes.

Ekta Kapoor: Yeah! Big time!

Karan Johar: She was known at that point of time, but now of course she is much older. Everyone was told to stay away

> **I have a lot of virtues, but patience is not one of them.**
> *–Ekta Kapoor*

from Ekta because she had been creating confusion.

Sunita Menon: She is a brat!

Ekta Kapoor: She believes I am creating confusion for nearly 90 per cent of the time.

Karan Johar: Were you really meaning to cause all that confusion?

Ekta Kapoor: No. You know what happened. I used to be called a motor mouth. I used to utter whatever came to my mind. I never realized what I had told to someone. Of course, I have got into major trouble.

Karan Johar: So, that's where the plots of TV serials come from? Ekta's past!

> **I used to be called a motor mouth.**
> *–Ekta Kapoor*

Karan Johar: Oh dear! Where do these plots and sub-plots come from? Were they from Ekta's manipulated concepts?

Ekta Kapoor: I have manipulated the concepts partially from Karan's films and partially from myself.

THE SILLY QUESTIONS

Karan Johar: I like that! Does she come to you for stupid little issues? 'Should I take a flight today or tomorrow?'

Sunita Menon: Yeah! I go hysterical sometimes. Mundane issues that are insignificant. I have had bad days. There were some intense and profound things. She fluctuates between profound, intense, wacky, funny, and such sort of things.

Karan Johar: I believe she alone comes to redress the trivial issues. I recollect what you and I had when a lady inquired Sunita whether she would be invited to Tina Ambani's party that night? Sunita, do you have to answer similar questions?

Sunita Menon: I have kept a straight face. What do you say? I replied in the affirmative. She was on that night guest's list. If that is your criteria in life, what makes you happy? Life is a recourse to liberate from social rituals and norms. It does not matter. Every equation changes in life. You will encounter problems if you give serious thought to them. I will reiterate that you have unveiled much more in your life. My humble request to the audience is to cheer Ekta up for her behaviour. There is art, there is painting, there is music, there is writing, there is poetry, there is dancing.... Many faculties she could access.

> **You will encounter problems if you give serious thought to them.**
> *–Sunita Menon*

Karan Johar: And being on the Ambani guest list is not a..

Sunita Menon: No! That is just one of the things in life. It does not make you special at all. Truly! You have to emancipate from the bondage as a human being.

Karan Johar: Tell me another silly question you were asked. Like this one.

Sunita Menon: I recollect one such question – 'When shall I lose weight?' That is perennial.

Karan Johar: You are supposed to predict when someone loses weight?

Sunita Menon: It could be a serious prediction. 'My daughter had to get married. She was 17 kilos overweight. When will she lose weight?' Mothers and daughters or overweight people always inquire when they will lose weight?

> I get many silly questions. 'When shall I lose weight?' is perennial.
>
> *–Sunita Menon*

Karan Johar: My God! That is so ridiculous! Ekta, what is the silliest question you have posed to Sunita?

Ekta Kapoor: When will I lose weight?

Karan Johar: That is fantastic! That truly is! Have I ever asked you that? Once, right?

Sunita Menon: Yes, you did. You said my face is looking puffy.

Karan Johar: OK, Ekta! We will go for a second opinion to the doctors.

Ekta Kapoor: Yeah!

Karan Johar: Do you approach other numerologists, astrologists or tarot readers?

Ekta Kapoor: No tarot readers.

Karan Johar: Just other astrologers?

Ekta Kapoor: I meet Pandit Janardhan. He has been like a family astrologer. Now, I have stopped meeting any of them. Sunita is my main advisor.

Karan Johar: Advisor?

Ekta Kapoor: I shall seek the second opinion from Pandit Janardhan, other than that I never rely on anyone. Their prediction loses sanctity. I have to rely on one person whom I trust. You cannot trust everyone.

Karan Johar: Sunita, at one point in time, does it bother you that she goes to see others?

Ekta Kapoor: She sends me.

Sunita Menon: I have sent her.

Karan Johar: You send her?

Sunita Menon: I believe in one thing. It is like a baggage to carry. I like travelling light. I am very unconventional in that way. I tell her, 'Please go and check out' because sometimes, she may get hysterical – 'I want to make this movie' or the other with some concept. I have told her to meet them and find out whether it is feasible. I have advised her to approach five different professionals and arrive at a decision.

> I have sent Ekta not once but several times to other psychics.
>
> *–Sunita Menon*

Karan Johar: So, actually, you have sent her?

Sunita Menon: I have sent her not once but several times.

The 'K' Factor

Karan Johar: Tell me to assuage my curiosity – what is this 'K' factor all about? The release of *Kuchh Kuchh Hota Hai* made me stick with it. Were you told this right in the beginning? *Hum Paanch, which* was your first successful big show on television, did not begin with the alphabet 'K'. Did you think, Sunita, whether *Kum Panch* would work?

Ekta Kapoor: *Kum Paanch*!

Karan Johar: I know it sounds very suspicious.

Sunita Menon: It sounds very problematic. People would not endorse it.

Karan Johar: No, I do not mean that. It could have been called K. Why? How come that worked?

Sunita Menon: Well, you see, numbers and alphabets that work for you accentuate your good luck. Do you know what I

> If Ekta names something with K and never works hard, it will end up in failure.
>
> – *Sunita Menon*

am mentioning? She names something with K and never works hard will end up in failure. I remember once a director had approached me three days before the release of his film. It was a tacky film. I do not mean it in a bad way.

Karan Johar: Tell me the name. I am only interested in the name.

Sunita Menon: No, I would not. It was a very badly produced debut. It was awesome when I went for the trial. Oh my God! Everything was worked out three days before its release. He asked me about its name. I could not control my emotion and share it with him. I knew I was hurting his sentiments. I told him, 'OK' and asked him to make other films. His film flopped when it was canned two days after release. He called me up after ten days and remarked that I had lied to him by saying that the film would make its mark. I replied that he would make other films as well, but the to-be-released would be OK. I did not want to hurt him. The reality was that the film was technically below par with poor performance of the actors.

Karan Johar: Was the film with the alphabet 'K'?

Ekta Kapoor: No.

Sunita Menon: I am not getting into that factor. Neither will you get the name, but you have believed what it was. How can you be optimistic from a person like me? Would you tell a girl of 23 or 24 years of age your forecast that she would never marry until she was 38 or 40? Or that her marriage would fall apart when somebody died after being bedridden for some time? Whether she would not beget a child or similar such issues before hand? Whether she would never go abroad or never really take into her career? How can you interpret other than showing her hope? When you say good things in some way, I hope it would certainly come true. I abide by such a policy in my life. I do not care if people would call me a fraud or pseudo-professional.

Karan Johar: Because there is something called as free will.

> **Would you tell a 23-year-old girl the forecast that she would never marry until she was 38 or 40?**
>
> *–Sunita Menon*

Sunita Menon: Of course. You have to exercise that with your mind, willpower and visualization. We have come across some talented people who have seldom made their mark. Unfortunately, they do not have the willpower. Those who have will certainly rock the world, for they have the will to accomplish anything by hook or crook.

Karan Johar: So they are out there.

Sunita Menon: Yes, absolutely.

Karan Johar: Ekta, will you ever leave the alphabet 'K' for anything in the world?

Ekta Kapoor: No!

Karan Johar: Never?

Ekta Kapoor: Never.

Karan Johar: Now, it has made an impact on you.

Ekta Kapoor: Yes, it is my firm belief now. It is not my superstition.

Karan Johar: We will run out of 'K' titles between Rakesh Roshan, you and me. Everytime I want to register a 'K' title, I look at the Balaji titles. May be I can borrow one from Ekta.

Ekta Kapoor: They are yours, Karan!

Sunita Menon: So sweet!

EKTA AT WORK

Karan Johar: OK. Thank you, Ekta! I have heard about you as a tyrant at work. Balaji shudders at the mention of your name. Is that true?

Sunita Menon: I have told her she has the loveliest oval face, resembling angels. But she is so deceptive. I have almost shuddered when she has lost her temperament. Something might be wrong in her office. I have thought her to be the same child I have known.

Karan Johar: What gets you so angry? Do you feel that you are overworked and found your staff as an outlet to discharge your pensive mood?

Ekta Kapoor: No, nothing like that. It is basically like 10 people associating to do one thing. It is a teamwork that goes on. You have the conceptualizer, the screenplay writer, the dialogue writer, the director, the actor, the cameraman, the cinematographer and eventually the editor. One person messing up the output of the team is unbelievable. It cannot be a mistake other than casual approach to the problem. One feels bad eventually!

> **One person messing up the output of the team is unbelievable.**
> – Ekta Kapoor

Karan Johar: Yeah!

Ekta Kapoor: I am answerable to the audience if my show goes off the air. It is the breadwinner for my people on the sets. We return home with our earnings. You cannot take work in a lighter vein. I dislike making changes. You can re-shoot or re-edit a film, but not a live show on television. You have to meet the deadline. We call the competent and dependable professionals to support our debut. A mistake is understandable when you really want to present something best. You can ignore that. If somebody errs when they return four hours late after meeting people at the party, then things like that would keeps me agitated.

Karan Johar: You cannot take that?

Ekta Kapoor: I cannot. I am supposed to be my boss. I do not think of it. I think of myself as one of the colleagues. I have to check the creativity of the show. I have a channel with vast audience and over 1,000 investors who have infused funds to keep things on – I am answerable to all of them.

Karan Johar: I completely understand your problem. Apparently, you are answerable to your staff by regulating the fees to be paid for their work.

Ekta Kapoor: In fact, I pay the highest perks in the industry.

Karan Johar: You do, but the perception is completely contradictory to that.

Ekta Kapoor: I am so shocked about that development. What I say is that the workforce of every department should feel euphoric with Balaji Television Company.

Karan Johar: Because you pay them well?

Ekta Kapoor: I pay them well and on time.

Karan Johar: Well, then, I do not know what made them grumble. I think people, who do not have inroads into Balaji probably speak things like that.

Sunita Menon: Lot of things have been spoken about her, which are untrue. I have heard such ridiculous comments.

Karan Johar: Like what?

Sunita Menon: Once, somebody reported that she threw a paperweight at the person. It was rubbish!

> **I pay the highest perks in the industry! And on time!**
> – *Ekta Kapoor*

Karan Johar: My God! Ekta, I am scared! I shall hope I do not pose questions that will make you throw paperweights at me!

Sunita Menon: I told her not to give me this bullshit. That is not Ekta. What about rolling to the temple incident? Yeah! Somebody, I believe a famous designer, called me to take his name.

Karan Johar: Sunita! Are you taking anybody's name on the show?

Sunita Menon: Behave yourself.

Karan Johar: OK.

Sunita Menon: He told often whether we would roll down the Siddhivinayak temple? I replied that we would love to do so, but it would be rather difficult to do at 7 am in the morning. My God! Where would I find a place in Bombay, traffic snarls et al, to roll? We would roll on each other's top, but not in front of the shrine!

Ekta Kapoor: You would be bruised, but I can manage with my car!

Sunita Menon: I mean both of us would not have managed. I told often that such an act would entertain us imagining the sweet image of Lord Ganesh. Thank you for making us laugh. We went to Tirupati! We rolled and come back!

Karan Johar: Oh God! What?

Sunita Menon: Yeah! We were like these little tops rolling all over the place. It is presumed to have some fun, if the two of us go to some pilgrimage, obviously to roll somewhere.

> I quite like the idea of being a muse.
>
> – *Ekta Kapoor*

Karan Johar: That is very hilarious. Incorrect perceptions about Ekta Kapoor have been clarified by Sunita, the psychic and her muse. Sunita Menon with Ekta Kapoor. Alright! I would quite like the sound of that.

Sunita Menon: Sounds quite catchy.

Ekta Kapoor: I quite like the idea of being a muse.

EKTA ON 'REGRESSIVE' SERIALS

Karan Johar: Yes, why not? Let's talk a little sharp again. We have meandered in between and spoken about various interesting things. Ekta, what do you say to the masses, besides those critics on your work and shades of opinions?

Ekta Kapoor: I think anything popular is sure to come down.

Karan Johar: Are you telling something particular?

Ekta Kapoor: I think it is a pure cliché. Watching someone in a sari or a *Mangalsutra* does not qualify her to be regressive. You cannot judge that person by costumes. I have never projected any woman touching the feet of her husband in my show. It will reciprocate the due respect she paid to her husband. We have portrayed the aspect of mutual respect in our shows. It will certainly be the problem for the people who believe such depiction as regressive. The Indian mass has a different perception, especially so with 80 per cent of the populace. We seldom teach what they want to watch, other than the programmes of their choice. We have shown daughter-in-laws getting married again to boys, probably in the same family. Such developments cannot be labeled as regressive.

Karan Johar: Sure!

Ekta Kapoor: We have shown Ba going to Paris and doing a fashion show at 80. No one else

> My shows are not regressive – I have never projected any woman touching the feet of her husband in my show.
>
> –*Ekta Kapoor*

would have demonstrated such performance. That experiment has worked with people. So, the myth of regression haunts everybody. People stop watching the show the moment you show something regressive. They say, 'How can you show such a powerful woman going and doing something so stupid?'

Karan Johar: Do you think this as just media jargon or people with idle minds who want to malign your image because you are successful?

Ekta Kapoor: More than that, I think it is like an urban legend. It grows from year to year, from person to person and will overpower the masses like a semi-truth.

Karan Johar: Well, it is like what happened to me. I have made three films. It was clubbed like 'bubblegum genre' or 'feel good genre' of films. I have gone through that predicament.

Ekta Kapoor: Absolutely! *Kasauti* was a love story. It was not a *Saas Bahu* saga and was without a single scene depicting that. Still, it was called one of the *Saas Bahu* serials. I have accepted it. It is OK, if you want to say that.

> To my cynics and critics, I would say, 'Start watching my soaps! You might just enjoy it!'
> – Ekta Kapoor

Karan Johar: How do you assuage the cynics and critics who were out there?

Ekta Kapoor: Start watching!

Sunita Menon: I love that!

Karan Johar: Get a life!

Sunita Menon: Way to go!

Ekta Kapoor: You might just enjoy it!

RAPID FIRE

Karan Johar: Chill out! We have the *Rapid Fire Round*. I throw a volley of questions. I shall decide the winner who has answered my round better. I will be the judge.

Sunita Menon: OK.

Karan Johar: The winner shall get the *Koffee with Karan koffee hamper*.

Sunita Menon: Let her win that.

Ekta Kapoor: Sunita! You are going to win.

Karan Johar: I will decide the winner. Sunita! Are you ready? Which of these couples will be the first to make it to the cinema altar? – John and Bipasha, Vivek and Aishwarya, Shahid and Kareena or Lara Dutta and Kelly.

Sunita Menon: John and Bipasha.

Karan Johar: Which of these couples will be the first to split, if they have to? John and Bipasha, Vivek and Aishwarya, Shahid and Kareena or Lara and Kelly.

Sunita Menon: I do not want to answer. You are being a bad boy. Not done!

Karan Johar: OK. God bless them. I hope none of them will split.

Sunita Menon: Let them be happy.

Karan Johar: All right! Who will be the next Shahrukh Khan?

Sunita Menon: He had not appeared so far.

> **John and Bipasha will be the first to make it to the cinema altar!**
> – *Sunita Menon*

Karan Johar: Rani, Kareena, Preity, Aishwarya – who will be the reigning diva of Bollywood? I hate that term; I am sorry.

Sunita Menon: Right now, I will look at Rani.

Karan Johar: She has a bright future. Superb! OK. What are the chances that one of these actresses will make a dramatic return? Juhi Chawla, Karishma Kapoor, Madhuri Dixit.

Sunita Menon: None!

Karan Johar: Vivek, Shahid, Zayed, John. Who has a brighter future?

Sunita Menon: I would not like to answer.

Karan Johar: I hope one of them does.

Sunita Menon: All of them will, but I am not going to answer.

Karan Johar: What kind of a girl will Abhishek Bachchan finally marry?

Sunita Menon: Somebody who will completely fit into his family. Else, he will not marry.

Karan Johar: Do you think it will be an arranged alliance?

Sunita Menon: No, he will fall in love with a person, who will be very conventional.

Karan Johar: From India?

> **Abhishek Bachchan will fall in love and marry someone who will be very conventional.**
> –*Sunita Menon*

Sunita Menon: Yeah. She might have studied abroad, but from India.

Karan Johar: When do you think that will happen?

Sunita Menon: Still time.

Karan Johar: No years there?

Sunita Menon: No. I am not sharing with you.

Karan Johar: Do you think Salman Khan will ever get married?

Sunita Menon: Yes. He will make a good husband.

Karan Johar: Oh!! He will?

Sunita Menon: Yup!

Karan Johar: Great! Who is the next star son or daughter that you would put your money on?

Sunita Menon: Right now, I am not looking at anyone.

Karan Johar: Nobody in the near future?

Sunita Menon: Not right now.

Karan Johar: OK. Which thing Ekta should avoid?

Sunita Menon: Never try to lie, because she is so transparent.

Karan Johar: OK. Which thing Karan should avoid?

Sunita Menon: Stick to that genre of work you have adapted. You have attempted to do art-supportive films. You have fooled yourself.

Karan Johar: I want to be critically acclaimed.

Sunita Menon: Few people criticize you. Let me tell you that art filmmakers would love to step in your shoes. They want to usurp you from the position for money and success. You can drift to commercial cinema! Most of them do not give immediate returns. They will lead you to struggle and make your life extremely tense. Don't you feel that you are in an abandoned genre? Stick to what you are doing.

Karan Johar: Thank you. Your prediction of my show?

Sunita Menon: Rocking!

Karan Johar: OK. Let us make it the way to go! Thank you! Fantastic! Thank you, Sunita. You have performed rather well. You have refrained from answering a few questions.

> **Salman Khan will make a good husband.**
> –*Sunita Menon*

Sunita Menon: I believed that you would become wicked.

Karan Johar: I promise to be more wicked with you. Ekta.

Ekta Kapoor: Please! I want to go home.

Karan Johar: **The worst you have heard or read from a critic?**
Ekta Kapoor: **Modern Day Nirupa Roy!**

Karan Johar: Don't you want to win my koffee hamper?

Ekta Kapoor: You know, Karan, at this present moment, no!

Karan Johar: OK! The worst you have heard or read from a critic?

Ekta Kapoor: Modern Day Nirupa Roy!

Karan Johar: Who called you that?

Ekta Kapoor: Should I say it?

Karan Johar: Yeah! Of course!

Ekta Kapoor: No. She was working in a movie.

Karan Johar: What is the weirdest marriage proposal you have ever received?

Ekta Kapoor: Do you remember? You accompanied him while flying.

Sunita Menon: The Sardar!

Karan Johar: Oh, yeah! My God!

Ekta Kapoor: It was the weirdest! You have asked me by calling up.

Karan Johar: Obviously. You have declined.

Sunita Menon: I sure hope so.

Karan Johar: She was not saying it but I wondered suddenly. All right. How do you relate on being the daughter of the would-be mother-in-law?

Ekta Kapoor: I think it will justify her politically.

Sunita Menon: I will send her flowers.

Ekta Kapoor: I will be very nice to her on the face.

Karan Johar: I like that! The finest actor or actress on Indian television today?

Karan Johar: **The finest actor or actress on Indian television today?**
Ekta Kapoor: **Smriti Malhotra.**

Ekta Kapoor: Smriti Malhotra.

Karan Johar: She played Tulsi of *Kyunki Saas Bhi Kabhi Bahu Thi.* Well done! The finest actor in Hindi cinema today is?

Ekta Kapoor: One and only Shahrukh Khan!

Karan Johar: I endorse that! Great! The hottest hunk in India is?

Ekta Kapoor: John Abraham.

Karan Johar: Your personal favourite show on television?

Ekta Kapoor: *Kasauti Zindagi Ki.* My own show and 'Friends'! Karan, I love 'friends'.

Karan Johar: That's the sitcom. A TV show that you wished you had produced?

Ekta Kapoor: *Desh Mein Nikla Hoga Chand.*

Karan Johar: Great! If an actor opined, you would (a) kill the character, (b) kill the actor, (c) ignore it, or (d) reduce remuneration.

Ekta Kapoor: I would opt for (b) but will stick to (a).

Karan Johar: What is Ekta Kapoor's worst nightmare?

Ekta Kapoor: Having to wake up with my family not by my side.

Karan Johar: That would be anyone's worst nightmare. Five years from now, Ekta Kapoor would be?

> **Karan Johar: Your personal favourite show on television?**
> **Ekta Kapoor: Kasauti Zindagi Ki.**

Ekta Kapoor: Hopefully, doing good films too!

Karan Johar: OK, great! Sunita that one is for you.

Sunita Menon: Yes.

Karan Johar: All right. Which film actress would make a perfect *Tulsi?*

Ekta Kapoor: Rani Mukherjee! Any day!

Karan Johar: OK! Great! Wonderful! Very quickly then. *Tulsi* or *Parvati?*

Ekta Kapoor: Oh! No. That is a tricky one.

Karan Johar: OK, one?

Ekta Kapoor: *Parvati!*

Karan Johar: *Parvati.* Love or money?

Ekta Kapoor: Money!

Karan Johar: Way to go, Ekta! *Saas Aur Bahu?*

Ekta Kapoor: Depends who I am.

Karan Johar: Jeetu-ji as a dancer or Tushar as a dancer?

Ekta Kapoor: Tushar as a dancer.

Karan Johar: Way to go! Poor father! What happened to him? Good husband or high TRP's?

Ekta Kapoor: Good husband.

Karan Johar: All right, wonderful! Well, Ekta I am kind of stuck. I do not know who will win the *Rapid Fire Round*.

Karan Johar: Do you think it is Sunita?

Ekta Kapoor: She will be.

Sunita Menon: No, it will be Ekta.

Karan Johar: I think Ekta. You are bonded by karma to win my koffee hamper.

Ekta Kapoor: Thank you so much!

Karan Johar: Congratulations! This is for you. You have to eat that chocolate.

Ekta Kapoor: Sunita and I will share that hamper.

SURPRISE GUEST – MANISH MALHOTRA

Karan Johar: The next segment will be full of fun. We have a surprise guest on our show. Someone who, of course, comes to you for advice.

> **Karan Johar: Love or money?**
> **Ekta Kapoor: Money!**

He is also a friend of yours, Sunita. Ekta, it is someone you are very friendly with. Sunita, I will play that with you.

Sunita Menon: Why does he do this on camera? I want to have a word with you now.

Karan Johar: No. This is not a game.

Sunita Menon: Now, what are you up to?

Karan Johar: I am trying to make you guess, who this special guest is? OK. He is a close friend of yours.

Sunita Menon: I have a lot of them.

Karan Johar: All right, this is a man, who is close friend of yours.

Sunita Menon: I have a lot of male close friends.

Karan Johar: All right, I like that. I wish I had got him earlier.

Sunita Menon: I do not understand.

Karan Johar: He is someone who always sought your advice. You might not be aware of him. He is extremely in vain, personified vanity. Sometimes, he seems to be self-obsessed. Tell me who he might be?

Sunita Menon: I do not know.

Karan Johar: Come on! Introduce him to the show.

Sunita Menon: My favourite man, Manish Malhotra.

Karan Johar: Welcome, Manish Malhotra, to *Koffee with Karan*!

Sunita Menon: You think I am helpless. I am self-obsessed.

Karan Johar: Yes, you are both.

Manish Malhotra: I have no reason to be

Karan Johar: You have every reason to be.

Manish Malhotra: Of course.

Sunita Menon: He knows it.

Karan Johar: God, we always applaud Manish for no rhyme or reason.

Manish Malhotra: You should appreciate me for taking part in the show.

Karan Johar: OK! Well done! Manish, you are the perfect choice to be the special guest. You are so close to Sunita. You adore Ekta. We are attached to one another in the profession. Ekta and I have this big karmic connection. Sunita and you are my advisors. You are Sunita's client or friend?

Manish Malhotra: Friend!

Karan Johar: Yes. We are the awesome and foursome combo!

Sunita Menon: Sunita is here with her clique.

Ekta Kapoor: Absolutely!

Karan Johar: We are like one family. How do you perceive Sunita Menon?

Manish Malhotra: I think Sunita is the coolest person I have ever met. She is just not judgmental. You can talk to her about anything under the sun. She is ready to party, which is very rare. I think she is beautiful. She is very sensuous. I really love her. Will you marry me?

Karan Johar: We will talk about that after the show.

Manish Malhotra: She keeps on rejecting me.

Karan Johar: I am sorry I have to break this mutual admiration society for some time.

Manish Malhotra: We just love each other.

> I think Sunita is the coolest person I have ever met!
> – *Manish Malhotra*

Sunita Menon: That we do!

Karan Johar: OK. I said stop.

Sunita Menon: Sorry.

Karan Johar: OK. I will return to Ekta. How do you perceive the most successful Indian woman?

Manish Malhotra: I have known her since ages. The best thing

Manish Malhotra: We find something about Ekta as superstar!
Sunita Menon: Princess!

about her is that she hasn't changed a bit. She hails from a good family. She had been a star since her birth. We find her as superstar.

Sunita Menon: Princess.

Manish Malhotra: She was and will remain as Ekta Kapoor, before she became so. She is brilliant.

Karan Johar: She complained that she was not well dressed, quoting you.

Sunita Menon: I do not think she needs clothes.

Karan Johar: Is it so?

Sunita Menon: She is such a persona herself in the sense that she does not need to be well dressed.

Karan Johar: Would you like to change something in her?

Manish Malhotra: Lots!

Ekta Kapoor: This is Manish's outfit.

Manish Malhotra: She is well dressed for the show.

Karan Johar: Otherwise, what else you would like to change?

Manish Malhotra: I think she has a stunning face. Her house is full of her photographs.

Karan Johar: So, you are another vain person!

Manish Malhotra: Well, she has reason to be. I do not, but she does.

Ekta Kapoor: Oh really! Now what do you want me to say?

Karan Johar: OK. Now this can get even sicker.

Manish Malhotra: Karan, I think one compliment for each of us would not be bad.

Karan Johar: It is allowed. Sunita, what would you like Manish to change?

Sunita Menon: Sometimes, he is over-emotional about development. I want him to change that for his own good, not for anyone else. It will hurt him more than anyone else. He is loyal, passionate and firm in opinion. He will be a dependable friend for his amazing loyalty. He will get hurt if he fails to get the same from friends. I always remind him that such thing is unavailable in the universe. So he should not get hurt.

Karan Johar: Ekta, anything you perceive different from what Sunita commented upon? You have adjudged him on the social level for years.

> **Manish is over-emotional and that will hurt him more than anything else.**
>
> *–Sunita Menon*

Ekta Kapoor: I dislike him reiterating that he belongs to a middle class family.

Karan Johar: Yes, often his mother complains the same. I just saw him drive his Mitsubishi Lancer with designer glasses.

Manish Malhotra: That is untrue!

Sunita Menon: He still says he belongs to a middle class with designer wear!

Ekta Kapoor: As long as he knows that he is grounded by heart, it does not matter.

Manish Malhotra: But I am!

Ekta Kapoor: The rest does not matter.

> **Manish still says he belongs to the middle class with designer wear!**
>
> *–Sunita Menon*

CONCLUSION

Karan Johar: Thank you, Ekta. Thank you, Sunita. Thank you, Manish. Thank you for being on my show. You will find a koffee mug there. Please sign it.

Manish Malhotra: OK.

Karan Johar: Remember, this personally autographed mug could be yours only if you participate in the *Koffee Quest* contest. Let us go to the koffee wall. It lies there till someone wins it.

•••

Sushmita Sen & Sanjay Dutt
The Diva and The Hunk

She is the ultimate diva. She is a head turner. She has influenced men across the universe. No wonder, she was crowned Miss Universe for the Year 1994. She inherits the crown as a style icon with sex appeal. Yes, I am speaking about Sushmita Sen. She can actually turn you on with just her talk! Welcome the woman, Sushmita Sen.

SUSHMITA SEN

Karan Johar: Wow! Welcome to my show, darling!

Sushmita Sen: It is my pleasure.

Karan Johar: The pleasure is all mine.

Sushmita Sen: I love that black watch you are wearing for the show – Frank Mueller, is it?

Karan Johar: Oh my God! You do know it, don't you?

Sushmita Sen: Yes. I always ask before the show.

Karan Johar: Well done! Let us get into what I said about you during the introduction – I called you the ultimate diva.

Sushmita Sen: The man has got great taste!

Karan Johar: Well, call it a media lingo or just stuck with the whole tag. Do you agree? Do you think yourself to be a diva?

Sushmita Sen: The definition of a diva is unclear to me. I would like to think it for Madonna, the woman that I totally admire and love, who has been glorified to be a diva.

> *Karan Johar:* I called you the ultimate diva.
> *Sushmita Sen:* The man has got great taste!

Karan Johar: Madonna, yes.

Sushmita Sen: Now if you go by that definition, thank you so much. I would like to know whether we have any other hidden agenda. I will let you know on being comfortable with the definition.

MISS UNIVERSE

Karan Johar: You were crowned Miss Universe for the Year 1994. Subsequently, you went on to become a mainstream film actress. Did it bother you or did the title keep you only as pretty face in the mainstream cinema?

Sushmita Sen: No, Karan. The year I won the pretty face competition, I had Aishwarya Rai as Miss India, the most beautiful woman next to me. I had Carolina Gomez at Miss Universe. However, people never really looked at the way I appeared. So, it was never like "Wow! She's so gorgeous." I thought Ash had a lot more problems than me. I had a more person-to-person connection. I wished to enjoy being just a pretty face. It seldom happened to me!

Karan Johar: Oh dear! You do not mind being called just a pretty face?

Sushmita Sen: Oh, absolutely not! I do not mind even the truth!

> I wished to enjoy being just a pretty face. It seldom happened to me!
>
> *—Sushmita Sen*

Karan Johar: All right. You could have answered that question so.

Sushmita Sen: I could have got 10 out of 10! I have decided to remain diplomatic on your show!

Karan Johar: No. I dislike you to fall into your own trap. You spoke about Aishwarya. I will go right there. The year you won Miss India, it was a complete shock to everyone in India.

Sushmita Sen: Including me.

Karan Johar: Yes. Aishwarya was touted to be the winner for the Year 2004. She happened to be crowd-friendly. Everyone foresaw her to be the winner. It was very simple.

Sushmita Sen: Correct.

Karan Johar: That was what I heard in an opinion survey – and that one of the contestants, Sushmita Sen, knew that she would win the competition. I thought you were lying when you revealed of being shocked.

Sushmita Sen: No. I was shocked, Karan. I withdrew from the Miss Universe contest knowing that Ms. Aishwarya Rai had entered the pageant. I believed her to be beautiful and emerge as Miss India. I returned home saying, 'I tried, mamma.' Thank God for my mother. She explained that there is something in life what one calls as an upset.

Karan Johar: Yes.

Sushmita Sen: You will never know that someone will upset you. She told me to return on having lost to the woman I thought to be beautiful. That was fine. I went for the pageant due to my mom. I was shocked when I won. I told her often not to come for the pageant and get us embarrassed. She had missed out a moment, which she did not when she went for Miss Universe. She watched with fascination.

> It was a complete shock to me when I won the Miss India contest and not Aishwarya!
>
> *—Sushmita Sen*

Karan Johar: Well done! Let us revert to the pageant. You might have gauged your performance that night, Miss India particularly. Did you think you deserved to win the pageant?

Sushmita Sen: Oh! Most definitely without a second thought.

Karan Johar: Why do you think that when you compare your on stage performance to Aishwarya that night?

> **I deserved to win the pageant – most definitely without a second thought!**
> *– Sushmita Sen*

Sushmita Sen: I do not compare myself to her performance. She was fabulous on stage. I was my best, which qualified me to the pageant. Everybody thought me to be luckier. My shooting star went right over my head because the dash of luck favoured me to gain the mileage among 20-30 contestants, who had worked very hard to get the glory.

Karan Johar: So luck favoured you that night. Thank God!

Sushmita Sen: Well, that night luck was a gentleman, not a lady!

SANJAY DUTT

Karan Johar: All right. Can we expect a gentleman to join the show?

Sushmita Sen: All right! Well, he knows when to pass on the compliment. Who is this man?

Karan Johar: All right, my next guest would be a head-turner and a bed-turner.

Sushmita Sen: Wow!

Karan Johar: Every woman who wants to mother or brother or do whatever else to him has claimed him to be the original rock star. We too have endorsed him. Let us welcome the very stylish superstar, Sanjay Dutt.

Sushmita Sen: There he is!

Sanjay Dutt: Hi!

Karan Johar: Hello. Welcome to my show!

Sushmita Sen: How are you?

Sanjay Dutt: Good.

Karan Johar: OK. Very true – head-turner, bed-turner – whatever you perceive!

Sanjay Dutt: I think not in bed, just a head-turner.

> **I am a head turner, not a bed turner!**
> *– Sanjay Dutt*

Karan Johar: Do you agree with that?

Sanjay Dutt: Yes. She is more of a head turner than me.

Karan Johar: All right. Welcome to the show!

THE UNENDING BATTLE

Karan Johar: Sanju, it has not been easy for you. You have faced hell from the fraternity. You have faced upswings and downswings on a personal level in your career. I can recall many such incidences. What keeps you going?

Sanjay Dutt: One has to remain a fighter in life – look at the problem; face that instead of running away. I did the running away a bit, resorted to addiction and similar habits, but in vain. Ups and downs happen. You want to climb when you are down.

Karan Johar: It takes a lot of guts to combat a situation. You have emerged successfully. Not many people have the capacity to do that. You have spent much time in jail. You have been the drug addict earlier. How do you recollect the previous developments?

> One has to remain a fighter in life – you want to climb when you are down.
>
> – *Sanjay Dutt*

Sanjay Dutt: I have no regrets, Karan. I have got lessons from life and I have learnt from them – my drug phase followed by my imprisonment. I do not have any ill-will against anybody. I have realized that I would have done the same had I been in their position. It would not be easy to associate with an imprisoned guy. So, I forgave the people responsible for my predicament.

Karan Johar: Do you think the industry was fair to you and loved you?

Sanjay Dutt: Absolutely. They welcomed me with open arms on my return. I can never forget my family and supporters. One was your dad, who was always there. I love him wherever he is.

Karan Johar: Thank you. Do you feel any kind of regrets in that phase? Have you gone through turbulence, when people were harsh to you?

Sanjay Dutt: I recall an incident about how my dad used to frequent the jail. He used to assure that I would be bailed out some day. Six months went like this. I asked him what was he doing? He held me with tears welling from eyes. He replied that he was helpless. The incident shattered my conscience.

Karan Johar: Oh dear!

Sanjay Dutt: I mean he had just showed me his helpless condition. I acknowledged his position and continued to remain imprisoned. I did not know when I would be discharged. However, God is great!

Karan Johar: Well done. You have been a brave man.

CATCH ME, IF YOU CAN

Karan Johar: Let us revert to Sushmita. Are you ready?

Sushmita Sen: Yes.

Karan Johar: How do you find life?

Sushmita Sen: Interesting!

Karan Johar: What happened with so many relationships? Is it commitment phobia or boredom that always seeps in? What is it?

Sushmita Sen: It is not boredom. Sometimes, you will grow with the relationship and people. People outgrow you. It is a very natural process. Some people could hold your attention for a long term. It could be for lifetime. People celebrate 20 years of marriage with the next day for a toss. We do not have any guarantee. I think the relationships are there to grow. Sometimes, they do last, otherwise not. No boredom really.

Karan Johar: Someone holds your attention? You are trying to get away from such relationships?

Sushmita Sen: I like to be brave and clear.

Karan Johar: In a serious relation?

Sushmita Sen: No, I am not.

Karan Johar: Are you missing a serious relation?

Sushmita Sen: No – I will breathe for a while. I definitely think I need to get my space. I also think I am older than I was at 16 when dating was fun. I need a lot more from the man who loves me. It will not be so easy. So, I shall take my time.

Karan Johar: All right. Let us ask the man what he thinks of a relationship. There have been

> **I just love for me being loved!**
> *–Sanjay Dutt*

so many, Sanju! I do not want to get into names. What keeps you going in that respect?

Sanjay Dutt: Karan, I yearn to be loved. I love somebody to hold and cuddle me and treat me like a son! I just love for me being loved!

Karan Johar: Like you being mothered as well?

Sanjay Dutt: Yes, that will keep happening.

Sushmita Sen: OK. That was an honest reply.

Karan Johar: Yes, that was. I am enjoying this!

Sanjay Dutt: But Sush is right. Today, it is different. I am more romantic.

Sushmita Sen: Really! Do you have someone in your life?

Sanjay Dutt: Many of them!

Sushmita Sen: Oh God! I tell you – some people have all the luck! Was that a Miss Universe answer?

Karan Johar: Yes, that was. What about the marriage? There have been two.

Sanjay Dutt: Karan, marriage is a commitment. You have to acknowledge that. The golden days are over. There was Nargis and Sunil Dutt, my mom and dad. Women used to cherish their spouse a lot. Today, I have not seen a happy marriage – I do not know why.

Karan Johar: Do you think the institution of marriage is dead?

Sanjay Dutt: I think it is. I am afraid people have lost confidence to keep the pledge they make.

Sushmita Sen: Objection! I do not think the institution is dead.

Karan Johar: The nice men are.

Sushmita Sen: Well, I do have a very lovely man sitting next to me. I believe the whole concept of marriage has changed. His belief is that a woman leaving her parents to settle down with husband had to cherish

> **Sushmita Sen: Do you have someone in your life?**
> **Sanjay Dutt: Many of them!**

a lot, blah blah; otherwise, not good. Today, the concept of the marriage is more equal. Sweetheart, it is a concept. 'What are you doing this weekend? If you tend to the baby, I shall do this. Otherwise, stay back this Friday – I will go.' It is a concept very hard to look after. So the whole concept of marriage has been misunderstood.

> I think the institution of marriage is dead.
> –Sanjay Dutt

Karan Johar: Well, we speak about mutual adjustment. What I mean is fidelity.

Sushmita Sen: We shall seldom find the concept of adjustment.

Karan Johar: No. Fidelity is the catchword in marriage. Adjustment is an effective word.

Sushmita Sen: Do you mean that the institution is alive?

Karan Johar: What about the fidelity? How can one be faithful to a lover or spouse?

Sanjay Dutt: No. It is the question of adjustment that one finds very difficult.

Sushmita Sen: Karan, I want to interfere – may I?

Karan Johar: Please.

Sushmita Sen: Fidelity is not hard, difficult or impossible. It just depends upon what you mean out of it. Fidelity had been a concept of what people think is the physical aspect of a relationship. I choose to disagree. A man up from the bed with the self-image in the mirror does not lead him anywhere. However, it would certainly reinforce his commitment to her, when he minds about *her* image on the mirror, while he was up from the bed.

Karan Johar: Yes, I understand that.

Sushmita Sen: I believe it is the presence of mind, which conditions fidelity. I cannot live with someone else on his mind.

> I cannot live with someone else on his mind.
> –Sushmita Sen

Karan Johar: OK. Wonderful. The unique relation shall condition other relations!

Sushmita Sen: Karan, please have some koffee!

Karan Johar: Have you found any relation dear?

Sushmita Sen: Yes. I had a Hispanic singer from Puerto Rico. I will not name him. My first relationship came from China. I prefer to remain as more of a South American-Asian or Asian about my nationality.

Karan Johar: Why did you ignore the Hispanic singer?

Sushmita Sen: I did not. It was a beautiful relationship. I

> **Every relationship ends. I have no regrets.**
> –Sushmita Sen

believed to have come closer to finding a companion. He remained indifferent. It was a lovely contradiction. Every relationship ends. I am sure you dare not venture to know about his name. I have no regrets.

Karan Johar: You were tied up at one time, but felt uncomfortable?

Sushmita Sen: Oh! but I love him!

CHIVALROUS SANJAY AND MORBID MEDIA

Karan Johar: The film fraternity is a small world. Sanjay, I recollect an incident where you bashed someone at London show.

Sushmita Sen: Let me tell the story. I was being harrowed by a gentleman photographer in London or somewhere across the UK.

Sanjay Dutt: In Manchester.

Sushmita Sen: He has great memory! The gentleman photographer kept on coming to me. I told him not to pester me. Sanju saw that

> **Sanju pounced on the pesky reporter and seized his camera when he attempted to shoot!**
> –Sushmita Sen

incident and inquired whether I need help. I replied, 'No, I am fine.' Sanju pounced on him and seized his camera when he attempted to shoot. Sanju jostled him physically and kept him off. The incident got reported beyond proportion because the reporter was affiliated to India's mainline print media.

Karan Johar: Was it reported as fair at that point of time?

Sushmita Sen: No.

Karan Johar: Do you believe the incident had any domestic repercussions?

Sanjay Dutt: No.

Sushmita Sen: It seldom has influenced me.

THE 'SANJAY' FACTOR

Karan Johar: There is no affair between Sanjay Dutt and Sushmita Sen. Sanjay seems to be a name associated with Sushmita in the past. Let me ask Sushmita about her fetishes with Sanjay.

Sushmita Sen: Interesting question. I am so glad you have noticed.

Karan Johar: Yes. Well, there is Sanjay Kapoor and Sanjay Narang and alleged names linking you up with Sanjay Dutt.

Sushmita Sen: You have missed quite a few – never mind!

> *Karan Johar:* Sanjay Kapoor, Sanjay Narang and allegedly Sanjay Dutt?
> *Sushmita Sen:* I will move on to another alphabet; S has failed to work!

Karan Johar: A few more Sanjay(s) there? Sushmita! Does that name attract you or the men lobbying for you?

Sushmita Sen: Obviously, the men. I can always change the name, but the man. I do not know about Sanjay (s). None of them seem to work out.

Karan Johar: Do you find the names out of context?

Sushmita Sen: No. I will move on to another alphabet; S has failed to work.

Karan Johar: Is it so?

Sushmita Sen: The Sanjay (s) were different, nice and remain fabulous men. Let us not push it. I always believed before entering the profession to have spoken about Sanjay Dutt, even before I met him. He had been one of the most good-looking, softhearted personas, which any woman seeks for life.

Karan Johar: Do you mean vulnerability was at its peak?

Sushmita Sen: I have committed to the issue of linking with the name, but not him by persona. Things came to a pass when he was not ready to get married. I, too,

> I just have been lucky to have met some incredible men in my life!
> —*Sushmita Sen*

just have been lucky to have met some incredible men in my life, God bless them!

THE SPIRITUAL AND THE RELIGIOUS

Karan Johar: I am going to revert to the spiritual aspect. I have heard about regression into previous life. You have been to *Shivnari*. Share with us about your interesting experience.

Sushmita Sen: I just do not know about that.

Sanjay Dutt: A friend of mine lives in *Gangavati*. He told me about *Shivnari*. It will take two hours to reach from Chennai. Nobody knows him except Rajanikant.

Sushmita Sen: OK.

Sanjay Dutt: It is a small village. If you give your thumb impression......

Karan Johar: They will find you a leaf.

Sanjay Dutt: Yes, they found my leaf and told that my dad's name was Balaraj Dutt. My mother's name was Fatima Hussein. I told my father's name was Sunil Dutt, but I do not know about my mother.

> In Shivnari, they told me that in my past life, I was a king in the Ashoka dynasty!
>
> –Sanjay Dutt

Sushmita Sen: Amazing!

Sanjay Dutt: I tried to say no, but he said it was impossible. I got my leaf and he said that in past my life, I was a king in the Ashoka dynasty.

Sushmita Sen: He told you that?

Karan Johar: My God! You were always a king.

Sanjay Dutt: He continued that my wife had an affair with the minister. She sent me away to the battlefield to get me killed. I was found to have returned vanquishing my enemies. Later, I killed the minister and my wife. I became the devout of Lord Shiva, went into penance in a forest and died of starving.

Karan Johar: My God!

Sanjay Dutt: My belief was justified to have been born in a good family and living my own life without anybody's interference. I have this career and am repenting for the killing *en masse* of my previous life.

Karan Johar: So it was pay-back time in this birth?

Sanjay Dutt: It was great!

Karan Johar: My God! That is an interesting story. I have even heard of some dreams to have transformed me to the occult world.

Sushmita Sen: Yes, I had an accident on *Paisa Vasool* sets and landed in bed with traction. I suffered from dislocation of the lower disk on my back. I woke up with a dream and saw a black stone with white eyes and red forehead. I did know what it was. I saw clearly and asked my sister, mother and everybody about the silhouette. They replied it as Vaishno Devi. Everybody believed that I had been summoned by the goddess. I went to Jammu with a dislocated lower disk. I flew from Katra for my darshan. The chopper could not fly due to inclement weather. I walked and returned after darshan. I returned to Jaslok hospital, when the doctors reported me to have recovered as though I never had my spine injured.

> When I injured my spine, I dreamt about Vaishno Devi. After my darshan, the doctors reported 100% recovery!
> *–Sushmita Sen*

Karan Johar: My God!

Sushmita Sen: Things happen to the people who have faith in certain thing. Your belief in some thing will certainly materialize. It is a fact to be reckoned with.

Karan Johar: OK. I heard that when you were imprisoned for the longest term, you worshipped the deities. What did you do?

Sanjay Dutt: I read Ramayana, Mahabharata, stories related to one's encounter with the hard task master Lord Saturn and redressal by goddess Vaishno Devi. You know, Karan, my bail was being argued in the apex court of law. I wanted to celebrate in jail during Dussehra.

Karan Johar: In jail?

Sanjay Dutt: Yes, they allowed me to conduct puja from two local pundits. They were imprisoned over alleged fraud.

Karan Johar: What did you say to them in the jail?

Sanjay Dutt: I met the pundits who told me to pray until we were bailed out. They initiated me into prayer. They told me to

> When in jail, 2 pundits told me that I would be out of jail before 11 days – I was discharged on the ninth day!
> *–Sanjay Dutt*

bathe by 3 am and pray using that mantra. It would take me two hours and that I would be out of jail before 11 days on austerity measures. I asked why? One of the pundits replied that that was the opportune time when goddess mother bathed on the banks of Ganges and that I should touch her feet for help. She would then find some way out. I went on doing this for the said period. Fortunately, I was discharged on the ninth day.

> **Who could think that you two, the two sex icons, have walked down the spiritual path?**
>
> *–Karan Johar*

Sushmita Sen: Wow! My God!

Sanjay Dutt: The pundits repeated **the proce**dure and were bail**ed the** next day.

Karan Johar: It is almost like they came there for you!

Sanjay Dutt: Exactly.

Karan Johar: Did you ever get in touch with them?

Sanjay Dutt: I never saw them. I do not know where they went.

Sushmita Sen: Incredible!

Karan Johar: Any follow-up to your spiritual side?

Sanjay Dutt: Absolutely! I pray a lot. I believe in goddess Mother a lot. I am a devotee of Lord Shiva.

Karan Johar: OK. You have Shiva-ji's tattoo!

Sushmita Sen: This is stunning!

Karan Johar: Who could think that the two sex icons, Sanjay Dutt and Sushmita Sen, have walked down the spiritual path?

On the Matters of the Heart

Sushmita Sen: Sanju, have you ever regretted being with a woman?

Sanjay Dutt: Never.

Sushmita Sen: For me, every single time, I am a lover. When you are in college, the stuff is different.

Sanjay Dutt: I had my relation when you, Sush, became an adult. I have believed in those memoirs.

Sushmita Sen: If you are in love with every single woman of your choice, whom are you going to marry? How do you know which one to marry?

Karan Johar: Well, he had been married.

Sanjay Dutt: I have a big heart, Sush. I love these heart attacks!

Sushmita Sen: So marriage is a heart attack? I see that the men understood the joke very nicely!

> **I have a big heart. I love these heart attacks!**
> *–Sanjay Dutt*

Karan Johar: 'Marriage is a heart attack' – I like that statement. Sanjay! Did you stop smoking?

Sanjay Dutt: No, I have not.

Rapid Fire

Karan Johar: Let us have the *Rapid Fire Round.* I will throw the questions at you. You have to answer them at a quick pace. The winner will have *Koffee with Karan koffee hamper.*

Sushmita Sen: How exciting!

> *Karan Johar:* Three words to describe you.
> *Sanjay Dutt:* Sexy, a man, and a tiger!

Karan Johar: I am sure you have been yearning to win it. I will decide the winner. I will start with Sanju. Be fast, this is your *Rapid Fire Round.* A person outside your family whom you cash in on for life?

Sanjay Dutt: Uncle Yash!

Karan Johar: Three words to describe you.

Sanjay Dutt: Sexy, a man, and a tiger!

Sushmita Sen: Oh, my God! You are perfectly right!

Karan Johar: All right. Well done, Sanju. Three words to describe Sushmita Sen.

Sanjay Dutt: Lovely, elegant, a tigress!

Karan Johar: The toughest thing about being Sanjay Dutt?

Sanjay Dutt: Being kind.

Karan Johar: The best thing about him?

Sanjay Dutt: Kind again.

Karan Johar: Your kindness is your virtue. That factor which really turns you on in a woman is? Don't say her smile; I have heard that before.

> *Karan Johar:* What really turns you on in a woman?
> *Sanjay Dutt:* Her feet!

Sanjay Dutt: Her feet.

Karan Johar: Her feet? What is this about the feet?

Sanjay Dutt: I do not know.

Karan Johar: So you really look down and work your way up! The sexiest woman alive in India is?

Karan Johar: The art of living, according to you is...
Sanjay Dutt: The art of giving.

Sanjay Dutt: Mallika Sherawat.

Sushmita Sen: Now, he has just lost that hamper! You try to give it. I am not parting with that.

Karan Johar: The last time you cried?

Sanjay Dutt: I cried about five months back. I could not see Yash uncle the way I saw him in hospital. I was born in his lap!

Karan Johar: The art of living, according to you is...

Sanjay Dutt: The art of giving.

Karan Johar: Expand.

Sanjay Dutt: It gives you meditation, it teaches you how to breathe deeply breathing; it really works.

Karan Johar: A strange rumour you have ever heard?

Sanjay Dutt: That I had an affair with a donkey!

Sushmita Sen: Oh God! I have to leave this show now.

Karan Johar: You had an affair with donkey?

Sanjay Dutt: Yes, sometime back *Stardust* reported that – that I had an affair with animals!

Sushmita Sen: Oh God!

Karan Johar: Very quickly then, these are what I call choices. Sunil Dutt as a politician or Sunil Dutt as an actor?

Sanjay Dutt: Actor.

Karan Johar: *Munnabhai* or *Vastav*?

Sanjay Dutt: Munnabhai.

Sushmita Sen: What is that *Magic ki jhappi*?

Karan Johar: The strangest rumour?
Sanjay Dutt: That I had an affair with a donkey!

Sanjay Dutt: *Jadoo ki jhappi.*

Karan Johar: Suneil Shetty or Abhishek Bachchan?

Sanjay Dutt: Karan!

Karan Johar: Sex or romance?

Sanjay Dutt: Romance.

Karan Johar: Sushmita in a sari or Sushmita in a dress?

Sanjay Dutt: In a sari.

Karan Johar: Sushmita or Aishwarya?

Sanjay Dutt: Sush!

Karan Johar: Shahrukh Khan or Salman Khan?

Sanjay Dutt: Difficult. Salman.

Karan Johar: *Rudraksh* or *LOC*?

Sanjay Dutt: None.

Karan Johar: All right Sanju. Well done!

Karan Johar: *Rudraksh* or *LOC*?

Sanjay Dutt: None!

Sushmita Sen: Now comes my *Rapid Fire*. See how much time I will take!

Karan Johar: 'Shahrukh and I have set the screen on fire.' Complete the sentence. 'We share a great chemistry, when I teach...'

Sushmita Sen: '..chemistry; that's what happens!'

Karan Johar: All right. Favourite part of your own body.

Sushmita Sen: My heart, most definitely.

Karan Johar: One thing that makes you feel really sexy?

Sushmita Sen: Looking at the mirror.

Karan Johar: Three things that turn you on in a man?

Sushmita Sen: (a) A sense of humour, (b) His intelligence and, (c) His attitude with children is a big turn on.

Karan Johar: All right. The sexiest thing about Sanjay Dutt is?

Sushmita Sen: The sexiest thing about Sanjay Dutt is that blend of being an old masculine, tattooed guy with a very soft heart within. I find that as the sexiest thing about him. Sorry to disappoint you, Karan! That is the answer.

Karan Johar: One thing that makes you feel really sexy?
Sushmita Sen: Looking at the mirror!

Karan Johar: How do you feel on being naughty with Sanjay?

Sushmita Sen: Well, that is very simple. I do not need to answer.

Karan Johar: All right. If a woman made a pass at you, you would?

Sushmita Sen: Say thank you.

Karan Johar: If an ex-boy friend would like to see you again?

> **My epithet would say, 'She has lived.'**
> –Sushmita Sen.

Sushmita Sen: He is in Miami right now. I would tell him that I would go when he reached there!

Karan Johar: Sushmita Sen's epitaph would say.....

Sushmita Sen: 'She has lived.'

Karan Johar: Miss universe or the National award for performance.

Sushmita Sen: Come on, both!

Karan Johar: Sex or money?

Sushmita Sen: Both.

Karan Johar: Sanjay Dutt or Salman Khan?

Sushmita Sen: That is mean. Salman as friend and Sanju as man.

Karan Johar: OK. Rekha's *Diva*-ness or Sushmita's *Diva*-ness.

> *Karan Johar:* **Amitabh Bachchan or Abhishek Bachchan?**
> *Sushmita Sen:* **Abhishek**

Sushmita Sen: Very smart, Karan! **Definitely Rekha's** *diva*-ness.

Karan Johar: All right. Amitabh Bachchan or Abhishek Bachchan?

Sushmita Sen: Abhishek Bachchan, definitely.

Karan Johar: I am at loss. I do not know whom should I confer this hamper to.

Sushmita Sen: I know. Please give it to him. He deserves it. He had three out of four answers on Sushmita!

Karan Johar: All right. Let us give it to the man. Congratulations on winning, gentleman. It was not me, but Sushmita was the judge. I will add to the result that you have answered spectacularly well, Sanju! Sushmita! You look more spectacular! Do you agree?

Sanjay Dutt: Absolutely!

Yeh Jo Public Hai

Karan Johar: Sanjay Dutt wins the rocking *Rapid Fire round*. We went to a host of men and women to ascertain whether Sushmita and Sanjay (respectively) have sex appeal. Let us see the response.

Sushmita Sen: Let us not delay anymore!

Karan Johar: Always ready for the praise, aren't you? Let us have a look.

Sushmita Sen: The Sush effect!

THE SUSH EFFECT

Vivek Oberoi: Sushmita is attractive.

John Abraham: Gorgeous.

Farhan Akhtar: Sensual.

Uday Chopra: Desirable.

Hritik Roshan: Diva.

Abhishek Bachchan: The ultimate diva.

Farhan Akhthar: I like her smile very much. It lights up her face.

John Abraham: Her persona. Her Attitude.

Dino Morea: Her raw sex appeal. Her eyebrows, her eyes.

Hritik Roshan: The way she basically carries herself.

Uday Chopra: Her hair does really turn me on.

Abhishek Bachchan: It is her countenance.

Sunil Shetty: Sushmita is the universe.

Farhan Akhthar: The way she walks, the way she speaks.

Fardeen Khan: Whole package is sexy.

Zayed: She has overwhelming sex appeal; whether it is 15 or 50, men like her.

Sushmita Sen: Go on, Zayed!

Uday Chopra: She makes a man feel like a man.

John Abraham: Sensuality will be at the brim when she stands in front of you.

Male: She is absolutely warm and lovely.

Manish: She emerges always happy, which proves to be auspicious.

Hritik Roshan: Very sexy with intelligence to match. It turns her very attractive.

Suneil Shetty: She has tremendous confidence and is very intelligent.

Abhishek Bachchan: Sushmita does not give a damn.

Boby Deol: A good actress.

Hritik Roshan: A song she enacted in *Fiza* – 'Mehboob mere' completely blew my mind.

Fardeen Khan: She was the bomb in that song.

Uday Chopra: The song in *Main Hoon Na*, where she had a tanned look was very sexy.

Vivek Oberoi: When you see her draped in suit and cuts that seldom make other women look nice. The style befits her very well.

John Abraham: Sushmita is one of the few people who probably could drape anything and it would make her appear good.

Sunil Shetty: It is about her attitude. The way she dresses, the way she talks, and the way she carries herself. She is extremely lively.

John Abraham: Sush, they have asked me to do a byte on you. You know I would rather bite you!

Fardeen Khan: You are the babe!

Abhishek Bachchan: I think she is one of the most wonderful human beings and a wonderful example for women in our country. I love her for that and do so for just being the person that she is. Keep going and stay gorgeous!

Sushmita Sen: I love you!

Karan Johar: Now, the response about Sanjay Dutt!

SANJAY DUTT

Esha Deol: Oh God!

Shilpa Shetty: Oh my God! Wow! Deadly Dutt!

Mallika Sherawat: Extremely innocent. Rock star!

Sushmita Sen: Mallika Sherawat!

Bipasha Basu: So, charming. Very charismatic.

Lara Dutta: Very intense.

Kareena Kapoor: The ultimate man.

Kajol: Little boy.

Riya Sen: Macho.

Esha Deol: Original stud.

Samita Reddy: His style.

Lara Dutta: It is his body language. His eyes.

Esha Deol: Cool tattoos on his body.

Kareena Kapoor: His hair.

Mahima Chowdhury: His whole physique.

Esha Deol: I wish I had done a scene with him during his youthful days!

Kareena Kapoor: I think he is every woman's ultimate fantasy.

Asita Paul: He has a certain style that nobody else has onscreen.

Amisha Patel: Every woman's fantasy, where you know they want to have that one really bad, really exciting moment in their life – that would definitely be Sanjay Dutt.

Kajol: I think of Sanjay Dutt as more than having a manly appeal. I think he has just got this little boy's cuteness, somewhere around the line that every woman wants.

Bipasha Basu: He is just too laid back – his walking, the way he talks; I think that's where his sex appeal lies.

Malaika Arora: You have just seen those crisp white shirts and blue jeans. He has got that perfect Marlboro man image.

Shilpa Shetty: He is one of those actors who is very nonchalant about his looks, image and the fan following.

Riya Sen: I like his awkward way of dancing; it is rather cute.

Samita Reddy: He has kind of captured the Hollywood look that really most actors aspire to.

Kareena Kapoor: Ever since my childhood, I have yearned to work with Sanjay Dutt. He is the hottest man forever.

Lara Dutta: Sanjay Dutt, indeed, is sexy.

Mahima Chowdhury: He has that distinct walk and distinct style of dancing – lanky looks forever!

Kareena Kapoor: The way he sports his hairstyle, the way he walks – people imitate his walk. They imitate the way he talks, the way he holds his cigarettes and the way he does everything.

Malaika Arora: Every women fantasy and every guy's ideal. They worship him as a hero.

Bipasha Basu: I heard you were a great friend, Sanju. I hope you will be my friend. We have worked quite a lot together. I will catch up with you whenever I am in trouble. Be there for me.

Mahima Chowdhury: Lots of love for Sanju.

Esha Deol: I do not think any clone will really remind me more of Sylvester Stone. I am a big fan of yours and his.

SUSHMITA SEN AND SANJAY DUTT COMBO

Zayed Khan: It is a hell of a combination.

Amisha Patel: A complete sizzler.

Farhan Akhtar: Visually, I think they will be good together.

Malaika Arora: It is a very unusual and very interesting pair.

Hritik Roshan: Perfect! I think that they would be really a match for each other.

Bipasha Basu: A killer combination.

Uday Chopra: She is a diva. He is a rock star. They will look very good together.

CONCLUSION

Sushmita Sen: Oh lovely! Bravo! Karan, you know how to make your guests feel. Thank you so much to every single person on that video. Guys and gals! You really spoke something unbelievable. Thank you so much!

Karan Johar: Do you think, Sushmita, that you deserve all the praise?

Sushmita Sen: Karan these people deserve a lot of praise for what they have done brilliantly.

Karan Johar: All right. And you Sanju, were you happy with what those hot women had to say?

Sushmita Sen: There was Mallika Sherawat, not to miss. He did shift once when she came on the set!

Sanjay Dutt: I just wanted to say thanks. I love you all and God bless!

Sushmita Sen: That's really amazing.

Karan Johar: Yes. Why did Vivek want to bite you?

Sushmita Sen: Very, very interesting. You know what I have thought about the men possessing beauty. They do not get into the nitty-gritty of what people may consider controversial. I think it is interesting to have a man speak about women irrespective of the woman he is with or without.

Karan Johar: All right. It has been wonderful chatting with Sanju and Sushmita. There is a mug right next to you. You should leave that autographed. Remember, this personally autographed mug could be yours only if you participate in the *koffee contest*. Any last thoughts, Sanju? We have tortured and trailed you enough!

Sanjay Dutt: No, Karan, it is great being here. I am so proud of you.

Karan Johar: Thank you!

Sushmita Sen: Thank you for letting me have such a wonderful guest besides me.

Karan Johar: All right. Everybody thought that the duo could make an amazing pair. So you should perform together in a film.

Sushmita Sen: Shake on that.

Sanjay Dutt: Absolutely.

Sushmita Sen: Got it.

Karan Johar: All right. Thank you. Let us walk towards the koffee wall with the koffee mug.

● ● ●

12

Rakhi Sawant
PETA's Brand Ambassador

She's truly a household name today whether she went about it in the wrong way or the right way. Who are we to judge? Because at the end of the day, her popularity is unprecedented. Ridicule her, mock her or love her, whatever you do, you cannot ignore her. Please welcome the girl of the season, Rakhi Sawant.

RAKHI SAWANT

Karan Johar: You are looking lovely today. How does it feel to be on the show.Are you wearing Manish Malhotra's designer saree?

Rakhi Sawant: Yes. I am feeling very good.

Karan Johar: So are you set?

Rakhi Sawant: I believe I look like some top actress, like Rani or Preity or Sushmita.

Karan Johar: Do you watch the show? You have been mentioned on the show for umpteen times.

Rakhi Sawant: Some have been given a good response, others said something else.

Karan Johar: Do you feel bad after hearing bad things about yourself?

Rakhi Sawant: No. This is life. Some people think well and others think badly (about me). It is their wish. They should think before uttering something bad about someone's achievements and hardships. They should see how much I have struggled.

Karan Johar: Right. I would like to render my apologies to you.

Rakhi Sawant: Not at all.

> **My parents don't like me.**
> – *Rakhi Sawant*

Karan Johar: I preferred to laugh on seeing the way you present yourself and your level of confidence. But after watching your reality show I thought that you are a very innocent and vulnerable person, very honest and frank. I have felt that the success you have achieved is the outcome of your hard work though you often tend to go overboard, even with your performance.

Rakhi Sawant: I can justify my behaviour. I have had a difficult childhood. My parents don't like me.

Karan Johar: Why? I have heard for the first time that parents dislike their own child.

Rakhi Sawant: They love me, but dislike my boldness and straightforward behaviour. I am an extrovert. They ask me not to be too bold or else I will not survive. Such things have been ingrained in me since childhood.

Karan Johar: You must have seen the movie.

Rakhi Sawant: My mother must have seen that. They allege that I was too straightforward. They have advised me, 'Be diplomatic.' I have just done my first year in college. I am not very educated. Moreover, the middle-class families have some problems. I have had to face many things in my life.

Karan Johar: Like what?

> **I do not know what the public likes in me.**
> *–Rakhi Sawant*

Rakhi Sawant: I am from a middle-class family.

Karan Johar: But you are no longer middle class today. You are doing quite well for yourself.

Rakhi Sawant: I have come forward due to my own free will. The public likes me a lot. I do not know what they like in me.

Karan Johar: I am still curious about the relations between you and your family. You have replied in an interview that you want to live alone. Why don't you live with the family?

Rakhi Sawant: I want my peace of mind when I return from shooting.

Karan Johar: So, does your mother cry a lot when controversies or issues happen?

Rakhi Sawant: I never created these controversies. Accidents happen with me. I never do it intentionally. My mother screams a lot. My father joins her. I have decided to stay apart and spend my life. I would not like to even get married.

Karan Johar: Why? Every girl wants love. You have become too emotional.

Rakhi Sawant: I cry sometimes. I get very emotional about my family and house. The manner in which I have lived my life, no girl should lead such a life. I have struggled a lot in the industry.

> **My mother screams a lot. My father joins her.**
> *–Rakhi Sawant*

Karan Johar: Has it been very difficult for you?

Rakhi Sawant: Yes. When I was 10 years old, my father left us.

Karan Johar: He left you all?

Rakhi Sawant: Yes. That led us to live our own lives. The responsibility came on me. I could not even study much and was forced to take care of my brother and sisters.

Karan Johar: Did you look after them?

Rakhi Sawant: I forgot my life. I could have become a lead actress. But I cannot even speak English properly.

Karan Johar: Is it not necessary for an actress in the industry to speak good English?

Rakhi Sawant: No. This is Hindi cinema. It is important to enact, dance and emote well.

Karan Johar: You will not become a star overnight by speaking good English.

> **When I was 10 years old, my father left us.**
>
> –*Rakhi Sawant*

Rakhi Sawant: But because of all these problems, I was left behind.

Karan Johar: How do your male relatives react to your skin-show?

Rakhi Sawant: They do not even talk to me. Nobody in my family is on good terms with me.

Karan Johar: Because of you?

Rakhi Sawant: Yes.

Karan Johar: Do you think there are double standards?

Rakhi Sawant: Yes. I cannot meet any of my cousins. Because I have entered the film industry which is not considered a nice place.

Karan Johar: You wear short clothes. And your name is embroiled in many controversies.

Rakhi Sawant: I have replied that I want to live my life. Keep good relations with me, if you want to proceed or forget me. Be happy; I am happy in my house. Today, the same people call Rakhi Sawant when their kids go to school. They boast about me being their sister or daughter, but in vain.

Karan Johar: But you don't care about them?

Rakhi Sawant: No, they were not there with me during difficult times, yet, I do not say anything to anyone and I respect them even today. I welcome and summon them

> **This is Hindi cinema. It is not necessary for an actress to speak good English.**
>
> –*Rakhi Sawant*

to my house. We sit across and talk, because life is short.

Karan Johar: Did you think of exposure at a young age? You expected that you would participate in dance shows and project a sexy image?

Rakhi Sawant: No.

Karan Johar: But it did happen, did it not?

Rakhi Sawant: No. I was a very simple girl. My hair used to be tied in two braids. I wore Indian dresses. My face was not so good. My body was not so good.

> I was a very simple girl. My hair used to be tied in two braids.
>
> –*Rakhi Sawant*

Karan Johar: So, you have worked on your body?

Rakhi Sawant: I worked hard on my face and body.

Karan Johar: Did you resort to the plastic surgery?

Rakhi Sawant: My lips were very thin. My doctor Rashmi Shetty enhanced my lips with silicon treatment.

Karan Johar: Did you switch the treatment elsewhere as well? What do you want to say?

Rakhi Sawant: It is believed that doctors will give you what God did not. Heroines and models resort to the treatment. Why not Rakhi Sawant?

Karan Johar: This is it, Rakhi! Rakhi chooses to speak the truth!

Rakhi Sawant: Absolutely.

Karan Johar: You don't like it?

Rakhi Sawant: Yes, I do.

Karan Johar: You have a boyfriend?

Rakhi Sawant: Yes. His name is Abhishek.

> I believe that doctors will give you what God did not!
>
> –*Rakhi Sawant*

Karan Johar: Are you still with him?

Rakhi Sawant: Yes. We are good friends. We are just friends. I am not going to marry him.

Karan Johar: Why?

Rakhi Sawant: I have decided that I will not get married or beget kids.

Karan Johar: Why?

Rakhi Sawant: I have made up my mind. I have witnessed how my parents get separated.

Karan Johar: Since childhood... Are you scared?

Rakhi Sawant: I am scared. Nowadays, you see divorces follow soon after marriage. I believe more in a live-in relation.

Karan Johar: But your mother does not have any problems? She does not like your boyfriend?

Rakhi Sawant: She has her own problems. She does not see the need for such a relationship and feels that it will affect my career. She says, 'I have to go ahead.'

Rakhi Sawant: Lots of work should be compensated with little love.

> **I have decided that I will not get married or beget kids.**
> –*Rakhi Sawant*

Karan Johar: What is the status of the episode with Mika? Mika made a video on your name. What do you say? Do you want to bring the curtains down?

Rakhi Sawant: I have ended it, but he is stretching it further. Sometimes, he comments that I was a boy earlier. Some 50 surgeries cannot happen in one body.

Karan Johar: How can that happen?

But even I heard a rumour that you were Rakesh Sawant

Rakhi Sawant: But that is my brother!

Karan Johar: Is it? So why did he spread that? Did you see the video he made?

Rakhi Sawant: He thought the kissing publicity had lessened, so he had to try something new.

Karan Johar: Why did he kiss you?

Rakhi Sawant: He should have kissed a garbage woman. I do not know why he did, but I never troubled him.

Karan Johar: Did you know him?

Rakhi Sawant: Yes. I had compered a show with him. He invited me on his birthday and abused me. He exploited me a lot by creating controversies using my name.

> **Mika commented that I was a boy earlier and my name was Rakesh Sawant!**
> –*Rakhi Sawant*

Karan Johar: Perhaps, he did get a lot of publicity.

Rakhi Sawant: He got many shows. He mobilizes money from the incident. He should not do such a thing.

He is a good singer, renders good music. He does not have any other work. He should not have done such things.

Rakhi Sawant: I would have never taken his name if you had not mentioned him. I have much work to do in my life.

Karan Johar: You have commenced singing. What was that song?

Rakhi Sawant: I have sung the number for the first time. Why can't I sing when Amitabh Bachchan, Sanjay Dutt, Shahrukh and Aamir could? You should sing here.

Karan Johar: Yes.

Rakhi Sawant: You will get trapped.

Karan Johar: Has this song become popular?

> **Mika mobilizes money from the (kissing) incident. He has no other work.**
>
> *–Rakhi Sawant*

Rakhi Sawant: Very popular. People like a lot.

Karan Johar: I am not a singer. Neither can I sing in the bathroom. I cannot sing here. Where were you trained?

Rakhi Sawant: DJ Shezwood made me sing.

Karan Johar: Who is he?

Rakhi Sawant: He gave the music and encouraged me.

Karan Johar: People tolerate you through that number?

Rakhi Sawant: DJ told me that whatever I do, they will will tolerate it. I am talented and speak upright.

Karan Johar: People fear a girl, who speaks fearlessly the truth?

Rakhi Sawant: I do not fear anyone except Jesus. I am very straight forward.

Karan Johar: You believe in Jesus?

Rakhi Sawant: I do.

Karan Johar: I saw an image of you becoming a lioness.

Rakhi Sawant: I am a brand ambassador for PETA.

Karan Johar: Are you a vegetarian?

> **Why cannot I sing when Amitabh Bachchan, Sanjay Dutt, Shahrukh and Aamir could?**
>
> *–Rakhi Sawant*

Rakhi Sawant: I refrain from commenting. I want to explain: *'There was a cage there. I was kept inside for an hour. I moved around with difficulty. I had been filled with colour – a lion's costume for five hours. Yes. My hair got spoilt with the crimping.'*

Karan Johar: Were you growling inside?

Rakhi Sawant: Yes. I have felt that humans do not spare other beings.

Karan Johar: Why will they spare animals then?

Rakhi Sawant: I just wanted to say – do not do this to animals.

Karan Johar: I have heard you were trapped in another cage for 90 days?

Rakhi Sawant: That experience had been very torturous. I shudder when I recollect.

> **Whatever I do, people will tolerate it.**
> *–Rakhi Sawant*

Karan Johar: Everybody witnessed your innocence and vulnerability. How do you feel about those days?

Rakhi Sawant: I cannot forget that show in my life. It gave me a new life. It gave me love and respect because of which I am actually on this show today. However much I praise it, it is not enough. People did not know me; they defamed me by calling me 'An Item Girl.'

Karan Johar: You feel you had a cheap image earlier?

> **I feel that humans do not spare other beings.**
> *–Rakhi Sawant*

Rakhi Sawant: I was made cheap.

Karan Johar: Now you feel you have got class?

Rakhi Sawant: Yes. This is such a big show – only celebrities come here. Big stars come here. My fate is good. Thanks for respecting me. I am grateful from the bottom of my heart. You have my blessings. May your show go on for years. I am very happy to come on to this show. I would not have been so happy even after sitting in the parliament house. My reality show was very good. It gave me a new life. I am regaining this life; people love me. Parents get their kids to meet me wherever I move. Every child wants to be Rakhi Sawant. They love me, take my autograph. I like it a lot.

Karan Johar: You have become emotional again.

Rakhi Sawant: Yes. The press had defamed me much. My daddy told me that I was no more his daughter. Mummy left me and inquired what was this all about. You can understand what a girl goes through. I just took the name of the Lord and said that it was all right if no one was with me. It is enough that the Lord is there. I got the reality show. People saw me. I did not know

> **'Big Boss' gave me a new life.**
> *–Rakhi Sawant*

what would be shown. I wore a short costume and danced. I reached inside and didn't know what would happen. I did not presume my image could have been reduced to that of a maid – that I would have to wash everyone's underwear!

Karan Johar: Did you wash underwear?

Rakhi Sawant: Yes. I washed everyone's clothes. Everyone started calling me 'Sawant Laundry.' I thought I would get the royal treatment. I did not know how to work. Sweep, clean... I did not know anything. I was not told anything; that we would have to cook and eat ourselves. The contestants would have to cook.

Karan Johar: But you did well and everyone loved you on that show.

Rakhi Sawant: Thanks. I want to say something.

Karan Johar: Please say.

Rakhi Sawant: Everyone has changed his/her attitude on hearing that I would be on your show.

Karan Johar: Is that so?

Rakhi Sawant: Those who used to ignore me have greeted me. They have looked at me with respect. I am surprised at the way people behave. I will never change. I am thankful to you for summoning me.

Karan Johar: We have done something special for you. We have a *Rapid Fire Round.*

Rakhi Sawant: I will surely participate.

Karan Johar: You will win the hamper. Some people have asked you *Rapid Fire* type questions. But first let us see what they think about you.

PEOPLES COMMENTS

'I find her very hot. There is a spark in her dance. She dances very well. She exposes a lot, but OK.' 'She is very gutsy, hat's off to her.' 'She exposes a bit too much, but that's okay' 'She is very frank but should learn to be a little diplomatic.'

People's Rapid Fire

Q: If you were on a deserted island, which three men would you take with you?

Rakhi Sawant: Amitabh Bacchan, Shahrukh Khan and John Abraham

Q: What would you do with them on the deserted island?

Rakhi Sawant: What would I do? Is there any need to reply?

Q: What do you think of the video Mika made about you?

Rakhi Sawant: (Does a boxing gesture)

Karan Johar: Is this your reaction?

Rakhi Sawant: Yes.

Karan Johar: Very good.

Q: If you had to choose a director from Bollywood to work with you would you choose?

Rakhi Sawant: (runs towards Karan), Sirrrrr! Please give me a break! I will reiterate that you are a very good director. I also like Sanjay Leela Bansali a lot.

Karan Johar: I am the second choice?

Rakhi Sawant: No. You will be my favourite. Mr. Sanjay called me on the set while he was shooting for the film, *'Sawariya'* as I was coming out of 'Big Boss.'

Karan Johar: I know.

Rakhi Sawant: I went there and he stopped the shoot and told me, 'I am a big fan of yours.' Rani, who was there, screamed aloud. I felt very good. Such big stars!

> **Sanjay Leela Bhansali told me, 'I am a big fan of yours.'**
> *–Rakhi Sawant*

Q: What do you think of the casting couch? Has it happened to you?

Rakhi Sawant: Yes, it does exist and I have faced it.

Q: Rakhi, how do you maintain your sexy, voluptuous body?

Rakhi Sawant: I avoid oily foods. If you want a body like mine, then you should visit doctors, take botox and then you shall get a glamorous body. You understand? I am just kidding! No. It is just dieting and lot of work in the gym.

Q: Who is sexier than you?

Rakhi Sawant: Mallika Sherawat

Q: Who inspired you to come in the movies?

Rakhi Sawant: (Mimics a running movement)

Karan Johar: What are you doing?

Rakhi Sawant: Sir, you understand? Angry young man! Everyone likes him.

Karan Johar: Now my questions.

Rakhi Sawant: I want to say something before this.

I am not speaking in English. I can understand it. But if I speak English neither the public nor you will understand it. So, I thought I would speak in Hindi. Please forgive me.

Karan Johar: Why not? It is our lingua franca.

KARAN'S RAPID FIRE

Karan Johar: In one word, your response to men who find you sexy?

Rakhi Sawant: Right. They think right!

Karan Johar: What would you do, if you became Ravi Kissen?

Rakhi Sawant: 'Life will end, but still we have so much ego.' (says it is Bhojpuri) Yes, being Ravi Kissen will be very nice.

Karan Johar: On a scale of 1 to 10 how would you rate these heroes on their sex appeal? Salman

Rakhi Sawant: 9

Karan Johar: Shah Rukh Khan?

Rakhi Sawant: 5

Karan Johar: How many marks will you give him? Why, are you angry with him?

Rakhi Sawant: No. He doesn't reveal much. Only his shirt buttons are open. He just emotes on his face, but I like him a lot.

Karan Johar: Aamir Khan?

Rakhi Sawant: 5

Karan Johar: Saif Ali Khan?

Rakhi Sawant: 8

Karan Johar: Hrithik

Rakhi Sawant: 10, I like him!

Karan Johar: John Abraham?

Rakhi Sawant: 10

Karan Johar: He's sexy? He exposes a lot?

Rakhi Sawant: Yes. Sorry, Bipasha, but I like him a lot!

Karan Johar: Which Bollywood hero would you want for a romantic date?

Rakhi Sawant: John

Karan Johar: Which hero as a bodyguard?

Rakhi Sawant: Salman

Karan Johar: Which hero would you want to entertain you, if you were depressed?

Rakhi Sawant: Amitji

Karan Johar: Which hero for a kiss?

Rakhi Sawant: Nobody. I don't like to kiss or like anyone to do so or touch me.

> **Cricketers' wives should be allowed to accompany them during the matches. Then, we could win the world cup.**
> *–Rakhi Sawant*

Karan Johar: So do you never kiss?

Rakhi Sawant: Who said that?

Karan Johar: You just said you don't like to kiss.

RS: Everyone is booked. Some are getting married, while others have girlfriends.

Rakhi Sawant: So what can I say?

Karan Johar: OK. What would you do if you were in charge of the cricket team?

Rakhi Sawant: I would be very strict. I will not let them go to discos and flirt with anyone. I would ask the guys to sit and practice in front of me.

Karan Johar: Do they practice correctly?

Rakhi Sawant: Their wives should be allowed to accompany them during the World Cup and similar matches. Then, they would not make mischief or take booze or anything. They would reach the cricket grounds and sleep on time at the night. We could win the World Cup.

Karan Johar: Normally, they do not allow their wives, but your take is completely different! But I agree with you.

Rakhi Sawant: Yes, they should allow their wives.

Karan Johar: Sorry to interrupt. They think that they will become weak.

Rakhi Sawant: You understand in what way will they become weak and play poorly. They will say they are tired, but it will be the same – whether they take their wives or other's wives.

Karan Johar:. What would you like to change about your body?

Rakhi Sawant: Nothing, because I have changed. I am fine as I am.

Karan Johar: The sexiest actress among Aishwarya, Kareena, Priyanka?

Rakhi Sawant: Aishwarya.

Karan Johar: The best male body among Hrithik, Salman, John.

Rakhi Sawant: John

Karan Johar: You did well, you deserve the Koffee with Karan hamper

Rakhi Sawant: Thanks I have been wondering whether I would win, whether I would be able to even say something. It's unbelievable!

Karan Johar: You got it. You have pinched yourself. Are you happy?

Rakhi Sawant: Yes

> **The people in 'Big Boss' had never thought there could be such a personality as mine.**
>
> *–Rakhi Sawant*

Karan Johar: Back to the reality show, do you keep in touch with others?

Rakhi Sawant: Yes, after the reality show, when everyone went home, sometimes I spoke to Rahul Roy. Carol also calls, but did not understand me in the house. She understands me now and Ravi Kissen, too, who responds on time.

Karan Johar: So, Carol had not understood you?

Rakhi Sawant: Not in the beginning.

Karan Johar: You are a different personality type.

Rakhi Sawant: She had not seen a personality like me. I speak directly – in your face. They had never thought there could be such a person.

Karan Johar: She is here with us now...Let's welcome the very gracious, Carol Gracias.

Rakhi Sawant: Yes.

Karan Johar: Are you shocked and frozen? Okay, Carol how does it feel to be on the show?

CG: Very exciting! Very excited to see you

Rakhi Sawant: And not excited to see me?

CG: But I did speak to you on the phone. But it is nice to see Rakhi, she is so funny!

Karan Johar: But she was just saying right now that you were not very close during your time together in the house....

CG: It's true sicne we were from different backgrounds. My knowledge of Hindi is poor. Also the things Rakhi said or did were misunderstood at times...

Rakhi Sawant: But I like her a lot. She would make omelettes for everyone.

Karan Johar: But you had commented that no one knows Carol while everybody knows you.

Rakhi Sawant: That was in the beginning. We did not become friends until I returned back to the house.

CG: But what she said is true. Even I knew who was Rakhi Sawant. I am not as famous as her!

Karan Johar: So you felt bad about saying that?

Rakhi Sawant: I realised that I liked her a lot.

CG: We had a couple of chats. She's lovely, she's funny and honest. She is proud of where she comes from.

Karan Johar: That's the way she is.

CG: I call her once in a while to see that she is not in trouble.

Karan Johar: She landed herself in front of the jail, didn't she?

CG: Yes, but again her intentions were good.

Karan Johar: Did you not think to take permission?

Rakhi Sawant: We had permission. The jailer had given us the requirements like computers, blankets, blood sugar testing machines, etc. I was not mad to stand with all that equipment over there. I got delayed due to the ocean of traffic and I was not allowed to proceed. We had been given the date of 28th. I had spent so much money, say some Rs. 7-8 lakhs.

Karan Johar: Okay, did you know about her new song Carol?

Rakhi Sawant: I had invited Carol, but she seldom came. I was very upset. I had invited everyone but...

CG: I am not that kind of person! It's not my scene.

Rakhi Sawant: I know but I love you still! You still don't understand me Carol!

Karan Johar: Did no one come?

Rakhi Sawant: No. Ravi was away from Mumbai. I cannot understand that – even after coming out. They go to parties, but they did not come to mine. I was not doing anything, just flying like Super Girl. I had invited you to lunch.

Karan Johar: So do you feel that everything changes after a reality show?

Rakhi Sawant: Not for me. For me, everything has changed. My life has turned from negative to positive. I have become a heroine from an item girl.

> **I have become a heroine from an item girl.**
> *–Rakhi Sawant*

Karan Johar: Do you think you cannot assume mainstream roles? Main heroine roles, which do not meet your image?

Rakhi Sawant: I am doing it, boss. I am doing mainstream films with good roles.

Karan Johar: You are?

Rakhi Sawant: Earlier, everyone called me for item numbers. I was called for revealing scenes. Now, life has changed.

Karan Johar: You told us earlier what is seen would certainly sell?

Rakhi Sawant: I still do. People tolerate and understand that I am like this across the country. They say, 'She is one of a kind, she is unique.' I enjoy that a lot. I have become a heroine, so tolerate me now.

Karan Johar: Okay, now my next guest is the 'Ashiqui' boy, who won the reality show. Please welcome the 'Baba'- Rahul Roy. Is he a sage?

Rakhi Sawant: Sage?

Rahul Roy: I think everyone saw the spiritual side I was trying to follow.

Karan Johar: Rakhi, even you had no effect on Rahul!

Rakhi Sawant: He used to chant in a corner. I wondered what he did, but did not know that he was chanting for victory.

> **During 'Big Boss,' Rahul Roy used to chant for victory in a corner**
> *–Rakhi Sawant*

Karan Johar: What would you like to say to Rahul?

Rakhi Sawant: About what?

Karan Johar: Anything.

Rakhi Sawant: You seldom do good by winning the money. You should have shared the prize money. We have tolerated you as much as you tolerated us.

CG: But I want the share of money that Rakhi took for coming back to the show

RS: But I spent it all on the computers!

Rakhi Sawant: He did not even throw a party. What a miser is he!

RR: For Rakhi, I would like to say that she was amazing. It was difficult to understand each other. I had some maturity to survive. I thought Rakhi was trying to demand attention. But then I realized there was no pretense. That is the way she is! For Rakhi Sawant as long as there is dance and music, her life is set. She is also a very good cook.

> **Rahul is a big miser!**
> –*Rakhi Sawant*

Karan Johar: What would you like to say to Carol?

Rakhi Sawant: She is a very good girl. I love her a lot. I like Carol a lot; she is very honest. I love her from my heart. I do not love anyone else. Don't misunderstand me since we are girls!

RR: I would like to defend Rakhi as she has always maintained that she like Carol as a human being.

Karan Johar: Do you think you like Carol because she see her as an aspiration figure?

Rakhi Sawant: No. I am proud that I speak in Hindi. The best part about Carol is that anyone who asked for anything, any help, was given that. She would not think of hesitating. I liked that trait about her. What was the need for her to massage if anyone had body pain? She did it for me and even I reciprocated. Our equation has been very good.

Karan Johar: You won't get a masseur.

> **I like Carol a lot; she is very honest.**
> –*Rakhi Sawant*

Rakhi Sawant: I like Carol a lot. I cannot forget her massages, you understand? Just kidding!

Karan Johar: Give a parting shot to the camera.

Rakhi Sawant: I would say that I am very happy to be on your show. I shall sip coffee and give up tea from today!

Karan Johar: Sign on the mug in front of you.

● ● ●

13

Sunny & Bobby Deol
The Deol Duo

He is a superstar; extremely media-shy, introverted and likes to keep a low profile. Many women say that in an industry full of boys, probably he is the only man. My first guest is Sunny Deol. I was surfing the net the other day and read about an interesting anecdote – that the northern part of the peninsula could not proceed without *Dhols* and *Deols*. Let us discover the inner world of Sunny Deol.

SUNNY DEOL

Karan Johar: Welcome to *Koffee with Karan*! One does not see you very often on television. I have introduced you as extremely media-shy. Is that true?

Sunny Deol: Indeed, that is true.

Karan Johar: Were you anxious about this interview?

Sunny Deol: I did get nervous for just a few seconds, although I know what to do!

Karan Johar: I am nervous too because we have seldom interacted before. I have done a lot of research over a period of time. I have found out that you were extremely uncouth during your teens. You packed off with many women, often to London. Is that true?

> **You do a lot of stupid things during teens!**
> *–Sunny Deol*

Sunny Deol: No. You do a lot of stupid things during teens. I wonder what the hell I did when I recollect those dark days. But one does miss the amount of fun one has during those days! I would like to iterate that I am quite shy like other men, but I wanted to join films. Being my dad's son, it was very difficult at home to be treated normally. I was treated either nicely or over nicely by the family and friends. I just wanted to move to such a place where nobody knew me and I could break my shyness before joining the film career.

Karan Johar: I believe that you went to London, but did not pack off in haste. Did you pursue a course in acting there?

Sunny Deol: Yes. I was in Birmingham (UK). I was in *The Old Rep Theatre* to do my rehearsals. I was there for a year-and-a-half.

Karan Johar: Oh, really! Do you think that helped when you returned home to face the camera?

Sunny Deol: Definitely because I had never been to a studio or for an outdoor shoot, except accompanying Dad once or twice for outdoor locations. I had been running away from crowds.

Karan Johar: So you ran to London?

Sunny Deol: I was much at ease when I had practiced on the stage with fellow artistes – I shed off my shyness. I was extremely confident

> **I am quite shy like other men !**
> *–Sunny Deol*

about the metamorphosis in me. I could not believe how my personality had developed when I worked professionally while studying! It was just a support to compensate my emotional upheaval. It made me confident, 'Yes, I am ready.'

Karan Johar: Of course, learning never ends.

Karan Johar: Your wife, interestingly, taught you about the Shakespearean dramas! One cannot imagine Sunny Deol the action hero and his wife have studied Shakespearean lessons in drama together. Is that true?

> **I met my wife in London; she used to help me on Shakespearean lessons!**
> *–Sunny Deol*

Sunny Deol: Yes. She used to help me on Shakespeare. I was extremely unaware about his works. Moreover, the language, the usage of medieval English was perplexing. I was not confident how to spell it out. So, her company saved me from the hardships in mastering Shakespearean dramas.

Karan Johar: OK. Do you still remember any of the lines you studied? Do you want to share those lines while you were on 'love tuition' on the playwright?

Sunny Deol: I think I was doing Othello at that time, but I do not remember anything!

Karan Johar: Do you think your spouse bailed you out as an actor during vocation?

Sunny Deol: Yes, she did. She was of great help when I had my apprenticeship.

ON BROTHER BOBBY

Karan Johar: You have an extremely close equation with your brother, Bobby. You are almost like friends. Yet, of course, there is that line of respect. Tell us how you have tallied Bobby.

Sunny Deol: We are so close to each other! He is like my son. The bond we have in our family – there is so much love! My presence on the show might have kept him nervous. I may become pensive and brooding when he walks in.

Karan Johar: Wonderful. He is the only one who could wear your clothes – and you are so possessive about your clothes. Apparently, he is the only one you lend your clothes to.

I used to find my wardrobe used when I was not around at home!

—Sunny Deol

Sunny Deol: Yes, initially it was difficult, but slowly I got over it. I used to find my wardrobe used when I was not around at home. Initially, I used to admonish him.

Karan Johar: And then you relented, because it was Bobby.

Sunny Deol: Yes.

BOBBY DEOL

Karan Johar: We have Bobby Deol as our next guest. He is cool, sophisticated. He is the hip factor of the Deol family. He can dance non-stop, making his Dad and brother move to his tunes. Let us call Bobby Deol. Welcome, Bobby, to the *Koffee with Karan* show. Do you make your brother and father dance to your tunes?

Bobby Deol: I did earlier on! Now, I have become a father – I know how it feels!

THE YOUNG BRAT

Karan Johar: We just discussed your equation with your elder brother. We know how you are close and have been together through the entire journey. You were getting slapped at the tender age of 11 – you did such intolerable mischievous acts! What do you say?

Bobby Deol: He was right when he did that. That was the only time he did that.

Karan Johar: Why did that happen?

Bobby Deol: I was poor at studies. I was not doing my homework.

Karan Johar: So you got a slap from Sunny Deol! It was unforgettable, was it not?

Bobby Deol: I remember he slapped me and I hit the cupboard behind me.

Karan Johar: Oh! God! I discussed with him that you were the only man to have shared his clothes because Sunny was so possessive about his wardrobe.

Bobby Deol: I used to wear his clothes when I was in the tenth standard. I remember one time when I sneaked into his cupboard

I was poor at studies. I was not doing my homework. Sunny slapped me!

—Bobby Deol

during the farewell party at my school. There were faded jeans, besides green jeans, green shirt with leather tie. I used to pick up his jeans, which he never knew he had bought because he had many clothes in his wardrobe!

> I used to pick up his jeans, which he never knew he had bought because he had many clothes in his wardrobe!
>
> –Bobby Deol

THE BROTHERHOOD

Karan Johar: I think there is some affinity **between** you brothers. You, Bobby, looked at him like a father figure **role in** your life. You have believed him to be someone older to whom you were indebted. It has bonded you so well that it has mobilized you to think 'I love him so much that I will do anything for him; to that he would reciprocate at any time.' True. Sunny, you have put your career on the hold for a long period when Bobby was launched. There was an appreciable lull when *Barsaat* got delayed. You refrained from doing a lot of work.

Sunny Deol: One doesn't take it that way. A film was being made – it had to be made the way it should have been.

Karan Johar: One does not think of things as careers. Were you passive about your family?

Sunny Deol: No, one does not think about the family. My goal was Bobby's debut film. I had nothing else.

Karan Johar: You had an upswing followed by downswing with your maiden film. You changed the script and the director was responsible for the outcome.

Sunny Deol: Yes, I went through that change. Dad wanted to do something. You know that when you try too hard, things will certainly take a U-turn – things, which are easy to handle, will become difficult to pursue. It needs appreciable time to set the things right. I think it was somewhere during 1991-92 when I had my first photo opportunity.

> My goal was Bobby's debut film. I had nothing else.
>
> –Sunny Deol

Karan Johar: How did you feel when you saw Bobby onscreen for the first time?

Sunny Deol: Oh! I loved him.

Karan Johar: Did you feel he deserved to be on the celluloid?

Sunny Deol: Yes, definitely.

THE MEDDLING MEDIA

Karan Johar: We have to analyze the difference in terms of the characteristics of Sunny and Bobby – both have contrasting natures. Sunny, you being the shy guy, do you feel something brewing within your conscience to attack the media?

Sunny Deol: No. I do not have the will. I would love to be like everybody else. You should know how to get written and spoken about. I get agitated over the way the media projects me. Media personnel have tried to let me down irrespective of my performance on a number of occasions. I always try to forget the unsavoury things. I just run away from such developments.

Karan Johar: Do you agree, Bobby? Do you feel the media has worked in a rather unfair way vis-à-vis your family?

Bobby Deol: I think so. The media is actually making a mountain out of a molehill – that is the way they are. They do it to appease everybody. Quite often, they project that you are the best performer; then, they wait for your fall subsequently. Their modus operandi is quite weird. I seldom speak to the media on this aspect. I would rather speak when my movie gets released.

> I get agitated over the way the media projects me; I just run away from such developments!
> –*Sunny Deol*

Sunny Deol: Most of the time when I am interviewed, they ask, 'Oh! You are doing an action film!' I do not understand – is it bad doing an action film? Or is it bad doing a film? What is it? They always try to blackmail us. Or they say, 'Oh! You are doing a patriotic film!' Why they inquire so? I say it is a film.

Karan Johar: Why should you categorize it so?

Sunny Deol: They spelt out so much bullshit for *Gadar*. They diluted the text, music and content in such a manner that the industry wondered about what went wrong. Basically, it was a patriotic film done against Pakistan. The hype they gave ruined the very essence of patriotism. You cannot keep on watching

> Is it bad doing an action film? Or is it bad doing any film?
> –*Sunny Deol*

somebody beating a guy up. It was basically a love story. It had nothing against any faith or country. It was about a man for whom there is nothing bigger than his family. The family served as the bond. There is no country, no faith other than a family. It exists on a certain piece of a landmass. And if those people want them to be of their faith, they were ready to do so because they wanted to survive. The media blew up the core in such an irresponsible manner, which is unpardonable for any peace-loving citizen.

Karan Johar: For the public, *Gadar,* on record we all know is probably the biggest hit of Indian cinema. Do you perceive that the media biased things beyond limit for films like *Lagaan* or *Dil Chahta Hai* released in the same year 2001?

Sunny Deol: The media gave them so much of importance – it recurred on many occasions. My motto at the end of the day is to just do films, preferably better ones. Whatever the finesse of the film is, you are known for the work – not for what people talk or media say about you. That has always remained my motto.

> **There is no country, no faith other than a family.**
> *–Sunny Deol*

Karan Johar: Bobby, did it affect you when your brother's film *Gadar* was undervalued by the media?

Bobby Deol: It did. Anything biased for my brother would upset my temperament. But it is OK – it is the audience, the fans who dictate the outcome. They love your work, your film irrespective of what the media blasts out. That should be upheld at all costs.

Karan Johar: All right. We spoke about love stories under promotion like *Dilwale Dulhaniya Le Jayenge* or *Kuch Kuch Hota Hai.* Such films come in succession year after year. How do you rate them? The audience believe that such films remain regressive or repetitive in their concept.

Sunny Deol: I do not know much about how they interpret such films. I never read much about them. I portray the role of media as unfair when they label such films as unusual social masala – it is just not right! You should see whether people like them. People rant about rave reviews at the end of the day due to the proliferating multiplexes and similar theatres screening those films. Some television channel will say some bullshit on the premier day of release. Take it easy, man! You may say it is bullshit because of X-

Y-Z reason. What about the people who are going to watch with curiosity? Let them make up their mind. It is they who evaluate our production, performance,

> Some television channel will say some bullshit on the day of release. Take it easy, man! Let the people make up their mind!
> –*Sunny Deol*

music and shooting at home or abroad under arduous circumstances. Why are you influencing their mind? Let them make up their mind.

Karan Johar: Yes, it happens a lot of time. People go on the very first day – Friday(s). Suddenly, the news channels will probably kill your film.

Bobby Deol: There are so many channels that try to sneak into your personal life. That is how they work. They over-perform certain things, which is unfair.

Sunny Deol: Frankly, I really feel sorry for *Stardust*. It was the unique magazine with unbiased views. Today, the whole entertainment industry is a mere copy.

Karan Johar: So you feel the dailies, the periodicals, etc. only gossip on their front page or page 3 or entertainment supplements?

Sunny Deol: It used to be fun everywhere. Another periodical *Society* has proved reader-friendly. People love reading and want to be part of a magazine's readership.

Karan Johar: Media exaggerates a certain issue sometimes. Initially, there was a bit even with Shahrukh – they created this rivalry post-*Darr* between him and you, Sunny, for a long period. You never got to work with him again. Of course, today, you are bonding. He is always concerned and desires to know about the state of things. Did that bother you for the long?

Sunny Deol: It does. Sometimes, I do not know what should I say. Let us forget everything and move on in life. Everybody is doing well. How and what they did, why they talked so during 1993-94, I could not gauge. Shahrukh was new to the industry a decade back. He found it difficult to adapt to the genre of people, even though he had worked for quite some period. I belonged to a different category. I had abstained from gossiping with people and such routine. One does not know what happened. As he matured, Shahrukh understood the state of things.

> Today, the whole entertainment industry is a mere copy!
> –*Sunny Deol*

THE OPPOSITES

Karan Johar: Speaking about parties, Bobby, you and your wife Tanya are relatively social. One

> **I prefer going out and enjoying my parties!**
> *–Bobby Deol*

sees you in parties rejoicing. Has it a lot to do with Tanya's nature that makes you outgoing?

Bobby Deol: Yeah! I prefer going out and enjoy that period, Karan!

Karan Johar: One seldom notices you going out, Sunny, due to your introvert nature.

Sunny Deol: If one avoids such events, it does not mean that one dislikes them. I never drink. I am a little shy guy. I dislike to gossip. For me, after a full day's work, I try to relax somewhere where nobody disturbs me. I feel I have to ease out. I am an early-riser. So parties are basically for those who hang out until the wee hours.

Karan Johar: It is a wise decision that you've taken – even one seldom notices your wife anywhere.

Sunny Deol: We are basically, private individuals. We go out to friends' places quite often.

Karan Johar: You like intimate gatherings?

Sunny Deol: Yes, where we could chill out. Because throughout the 24 hours, people stare at you even when you are on the sets before cameras. They chase you when you walk around. So, there

> **For me, after a full day's work, I try to relax somewhere where nobody disturbs me!**
> *–Sunny Deol*

has to be some time when you remain aloof to chill out and relax. That is one of the reasons why I go abroad frequently – whenever I get a chance for two to five days. You just like to get away where I can sit down on a footpath. I can just go on

to a shop, eat anything, sit down anywhere – a place where no one will disturb me.

TROUBLING TIMES

Karan Johar: Unfortunately, you were involved in insignificant controversies in terms of breakups with filmmakers and other assignments. We are talking about Raj Kumar Santoshi. What happened there?

Sunny Deol: Nothing happened. I always wanted to make the film on Bhagat Singh. I commenced, but a lot of things just happened, which should not have happened. We lost substantial money. I am sure they too invested heavily, but in vain. I dislike speaking on the issue, which was so close to my heart. I always

wanted to play Bhagat Singh myself. I thought Bobby could be the right choice to act as Chandra Shekhar Azad. So, we chalked out the concept, but the film flopped. I wish they had enlivened the story.

Karan Johar: Unfortunately, there were two of the films on the same weekend, which robbed off the impact. You have worked with Raj Kumar Santoshi for *Ghayal* and *Ghatak* and have had an amazing working partnership.

Sunny Deol: We introduced Raj Kumar Santoshi to the celluloid world. Initially, we did two to three films and seperated later.

Karan Johar: Did it hurt you?

Sunny Deol: No. We have forgotten unsavoury developments as time has rolled on and proceeded afresh. What else could we do?

Karan Johar: Have you forgiven Raj Kumar Santoshi?

Sunny Deol: Yeah. I have forgiven and forgotten him with others.

Karan Johar: Bobby! There were no filmmakers' spat with you. Perhaps, there has been a spat with two Kapoor sisters – Karishma and Kareena. Not a very amiable equation there.

Bobby Deol: I do not know. I do not think anybody had a problem with me or me with them. I guess whatever happened was quite immature, if it did happen. Karan, you were there in Singapore. You witnessed a lot of things there. I guess with time you just forgive people and forget things.

Karan Johar: Does it make it awkward?

Bobby Deol: That is the sad part. I dislike being unfriendly with people. That is what I believe. So, when you have two people who are not looking at you or not interacting with you, it makes the general environment very awkward. I guess there is always a third person to be blamed for what happens.

Karan Johar: But does that ever stop you from working with them?

Bobby Deol: No, I do not think so. I guess I would love to work with them. Karishma is already married and has withdrawn from performing in movies, but definitely, I would like to work with Kareena.

Karan Johar: Would it be a problem if given an opportunity to work with Kareena?

Bobby Deol: No. I guess not.

Karan Johar: Will you accept to work with Raj Kumar Santoshi on an interesting script?

Sunny Deol: No. We have been discussing scripts quite a lot. Nothing seems to materialize.

The Director and His Muse

Karan Johar: You would have probably been one of the first people making a crossover to film world. Perhaps the film *London* that commenced with Gurinder Chadda might have been interesting. Bobby and you have worked in *Dillagi*. Initially, it was often called *London*. Today, the acclaim Gurinder Chadda has, do you regret about your film being a flop?

Sunny Deol: No, I do not. My fiscal position was unsound. Quite a lot of actors had entered the profession. They quit soon, leaving me to lurk around to produce the film. I just love to make films. My debut, *Ghayal,* had suffered a blow. I had the vision to do many things during the

> **While making *Dillagi*, I should have been more sensible from the financial side.**
>
> *–Sunny Deol*

London sojourn. People derided me saying, 'Why the hell is he doing something like this?' I should have been more sensible from the financial side. I should not have backed out – I should have just gone ahead amidst all the things that happening at that time.

Karan Johar: Sunny might have faced unsound finance condition with production. How did you support him, Bobby?

Bobby Deol: My brother never told me about his problems and he has always been like that. He wants to take away other people's problems. I was the youngest which made him treat me like a kid. I never saw the bad aspect of things – I was always kept away from it. Now, I have realized it and try to be optimistic, more responsible, and be there for him.

Karan Johar: So, you were always protected. Were you made to feel any crisis in the family at that time?

Bobby Deol: Never.

Karan Johar: Who does not like to have an elder brother like Sunny?

Bobby, were you burdened by the career graph of your father and brother? Huge success has eluded you. Do you feel extremely burdened on a day-to-day level?

Bobby Deol: Actually, I am lucky that I am in a family. I was a passive witness to the

> **I was the youngest so I never saw the bad aspect of things!**
> –Bobby Deol

predicament of my dad and brother in their oscillating career. I saw other actors around me who had big success for a while. You are happy when you do well. It does not mean you give up in the weaker moments. Everybody is a human being – they have to react so. I wish to improve.

Karan Johar: Perhaps there were insecure moments when you felt what happened?

Bobby Deol: Yeah! Sometimes, definitely – but I think with every passing year and day of life, you certainly become stronger.

SUNNY ON BOBBY'S ACTING SKILLS

Karan Johar: Bobby, you did shift genres. You did a lot of love stories. Subsequently, you moved on to action movies.

Bobby Deol: I have worked with lot of good filmmakers who did not produce quality films. I did films that were of a thriller kind and action films, which did well in the industry. I guess in this industry, one tends to get an image and the whole scenario is that distributors think 'If it is Bobby Deol, either it will be a thriller or an action movie!' I did get good offers. Things took a turn. Everybody said, 'You know how it is.' I have attempted to do love stories interspersed with action films.

Karan Johar: Yeah!

Bobby Deol: People used to talk about my long hair. They said, 'He won't work since he has long hair'. My biggest hit was with my longest hair – *Soldier*! It was like a slap on the silly critics!

Karan Johar: Sunny, did you advise Bobby often?

Sunny Deol: He hardly went through any difficult phase. You need a good subject and a good director can do justice to that – nothing beyond because I think he is a very good actor. I have directed him.

> **People said, 'He won't work since he has long hair'. My biggest hit was with my longest hair – *Soldier*!**
> –Bobby Deol

Karan Johar: Yes.

Sunny Deol: I think he is one of the best-looking guys we have in our industry.

> **I think Bobby is a very good actor – I have directed him.**
> *–Sunny Deol*

Karan Johar: Any specific film for which you have fired him by uttering, 'Why did you do this film?'

Sunny Deol: No. I like to advice on certain aspects, but I have avoided it quite often. I have made him realize about the number of mistakes at a later stage.

Karan Johar: Clearly, as you opined, Bobby is a good-looking boy. He has a long and bright future.

RAPID FIRE

Karan Johar: We will commence the *Rapid-Fire Round*. Do not take it seriously.

Sunny Deol: I am just looking where the guns are!

Karan Johar: There are no guns – my questions are all the ammunition that you need! I shall throw a volley of questions in anticipation of spicy and punchy answers. The winner will get the *Koffee with Karan koffee hamper*. Let me start with Sunny. Ajay Devgan, Akshay Kumar, Sanjay Dutt, Salman Khan – who do you think is the best action hero after you?

Sunny Deol: Salman.

Karan Johar: *Sholay, Chupke Chupke, Satyakam* – which is your favourite Dharmendra film?

Sunny Deol: All of them.

Karan Johar: If you had to recast Jai and Veeru from *Sholay* today, who would they be?

Sunny Deol: Abhishek and Bobby.

Karan Johar: An Indian film you wished you were a part of?

Sunny Deol: That is a tricky question. *Sholay* is the easiest answer.

Karan Johar: A film that you wish you were not a part of?

Sunny Deol: My own film, *Savere Wali Gadi*.

Karan Johar: The sexiest woman in India today is?

Sunny Deol: Everybody is

> **Karan Johar: A film that you wish you were not a part of?**
> **Sunny Deol: My own film, *Savere Wali Gadi*.**

so much made up with the media hype – you do not know the reality behind!

Karan Johar: What would change in Bobby?

Sunny Deol: Nothing – he is perfect!

Karan Johar: What does Bobby have that you don't?

Sunny Deol: Grace.

Karan Johar: OK. What do you have that Bobby doesn't?

Sunny Deol: Discipline.

Karan Johar: OK. When is the last time you cried?

Sunny Deol: I cry very often and very easily – I could cry even watching a film!

Karan Johar: What comes to your mind when I say......Punjabi men?

Sunny Deol: Deols.

Karan Johar: Critics?

Sunny Deol: Not fair.

Karan Johar: Films like *Murder* and *Julie*?

Sunny Deol: Earlier, they used to keep to the side, now they do so up-front!

Karan Johar: OK. How do you rate yourself as an actor on a scale of 1 to 10?

Sunny Deol: I would love to say 10.

Karan Johar: As a dancer on a scale of 1 to 10?

Sunny Deol: Zero.

Karan Johar: All right, quickly then – Raj Kumar Santoshi or Rahul Rawail?

Sunny Deol: Rahul Rawail.

Karan Johar: *Gadar* or *Sholay*?

Sunny Deol: *Gadar*.

Karan Johar: Arnold Schwarzenegger or Sylvester Stallone?

Sunny Deol: Arnold.

Karan Johar: Who is the most rocking Khan – Shahrukh, Aamir or Salman?

Sunny Deol: Salman.

Karan Johar: The desirable diva – Aishwarya Rai or Sushmita Sen?

Sunny Deol: Ash!

Bobby Deol: You cannot ask questions like this!

Karan Johar: Of course, I can! Very well done, Sunny! On to Bobby Deol for his *Rapid-Fire*.

> **I do not want to win!**
> *–Bobby Deol*

Bobby Deol: I do not want to win!

Karan Johar: Come on, Bobby. If you were struck in a lift with Karishma and Kareena, you would?

Bobby Deol: I would be quite happy!

Karan Johar: Why would that be?

Bobby Deol: We have so much to say to one another!

Karan Johar: The sexiest Indian actress you ever worked with?

Bobby Deol: I do not think they are sexy – they are just my good friends.

Karan Johar: None of them are sexy? You are quite mean to them.

Bobby Deol: They are all like guys. That is how they are.

> *Karan Johar:* **The sexiest Indian actress you ever worked with?**
> *Bobby Deol:* **I do not think they are sexy. They are all like guys!**

Karan Johar: The most romantic thing you have done for Tanya?

Bobby Deol: Once I really pissed her off quite badly. So, I came home and decorated the place. I called for some Italian food, lighted some candles and waited for her to walk-in. Later, she forgave me.

Karan Johar: How sweet! That's quite romantic. Who is Tanya's favorite hero?

Bobby Deol: It is her husband.

Karan Johar: Great! And after you?

Bobby Deol: My brother and dad.

Karan Johar: She is a loyalist. When was the last time you cried? I have been told that tough men seldom cry. However, you brother cries at the drop of a hat.

> *Karan Johar:* **Who is Tanya's favorite hero?**
> *Bobby Deol:* **It is her husband!**

Bobby Deol: I cry easily for myself. We cry whenever we get a chance! Actually, we get emotional about each other – it is just the way we are!

Karan Johar: One thing Sunny has that you do not?

Bobby Deol: He is the strength of my life. I do not think I could be that to people, but is amazing. I do not know. I just love him.

Karan Johar: Aishwarya or Sushmita?

Bobby Deol: Both.

Karan Johar: *Badal* or *Bichchoo*?

Bobby Deol: *Soldier*!

Karan Johar: OK, bhaiya's action or papa's comedy?

Bobby Deol: Papa's comedy.

Karan Johar: Lara Dutta or Priyanka Chopra?

Bobby Deol: Lara, my friend.

Karan Johar: Mallika Sherawat's sex appeal or Rani's histrionics?

Bobby Deol: Rani.

Karan Johar: Good. *Gadar* or *Sholay*?

Bobby Deol: *Sholay*.

Karan Johar: **What would you do if you were offered a film like *Murder* or *Julie*?**
Sunny Deol: **He would *Murder Julie*!**

Karan Johar: OK. What would you do if you were offered a film like *Murder* or *Julie*?

Sunny Deol: He would *Murder Julie*!

Karan Johar: Wonderful. One emotion you are going through?

Bobby Deol: When will this be over?

Karan Johar: Bobby, unfortunately your brother answered much better and he has won the round. Congratulations on winning the koffee hamper and answering so well in the *Rapid-Fire Round*, Sunny! Bobby remained non-committal.

DHARMENDRA

Karan Johar: Let us find the reason for the deep admiration you feel towards your father. Sunny, how would you describe him?

Sunny Deol: I believe him to be the last hero. He is a good-looking man. He has performed successfully in comedy, emotional and action films. He is one actor who had been responsible for superhits. I remember when his two to three films were released simultaneously; they ran successfully throughout the country. I do not know anything beyond my dad.

Karan Johar: Bobby, how do you describe him?

Bobby Deol: Everything that I have is from him. I do not find any word to describe him. I used to accompany him when I was a kid and I have found that people look at him in the eye because they never look at him as a star but as a macho man in the industry. He is an amazing human being. I am very lucky to be a part of this family.

Karan Johar: We asked your father to say something to you. We have it on camera.

> **The people who know everything do not blow their own trumpet.**
>
> *–Dharmendra*

Dharmendra: My sons Sunny and Bobby – this is the voice from my heart! This applies equally to the film industry cronies. You need to keep going; nobody will respect you the day you stop. The people who know everything do not blow their own trumpet – they keep on going and never turn back. I launched both of you. I love both of you a lot. You have grown up – times have changed. We are emotional and I think the world today is more practical than than emotional. So be wise, be good to the industry. This is the most beautiful industry – there is no business like show business. People must be thinking why I made them actors. I am a very emotional guy from a village, who had lots of dreams. The industry I dreamt only had the Kapoor family. I used to ponder over things such as when would I have kids to make them heroes and have my own film family. Everybody grew up as the time flew. I am very happy that you, my sons, are down-to-earth and affectionate to everybody and me.

I am proud that our family is a joint family – we learn from each other. Sunny is always protective, and not only towards Bobby; he behaves often like he is my father! He wants to do everything for me. He can do anything for my happiness, but cannot express himself. Do not expect much from others – you will face an acute loss. Live your life to the fullest extent. I do not expect anything from anyone. I have lived my life. I am fulfilling my emotional duties – I will do that it until I am alive. I know that my kids will do similarly.

THE SOFT MACHO MAN

Sunny Deol: I am proud that I have a father like him. He gets me going.

Karan Johar: That is something about you that a lot of people probably would not realize. There was a phase when people said, 'Oh, my God, Sunny can bash you up! He has a short temper!'

Sunny Deol: I know it is so, but I cannot understand why – it makes people stay away from you.

Karan Johar: You dislike it?

Sunny Deol: Yeah! Sometimes, you are left alone. I just wonder why it is so. Your brother runs away from you.

Karan Johar: Does that happen?

Bobby Deol: I am scared that he will say something. Discipline! That is one thing.

> **I am scared that Sunny will say something. Discipline! That is one thing.**
>
> *–Bobby Deol*

Karan Johar: So are you scared of your brother?

Bobby Deol: I am not. I just respect him very much. I could not understand him when I was a kid. Now, I would love to go out for dinners with him, and tell him 'let us go out and eat.' I have some habits, which he disapproves of. I keep a distance because of that. It is not that I do not want to be near to him. We have never communicated with each other – we should communicate more easily.

CONCLUSION

Karan Johar: I think you should. Well, it was wonderful chat with both of you. Thank you so much for sparing time for my show. I know that you seldom appear on television together. Thank you so much for your cooperation. It has been absolutely wonderful. There is a mug right next to you Bobby with silver pen aside. You have to lift and affix your signature. This personally autographed mug could be yours only, if you participate in the *Koffee with Karan* quest contest. Let us proceed to the koffee wall. Thank you so much.

● ● ●

14

Shabana Azmi & Shobha De
Beauty with Brains

She truly is an institution. Her acting performances have not only left an indelible impression on cine-goers and made everyone aware of her unattainable standard as well. Otherwise, in the selfish world of actors, you will not find an actor who thinks beyond the horizons of celluloid. She invests her passion to work for socio-political and human causes. We have Shabana Azmi as our guest.

Shabana Azmi

Karan Johar: Good evening, Lady!

Shabana Azmi: Good evening!

Karan Johar: Welcome to the show. How do you feel?

Shabana Azmi: Well, I have not taken enough time to be adept on your show.

Karan Johar: It is a pleasure to present myself to different environs.

Bollywood on a World Platter

Karan Johar: Perhaps you might have been exposed to the hype and hoopla surrounding stars making their debut in Hollywood. What about your foray into Hollywood?

Shabana Azmi: Hindi film industry is being noticed in most cases except my recent debut in Hollywood! I did a film called *Waterborne*. I finished shooting in September 2004. The Hollywood people do not know anything about our Hindi films. It is a pity. I shall believe we are 'en route' to the pinnacle. Perhaps Britons are quite aware of Hindi films but those in the US remain cut-off from us.

Karan Johar: Well, I expect you to share with us some unbelievable facts. Indian media went mad on glorifying Aishwarya. They highlighted her debut on a day-to-day basis with all the offers coming in from Hollywood. They wonder why her projects have not materialized. Do you believe in such media hype and hoopla?

Shabana Azmi: I believe the media will help eventually because we had a lot of Indian film fraternity people on the jury in the Cannes International Film Festival. In fact, I was in Cannes and I felicitated James Spader for his debut on *Sex, Lies and Videotape*.

Karan Johar: Oh really!

Shabana Azmi: Yes. Mira Nair and Mrinal Sen were on the jury. Yet, it never created such hype in India as in the case of Aishwarya because she hailed from mainstream Hindi cinema. It is the glamorous world – I believe it is wonderful, because that is how it gets noticed.

> I felicitated James Spader for his debut on *Sex, Lies and Videotape* in Cannes.
> –*Shabana Azmi*

Karan Johar: Do you think she was a deserving member on the panel of judges, being an actor herself?

Shabana Azmi: Firstly, it is wonderful being a young actress. It is unfair for the jury to ignore such actresses. Let me tell you about the time when I chaired the jury in Montreal some years ago. I was the only woman and as a token of respect, the organizers elevated me as the president. The members of the jury were film critics, directors, producers and writers – but none were actors. They elevated me to the status of a queen! Making the members subordinates, I believe, is one of the great mistakes committed by the organizers. The subjective judging of a film had certain factors – we had to erect some kind of framework to evaluate a performance.

> In Montreal while chairing a jury, I could hear their conscience saying, 'You third world actors – you are going to tell us?'
>
> *–Shabana Azmi*

Karan Johar: Yes, of course!

Shabana Azmi: Suddenly, we came across a factor – prejudices – on their faces! I could hear their conscience saying, 'You third world actors – you are going to tell us?'

Karan Johar: Oh, God!

Shabana Azmi: It was so amazing – I seldom experience that in India. The culture, however, in Montreal supposedly was much more westernized. We faced prejudices against women, especially gender prejudices against actors of the third world. It was nice that somebody like Aishwarya, so young, went there amidst the Indian media hoopla. I celebrated the occasion.

Karan Johar: Such prejudices exist at home. There is a common factor about the acting fraternity that one believes quite frequently – the journalists or members of the media are nice to you provided you create such a relationship in tandem. Do you agree that that happens at some point of time?

Shabana Azmi: I am sure that happens. We have to remember that the media representatives are human beings, and just like us, they too have favourites and prejudices.

> We have to remember that the media representatives are human beings, and like us have favourites and prejudices.
>
> *–Shabana Azmi*

Karan Johar: Yes.

Shabana Azmi: However, we try to remain objective. The fact is that we are prejudiced. So, why do we treat the media with indifference?

Karan Johar: All right. We should take pride in our prejudice!

Shabana Azmi: Yes, I think so.

Shobha De

Karan Johar: All right! Media brings me to my next guest, the fellow Queen Marian – Shobha De. She is a successful columnist, author and opinion maker. You can admire or hate her, but cannot ignore her opinion. Let me bring on Shobha De. Hello! Good evening. Welcome to *Koffee with Karan!*

Shobha De: Hello!

Shabana Azmi: Hello, my dear!

Shobha De: Hello, my darling from one Queen Marian to another!

INDIVIDUALITY Vs BRANDING

Karan Johar: Shobha, you have been a successful columnist, an author and an opinion maker. It will certainly bother you on a cerebral level when people call you a socialite or a Page 3 specialist!

Shobha De: I think it goes on with the turf. I really do not care much about the definition on the whole. So I do what I need to do – what I am good at, what I am known for, or what has taken me some 25 years for honing my skills is perfect. It is not my problem how I have been categorised or labeled.

> I do what I need to do. It is not my problem how I have been categorised or labeled.
>
> *–Shobha De*

Shabana Azmi: Shobha, is that true?

Shobha De: Completely.

Shabana Azmi: I think we are conscious of the images we have – I am pretty conscious of my own image and I do not think that it does not hurt.

Shobha De: I honestly say that it does not, because it is very important to know who you are, why you do what you do, and see yourself as a social communicator. I see myself as someone who

> **I am called a candy floss filmmaker by my opponents!**
> *–Karan Johar*

has chronicled a changing and inspirational India. It is not my problem if the other person could not get it.

Karan Johar: I endorse what you say but I am called a candy floss filmmaker by my opponents and it does bother me.

Shobha De: It is like describing Ratan Tata or Narayana Murthy on page 3. Sachin Tendulkar is on page 3. It depends on what you mean by the page 3. I think page 3 is for most of the achievers. I do not gauge the observation as a let down for any budding personality, but work it out as an occupational hazard – it is a part of what you do.

Karan Johar: OK.

Shobha De: People would christen me as the columnist if I walked around in *khadi kurta* with

> **People would christen me as the columnist if I walked around in *khadi kurta* with a jhola!**
> *–Shobha De*

a jhola. I would not do that. I have never conformed. I have believed in dressing so as to qualify me to look as a normal human being. If the people refuse to accept me, then I will say, 'Sorry if you cannot handle me so!'

Shabana Azmi: Beautiful!

PROFESSIONAL VS POPCORN JOURNALISM

Karan Johar: All right. I will speak next about the way professional journalism has moulded the society. Well, Shobha, you were the editor of *Stardust*, which is something that very few people know about. She is responsible for this popcorn journalism, which exists today in a huge, huge way.

Shabana Azmi: Did you start calling me Bahana Azmi by the way?

Shobha De: Yes, I did.

Shabana Azmi: It stuck on me forever!

> **Shabana Azmi:** Shobha started calling me 'Bahana Azmi!'
> **Shobha De:** I do not remember – but it sounds good, so I shall take credit!

Karan Johar: Is that what people call you?

Shabana Azmi: Bahana Azmi. And she is my pal! Imagine my school friends and college mates!

Shobha De: It is an occupational hazard, honey! It was another life and another *janam*! I do not know whether I did it or not, but it sounds good, so I shall take

credit! It was a magazine at any rate. It was the first fan magazine brought out of India. It had a prototype in Hollywood. It had 'Photoplay' and magazines in that genre. I have enjoyed my ten-year tenure very much. Today, I see the 'stardustization' of media across the board. It has spread on to the mainstream newspapers.

Karan Johar: Newspapers. Yes!

Shobha De: Are people using *Stardust* lingo or its stories? Is the same kind of writing appearing on the front page? Indian politics has been 'stardustized'. Sports has been 'stardustized'. Show me any sector of existence untouched by Stardust?

Karan Johar: Oh my God! Shabana, I need to know your take on film journalism. Everyone looks at you as a brilliant actor.

Shabana Azmi: I do not think the actor figures or the actor's crafts figures at all in film journalism. It is about their persona, their style, or their personal profile. I do not think anybody even expects or cares that there is something called craft; something called technique. Karan, showbiz essentially is about vicarious thrills across the world, not just in India. Showbiz without masala is a cold business.

Shobha De: The serious trade magazines, which attempted to analyse an actor's craft have failed spectacularly. It is not only the scenario in India, but elsewhere in the world as well. It is the sort of a very niche market. Most of the publishers seldom invest behind the venture, especially in India. You had publications analyzing the business, three decades ago – the industry, the craft etc., of film making, but they are just dead.

Shabana Azmi: I disagree with what you say. I have a problem with something – small budget films that just do not have a stake.

Shobha De: Who's going to compensate? Who is going to subsidize?

Shabana Azmi: No, I feel Karan Johar can very easily subsidize a small film!

– a two crore film would be what one set of yours would cost.

Shabana Azmi: You can easily lend that rupee two crores for a film, for I have worked in small budget films. I am working with more films and I know how impossible it would be to release them. I do not think audiences have dried up. I believe that you would not find the correct infrastructure to market such films. Whether it relates to film, music, or journalism, the budget varies from project to project. I totally welcome what is commercial, which is celebrated.

> **I totally welcome what is commercial, which is celebrated.**
> *–Shabana Azmi*

Karan Johar: What will be popular, as they say.

Shabana Azmi: I am afraid of failure. To say it ended in failure because it hardly has any readership – that it has no audience who could not justify the truth.

Shobha De: I agree in principle about what she says, but there is a prototype – business model for everything.

Shobha De: A publisher looks at what he does as a business proposition. Unfortunately, neither you nor anybody will involve in the business for charity. Obviously, you want the return for investment in any venture, as the basic principle of life.

Shabana Azmi: Shobha, I am saying that you will not lose money. The mode of cross-subsidy exists in every society, provided you are ready to invest at proper time. The rich will subsidize the poor in any democracy, in any sane civilized society. It will probably come by independent filmmakers persuading Karan Johar! There is value in it for Yash Chopra and Subhash Ghai as these films will win awards or win you different kind of acclaim.

Karan Johar: Acclaim!

Shabana Azmi: Let me get back. Karan! Everybody ignored us at the initial stages when Smita Patil and I worked for a film. They attributed it as small budget film. They labeled us something else, when we ventured ahead. You had people from the mainstream like Rekha, et al, who had worked with Shyam Benegal. Something was

> **Nobody will involve in the business for charity.**
> *–Shobha De*

available at that time. They were getting in the mainstream cinema. I believe it was a very healthy interaction.

Karan Johar: I completely agree.

Shobha De: It is a perfect cycle for all of us.

Shabana Azmi: Today, we hardly find any audience for anything else than mediocrity. I believe something wrong is with the state of cinema in India today.

> We produce a small budget film and cry later about the shoestring budget for marketing.
>
> *–Shabana Azmi/Shobha De*

Karan Johar: Do you agree with her comments?

Shabana Azmi: I disagree with her. Definitely, we need to find an audience. Usually, we commit some mistakes. We produce a small budget film and cry later about the shoestring budget for marketing. Suave marketing alone could get you substantial audience. I have been recommending to the concerned authorities (Ministry of Information and Broadcasting, Government of India) to establish a coherent distribution network to produce documentaries, which lie sealed in a can for over two decades. What is the fun of storing such films? A lot of producers produce such films to glorify the aesthetic sense. We have to get it right. Who shall bell the cat?

Shabana Azmi: There will be massive audience.

Shobha De: Who will stake with them at the juncture?

Karan Johar: I believe a good film shall always find an audience. Unfortunately, we have come across a vicious circle.

Shabana Azmi: No. Karan! Let me share the position when Hindi cinema took off to international festivals – Cannes. I have often faced problems.

Karan Johar: When film *Devdas* went to Cannes?

Shabana Azmi: Yes.

Karan Johar: Don't you think the film deserved to be in Cannes?

Shabana Azmi: No. *Devdas* had enough money to go independently to the international market. The filmmakers or the CII could have influenced it to get into Cannes on its own rather than the Government of India.

Karan Johar: Government of India?

Shabana Azmi: The authorities in the Union

> **Karan Johar:** Don't you think the film *'Devdas'* deserved to be in Cannes?
>
> **Shabana Azmi:** No.

Government need to support independent film producers because their films never see the light of the day.

Karan Johar: Unfortunately, the bureaucrats are stymied.

Shabana Azmi: They have enough money privately. The game should proceed. Of course, they anticipate rich dividends. I am not attributing that film *Devdas* does not deserve to go to the Cannes Festival. Why did the authorities take that film which is a mainstream film? Why did not they try to encourage different kind of cinema on such an occasion? They need to support such varieties.

Karan Johar: Shobha, do you think *Devdas* deserved to be screened at Cannes?

Shobha De: Not at all. I do not think of rich dividends, either. *Devdas* was just another huge budget film with great costumes. I do not think it had been represented in any way. First of all, it was a total travesty of a classic book. Too many liberties were taken with the original story.

Shabana Azmi: She is married to a Bengali!

Shobha De: There was a huge media outcry in terms of representation. It was just

> **Devdas does not fit the bill even in the category of mediocre films!**
> *–Shobha De*

another big buck film. Frankly speaking, I do not think it deserved any of the dividends – it did not deserve the hype. The music was nice. The girls looked pretty. The matter ended there. Certainly, it did not deserve to be showcased representing Indian cinema at such a glamorous event. It does not fit the bill even in the category of mediocre films. I am afraid I am not one of the *Devdas* fans!

Shabana Azmi: The rich dividends came because it was *Devdas*. It was contrary to the image of India in the west as mystical despite the spate of famines and droughts that gets on my nerves.

Karan Johar: And no elephants and no snake charmers there?

Shabana Azmi: Suddenly, they said, 'Oh! My God! All this opulence and glamour!'

Shobha De: The film *Dil Chahta Hai* in that case was a cutting edge film.

Karan Johar: Sure as a breakthrough film for our lifestyle and urban nature.

Shobha De: The urban India is well represented there. What about *Devdas?* It was just a costumer-based drama with pretensions.

Shabana Azmi: I have enjoyed watching the film.

Shobha De: I too have enjoyed watching it. Does that make it a great film? No.

Karan Johar: We have discussed the state of commercial cinema in India and the cinema in general.

> **I too have enjoyed watching Devdas – does that make it a great film? No.**
>
> *–Shobha De*

Shabana Azmi: Something very interesting – I spoke to Rishi Kapoor this morning. He told me that the time was opportune to proceed in the industry because every genre of films was being made. For the first time, you could notice a spate from the big, the musical, to the small budgeted art film to the middle of road kind of films. Shobha says pretending to be, but actually nothing of such sort – the whole lot of them owe to the industry.

Karan Johar: There is lot of scope now.

Shabana Azmi: I really think that as an actor, I have been born at the right time and the right place because ten-fifteen years ago; a girl aged 28 was too old. I have got the best parts in the industry after I turned forty – whether it was *Godmother, Saaz, Fire, Mrityudand.* I have just done a film called *Morning Raga* in which again I act as the protagonist. Those films would not have been available some ten years ago. So, it is a great time to be in films as an actress.

Karan Johar: I do agree, but why week after week when I enter the cinema hall do I return disillusioned? I have been disappointed with what I have watched. You speak about a few films in a year, but our industry churns out over four hundred or five hundred films every year. Why do I still feel when I walk out that why did I spend my hard earned money?

Shabana Azmi: I think that is true of any time.

> **I have got the best parts in the industry after I turned forty!**
>
> *–Shabana Azmi*

Shobha De: That is pretty interesting what Shabana has commented upon, as she had been an exceptional actor. That is why she gets such amazing roles. I imagine the ceiling age limit for any actress should be between 16 and 21 years of age. Today, alarmingly, young girls get into the industry. The industry is very cruel to women species. Whether it is Bollywood or Hollywood, there is hardly any difference to be

> **The industry is very cruel to women species!**
> –Shobha De

accounted for. There is one token film just before the Hollywood Oscar nominations, which has a Meryl Streep or a Susan Sarandon or somebody else. Where are the films of a certain age category other than them? They do not exist.

Shabana Azmi: No, but the portrayal of women in Indian cinema has, of course, come of age. It is fair. I would say the position is far better than it ever was. We have a long way to go, babe.

Shobha De: Karan! Girls in their late thirties or early forties are being offered motherly roles. They are playing moms to twenty plus guys. Frankly speaking, I find that insulting and ridiculous. It is obscene, but guys in their sixties are still playing college students. What are we talking about?

Karan Johar: What happens when you get offered in the mainstream cinema is that offers for such motherly roles and such will repeat forever.

Shabana Azmi: I did not perform when I was offered mega bucks – more money than I ever got as a lead actress. I would not acknowledge it. I would not compromise. It does not interest me – although I have got nothing against motherly roles. I am doing mother's role for the sake of Jesus Christ!

Karan Johar: Yeah!

Shabana Azmi: Where would you draw the line? What sort of role would you ignore? I do not know, Shobha, unless it is being executed in letter and spirit.

Karan Johar: Would you have played the role as the mother in *Khabie Khushi Khabie Ghum*?

> **I have got nothing against motherly roles. I am doing mother's role for the sake of Jesus Christ!**
> –Shabana Azmi

Shabana Azmi: Maybe not in *Khabie Khushi Khabie Ghum*, but I would have definitely done the role in *Kal Ho Na Ho*.

Karan Johar: Why not *Khabie Khushi Khabie Ghum*?

Shabana Azmi: Because she was subservient to her husband for a pretty longer period and she got only one moment to claim. My mother loved it – she clapped when Jaya Bachchan made that statement!

> *I would have happily done the role of the mother in Kabhie Khushi Kabhie Ghum – sobbing my way through pain and standing with a thali in hand!*
>
> *–Shobha De*

Shobha De: I would have happily done it, Karan!

Karan Johar: You spelt out that you would have happily accepted the role. Would have happily been the subservient woman to her husband in *Kabhie Khushi Kabhie Ghum*?

Shobha De: Sobbing my way through the pain? Standing with a thali in my hand? I would have had lots of fun!

Karan Johar: Shabana, would not you have accepted it as a challenge? You have interpreted it as a role calling for certain subservience, but that is contrary to your self-image. Would not you have enacted a role that would have broken that mould?

> *Jayaji, I hope you are not listening!*
>
> *–Shabana Azmi*

Shabana Azmi: No; I have played the role of a subservient woman – it is not that I have not performed it. There is a transition that is far more interesting to play – somebody who starts from being subservient and finally reaching the other end. Jayaji, I hope you are not listening! I mean, that's really in retrospect.

HANDLING CRITICISM

Karan Johar: We should speak to some creative persons about the word 'criticism'. How open are you to criticism? I do not think you have heard too much of your onscreen performances, Shabana. What will you do if you get such offers? The social causes that you take up – like slum rehabilitation and similar other causes – the people have said that Shabana Azmi has been doing this for publicity. We were talking about the media earlier. How do you deal with such criticism?

Shabana Azmi: You know, it seldom happens. It happened twenty years ago, when I was a suspected do-gooder, who used to suddenly appear on the scene from nowhere. Now, it is perfectly all right. I had been watching how I was different from every other actor. It was perfectly all right for people to go skeptical. No such development took place when I undertook a hunger strike for the slum dwellers.

Karan Johar: Yes.

Shabana Azmi: We never had an actor really during her prime youth to go and sit vigil across the road. Obviously, it was something people were unfamiliar with – sitting for five days at a stretch. I got a couple of brickbats, but Javed alerted me about some or the other controversy. Indeed, that happened which disheartened many of the film actors.

> It will much easier to work for things which you are quite capable of handling – say blindness or cancer.
> –*Shabana Azmi*

Karan Johar: From doing the same thing?

Shabana Azmi: They would have done so by announcing their names. Instead, they wondered whether it was too dicey. It will be much easier to work for things which you are quite capable of handling, say blindness or cancer – with which I was not actually involved in the beginning.

Karan Johar: You were right there on the scene.

Shabana Azmi: The fact was that it was consistent work. I undertook the work year after year, which changed the scene completely.

Karan Johar: Criticism. Shobha, we take up newspapers in the morning, read your column and you have something to say. We cannot ignore your comment. Sometimes, we find people even seek your approval. Are you open to their criticism? How would you take such criticisms?

Shobha De: Oh! My first book came out when contributors churned out new stories. I received a record number of worst reviews anybody had in post-independent India! I believe we have received some 235 reviews for the book.

> For my first book, I received a record number of worst reviews anybody had in post-independent India!
> –*Shobha De*

Karan Johar: Bad review?

Shobha De: These really trashed me so thoroughly that had I been discouraged not to venture ahead. I paid serious attention to the reviews. Some of them came from people for whom I have high regards. Others were childish, stupid and I understood that because I had been at the giving end for an appreciable period. It was an opportunity for them to air their grievances, whose sentiments I had hurt inadvertently. It was their big chance to challenge me. Such virulent attacks remain fair as long as you see their criticism in the right perspective and learn to deal with them accordingly.

> **Nobody in the world is unbiased!**
> *–Shobha De*

Karan Johar: Do you treat such comments as unbiased?

Shobha De: Nobody in the world is unbiased – but I have an obligation to my readers. The reason why an editor hires me is to write a column because it is a sacred space, which I would seldom abuse. I have to substantiate facts in a responsible and fearless manner, as frankly and fairly as possible. That is my job.

Karan Johar: Shabana, how do you react to Shoba's columns?

Shabana Azmi: She is a very clever and interesting writer – she has her way as a spicy writer! You may or may not agree with it. She can hook you from her first line onwards. I have, in fact, called her a couple of times and told her to have really enjoyed what she had interpreted. She is very tongue-in-cheek at times, which is very interesting as long as it is not turned on me!

Karan Johar: I have never been at the receiving end of any of your criticism.

Shobha De: You are speaking too soon! Just kidding!

Karan Johar: If you don't like my film, promise me that you won't write after my show!

Shobha De: It depends whether you gift me a diamond bracelet! Even being a friend is not protection enough!

Shabana Azmi: I agree!

> *Karan Johar:* I have never been at the receiving end of any of your criticism.
> *Shobha De:* You are speaking too soon! If you make a lousy movie, I am going to call it a dud.

Shobha De: I am sorry – I am true to what I write. I have had a track record of twenty five to thirty years. My bond is with my readers. I owe it to them to what I say. You could be my best friend. Sorry, honey! If you make a lousy movie, I am going to call it a dud.

Karan Johar: If you come face-to-face with someone about whom you had written that morning, how would you react?

Shobha De: I comment on the public utterances of public figures. I also blast off about their public conduct in a public place watched by the sundry. I am not going into their private lives.

> **I have every right to comment as a watchdog of the fourth estate, as a journalist to tear public figures apart if they misbehave!**
>
> *–Shobha De*

These are the people who are accountable because we want them to care for us. We have voted for them to remain where they are. When we see them behaving in such a manner that is contrary to the pledge made, I have every right to comment as a watchdog of the fourth estate, as a journalist, a commentator to tear them apart. That is what I owe to my readers!

Rapid Fire

Karan Johar: I have a *Rapid Fire Round*, which has loads of fun for the contestants. Eventually, I shall decide about your performance. It is a small game with the koffee hamper as the dividend. I am going to start with Shabana. You should answer with pun and fun. A recent Indian film you wish you were a part of?

Shabana Azmi: None.

Karan Johar: A female actor of the current lot you think has tremendous potential?

Shabana Azmi: Tabu.

Karan Johar: You have to name another besides Tabu.

Shabana Azmi: I think lots of them. Manisha Koirala.

Karan Johar: All right! Someone younger?

Shabana Azmi: Someone underrated? I think Urmila Matondkar.

Karan Johar: What would be your ideal cast for *Arth* in 2004?

Shabana Azmi: Tabu, Kareena and Aamir Khan.

Karan Johar: The sexiest man in India?

Shabana Azmi: I will find him the sexiest who would wear a sherwani and speak immaculate

Karan Johar: **What would be your ideal cast for *Arth* in 2004?**
Shabana Azmi: **Tabu, Kareena and Aamir Khan.**

English or a three-piece suit and speak chaste Urdu with intonation!

Karan Johar: I have seen your husband do that. He wears the sherwani and speak immaculate English.

Shabana Azmi: Of course, he is not the sexiest man in India.

Karan Johar: So, no man turns on Shabana Azmi at all today?

Shabana Azmi: Dilip Kumar.

Karan Johar: Who turns on Shabana Azmi?

Shabana Azmi: Dilip Kumar.

Karan Johar: All right! The sexiest politician in India today?

Shabana Azmi: Sonia Gandhi.

Karan Johar: Ah…. All right. An overrated actor in India?

Shabana Azmi: I will not lose friends talking about that.

Karan Johar: An underrated actor?

Shabana Azmi: Deepti Naval.

Karan Johar: The depiction of politics in Indian cinema?

Shabana Azmi: It is completely stereotypical.

Karan Johar: The depiction of sex in Indian cinema?

Shabana Azmi: It is bordering on the obscene.

Karan Johar: Depiction of romance in Indian cinema?

Shabana Azmi: Yash Chopra.

Karan Johar: Three words to describe the new government?

Shabana Azmi: Huge welcome change from the predecessor government. I am glad that the Left parties are an important part of the ruling party. They have many promises to fulfill.

Karan Johar: Deepa Mehta, Mira Nair, Aparna Sen – your favourite woman director?

Shabana Azmi: I would say Aparna – I have worked with Aparna. I think she is one of the most intelligent women I know. I have enjoyed very much working with Deepa. I would love to work with Mira Nair.

Karan Johar: Depiction of romance in Indian cinema?

Shabana Azmi: Yash Chopra.

Karan Johar: Very quickly then – *Lakshya* or *Dil Chahta Hai*?

Shabana Azmi: *Lakshya*.

Karan Johar: Om Puri or Nasiruddin Shah?

Shabana Azmi: Nasiruddin Shah.

Karan Johar: *Masoom* or *Arth*?

Shabana Azmi: *Arth*.

Karan Johar: Rituparno Ghosh or Mani Ratnam?

Shabana Azmi: Rituparno Ghosh.

Karan Johar: Sonia Gandhi or Manmohan Singh?

Shabana Azmi: Sonia Gandhi.

Karan Johar: All right. Well, that was fun, was it not?

Shabana Azmi: It was not so bad!

Karan Johar: All right. Now, it is Shobha's turn. The worst Indian film you saw recently?

Shobha De: *Bride and Prejudice*.

Karan Johar: An overrated actor in Hindi cinema?

Shobha De: Aamir Khan.

Karan Johar: An underrated actor in Hindi cinema?

Shobha De: Irfan Khan.

Karan Johar: Page 3 is? Complete the sentence.

Shobha De: Always a good read.

Karan Johar: The next deserving statue at Madame Tussauds would be of?

Shobha De: Whoever gets the desi rupees into paying 18 euros to see a wax figure!

Karan Johar: If you had to cast the lead of your book *Starry Nights*, whom do you take?

Shobha De: I cannot think beyond Rekha.

Karan Johar: The sexiest man in India is?

Shobha De: P. Chidambaram.

Karan Johar: The worst reaction for your column?

Shobha De: Amar Singh.

Karan Johar: The current rumour afloat?

Shobha De: That Manmohan Singh is not in fact, hands-on prime minister!

Karan Johar: *Masoom* or *Arth*?

Shabana Azmi: *Arth*.

Karan Johar: An overrated actor in Hindi cinema?

Shobha De: Aamir Khan.

Karan Johar: The next deserving statue at Madame Tussauds would be of?

Shobha De: Whoever gets the desi rupees into paying 18 euros to see a wax figure!

Karan Johar: The best-dressed Indian woman?

Shobha De: Muzzafar Ali's wife.

Karan Johar: The worst dressed Indian woman?

Shobha De: Aishwarya Rai.

Karan Johar: Godrej, Ambani, Birla – your favourite industrialist family?

Shobha De: Yash is a serious cutie. I want to adopt him. Then, the Godrej's; I have known them for over thirty years. And the Ambani's, I like their guts and dare.

> **Yash Birla is a serious cutie – I want to adopt him!**
> *–Shobha De*

Karan Johar: Shabana Azmi is.... Complete the sentence.

Shobha De: Hugely talented, though even she doesn't know how much. She can never be anything but great.

Karan Johar: My sentiments exactly if that means anything.

Shabana Azmi: My God! You have touched me.

Karan Johar: Page 3 or editorials?

Shobha De: Why pick? Editorials are Page 3 specimens now!

Karan Johar: All right! Yash Chopra glamour or Ram Gopal Verma's reality?

Shobha De: More glamour in Ram Gopal's reality.

Karan Johar: Politicians or film actors?

Shobha De: I have no time for either!

Karan Johar: OK. Shahrukh Khan or Hrithik Roshan?

Shobha De: Shahrukh Khan.

Karan Johar: Socialites or journalists?

Shobha De: Does one have to pick? I mean without socialites, what would the poor journalists do?

Karan Johar: That is the end of my Rapid Fire round. Very well done. Now who is the winner?

> **Without socialites, what would the poor journalists do?**
> *–Shobha De*

Shabana Azmi: We are confident that we will not going to fight over that hamper.

Karan Johar: Well, you are two lovely ladies. I will not choose a winner. Both of you won my coffee hamper.

Shabana Azmi: All right!

POLLING TIME

Karan Johar: We normally go to people to find out their opinion. We inquired from some women about their reaction. You know some people. Some are prominent women from various walks of life. We have approached a common friend – he is the only man in our segment who had something to say. Shobha and Shabana are attractive, inquisitive, sensitive and successful women in their fields. Shobha, like Shabana, really has brains. If you ask me whether she had balls than brains, I would say in the affirmative. Shabana is the other way – Shabana has more brains then balls.

SHABANA AZMI

Kajol: Shabana Azmi is definitely opinionated. She, you know, acts on her opinions.

Tabu: I really admire her for taking up the causes that she really believes in.

> **My only disappointment is that Shabana has been too politically correct, almost like a textbook case.**
>
> *–Kajol*

Farah Khan: She comes on television as an activist. She wants to address any gathering, waving the tricolour on a silent march for the cause. I think it takes a lot of courage with guts. I do not think any of us would step out of our air-conditioned homes or cars to walk down the dusty roads to secure rights for somebody.

Ekta Kapoor: I see a person who is not one dimensional in life. She is somebody who lives a full life. She is responsible to her family. She frames her own opinion. Being an activist, she cares for the weaker section of the society. She takes on good causes as part of her ethos. In *Arth*, she championed for women's rights.

Tabu: *Arth*, in which she had performed with unbelievable acting, was really something much ahead of her time.

Kajol: She stirs your conscience when you watch her. She is absolutely honest in whatever roles she adapts. Her onscreen chemistry remains innately powerful. My only disappointment is that she has been too politically correct, almost like a textbook case.

SHOBHA DE

Kajol: Shobha is mellow and more controlled. She is a complete Capricornian. I think she is another empowered woman in an apolitical environment, predicting something positive. Thank God for Shobha De!

> I think *Surviving Men* should be emulated like Biblical principles!
> —*Ekta Kapoor*

Tabu: Her opinion makes a remarkable difference.

Ekta Kapoor: I think *Surviving Men* should be emulated like Biblical principles. Because every young girl who gets married, it is the most awesome book with unprecedented analysis on men vis-à-vis women. Every diligent citizen realizes her waves of positivity when they begin to assimilate her vibes through her acidic remarks in the columns.

> Sometimes, I feel her columns are much biased. I think the next one will be me!
> —*Farah Khan*

Farah Khan: Sometimes, I feel her columns are much biased. 'Oh, God! Help that poor person in the column!' I think the next one will be me!

SHOBHA AND SHABANA

Kajol: I admire her in lots of ways because she is quite aware where the rights of women are concerned. Shobha is willing to reinvent herself every five years. She always re-invents herself – either with a new haircut, or a new husband, or with a new name or surname, like the Indian Madonna!

Farah Khan: She is an extremely beautiful lady. She is very classy without any knowledge about films. Shobha and Shabana happen to be the survivors of nature's onslaught and the champions for the needy – irrespective of positions.

> **I hope I can be at least one-tenth of you women!**
> *—Ekta Kapoor*

Ekta Kapoor: I hope I can be at least one-tenth of you women!

Karan Johar: We thought you heard many nice things about yourself.

Shabana Azmi: Ah, really!

Shobha De: More, Karan!

Karan Johar: You want more? All right!

Gautam Rajadhyaksha: Hi, Shobha! Hi, Shabana! I think I am the only person who knows right from your school days. You have a lot of similarity regarding traits and values. I am so glad that I have known about your affinity with our socio-cultural values. Shobha and Shabana are really the women of the brigade of rights' loving women. They are formidable personalities. The influential men and women are rather frightened about their approach to the cause. Your images, ladies, substantiate the truth. You speak your

> **A secret – both of you get tongue-tied often with a sense of instant rapport!** ·
> *—Gautam Rajadhyaksha*

mind. You come up or write or react in a way that would evoke a certain kind of fright. A shocking revelation – you get tongue-tied often with a sense of instant rapport. So, therefore, I think the audience should know that both of you are not so formidable, but quite sweet in general.

Shabana Azmi: That is very incisive of him, really.

Shobha De: Really, that was lovely. I am definitely a woman's woman.

Karan Johar: Anything you want to share with us on their comments?

Shobha De: I think it was all pretty fair. It is something that one needs to pay attention to.

Karan Johar: Well, that's great then, if it had made any kind of difference. And what about you, Shabana?

Shabana Azmi: I am overwhelmed. I was deeply touched by what Ekta and Kajol have observed.

Karan Johar: All right! Well, thank you so much for being on the show. I had the best time!

Shabana Azmi: Yeah! It was fabulous. I enjoyed it very much.

Karan Johar: It is just the way I wanted it. Thank you for sparing your valuable time. Shobha, you will find a koffee mug right there. You should sign the mug with the silver pen. Remember, this personally autographed mug can be yours only if you participate in the koffee quest contest. Let us proceed towards the koffee wall. Thank you so much.

• • •

Abhishek Bachchan & Preity Zinta
The Livewires

He is the son of a living legend. He is probably the most eligible bachelor in the country. Every mother wants to marry her daughter to him. Every daughter wants him to suddenly emerge on the Indian celluloid as the sexiest man. The girls just could not get enough of him. He is ready to bed, wed and knock you dead.

ABHISHEK BACHCHAN

Karan Johar: Let us welcome Abhishek Bachchan on the show. Hello and welcome, Abhishek, to *Koffee with Karan.*

Abhishek Bachchan: Thank you, Karan.

Karan Johar: How does it feel to revisit the show?

Abhishek Bachchan: Not too happy.

Karan Johar: Why? Are you unhappy? You are back on popular demand. We got emails, snail mails, and phone calls galore to bring junior B back with a daring and ebullient girl. Why do you think that has happened?

Abhishek Bachchan: They justify that since I did not win the *Koffee with Karan koffee hamper* last time, they availed me an opportunity. So, I am back.

Karan Johar: Do not tell me you are still sulking!

Abhishek Bachchan: Actually, I am.

THE MOST ELIGIBLE BACHELOR

Karan Johar: We will talk about your new single, sexy status. What does it really feel like? I am quite shocked. You were just a brat, who was my childhood friend. You are sexy. Do you believe it? You have women hitting on you all the time.

Abhishek Bachchan: No!

Karan Johar: Of course, you do. Your father is not here. Come on man, talk to me.

Abhishek Bachchan: No, really, I do not.

Karan Johar: Of course, you told me. I have a lie-o-meter.

Abhishek Bachchan: No.

Karan Johar: Contemporary heroines do not hit on you?

> It is very embarrassing that people have labeled me as a sex symbol.
>
> –*Abhishek Bachchan*

Abhishek Bachchan: They hit me like I told you the last time.

Karan Johar: They hit you. That ended well. The whole world wants to know. You are the eligible bachelor. They say you are sexy. Acknowledge it or justify what they want from you. Come on, talk to me!

Abhishek Bachchan: It is very embarrassing.

Karan Johar: Do you mean about the sex appeal?

Abhishek Bachchan: No.

Karan Johar: Then?

Abhishek Bachchan: Just, to think that people have labeled me so. Every actor should remain pure at heart rather than conducting himself to the whims of the public.

> Every actor should remain pure at heart rather than conducting himself to the whims of the public.
>
> —*Abhishek Bachchan*

WINNING THE SCREEN AWARD

Karan Johar: You have scored *minus two* for boring answers. OK. Come on, continue. We shall have a lady to join you. Congratulations on your first major award. You have won your first SCREEN award for your splendid performance in *Yuva*. You won the supporting actor award, did you not?

Abhishek Bachchan: Yes.

Karan Johar: The very interesting point the host of the show, Sajid Khan, sought to know was how would you fit the bill as supporting actor? There was no main character in the film, other than supporting ones like Vivek and Ajay. You were just supporting the director.

Abhishek Bachchan: It was very sweet of Sajid. I remember when the movie was released, he told me so. The film *Yuva* depicts the career of three young men. After watching the film, I feel the main protagonist was none other than Ajay. The supporting actors have parallel roles independent of one another. I feel honoured on his recommendation to show my debut in such a film.

Karan Johar: Let us talk about the real feeling about winning your SCREEN Award. Did you want to just wake up and yell out and say, My God! I have won my first major award!'

Abhishek Bachchan: I shall tell you a secret – I was asleep.

Karan Johar: Were you asleep while getting the award?

Abhishek Bachchan: No. Not that. The show was earmarked to commence at 6 p.m. sharp. I remember it was 7.30 p.m. Dad walked

> In *Yuva*, the main protagonist was none other than Ajay.
>
> —*Abhishek Bachchan*

into my room. He told me to wake up. I replied that I had been shooting continuously, so I was relaxing for the night. I had to admit I was very apprehensive to go.

> **I was fast asleep when I got the SCREEN award!**
> *–Abhishek Bachchan*

Karan Johar: Were you apprehensive to win the first major award? Why?

Abhishek Bachchan: Nobody knew whether I would win the award.

Karan Johar: Nobody knew, are you sure?

Abhishek Bachchan: I did not know.

Karan Johar: OK. Congratulations! You deserve that award. Your performance was brilliant in *Yuva.*

PREITY ZINTA

Karan Johar: You know who our next guest is?

Abhishek Bachchan: Yes, I do.

Karan Johar: OK. She has been whistling from behind. She will do so, when she arrives here. All right, I am not going to introduce her. She had been on the show before. I want you to introduce her, who has been part of your life quite recently.

Abhishek Bachchan: OK. Karan's next guest is somebody whom I consider to be very special and a very good friend. She is Preity Zinta, a very talented actress. And more importantly, she is a wonderful human being. It is great fun, indeed.

Karan Johar: Who suddenly stopped talking after I introduced her the last time as somebody who talks, talks and talks!

> **I call Preity Zinta the new Basanti!**
> *–Abhishek Bachchan*

Abhishek Bachchan: Which, actually, is a record to get Preity Zinta to stop talking! It is a feat, which should be entered into the Guinness Book of World Records. So, ladies and gentlemen, without much appreciation, I would like to invite on to stage the new Basanti!

Karan Johar: You call her Basanti. We call her Basanti. Well, let's welcome the Basanti of Bollywood, Preity Zinta. Hello darling! Welcome back.

Preity Zinta: Thank you.

Abhishek Bachchan: Where would you like to sit?

Preity Zinta: Here is good, thank you.

Abhishek Bachchan: Are you comfortable? Can I get you something? Some tea?

Preity Zinta: I want some tapes to shut your mouths! Since you have called me talkative, now I will become passive.

Karan Johar: All right, we are not interested now. What happened has happened.

Preity Zinta: No, it's nice to be on the show.

Karan Johar: Excuse me.

Abhishek Bachchan: Can't you see we are talking?

Karan Johar: Excuse me, you are talking to me, this is my show. And I am not talking to you. Now, I am talking to her.

Abhishek Bachchan: Listen, you have called us back, so we will do what we want. Last time, we said what we had to say.

Karan Johar: All right.

Abhishek Bachchan: We've nothing to say; we are here just to catch up.

> **Abhishek rocked in *Yuva*.**
> *–Preity Zinta*

Preity Zinta: Yeah!

Karan Johar: Hello, Preity! Welcome back to *Koffee with Karan* again.

Preity Zinta: Thank you Karan.

Karan Johar: How does it feel to be back on this sofa?

Preity Zinta: Well, it is great.

PREITY ON THE SCREEN AWARDS

Karan Johar: We were chatting about Abhishek initially. I was just congratulating him on winning his first major award for *Yuva*. Have you congratulated him?

Preity Zinta: Yeah, I thought that was awesome. I saw *Yuva*, Abhishek – you have rocked in *Yuva*.

Karan Johar: The very show he won it in - at the very award ceremony he won for *Yuva* – you lost for *Veer Zara*. Your sentiments?

Abhishek Bachchan: Nobody loses; it is all about participating like you spoke in the last show, Karan. Exactly.

Preity Zinta: You win some, you lose some.

Karan Johar: Well, I always say that you never really win the silver; you lose the gold. So how did you feel really, Preity, not winning for *Veer Zara*? It was a major film of the year.

> **Although *Veer Zara* did extremely well, I would still vote for *Yuva*.**
>
> *–Preity Zinta*

Preity Zinta: OK. I believe the film did really well. I was really appreciated by the people concerned. The award does not belong to the choice of the people, though I would still vote for *Yuva*.

Abhishek Bachchan: I shall translate what Preity said. 'I cannot be the one who lost. Rani was nominated. She was the best supporting actress. She should have won the best actress award. I could not show up.' Right? That was the translation.

Karan Johar: Is that were you thinking, Preity? Well done.

Preity Zinta: No.

Karan Johar: You said that it was an unpopular choice. Do you think the jury was unfair?

Preity Zinta: No, no, jokes apart, I don't want to get into any of that.

Karan Johar: Why?

Preity Zinta: Because on your show, I would rather prefer you to press the lie-o-meter. Twenty people have performed after I left the scene.

Karan Johar: OK. How could you not win the award for *Veer Zara*?

Preity Zinta: I have won *Jodi No. 1*.

PREITY – THE RESERVED

Karan Johar: Was it with Shahrukh? Let us revert to your antecedents. You have had problems for some time. There were times when you were not even acknowledging each other.

Preity Zinta: That was not the true picture.

Abhishek Bachchan: No, that's not true at all.

Preity Zinta: We were very cordial.

Abhishek Bachchan: We worked together though Preity seldom acknowledged me.

> **Preity seldom acknowledged me although we worked together.**
>
> *–Abhishek Bachchan*

Preity Zinta: You know I am trying to be very proper and nice. So, do not ruin things.

Karan Johar: Lovely Preity, there was a time, when there was discomfort. Something to do with his former girlfriend?

> **I did not know Abhishek nor believed in getting friendly with him.**
> *—Preity Zinta*

Abhishek Bachchan: No, it was not that.

Karan Johar: There must have been in the history.

Abhishek Bachchan: We dined together last night. I remember what I said on the national television.

Preity Zinta: Well, I will not listen. I wished him everytime I met him. I did not know about him nor believed in getting friendly with him. I did not know him that well.

Karan Johar: Of course, there was a problem. The media roared when you distanced away from Karishma, your former girlfriend. Do you feel that as the reason for discomfort?

Preity Zinta: No, that was not. I did not know them. If you do not know somebody, you just stay away. Do you know why?

Karan Johar: You wanted to distance yourself from Karishma and her boyfriend.

Preity Zinta: Yeah, exactly.

Karan Johar: Did that bother you at times that Preity had abstained from wishing you? She was your contemporary.

Abhishek Bachchan: It did not make any difference.

Karan Johar: No?

Preity Zinta: Keep quiet. You complained last night about the way you were upset.

Abhishek Bachchan: No. I just thought that you behaved badly.

> **I wanted to distance myself from Karishma and her boyfriend.**
> *—Preity Zinta*

Preity Zinta: Really?

Karan Johar: Preity is not a badly behaved girl. I consider her to be one of the best-behaved girls.

Abhishek Bachchan: Yeah, because you are Karan Johar. She has to suck up to you.

Preity Zinta: Totally.

Karan Johar: That is untrue.

Abhishek Bachchan: I am just kidding.

Karan Johar: Preity is one of the best-behaved girls. In fact, I used

> **Preity is possibly one of the few actors in the industry who always have their protocol.**
> *–Abhishek Bachchan*

to wonder why she was not nice to me, even though I was Karan Johar. Why did she not wish me?

Abhishek Bachchan: Can I talk to her? I had to vouch for something. She is possibly one of the few actors in the industry, who always has her protocol.

Preity Zinta: Thank you.

Abhishek Bachchan: No, really, seriously, I have told you earlier.

Karan Johar: How did you hit that?

Preity Zinta: Thanks to you and the rumour that you have created.

SMOKE AND FIRE

Karan Johar: It did not happen when we spoke about that the last time. Tell me, the disturbing rumour afloat is the fun. I believe it has just brought you closer as friends.

Preity Zinta: I think I love Abhishek. I really do.

Karan Johar: Is that a declaration or what?

Preity Zinta: We hung out when I met Abhishek for the first time in Aditya Chopra's house. I conversed with him that evening.

Karan Johar: You really thought him to be the chilled out, cool guy?

> **I think I love Abhishek; I really do!**
> *–Preity Zinta*

Preity Zinta: Yeah. Abhishek was so chilled out when I came out of the house.

Abhishek Bachchan: You did not say, of course, that I dropped you home that night, with you in the car, Karan?

Karan Johar: OK. I was inside the car.

Preity Zinta: I believe you have a selective memory.

Karan Johar: OK. You thought he should have been cool. I believe you were kind of a hit with each other.

Preity Zinta: And we are Aquarians!

Karan Johar: All right! What about you? How did you perceive Preity when you broke ice with her following such an encounter? I hope you guys are really friendly.

Abhishek Bachchan: Well, when you do not know somebody on a personal level, everybody tends to shape up opinions, which is unfair.

Preity Zinta: Yeah!

> **I knew Preity was going to be really cool and would be great fun to be with!**
>
> *–Abhishek Bachchan*

Abhishek Bachchan: I had a very set notion of what Preity Zinta should be like.

Karan Johar: Really? What was that?

Abhishek Bachchan: I noticed something nice when I saw her conducting herself in the public through her interview.

Preity Zinta: I know.

Abhishek Bachchan: I have found her to be fiercely independent in the profession. Somebody who knows her *modus operandi*, knows what she wants to do. She seems to be chilled out. She might have lived in a bubble or she was on guard. It was like what you saw is what you got. I always thought that after that evening. At first, we hung out and began to meet on a regular basis. The same thing came across. I knew Preity was going to be really cool and would be great fun to be with. I mean, we never had the opportunity to hang out before – we have only worked together. I knew that Preity would certainly rock.

Karan Johar: Preity, have you ever been attracted to Abhishek?

Preity Zinta: Yes, Karan! He has been ignoring me.

Karan Johar: Oh God! Be serious. No attraction, not even the slightest bit?

Preity Zinta: No. I have the immediate comfort zone with Abhishek. It was before we could look at each other. A mad conversation flew around the air. We just hit off as best friends.

Karan Johar: It could have been a great relation for lonely hearts? It never happened.

Preity Zinta: It could have rocked. I love him too much to get together. You have to fight once you get together.

Abhishek Bachchan: We hung out from the first day, but the tempo

> **Abhishek and I just hit off as best friends!**
>
> *–Preity Zinta*

weaned out later. It was instantly just, when we hit it off.

Preity Zinta: Yeah, we just became good friends.

Abhishek Bachchan: We were completely normal when we met. There was no pretense. She

> **If I look at Abhishek, I say 'Wow!'**
> *–Preity Zinta*

was just being the mad person that she was. She was quite mad than I was.

Karan Johar: Tell me. She was being mad. You were being mad. She was a rock chick. You were you this cool stud. Nothing happened. Were you attracted like a man to another woman?

Abhishek Bachchan: No.

Karan Johar: An attraction is normal, I mean

Preity Zinta: Of course, it is very normal. I mean, if I look at Abhishek, I shall say 'Wow!' I must say that he has completely transformed since we met.

Karan Johar: Transformed?

Preity Zinta: I do not feel it that much in the sense of looks. I think there is another air to him even the way he appeared as a person. He is more cool, more relaxed, i.e., he has more confidence. I remember when Abhishek was really sweet in the last show. Saif jumped on to me and cried, 'Sweet! He is sexy!' Now, I can reply, 'Abhishek is really sexy!'

Karan Johar: Are you happy with the equation? Don't you feel missed out of the relation at all?

> **Preity will make you smile the minute you meet her!**
> *–Abhishek Bachchan*

Abhishek Bachchan: Not at all, Karan. In fact, I am just happy. You know, she is truly a special friend. She can say anything upfront and have a lot of fun. She is somebody to make you smile the minute you meet her. You can feel totally relaxed. She is very true and tells you on your face if she dislikes something. She is honest to have lot of fun around. People might think of her as being intense. You know the person who is passive would not have dimples or appear not so bubbly. You know, Preity Zinta remains bubbly, dimple faced, and smiling forever. She is really a kind of reclusive lady with fun radiating around her.

Karan Johar: OK. I have smelt of an equation that nothing bad will emerge.

Abhishek Bachchan: You better, because you are the only hopper.

Karan Johar: Did you get calls from the family after your encounter with Abhishek Bachchan?

Preity Zinta: Oh! My God! It was great! I am his fan and fan-o-meter. I know many of his fans from the calls I have received from women.

Karan Johar: You are lucky to see Abhishek Bachchan.

Preity Zinta: A lot of woman cried, 'Oh God! Abhishek!' I have replied to them as not seeing him. Really, we love him. So, I told them that I would inform them whenever I met him.

Abhishek Bachchan: Please tell your mother that I am such a good friend. What was wrong with those people? Do not lie. Why did they think so?

Preity Zinta: He is fishing for compliments. OK?

Karan Johar: No. He knows. Do not worry for the big act.

Preity Zinta: No. I think my rumour with Abhishek went over the roof. There were some fortune-tellers, who spelt about our presence. The 'ROKA' is over.

> **Abhishek and my 'roka' is over!**
> –Preity Zinta

Abhishek Bachchan: What are you saying?

Preity Zinta: Yeah, yeah. My God! It had quite reached that stage.

Abhishek Bachchan: Karan, you are very influential.

Karan Johar: I spread the rumour far and wide.

THE BRICKBATS

Karan Johar: The girl with the dimple and boy with the puff, i.e., Preity Zinta and Abhishek Bachchan are finding which rumours were afloat.

Preity Zinta: The dimple is fine.

Abhishek Bachchan: What do you mean?

Karan Johar: Well, your puff is pronounced. I know a lot of people wanted it suddenly. I do not know why. Most actors in the fraternity face serious criticism. Preity Zinta is a huge star. She has a bubbly image on being a super star. Can she do more serious roles over a range? What do you feel when such criticism is being thrown at you?

Preity Zinta: I believe, Karan, that everybody is entitled to his share of opinion. When I watch a film, I have my own opinions. The opinion remains biased if I have performed for the friend of any journalist. A situation will brew if I fail to attend any party hosted by them. It is good to remain polite. I disagree with such biased opinions when it gets malicious. You can tell me, 'Preity, you were not that great in a movie.' I appreciate such criticism. When I abstain from your party and you report that my performance in the film was poor, I believe it is very wrong.

Karan Johar: I believe you were capable of doing various roles as an actor.

> **I disagree with biased opinions when it gets malicious.**
> –Preity Zinta

Preity Zinta: Yeah. Karan! You see, I have played the role of a prostitute, an unwed mother, a trainee sleuth of CBI, a grumpy sweet girl, a bubbly cherub, and an ace journalist. I believe my roles remained within the labyrinth of an Indian cinema. I am experimenting to accomplish whatever roles I have been assigned. I have also played the role of a schizophrenic in *Armaan*. But I will fail if I have not attained mastery over the role.

Karan Johar: Yeah.

Preity Zinta: I do not mind failing in my performance. I shall try to do better next time. You should adjudge whether I have fared well or not.

Karan Johar: There should not be bias as such.

Preity Zinta: No. There are no personal biases, because you are a journalist. I do not claim to be great for your criticism as a

> **I do not mind failing in my performance.**
> –Preity Zinta

journalist. You have the full right to criticize me as a responsible audience. You can scream at me because you have bought the ticket. I shall go there and try to perform better.

Karan Johar: All right. Well done. Abhishek! Criticism is on your way. The magnitude of criticism was high when you started. The people inquired about your performance level and your appearance. They said that you had put on weight at this age when you should be fit and muscular. You were somebody who had gone out of shape. You know about your voice modulation. People have questioned lot of such things. Did you reciprocate towards the detractors? Do you feel that you have learned from criticism galore?

Abhishek Bachchan: No, I do not like to do so. I shall thank them profusely.

Karan Johar: All right, did you agree with the comments made?

> **I thank the people profusely who criticise me!**
>
> *–Abhishek Bachchan*

Abhishek Bachchan: Initially, no. See, this industry makes you grow up very fast. I have realised that I remained an unprepared actor without any idea. It was like I was a child offered a toy. I jumped in and availed the opportunity to work with somebody like Mr. J P Dutta, which was unbelievable. You know, he used to treat me and Bebo as kids. He was taking care of us completely. We really had to do nothing in *Refugee*. He appeared controlled the show all the way. I realised to have a lot of work when I went on working outside production. You have to reorient your performance. I became very defensive at that point of time.

Karan Johar: I believe I had a certain amount of intrinsic arrogance with the actor, when I was young.

Abhishek Bachchan: I just used to brush them aside when the critics wrote me off. They were not performing at the box office with every successive movie. You tend to introspect about your being defensive with the audience as well. You know, we tend towards such opinion in the industry as 'Oh! They are journalists, critics or just somebody else. They buy tickets, watch your films and air their opinion about the film. Stop looking at it as a personal onslaught and look at it as a....'

Karan Johar: Are you trying to tell Preity that she should not take what the media blares at her, initially?

Preity Zinta: No, I think we have totally different points.

Abhishek Bachchan: She speaks about different things!

TÊTE-À-TÊTE

Preity Zinta: I would like to add here that when we had dined together, I told Abhishek, 'I feel really bad for your children.' So he told me that it would be quite tough for an outsider in the film industry.

Karan Johar: Yeah!

Preity Zinta: It is even tougher if you are the son or daughter of a superstar as your performance gets compared with other actors.

Karan Johar: Yeah.

Preity Zinta: I told him, 'I feel bad for your children as they will have your father or the grandfather or the grandmother to look into.' There will be Jaya Aunty, Amit-ji and I do not know whom Abhishek will marry.

> It would be quite tough for an outsider in the film industry.
> –*Abhishek Bachchan*

Karan Johar: So, he has accomplished great job by fighting against obstacles. I think you need to be applauded with the way you adapt. I heard about your appearance as shoddy, which shook me badly.

Preity Zinta: Yeah! It had been so even when I heard your name earlier that it was Abhishek Bachchan, so it shall be....

ON FLIRTING

Karan Johar: Have you seen him interacting with other women?

Preity Zinta: I have not. I have only seen him natural.

Karan Johar: OK. I will tell you something that struck me. Picture a scenario you do not know about this boy. He is Abhishek; you have never met him. He has been drinking in a nightclub or whatsoever when you walk in. He looks at you and you look at him. Both of you do not know each other. It is a hypothetical situation. You have liked his looks. What would you do? Would you like to converse with him? Remember, you are just two people; ignore your identity.

Preity Zinta: He wants us to entertain the whole world.

> I would never go up to a lady – I am too shy!
> –*Abhishek Bachchan*

Abhishek Bachchan: The thing is, Karan, I would never go up to a lady.

Karan Johar: Is that so?

Preity Zinta: You would not. That is so sad, because I would never go up to a guy.

Abhishek Bachchan: I am too shy. I refrain from going up to a lady.

Preity Zinta: I believe the man has to make the first move.

Karan Johar: OK. You have to pretend. What would you say?

Preity Zinta: OK. Come on, let us do something.

Abhishek Bachchan: I would sit by her. I have actually seen someone doing this. Somebody went up to this lady to give company in the bar.

> **Do you believe that love at first sight or should I walk in again?**
> *–Abhishek Bachchan*

Preity Zinta: OK. I will have a drink with him.

Abhishek Bachchan: A friend of mine took up the ice. I broke the ice with a friend of mine and asked his name.

Karan Johar: I believe you have replied and initiated the conversation.

Preity Zinta: What would you like it to be?

Abhishek Bachchan: Next. I will get up when she said to get up.

Karan Johar: Did he say that you have broken the ice?

Abhishek Bachchan: I got the simplest thing done for which I should credit, Karan, can I? Do you believe that love at first sight or should I walk in again?

Preity Zinta: Oh! Sorry honey, I am not wearing my lenses today.

Abhishek Bachchan: I would be saying that next.

Karan Johar: Is this the pick up line you would say, Abhishek.

Abhishek Bachchan: No, I do not know any pick up lines, Karan!

Preity Zinta: Yeah.

Abhishek Bachchan: I never managed to ask a lady out on date.

Preity Zinta: It is pretty disgusting if a guy comes up with a pick-up line.

Abhishek Bachchan: Say, I did not know anybody in such predicament. I found another guy hitting on Zinta and told her that I had hit him.

Preity Zinta: Yeah. Men deserve to be smacked, if they behave so!

> **I have never managed to ask a lady out on date!**
> *–Abhishek Bachchan*

Karan Johar: Tell me, Preity, what is the sleaziest pick-up line you came across?

Abhishek Bachchan: 'Do you want to become film actress?'

Preity Zinta: No, not that one. I have been very lucky and heard things like. 'I have met you before.' Or, 'Is that a lovely dimple or something else?' I never got sleazy pick-up lines.

Abhishek Bachchan: 'Have I seen you before?'

Preity Zinta: Yeah. Now that I am an actress, buy a ticket so that you could see me quite frequently!

Men deserve to be smacked, if they behave so!
–Preity Zinta

Karan Johar: All right. No sleazy pick-up. Well, what about you?

Abhishek Bachchan: I have never been tried.

Preity Zinta: What about you?

Karan Johar: Unfortunately, nobody has ever tried to pick me up. Let me know whether anybody has picked up so?

Preity Zinta: I believe – can I say this on TV?

Karan Johar: Yeah.

Preity Zinta: I believe somebody came to Karan. He was well built with photographs and everything. He came to Karan. I told him to do so if he needed a role in his movie. He replied to him to meet his assistant and wait for his answer after verifying his pictures. Karan looked at him after five seconds. He had been pleased to sit with him. It was as if the table was meant for him. He said, 'Karan! He has gone. I am ready to do anything!'

Abhishek Bachchan: Are you serious? This happened to you?

Karan Johar: Preity, that is something I told you behind the doors. Oh God! Thank you, Preity, for uttering things you were not supposed to. It is quite shocking, Abhishek.

Abhishek Bachchan: I am not virtually shocked.

Karan Johar: Were you not? We inquired about the sleaziest pick-up line ever heard of. Nothing of such sort happened. What about you?

Once, a lady walked in and asked me was she really a cute ass? I fainted!
–Abhishek Bachchan

Abhishek Bachchan: I remember there was not any sleazy pick-up. Yeah, there were direct offers.

Preity Zinta: Like?

Abhishek Bachchan: Once, a lady walked in and commented that she really had a cute ass?

Karan Johar: And what did she want to do?

Abhishek Bachchan: I fainted. I thought she was not speaking to me. I just inquired who she was. Did she actually speak to me?

Karan Johar: That is neither so bad, nor terrible.

Abhishek Bachchan: Yeah. My life was not that much exciting, Karan!

Preity Zinta: May be. It would have been terrible had she grabbed him and said so.

Karan Johar: So, did that happen?

Preity Zinta: Sorry, I am kidding.

Karan Johar: Did that happen?

Abhishek Bachchan: No.

RAPID FIRE

Karan Johar: We have a different take on the *Rapid Fire Round.*

Abhishek Bachchan: Oh! Come on.

Karan Johar: Yes, let us do it!

Preity Zinta: I have come for the hamper. We could share.

Abhishek Bachchan: No. My dad did not share it with me.

Karan Johar: Can you just give 30 seconds to explain the position?

Preity Zinta: OK.

Karan Johar: Please hold the buzzer on your hands.

Preity Zinta: Who answers first?

Karan Johar: I shall ask a question. You will press the buzzer – whosoever had the instant answer. I will reply, OK. I shall pass it on to the next person if you do not have the wittiest answer.

Abhishek Bachchan: Can you just demonstrate? It is fair enough.

Karan Johar: Are you willing to play this game with me?

Abhishek Bachchan: Anything for the coffee hamper!

Karan Johar: This time, you want it?

> I am ready to do *anything* for the koffee hamper!
> *–Abhishek Bachchan*

Abhishek Bachchan: I am ready to do anything, Karan!

Preity Zinta: Me too, Karan!

Karan Johar: You have behaved badly. OK. Brace yourself for the position. A silence follows when you are struck with Salman and Vivek in an elevator. How do you break the silence, Abhishek?

Abhishek Bachchan: OK. I am really nasty to you. I am trying to be witty.

Karan Johar: Yeah.

Abhishek Bachchan: So Vivek, please do not mind. Vivek, meet Salman and vice-versa.

> If stuck in a lift with Vivek and Salman, I would say, 'Vivek, meet Salman and vice-versa
> *–Abhishek Bachchan*

Karan Johar: All right. That is fine.

Abhishek Bachchan: I am really sorry. It was just fun.

Preity Zinta: No, I have got a better one.

Abhishek Bachchan: OK.

Preity Zinta: Vivek, meet Salman and Salman, beat Vivek!

Karan Johar: All right. We shall attend to a call on that later who won the answer. I will give Abhishek points as he came here as the first entrant.

Abhishek Bachchan: This does not reflect the position. We like both of them, for they are wonderful people.

Karan Johar: All right.

Abhishek Bachchan: It will be my hamper.

> Aishwarya is the most beautiful model.
> *–Preity Zinta*

Karan Johar: Abhishek won points. My second buzzer round question.

Abhishek Bachchan: I am ready to do anything – remember that, Karan.

Karan Johar: Aishwarya, Sushmita, Lara and Priyanka competing for the same beauty pageant. Who would get the crown and why?

Preity Zinta: Ash. She is the most beautiful model. I find her to be the most beautiful. Sorry guys. It is a beauty pageant.

Abhishek Bachchan: I will distribute it.

Preity Zinta: To all four of them, the crown?

Karan Johar: I never asked you, she won that point.

Preity Zinta: I have won. Keep quiet. Stop trying to get brownie points!

Karan Johar: All right. You have won that. You felt envious of competing with an actor the last time as your family was not included. Is it not so, Preity?

Preity Zinta: I think Tabu looks brilliant in *Maqbool*.

> I felt completely envious of Tabu in *Maqbool*
> *–Preity Zinta*

Karan Johar: Wish you had done that?

Preity Zinta: I do not know if I wish I could have done that. I have just looked at her. I wondered, 'Wow! Could I ever reach a stage where somebody else would look at me?'

Karan Johar: No reverence, I am talking about envy.

Preity Zinta: Yeah. I have felt completely envious. •

> **If an unattractive costar hits on me, I will say, 'Have you met Preity Zinta?'**
> –*Abhishek Bachchan*

Karan Johar: All right. It is great to have 2-1 now. Abhishek, brace yourself ahead and comment yourself whether a man or woman made a pass at you?

Abhishek Bachchan: No, thanks. She buzzed. I did not.

Karan Johar: Have you buzzed?

Preity Zinta: Please pass by.

Karan Johar: That is what your answer could be?

Preity Zinta: Yeah.

Abhishek Bachchan: So sad! I reply that that is a bad answer.

Karan Johar: Yeah.

Preity Zinta: OK. Please pass it to him.

Abhishek Bachchan: OK. Agreed. I would inquire whether he is willing to do 'anything?'

Karan Johar: All right. Abhishek, I will give you two points.

Abhishek Bachchan: Thank you.

Karan Johar: A co-star you were unattracted to, hits on you blatantly. Comment your way out of the situation.

Abhishek Bachchan: Have you met Preity Zinta?

Karan Johar: What does that mean?

Abhishek Bachchan: Just ask the question?

Karan Johar: Sorry.

Preity Zinta: I shall reply – wait for my action.

Abhishek Bachchan: Oh! Come on, she is just really bad.

> **I really dislike shooting steamy love scenes with Saif!**
> –*Preity Zinta*

Preity Zinta: What do you mean?

Karan Johar: Your performance had been poor.

An Indian co-star you dislike to make steamy love with and why?

Abhishek Bachchan: I have just pressed the button. It is the most pensive reaction.

Karan Johar: Press the button. I got to know the answer.

Preity Zinta: Thank God.

Karan Johar: You shall lead the race. Please answer.

Abhishek Bachchan: No, pass.

Preity Zinta: It has come to me.

Karan Johar: Exactly. Abhishek, that had really been so cool and uncool. Come on.

Preity Zinta: I think Saif fits the bill. I am performing with him in a movie. I believe I might have such scene with him.

Abhishek Bachchan: Oh, that's really a bad answer. Just merit on not answering, I should get that.

Karan Johar: I do not mean a scene you have performed with him Do you get really naughty? You think he is cool or attractive or sexy?

Preity Zinta: Abhishek, I want to win the hamper.

I do not share anything!
–Abhishek Bachchan

Abhishek Bachchan: I never thought about you in such manner.

Karan Johar: I will not give the hamper.

Preity Zinta: This is unfair. We shall share.

Abhishek Bachchan: I do not share anything.

Karan Johar: My seventh question to you. You were struck in a desert for many days. Would you succumb? Why?

Abhishek Bachchan: It is an animal instinct. 'Listen! We are stuck here. We will never get out. We have left our families behind. We must start afresh to remain civilized. Let us do it for the sake of mankind!'

Karan Johar: Great! Well done! 3-2, Abhishek, with that answer.

Preity Zinta: I shall answer that.

Abhishek Bachchan: You were going to?

Karan Johar: Your advice to the following film couples. Now, this is three-part question.

Abhishek Bachchan: OK.

Karan Johar: (a) Vivek and Aishwarya?

Abhishek Bachchan: No.

Karan Johar: (b) John and Bipasha?

Abhishek Bachchan: Leave John.

Karan Johar: Well done.

Abhishek Bachchan: Bips, I love you, I saw your show.

Karan Johar: 4-2. (c) Shaheed and Kareena?

Abhishek Bachchan: Hello.

Karan Johar: 5-2. Preity, come on.

Preity Zinta: Sorry, what to do?

Karan Johar: How do you react when caught by a camera in a compromising position?

Abhishek Bachchan: Yes, it was me. I am caught. I am a human being, so what? Sorry.

Preity Zinta: He cannot get a point. That is not witty.

Abhishek Bachchan: Of course, I should get a point.

Karan Johar: Do you have a witty reply?

Preity Zinta: No. I would not say anything.

Karan Johar: You still oscillate at 5-2. Abhishek, you would not gain points.

Abhishek Bachchan: Not good enough.

Karan Johar: All right. How do you react if an ad is being inserted in a matrimonial column?

Abhishek Bachchan: I will think about it that day when I do so.

Preity Zinta: 'Looking for a hero?'

Abhishek Bachchan: Yes, that should be it.

Karan Johar: OK. I will give you that Preity.

Abhishek Bachchan: No, I should get half, I said 'real.'

Preity Zinta: You cannot get half a point.

Abhishek Bachchan: 'Looking for my real hero.'

Preity Zinta: 4. Now, how much is the score?

Karan Johar: No, now it is 3-5. You are 3; he is 5. All right! Three more questions to go.

You can still win, Preity! Brace yourself ahead. You regret what you have not told to your former boyfriend?

Preity Zinta: 'Can I have my things back?'

Karan Johar: All right. A wonderful answer.

Abhishek Bachchan: Mind blowing, fantastic.

Karan Johar: A wonderful answer. 4-5. All right. Two more marks. You could still win, Preity. You lead by one point, Abhishek. An honest confession about yourself that you seldom shared with anyone.

Abhishek Bachchan: Is it so? I genuinely believed that I had every right to stay back when I entered the film industry. And I emerged often as the best.

> **Preity should seldom appear on *Koffee with Karan* because she talks too much!**
> *–Abhishek Bachchan*

Preity Zinta: But that is not witty.

Abhishek Bachchan: Yes. It is very hilarious. Have you not seen my films?

Preity Zinta: No, I am sorry.

Abhishek Bachchan: Have you not seen my films? You cannot give her this point. It is very unfair. Karan. It is too funny. Come on! See her films.

Karan Johar: One last question. The person who seldom wants to appear on *Koffee with Karan* and why?

Abhishek Bachchan: Preity Zinta because she talks too much and makes me look bad.

Preity Zinta: Do not give him the hamper.

Karan Johar: All right! This has been a very tiring buzzer round.

> **The *koffee hamper* means more to me than the SCREEN award!**
> *–Abhishek Bachchan*

Preity Zinta: No, this is very boring, Karan.

Abhishek Bachchan: Listen, I think I should win for the last one.

Karan Johar: I have the result.

Abhishek Bachchan: I am ready to do anything, Karan!

Preity Zinta: Me too!

Abhishek Bachchan: I need the *koffee hamper*.

Karan Johar: Preity, I am very upset. Look what you have done to my wonderful suit?

Preity Zinta: So, that is why you will give me the hamper. Is not it?

Karan Johar: Yes, now the winner of the *koffee hamper.*

Preity Zinta: Why are you pretending?

Karan Johar: Brace yourself. The winner is Abhishek Bachchan! Where is the hamper?

Preity Zinta: He has already stolen the hamper.

Karan Johar: You have already taken the hamper!

Preity Zinta: Give a 'thank you' note.

Abhishek Bachchan: He is a cheesy guy.

Karan Johar: Congratulations! How does it feel? Does it matter as much as your screen award did?

Abhishek Bachchan: Much more! You have no clue.

Karan Johar: OK.

Abhishek Bachchan: I have to tell you very honestly, I was really upset the last time when I was on your show. I did not win the hamper. I have believed often that I had earned it. Now, I am so happy. I shall thank my father and mother for their support. I would like to thank Karan Johar for presenting myself with such great work and potential.

Preity Zinta: And, most importantly, me!

> **I am lucky in love.**
> *–Preity Zinta*

Abhishek Bachchan: I would like to thank Preity Zinta, without whom this performance would not have been possible. I would like to thank Simi Aunty. She, however, remained my inspiration with the coffee makers around the world. Thank you so much. You have made me very happy. You really love me!

Karan Johar: You have lost it twice, Preity. Your sentiments?

Preity Zinta: Unlucky in hampers, lucky in love.

Karan Johar: I am sure. You are lucky in love. We have reached the last segment of the contest.

Abhishek Bachchan: Please tell me whether it has something to do with Mallika Sherawat at high speed.

Preity Zinta: What do you mean? Tell security to throw him out!

Abhishek Bachchan: Excuse me. I was very upset. I must say, 'Mallika, if you are watching this show, you are wonderful. I am a big fan of yours. Honestly, you have

> **Mallika Sherawat epitomised the Indian women for the Year 2005.**
> –*Abhishek Bachchan*

amazing guts with appreciable confidence. You epitomised the Indian women for the Year 2005. Baby, you have to see me run. I run almost like my dad!'

Karan Johar: OK. We have surveyed by visiting some seventy people. To café badly Mocha, to Fame Adlabs, colleges.

Abhishek Bachchan: All over the places in Mumbai?

Karan Johar: Yeah. Asked about the most eligible bachelor – Abhishek. Of course, who is the perfect Ms. Bachchan from the film fraternity? We had some very interesting observations.

Preity Zinta: OK. Let us see the survey.

F: Abhishek Bachchan! John Abraham?

M: Abhishek Bachchan.

F-F: Abhishek Bachchan. Abhishek Bachchan.

M-F: Abhishek Bachchan. Rahul Ghandhi.

M-M: Salman Khan. Zayed Khan.

F: Abhishek Bachchan.

M: Shahid Kapoor.

M: Abhishek Bachchan.

F: Abhishek Bachchan. He is the most eligible bachelor in India. I love him! He is single, and ready to mingle. He is the most handsome guy. He is very humble and hot, too.

M: Aby's baby.

F: He is naughty. He has the best smile ever. He has got a sexy physique.

M: All die for him. He is one of the hottest guys.

F: He is mad. He has got a perfect body. I really like his smile.

Abhishek Bachchan: She is the first lady, who said I had a perfect body.

F: He comes across a soft-spoken, levelheaded person. A gentleman.

Abhishek Bachchan: See the show, baby.

F: He is a charmer.

ON MRS. ABHISHEK BACHCHAN

M: She has to be very beautiful, someone very homely. He is the person who understands.

F: Somebody who is like Jaya ma'am. Bipasha Basu.

F: Aishwarya Rai. May be Preity Zinta. A nice beautiful, cute girl for him. He should marry someone like Rani Mukherjee.

M: Someone from the film industry.

F: I think a girl like Sushmita Sen will definitely match his personality. I think Rani Mukherjee or my friend will do. I am there; there is no other option for him.

> **We will be the only running couple – Mallika and Abhishek!**
> *–Abhishek Bachchan*

M: Should be a love marriage, definitely, with an actress. I guess, Preity Zinta.

F: Abhishek Bachchan, Preity Zinta – sweet.

M: I think he should get married to Preity Zinta.

F: I think they'll make a good match.

M: Preity is very cute. Both will look really cute together.

F: OK. No. He has got that rough look. He may be better with Sushmita.

Abhishek Bachchan: I am going away!

F: Preity is very bubbly. She does not fit with Abhishek Bachchan. I think she is too aggressive for him.

M: She is far too cute.

F: Both are really cute.

M: They resemble brothers and sisters.

F: I think she looks older to him, I do not know. I think she is too girly and bubbly, OK? He is like a man and she continues to be like a girl.

Abhishek Bachchan: Who is that? Rani.

F: Obviously, the best.

F: Abhishek and Rani make an awesome pair. I think they like each other, somewhere have a soft corner. No, he is too tall and she is too short. Rani Mukherjee is very good for Abhishek Bachchan. I think they would

gel easily. The family making life will be easier for him. They look like *made for each other*. So, I think Rani Mukherjee is the best.

M: Abhishek and Rani make a good pair.

F: No, she is too short, for him.

M: I think he pairs well with Rani Mukherjee.

F: I think he looks good with her.

M: Abhishek Bachchan and Priyanka Chopra will definitely look good together.

F: Abhishek Bachchan is too sophisticated for Priyanka Chopra. They are tall and are good looking with similar personality to pair well.

M: Abhishek is too good for Priyanka Chopra. No way.

Abhishek Bachchan: I am not too good for Priyanka Chopra.

M: He is hot, off screen, onscreen, or any screen.

F: Oh no! Abhishek Bachchan and Priyanka Chopra – no. Abhishek Bachchan and Priyanka Chopra pair well as she is dark and both of them have similar complexion. No! If he has no other choice, then Priyanka Chopra may meet his requirement.

M: Abhishek and Mallika Sherawat..... a complete mismatch.

F: Abhishek and Mallika Sherawat will be the best.

M: It would be a nightmare; never.

F: Abhishek is too cute to be with Mallika.

M: I think, Mallika Sherawat will be very interesting. I do not think Jaya Bachchan will like that pair. So, Abhishek will be kicked out of the house.

F: Abhishek and Mallika Sherawat look horrible together. I think she is more crazy for Amitabh Bachchan. You know, so it is better not to get married to Abhishek.

M: Abhishek Bachchan would be simple. She would be hot to handle. That is a very hot combination.

F: Yes, yes! No. She will be too bold for him. Yeah, I think, he will be running.

Abhishek Bachchan: We will be the only running couple – Mallika and Abhishek.

F: Yeah, they look good together, definitely.

Abhishek Bachchan: I would love to run with Mallika.

F: No way. Abhishek Bachchan, we love you. We think you should marry a girl who will give you the same love as we have for you. Abhishek Bachchan, this is for you!

Abhishek Bachchan: Preity, you lost.

Preity Zinta: Rani!

Abhishek Bachchan: I have two things to say.

Preity Zinta: You shall make a good pair with Rani.

Abhishek Bachchan: Preity, do not despair. I know you lost yet again. It is OK. Secondly, I want to say one thing to Priyanka. Uday and me have the biggest crush on you. And I could be a couple with you any time.

> **Uday and I have the biggest crush on Priyanka Chopra!**
>
> *–Abhishek Bachchan*

Preity Zinta: So, do you agree before the show gets over that I do not talk that much? He talks more than me.

Karan Johar: I am sorry – he is the clear winner in that department.

Preity Zinta: I have lost there, too.

Karan Johar: Sign that mug, darling. Please remember, this personally autographed mug could be yours only if you answer the questions on the *Koffee Quest* contest. Thank you, Abhishek. Again, thank you, Preity. Thank you for coming back.

Abhishek Bachchan: It was our pleasure. We had a lot of fun. I hope we have not scandalised many people.

Karan Johar: No, I am sure, you have not.

Abhishek Bachchan: It was all in jest and good fun.

Preity Zinta: There is no offence to anybody. I do not think it was meant like that.

Abhishek Bachchan: That is diplomatic.

Preity Zinta: It is not so.

Abhishek Bachchan: If you laugh at yourself, we shall laugh at people who make fun of us.

Preity Zinta: We thought it was only three of us. Us, you and the Star TV.

Abhishek Bachchan: Remember, we are ready to do anything to get the *Koffee hamper*, Karan! Anything!

Karan Johar: We are going to take that coffee mug. I cannot take both of you anymore. Let us take the coffee mug and proceed to the coffee wall.

Abhishek Bachchan: End the show, thank you.

● ● ●

16

Rahul Bose & Konkona Sen
Mr. and Mrs. Iyer

My guest is someone who has made her presence felt in a short time. She has been sincere, natural, and at ease. An unconventional appeal made her occupy the acme in the cinematic chart. Critics and sensible audiences love her. You might have seen her on *Page 3* or in *Mr. and Mrs. Iyer*. Here is an actress to stay. Let us welcome Aparna Sen's daughter and the National Award winning actress, Konkona Sen Sharma.

KONKONA SEN SHARMA

Karan Johar: Welcome to *Koffee With Karan*, Konkona!

Konkona Sen: Thank you!

Karan Johar: How does it feel?

Konkona Sen: I am so excited!

Karan Johar: Are you ready for the ride?

Konkona Sen: Except for the rapid fire!

Karan Johar: Are you worried about your rapid fire?

Konkona Sen: Yes, because all your guests get very nervous – I have seen that.

Karan Johar: I do not think you will falter, as you are a confident girl!

KONKONA ON HER SUCCESS

Karan Johar: How does it feel to be on page three? You are on page three because you are a successful mainstream actress.

Konkona Sen: I am surprised and grateful. I have no expectations from any movie – you never know. I have enjoyed it. You cannot please everybody. I am happy and I am very grateful because it is sheer luck!

> **I have no expectations from any movies!**
> –*Konkona Sen*

Karan Johar: When you got the script, did you think Madhur Bhandarkar was a mainstream filmmaker?

Konkona Sen: I did not know about him. I had only seen *Chandni Bar* and really liked it. He actually called to congratulate my mother on *Mr. and Mrs. Iyer*. I liked the concept of *Page 3*. I replied in the affirmative and heard the script later.

Karan Johar: I did not know that Kareena Kapoor had been offered the role before you. Do you feel that a film like *Mr. and Mrs. Iyer*, a wonderful and credible film made by your mother, could not fetch the audience despite getting a national award while you tasted mainstream success after *Page 3*? Everyone knows who Konkona Sen Sharma is today because of *Page 3*, not because of the film *Mr. and Mrs. Iyer*.

Konkona Sen: It does not really matter to me either way. People may not like my next movie. I am just grateful for the moment.

On Mainstream Cinema

Karan Johar: What are your views on accepting mainstream films?

Konkona Sen: I like those that are fun. I enjoy watching the occasional mainstream film. Most of them are not great. I would not mind trying one or two. I will be very good at it.

Karan Johar: Tell me which mainstream film you liked.

Konkona Sen: *Main Hoon Na.*

Karan Johar: Was it like a joyride?

Konkona Sen: It was a little long.

Karan Johar: Even *Kal Ho Naa Ho* was long but so much fun!

Konkona Sen: Yeah! I want to do all kinds of things.

Karan Johar: You have done some great films with Rahul Bose. You have done *Mr. and Mrs. Iyer.* I believe you are doing another film together with your mother?

Konkona Sen: Yes. It is called *15, Park Avenue.* The cast includes Rahul, Shabana Azmi, Waheeda-ji and lots of other great actors. I play a schizophrenic.

Karan Johar: Are you in any way closer to the character?

Konkona Sen: Yeah, I think I am!

Karan Johar: Do you know our next guest?

Konkona Sen: I wonder who he must be?

Rahul Bose

Karan Johar: My next guest is someone whose butt shot in *English August* was a talking point for quite some time. He has done an enviable lot of niche audience films that have left an indelible mark on the minds of sensible cine goers. Let us call the multiplex man himself, Rahul Bose! Hello and welcome!

Rahul Bose: Thank you!

The English August Butt Shot

Karan Johar: True butt shot! It got talked about quite a lot.

Konkona Sen: I do not remember the butt shot!

Rahul Bose: Someone asked me the other day in an interview whether I saw a man masturbating under a sheet for that shot. I replied that the film was much bigger than that!

> Someone asked me if I saw a man masturbating under a sheet for the butt shot in *English August!*
>
> – Rahul Bose

Karan Johar: Suddenly, the media picked up things like Rahul Bose and his naked butt!

> It is time to give one more butt shot!
>
> – Rahul Bose

Rahul Bose: Media was not so cynical a decade back. Now, I would have to eat my words to remain alive!

Karan Johar: Are you the most spoken about actor?

Rahul Bose: Time to give one more butt shot!

Mr. and Mrs. Iyer

Karan Johar: We were just talking about the terrific interaction the two of you have had.

Rahul Bose: Onscreen, of course, in *Mr. and Mrs. Iyer.*

Karan Johar: Was that a good experience?

Rahul Bose: Yes, it was.

Konkona Sen: The best! It was my best movie. I had the most fun on the sets.

Karan Johar: Wonderful! What about you?

Rahul Bose: It is very rare, Karan, that you get five or six factors coinciding beautifully – like a great director, a great story, a great role, great co-actors, and aligned socio-politically. It was like the alignment of planets once in a million years!

Karan Johar: We spoke about the divided audience for a film like *Mr. and Mrs. Iyer. Page 3* blared the audience as niche, which gave ultimate recognition en masse. Comment on the film that is not appreciated by the massive audience.

> *Mr. and Mrs. Iyer* was like the alignment of planets once in a million years!
>
> – Rahul Bose

Rahul Bose: *Mr. and Mrs. Iyer* was released in English. It could have been very well appreciated if the Hindi version would have been screened. It was a love story. Unfortunately, most of the audience were able to digest English but could not speak the language. That was the reason that it ran for some 14 weeks across the country.

Rahul Bose: There were terrible Hindi films made earlier that used to vanish from the screens in two days. Your audience reach will get stymied if you make any film in English or any vernacular language other than the *lingua franca*.

Karan Johar: Are you reducing your audience reach?

Karan Johar: Yes; we shall prune the reach by 80 per cent.

Karan Johar: How will the English film run? Quite recently a film called *Black* was made. Was it because of Amitabh Bachchan and Rani Mukherjee that it opened quite slowly and became a big hit? 70 per cent of the film was in English.

Rahul Bose: Nobody knew it was in English! Everybody thought it was a Hindi film.

Karan Johar: The problem was many people abstained from watching the film.

Konkona Sen: It was a nice film with dialogues in English and Hindi.

Rahul Bose: It had Amitabh Bachchan and Rani Mukherjee. We are speaking about a man who is a legend of modern cinema. There would have been people out to call it fantastic even if he did it in Swahili!

Karan Johar: Do you believe that films like *Black* made new inroads into the mainstream cinema?

Rahul Bose: I would be skeptical. It takes a certain kind of a filmmaker to pull out something like that. I see no reason why anyone should emulate the language of *Black* until such filmmakers emerge. You should do things in a film with honesty and joy. It does not matter if it is Icelandic or whatever it is being called.

THE GOOD, THE BAD, AND THE UGLY

Karan Johar: Rahul! How do you contrast between parallel cinema, art and commercial cinema?

Rahul Bose: Good and bad films coexist. Why slot it if you are making a good film?

> Why slot a film into parallel, art or commercial cinema? There are just good and bad films.
> *–Rahul Bose*

Rahul Bose: To make money, you have to look at the latest model of film that was the most successful in the market, and replicate that. Your impulses are clearly towards making money in such a case.

Karan Johar: You hang the quality and everything else if you are making a film just to make money, which means you have to follow the most successful formula.

Rahul Bose: Which makes it tried and it's not new. Any other kind of cinema made as valid should be good for the audience.

Karan Johar: Your take on this, Konkona?

> I have never identified with any of the characters of late!
> *– Konkona Sen*

Konkona Sen: I never think about it. On being an actor, I have to like the director, approve the script, etc. Who shall care for you after completing the film?

ROLE SELECTION

Karan Johar: I shall offer you a situation. A big mainstream filmmaker comes to you with an offer. Would you reject him for the lack of understanding about his script?

Konkona Sen: I have never identified with any of the characters of late.

Karan Johar: There is a commercial film like *Main Hoon Na* you have enjoyed. Will you do the role of a sexy chemistry teacher if it came to you?

Konkona Sen: Are you insane? No chance! I am Mrs. Iyer.

Karan Johar: You said that you were unable to lip synch in between breaks.

> Me a sexy chemistry teacher? No chance! I am Mrs. Iyer!
> *–Konkona Sen*

Konkona Sen: I have never tried it. It seems a little inane but if it's fun like *Main Hoon*

Naa with a sense of fun, then it is ok. I seldom believe you make films only with a message – you make them only for entertainment!

Karan Johar: Lip-synching songs is not a real situation. Could you identify various other aspects to endorse the view?

Konkona Sen: It depends on whether the movie has a great spirit of joy like *Main Hoon Na* or *Chicago*. I would like to do different kind of things, something unique, which is fun and big.

Karan Johar: So, you are not averse to it. Rahul! What about you? I recollect your performance in *Jhankar Beats* where you failed to identify with the environs you had to adapt. Can you tell us the reason? Did you feel that it was slightly a mainstream film?

> **People have walked out when songs flabbergasted them.**
> *–Rahul Bose*

Rahul Bose: I did *Jhankaar Beats* because of the perception that I was the intense actor for underplay.

Karan Johar: You did that to prove a point?

Rahul Bose: Yes, absolutely. I have horsed around a lot on stage and I had to get it off my back – so I did the film. I actually believe in films that grip me in their narrative. I definitely do not need songs! Am I against musicals?

Karan Johar: Definitely not! I think they have intrinsic grammar. Stick to what you do.

Konkona Sen: You should not have to forward songs, you know! That happens a lot.

Rahul Bose: I watched *Jhankar Beats* with my sister at home. She asked me to fast forward the song. I told her that I could not recollect the film but that the song carried the narrative forward. That was cool – there is no hard and fast rule. It is just when you sense there is a lack of integrity in the filmmaker when he puts in a song when you interpret it as rubbish. I have watched the mainstream films where people have walked out when songs flabbergasted them.

Karan Johar: What happens is that those people who walk out actually can return in any case to see the film again some other time.

Karan Johar: What would you say to Konkona playing

> **If Konkona was the sexy chemistry teacher, there would be beads of sweat on her brow.**
> *–Rahul Bose*

a sexy chemistry teacher? She walks in very dowdy with her hair tied up and glasses. Suddenly, a tall, good-looking student walks up. Would you believe that it is action TV?

Rahul Bose: The strings of sexuality – that she should be sweating – there would be beads of sweat on her brow

WORLD CINEMA

Karan Johar: The common perception, Rahul, about you is that you have a disdain for commercial cinema.

Rahul Bose: There is a perception, but it is not true. I am obsessed with 95 per cent of the cinema in the world. In the last 10 years, which Hollywood cinema have you watched, which is good apart from a few here and there?

Karan Johar: Hollywood is full of crap! I think it is just untrue.

Rahul Bose: Hollywood has no integrity. I have been screaming it from the rooftop. 90 per cent of it is abysmal with influences from Hong Kong cinema! Italian cinema, 99 per cent of it is crap!

Karan Johar: And Indian cinema?

> **90 per cent of Indian cinema is crap!**
> *–Rahul Bose*

Rahul Bose: It is the same. 90 per cent of the Indian cinema is crap if you go by the ratio and proportion. It is just there. The audience goes like – 'What am I doing? What am I watching this for?' What I like now is that the audience has decided that it does not want to watch crap.

COMMERCE VS CONVICTION

Karan Johar: Sometimes, actors like you like having a lot of responsibility and so do not do commercial films. Do you feel that? Because it takes someone like Shahrukh Khan to do a scene with a song-and-dance number with conviction. It takes a different thought process and is far tougher than playing a real situation.

Konkona Sen: Absolutely.

Rahul Bose: I think it is far tougher and a valid point. I believe it is valid if I walked into a film like *Street Vaibhavpur*. I have played the role of a slum dweller from Mumbai after acquainting with the people from the slums. In *Kaalpurush,* I had increased five kilos on my stomach to propel the character of a middle class Bengali guy. The archetype loser's gesture needed to be revamped with intonation– that influenced me to attempt this role. I believed I had the wherewithal to do that, the reason being that I had been a superstar and had to play the role with conviction. I have been cast as a Shahrukh Khan kind of person in a film.

Karan Johar: Oh, you were offered a film within a film. But otherwise, you won't be able to put your hands up and do the song with conviction. Tell us, Konkona, do you have to necessarily be convinced before going for it?

Konkona Sen: I would commence with laughter if I had to do that!

Karan Johar: Will you sing a romantic number in Switzerland wearing a chiffon sari?

Konkona Sen: I think people would laugh at me!

Karan Johar: Would you laugh at yourself?

Konkona Sen: I do not know.

Karan Johar: Would you laugh at that film?

Konkona Sen: I may laugh watching the people do so. I do not think I can enact such a role.

> **People would laugh at me if I did a romantic number wearing a chiffon sari!**
> –*Konkona Sen*

Karan Johar: You think Kareena or Preity would have done it better?

Konkona Sen: Whoever it is, yes.

Karan Johar: Rahul disliked opening his arms and singing a number for a mainstream film.

Konkona Sen: He does not have to do it again!

On Exposing

Karan Johar: Did you like the look of that butt?

Konkona Sen: I do not remember it from the movie.

Karan Johar: Sad, Rahul. She doesn't remember your precious butt!

Rahul Bose: It is pure denial. She will be aflame with desire!

> *Konkona Sen:* I do not remember Rahul's butt from *English August.*
> *Rahul Bose:* It is pure denial. She will be aflame with desire!

Karan Johar: Has there been a vibe between both of you?

Konkona Sen: A vibe? Yes, I love him.

Karan Johar: Have *Mr. and Mrs. Iyer* been up to tricks?

Are you admitting then that there has been an affair?

Konkona Sen: Officially, will I get a coffee hamper if I admit that?

Karan Johar: Not on celluloid, my dear!

Rahul Bose: Can you imagine it? We are comfortable talking with Karan. Having an affair – what do you think?

Konkona Sen: No, dear.

Karan Johar: Nothing happened?

Rahul Bose: Any idea that her mother made the film?!

Karan Johar: Reverting to the butt, to what extent would you go for skin show – are you crude?

Konkona Sen: I dislike thinking about it. I am crude mentally, but I cannot show skin. No. Maybe if I had a gorgeous body – super hot – I would have loved to flaunt it.

Karan Johar: I saw you at a party – a still of yours in the *Bombay Times* newspaper party, and there was a lot of skin show. You looked quite super hot. So, what happened there?

> **Maybe if I had a gorgeous body, I would have loved to flaunt it!**
> *–Konkona Sen*

Konkona Sen: I was a little bit uncomfortable. I did it just for fun, but I know why I had been in the joke. Oh God! But great script, great director, a convincing screenplay – I know all I can do is kissing.

Karan Johar: You do not mind kissing?

Konkona Sen: Yeah! I cannot do anything else like landing in the same bed.

Rahul Bose: She insisted that we kiss in *Mr. and Mrs. Iyer*.

Karan Johar: She wanted to kiss? Whatever reasons, who knows? Maybe she's aflame with the desire!

Rahul Bose: I was totally against such scenes that go against the story concept.

Konkona Sen: I shall tell you why. My mother and I loved the movie at that moment. When we were about to kiss suddenly, someone

> **Konkona insisted that we kiss in *Mr. and Mrs. Iyer*!**
> *–Rahul Bose*

comes – it was such a cliché. I mean it never happens. What could any onscreen kiss be? How could it be better than imagination? Why do you have to make it so good? It just has to be real. You just

> **I knew that brain is the biggest sex organ of the body – did you have another answer in mind?**
>
> *–Rahul Bose*

talked about realistic cinema. He is talking about the realistic approach.

Karan Johar: The man does not want it.

Konkona Sen: No, no, nothing like that, Karan. He wanted to stop it and said we should leave it to the audience's imagination.

Karan Johar: So much for realistic cinema!

Rahul Bose: The realistic cinema includes desires in the imagination. Which is the biggest sex organ of the body?

Konkona Sen: Brain!

Rahul Bose: I knew the answer. You had another answer in mind?

Karan Johar: Well, we will not discuss that! No skin shows for Konkona? No *Jism*?

Konkona Sen: I would use a body double happily!

Karan Johar: You do not mind?

Konkona Sen: I would approve of the body double.

Karan Johar: How much would you show, Rahul?

> **Rahul Bose: Skin show? For me, whatever the role demands! Konkona Sen: I am very scared for the rest of us, the audience!**

Konkona Sen: Well, he has already shown a lot! There is nothing of left to show anymore.

Rahul Bose: There is a fleeting glimpse of the full frontal in the film *English August*. I do not care. As far as I am concerned, whatever the role demands! Whatever!

Konkona Sen: I am very scared of this.

Karan Johar: Scared to see Rahul like that?

Konkona Sen: For the rest of us, the audience!

Paising A Toast

Karan Johar: Talk to me about talent. You think there is a lot of talent around the mainstream and parallel cinema. Sorry about the divide again. What kind of people do you like to look up to today?

Rahul Bose: Naseeruddin Shah.

Karan Johar: Oh God! Say someone who is not Naseeruddin Shah or Shabana Azmi. I am talking about the mainstream people. Now, we are on a mainstream show. Talk about Irfaan – I think he's good.

Konkona Sen: I like Boman Irani. Saif is good looking.

Karan Johar: Good looking? what about the acting?

Konkona Sen: He is a good actor.

Karan Johar: Very funny. You like Saif? Do you think nobody is talented?

Konkona Sen: Oh! I love Shahrukh and Kajol. I love Rani and I love Tabu.

Karan Johar: And what do you think about the level of acting that goes on in mainstream cinema?

Konkona Sen: Tabu is just fantastic. She's one of the best actors.

Karan Johar: That's the general level. I am going to get to Rahul. The level of acting, favourite talents?

Rahul Bose: I honestly think that actors are great in different roles. We have seen Robert De Niro really screwing up in some of the roles, hamming it up like in 'The Score'. I do not really think it as fair to say that this person is a good actor through and through. Yes, there are some really talented actors that we have. I totally agree with Konkona – I think Tabu is very talented, Saif has a fantastic flair for comedy, Aamir can bring about some spark of magic, Pankaj Kapoor in *Maqbool* did one of the finest performances in the world, and Irfan was fantastic. There are tons of people. Boman is a fabulous actor.

> I love Shahrukh, Kajol, and Rani. Tabu is just fantastic!
> –Konkona Sen

Karan Johar: Do you think there are certain overrated talents?

Rahul Bose: Where are they not? In books, in music – everywhere – in the same ratio.

Karan Johar: Anyone overrated who should not have achieved stardom but has?

Rahul Bose: No! I think the audiences have been very clear why they come and see a particular person – because he is a star, is sexy, a good actor, and is great at comedy.

Karan Johar: I think the audience needs a clean presence?

Konkona Sen: As you said, you like Shahrukh and Kajol. I saw *Dilwale Dulhaniya Le Jayenge* six months back for the first time.

Karan Johar: You had never seen it before?

Konkona Sen: I had never seen it before and my friends were mad about the movie.

Karan Johar: Lovely! I know! Initially Kajol had similar problems – 'I do not believe this. I cannot do this. I cannot react in that manner. I can't do this while singing a number. I am dancing like this. Why is he touching me? Why I am reacting like this?'

> I saw *Dilwale Dulhaniya Le Jayenge* six months back for the first time!
>
> –*Konkona Sen*

Konkona Sen: I remember that when we talked about it. I could not do it.

Karan Johar: Do you say, 'No, this is what I want to do because I want to achieve a certain comfort zone in my work'?

Konkona Sen: I do not know what I want at the end of the day. Eventually, I would probably want to direct a film, if I am lucky enough to do so. I do not have any agenda to build my career other than how I have been doing. I shall try to do the best. I do not mind doing something for fun, love or magic, merely by copying.

Rahul Bose: It's hard to tell because she had acknowledged doing something musical.

> I do not mind doing something for fun, love or magic merely by copying!
>
> –*Konkona Sen*

Karan Johar: Really? Which one?

Rahul Bose: It does not matter. It is full on musical sounds.

Karan Johar: This is really interesting because the grammar of the whole thing would be true to people busy in singing and dancing – something you do not want to do in films.

PAST REGRETS

Karan Johar: Have you done any single film where you were uncomfortable, wondering 'Oh God! Why did I do it?' Has it happened to you?

Rahul Bose: The two films that I could not work with the script were *Bombay Boys* and *Mumbai Matinee*. The films let me down. *Ricardo* was okay; *Bombay Boys* was nice. I loved the role in *Mumbai Matinee* but it did not shape me up very well. I could not do anything but stand by my performance in the film.

Karan Johar: All right! What about you, Konkona?

Konkona Sen: It has happened to me. My debut was a Bengali film, which I do not think worked. It was more about me because I was in college when it happened. It was between my first and second year of the course.

Karan Johar: Who was the director?

Konkona Sen: Subroto Sen. It was a Bengali film, my first film and it was a negative character. I was a psychotic wherein I had to act as obsessed with an oldie. I really wanted to kill his girlfriend, but I die.

Rahul Bose: You were pretty decent!

Konkona Sen: I do not think the film was bad.

Karan Johar: You did well for your role?

Konkona Sen: I was just uncomfortable. I had to do a lot of workshops. Subroto Sen was fantastic in that workshop with me. 'The poor girl, these are the only weapons she has and that is why she does it.' You had to find logic because I was dying thinking, 'Oh God! This is not me and I cannot do this.'

Karan Johar: You played a psychotic, a schizophrenic – you are quite a mad one!

THE NATIONAL AWARD

Karan Johar: Rahul, when *Chameli* gave Kareena Kapoor the Filmfare Award and *Mr. and Mrs. Iyer* gave Konkona the National Award and they entered the media glare, what did you feel?

Rahul Bose: I felt intensely jealous and hateful!

Karan Johar: That is the answer I wanted!

Rahul Bose: Just think – very carefully, I clean my mind of the malice and decide, at some point, to kill them!

Konkona Sen: Impending death!

Rahul Bose: The national award will be speared through her body and I shall hold the National award and twirl her around it!

Konkona Sen: It's like that with you.

Karan Johar: It is a certificate.

Rahul Bose: I will make it into a paper spear and just punch it through the ear into the brain!

> *Bombay Boys* and *Mumbai Matinee* let me down.
>
> –*Rahul Bose*

> I felt intensely jealous and hateful when Konkona won the National award!
>
> – *Rahul Bose*

Karan Johar: All right! What about Kareena? Poor thing! What will you do to her?

Konkona Sen: Similar treatment!

Rahul Bose: Yes. In fact, it was a movie with lot of crying by the passive male role. Honestly speaking, it had to make sense as I have never had such a thing.

Karan Johar: So you do not mind if the woman is on top?

Rahul Bose: Not at all!

RAPID FIRE

Karan Johar: You are moving on to my *Rapid Fire Round*. How do you feel about it on watching the show?

Konkona Sen: I know what the round is about. Everybody knows that Karan puts a volley of questions in anticipation of rapid-fire response. We have to answer really fast and whoever answers it better will get the koffee hamper.

Karan Johar: I have really hyped this koffee hamper.

Konkona Sen: A new *Film Fare* award!

> I do not mind at all if the woman is on top!
> –*Rahul Bose*

Karan Johar: Let me start with you, Konkona. If you answer wittingly, fast and intelligently, you win this! Konkona, brace yourself! Are you ready for the Rapid Fire Round?

Konkona Sen: No!

Karan Johar: The best female actor in the Indian cinema?

Konkona Sen: Shabana Azmi.

Karan Johar: A recent Hindi film you could have done?

Konkona Sen: *Maqbool.*

Karan Johar: The most overrated actor in Hindi cinema is?

Konkona Sen: I do not know.

Rahul Bose: Karan is really high-rated!

Konkona Sen: Oh, Karan in *Dilwale Dulhaniya Le Jayenge.*

Karan Johar: I am not overrated – not cool enough! The most underrated film you saw in recent times?

Konkona Sen: *Maqbool!*

Karan Johar: The best compliment you received for *Page 3*?

Konkona Sen: When I came out of the premiere and the media said 'You should not be on that side, but with us!'

Karan Johar: The worst review about yourself?

Konkona Sen: I do not remember anything.

Karan Johar: Any other criticism that has come your way?

Karan Johar: The most overrated actor in Hindi cinema is?
Konkona Sen: Karan for *Dilwale Dulhaniya Le Jayenge!*

Konkona Sen: Yes, someone said something about a pudgy face, which made me die.

Karan Johar: All right! The question you were asked most often after *Page 3* is?

Konkona Sen: 'How is it like being the daughter of your mother?' I swear it has nothing to do with *Page 3*, but everyone inquires about it regardless of whatever I do.

Karan Johar: OK. If you were asked to do a cheesy sex film, you would?

Karan Johar: **Worst criticism?** *Konkona Sen:* **Someone said I had a pudgy face, which made me die!**

Konkona Sen: Say yes, and everyone would believe me!

Karan Johar: OK. If you were really a *Page 3* journalist, what would your headline be for article on *Koffee With Karan?*

Konkona Sen: *Kontroversial Koffee With Karan.* I do not know! I cannot think of something witty. *Kontroversial* would be the key.

Karan Johar: OK. *Kontroversial Koffee With Karan?* What is the worst mispronunciation of your name you have come across?

Konkona Sen: There are many – Konakona, Kankona, Konkayna, Kankana. It is KONKONA!

Karan Johar: What is the best part of success for you?

Konkona Sen: I get to travel a lot. I just love it!

Karan Johar: If you were to get naughty with a Hindi film hero, who would it be and why?

Konkona Sen: Saif Ali Khan.

Karan Johar: The worst pick-up line ever used on you?

Konkona Sen: No one ever used pick-up lines on me

Karan Johar: Nobody tried to pick you up, Konkona?

> If I was asked to do a cheesy sex film, I would say 'yes' and everyone would believe me!
> –*Konkona Sen*

Konkona Sen: I have this persona – I can really put people off and scare them!

Karan Johar: Very briefly, your take on the following: David Dhavan comedies. You have not seen any?

Konkona Sen: I have not seen any but believe they are hugely successful and people love them.

Karan Johar: That is great! Very politically correct, Konkona. All right! Ram Gopal Verma's thrillers.

Konkona Sen: I am interested nowadays. I think at least some efforts are being made towards the horror genre, which is really sad in India.

Karan Johar: Yash Chopra's love stories.

Konkona Sen: Nice. I have not seen a lot but I cry buckets.

Karan Johar: Alright, very quickly then. Kajol or Rani – which Bengali beauty do you prefer?

Konkona Sen: Kajol.

Karan Johar: Shahrukh or Aamir?

Konkona Sen: Shahrukh.

Karan Johar: Yash Chopra or Sanjay Bhansali?

> **I have this persona – I can really put people off and scare them!**
> –*Konkona Sen*

Konkona Sen: Oh, my God! This is not fair – I do not know enough. Sanjay Bhansali after I saw *Black*.

Karan Johar: OK. Farhan Akhtar or Ashutosh Gowarikar?

Konkona Sen: Farhan Akhtar.

Karan Johar: Box Office or critical acclaim?

Konkona Sen: Critical acclaim.

Karan Johar: Well done, Konkona! Not bad!

Konkona Sen: That really was not easy.

Rahul Bose: Just pass me the hamper.

Karan Johar: All right. Rahul, brace yourself – not that you look uncomfortable, but anyway.

Konkona Sen: He had been practicing at home with my mother, I swear!

Karan Johar: A recent Hindi film you wished you were a part of?

> **Rahul has been practicing *rapid fire* at home with my mother!**
> –*Konkona Sen*

Rahul Bose: *Maqbool.*

Karan Johar: An overrated actor is?

Rahul Bose: An unhappy man.

Karan Johar: An under-rated actor is?

Rahul Bose: Pavan Malhotra.

Karan Johar: The sexiest woman is?
Rahul Bose: The most attractive is Arundhati Roy.

Karan Johar: The most overrated Hindi film of last year? Quite honestly, have I walked into a cinema and said that was supposed to be good and walked out.

Rahul Bose: No, I think the public has their finger on the pulse nowadays.

Karan Johar: All right! The sexiest woman is?

Rahul Bose: Well, definitely the one most attractive woman would be Arundhati Roy. For everything.

Karan Johar: Your take on (a) Remix music videos.

Rahul Bose: Iceland.

Karan Johar: (b) *Saas - Bahu* sagas.

Rahul Bose: Kalashnikov rifle.

Karan Johar: Would you kill them?

Rahul Bose: Not only kill them, the whole genre should be murdered.

Karan Johar: Celebrity talk shows?

Rahul Bose: Fun.

Karan Johar: The most absurd role you have ever been offered in commercial cinema.

Rahul Bose: A role in a film which had toilet humour wherein I had to sing and dance.

Karan Johar: Please give me names; otherwise, you are uncool.

Rahul Bose: I am so cool – it is unbelievable!

Karan Johar: Your take on the term 'crossover cinema'.

Karan Johar: Saas - Bahu sagas?
Rahul Bose: Kalashnikov rifle – I would not only kill them, the whole genre should be murdered!

Rahul Bose: It's a piece of crap. It means nothing. There is good cinema and bad cinema. If it is good cinema, you will go everywhere; if not, and then you will not.

Karan Johar: One thing you would like to see more in Hindi cinemas?

Rahul Bose: Spiderman.

Karan Johar: The thing you would like to see less in Hindi cinemas?

Rahul Bose: Shalini Madhavi.

Karan Johar: Who was she?

Rahul Bose: You alerted me not to ask questions!

Karan Johar: **One thing you would like to see more in Hindi cinemas?** *Rahul Bose:* **Spiderman!**

Karan Johar: A critic you wanted to kill and why?

Rahul Bose: None.

Karan Johar: Worst criticism ever read about yourself?

Rahul Bose: That I cannot act.

Karan Johar: Where have you read that?

Rahul Bose: It was for *Split Wide Open* or *English August.* When I got the award for *Split Wide Open,* the same person came up to me and said, 'Wonderful!' But I did not spare him; I retorted, 'You reported in a review that I could not act!'

Karan Johar: Your reaction when you hear a film star saying, 'I do not mind exposing, (a) if the role demands.'

Rahul Bose: They utter the truth.

Karan Johar: (b) 'We are just good friends.'

Rahul Bose: You say the truth.

Konkona Sen: What is this? You guys are real cynical!

Karan Johar: (c) 'I did not do the film because I did not have the dates.'

Konkona Sen: Lies!

Rahul Bose: That is one of the things that I could say in most probability if I do not want to do a film.

Karan Johar: **Worst criticism about yourself?** *Rahul Bose:* **That I cannot act!**

Karan Johar: OK. Quickly. *Chameli* or *Mr. and Mrs. Iyer*?

Rahul Bose: *Mr. and Mrs. Iyer.*

Karan Johar: Sanjay Bhansali or Mani Ratnam?

Rahul Bose: A wonder woman.

Karan Johar: Mira Nair or Gurinder Chadha?

Rahul Bose: Mira Nair.

Karan Johar: Konkona Sen or Kareena Kapoor?

Rahul Bose: Konkona Sen.

Konkona Sen: Say Kareena!

Karan Johar: All right. That is the end of the rocking *Rapid Fire*. The winner is Konkona Sen Sharma.

Konkona Sen: I knew it! I am so happy!

Rahul Bose: Keep the award and be careful.

Karan Johar: Really?

Rahul Bose: Yes, remember – speared and rotated round!

Karan Johar: All right, Konkona! You have won the coffee hamper.

Konkona Sen: You can keep it for me!

Karan Johar: No. Let me stand up and give the award to you.

Konkona Sen: Oh really, I cannot. My sari will fly off!

Rahul Bose: Her sari will come off?!

Karan Johar: We shall see a lot of skin!

Konkona Sen: *Julie*!

Karan Johar: *Murder*. We have something really fun

Karan Johar: Sanjay Bhansali or Mani Ratnam?

Rahul Bose: A wonder woman!

planned for our last and final segment. It is so much thrilling! You would get a lot of commercials only if you overacted like this!

Rahul Bose: You have mentioned that. I shall always buy your movies!

Whose Line is it Anyway?

Karan Johar: All right! We have a clipping from a very popular soap. Do you watch Star Plus soaps?

Rahul Bose: I watch these soaps all the time!

Karan Johar: You, Konkona?

Konkona Sen: No.

Karan Johar: This is a clipping like 'Whose Line Is It, Anyway?' We will turn the sound off. We want you to add them. Are you ready?

Rahul Bose: Me first!

Karan Johar: Yes, first you, Rahul. All right. So, let us have a look.

Rahul Bose: I have learnt how to bowl off spin, bowl leg spin and bowl a damn googly! It is so simple. Hold the ball; swing it this way. Keep your hand out. Wait for the ball to return. He gives away the secrets. Indian secrets! She gives away the secrets. Will she, won't she? Oh! Come on. Please tell me. I want to know. Will you tell me or should I go to Shane Warne? Otherwise, I will go to Mushtaq Ahmed or Anil Kumble! What is the secret of the googly? Oh! Come on! Tell me. 'It is this way, you fool!' she told him. You will have to hold your fingers around the seam!

Karan Johar: Well done!

Konkona Sen: I cannot do that!

Karan Johar: You went into a little cricket commentary. Are you ready, Konkona?

Konkona Sen: No.

Karan Johar: 1, 2, 3! Have a look!

Konkona Sen: I know I have sinus. I know it is awful, but you always tell it on my face. I know I wanted hair like you. Yes, you must have hair like mine. See the colour? I will slap my hand. It is stuck! Why is not my hand moving? Is my hair really dirty? It is not. Yes. I am stupid. OK. Let me just brace myself. I dare you to touch my hair. Hit me! It is going on for too long. OK. I cannot! I have given up. That was so much better. I cannot do it. I am giving up. I surrender!

Karan Johar: You do, do you?

Konkona Sen: All over! This hamper is his!

Karan Johar: OK. Konkona, you were terrible! Do you always need your lines in advance?

Konkona Sen: Yes, I am not doing 'Whose Line Is It Anyway?' right. I love them. I really want to be like them, but I cannot!

Karan Johar: What did you think about her performance?

Konkona Sen: I thought it was very good. I thought she got into the character, I thought she really understood the motivation. She was convincing.

Karan Johar: You did very well.

Rahul Bose: Thank you. It is just natural talent!

Konkona Sen: We are so happy for you and your family!

Conclusion

Karan Johar: Nice show. Are you obsessed by Kareena?

Konkona Sen: I think he is.

Karan Johar: You are. She is very happy with Shahid. What are your comments? We are talking about Kareena.

Rahul Bose: I am very obsessed with Kareena and Shahid.

Karan Johar: Oh, you are?

Rahul Bose: Come on! She had a great time.

Karan Johar: Do they make a good pair, Kareena and Shahid?

Rahul Bose: Yes.

Karan Johar: They look fabulous in love. It is great to see people in love. You are not in love?

Rahul Bose: No. It has been years!

Karan Johar: No relationship?

Rahul Bose: It has been without dating years.

Karan Johar: You did not take any girl out for dinner?. My God! And what about you, Konkona?

Konkona Sen: I have not taken any girl out for dinner as well!

Karan Johar: No boyfriends, no lover? All of 26 and no lover?

Konkona Sen: No boyfriend. Why are you telling my age?

Rahul Bose: I am so old .You look much older! I am really depressed for being old.

> **I am really depressed for being old!**
> — *Rahul Bose*

Konkona Sen: That is really sad!

Karan Johar: For this loveless duo, I feel very bad for you. I wish you both happy relationships, lots of love. Thank you for being on *Koffee With Karan*. Konkona, I am so sorry you were really quite bad at this.

Konkona Sen: The star world audience has us totally exposed! I quit the movies!

Karan Johar: Not good at all, not good. I have given away my hamper, what else can I do? Thank you, Rahul; you were brilliant. You were the cricket commentator totally. Fantastic! Anyway, thank you so much for being on *Koffee With Karan*. Thank you for coming all the way from Kolkata.

Konkona Sen: Thank you!

Rahul Bose: I have come from Peddar Road!

Karan Johar: That is not good enough! There is a coffee mug right next to you. If you could lift and sign it for us with 'lots of love' message. Remember, this personally autographed mug could be yours only if you take part in the *Koffee Quest* contest. Let us walk towards the coffee wall with that mug.

● ● ●

17

Priyanka Chopra & Arjun Rampal
The Beauty and the Feast

She is the latest A-category star turned model. She is sexy. She is earthy. She has got what it takes. She is known for her curves, charisma and controversies. You have praised her onscreen performances. She accepts them in her *Andaz*. Mention her alleged affairs and there will be an *Aitraaz*. Let us welcome Miss World 2000, Priyanka Chopra.

PRIYANKA CHOPRA

Karan Johar: Hellow!

Priyanka Chopra: Hello!

Karan Johar: Looking lovely, Priyanka!

Priyanka Chopra: Thanks a lot!

Karan Johar: I want you to meet a friend of mine lying here – it is called the lie-o-meter. I use this when I think you are lying.

Priyanka Chopra: This is amazing; though I wonder how many times in the show you are going to use that.

Karan Johar: You think I will?

Priyanka Chopra: I hope not!

Karan Johar: All right, then you have to pledge that you are going to say the truth and nothing but the truth.

Priyanka Chopra: I will speak the truth and nothing but the truth, so help me God!

THE BOUQUETS

Karan Johar: Career-wise, it has been wonderful for you, Priyanka. Suddenly, you are slotted with Aishwarya Rai, Rani Mukherjee, Kareena Kapoor and Preity Zinta. As I said, you are an A-list startoday. How does it feel?

Priyanka Chopra: It is very flattering and humbling as well. I do not come from a filmy background. I do not know people here. It has been just about a year-and-a-half since I came here. I did not expect it, but feel great that the industry accepts me.

Karan Johar: That is the right thing to say. Say a wrong thing.

Priyanka Chopra: That is difficult for me. I am trained to say the right thing!

Karan Johar: Yes, I know, Miss World, 2000. All right! You are affable and amiable. You get along well with the girls as well. You have a great rapport. Every other girl seems to have a problem with Kareena Kapoor.

Priyanka Chopra: No, I got along really well with her.

Karan Johar: How did you manage that?

Priyanka Chopra: I don't think I have to try. She is just really nice.

Karan Johar: Full marks on diplomacy

> **I am trained to say the right thing!**
> *–Priyanka Chopra*

> **I don't think I have to try to like Kareena – she is just really nice!**
>
> *-Priyanka Chopra*

again! Wonderful! You are saying all politically correct things. I do not like it, Priyanka.

Priyanka Chopra: I am speaking the truth.

Karan Johar: Tell me there about your sudden new stand – no exposure.

Priyanka Chopra: Well, It is a conscious decision. I do not think that it is required when you are performing. When I played the character in *Aitraaz*, I did not stoop to exposure. It was more the character that I played – it was the way I spoke and it was the actions, the deliberate moves and things like that.

Karan Johar: Yes. 'Show me you are an animal!'

Priyanka Chopra: Oh Lord! Do not embarrass me with all that. But I do not want to be known for that; I want to be known for much more.

Karan Johar: Are you trying to say that the girls who show skin will not make it to the big league?

Priyanka Chopra: No, I will never say that – that is how I started. I wore a bikini in *Andaz*. It is not something I am ashamed of or what I would want to do now.

Karan Johar: All right!

Priyanka Chopra: I do not think it is required. I would want people to notice my performance. I would want to be known more for the respect that I probably would command. You want people to look above that when you say so.

Karan Johar: OK. How do you manage to evade that theory on the set that Priyanka Chopra personifies glamour and sex appeal – and then suddenly when you come on the sets?

Priyanka Chopra: I make it very clear to my directors before I sign any film. It would not be nice to go on a set and say, 'I am not going to do this or say this or perform like this.' I shall justify that before I start the film.

> **When I played the character in *Aitraaz*, I did not stoop to exposure.**
>
> *-Priyanka Chopra*

Karan Johar: Recently, how many times have you refused so-called kissing scenes in films? Have not done any one?

Priyanka Chopra: Not even one.

Karan Johar: Anyone you want to kiss onscreen?

Priyanka Chopra: No. Those things I keep private.

Karan Johar: Anyone you want to kiss onscreen?
Priyanka Chopra: No. Those things I keep private!

Karan Johar: I like that! Congratulations, you have done great work in *Aitraaz*. Other films before that – *Mujse Shaadi Karogi* was, of course, a big hit, which really put you up there.

Priyanka Chopra: Yeah!

ARJUN RAMPAL

Karan Johar: It is wonderful to have another guest with us. Do you know who the other guest is?

Priyanka Chopra: Yes, I do. I do not want the lie-o-meter to come out!

Karan Johar: OK. You have had a good equation with him.

Priyanka Chopra: We have done two films together. We have got along. We have teased each other; we have fought, we got angry at each other and drifted apart.

Karan Johar: Do you get along really? Do you like each other?

Priyanka Chopra: Yes. I am very fond of him.

Karan Johar: The supermodel turned actor, gorgeous Arjun Rampal. Have women become weak in the knees because when they see him, they know that not much can happen? He is happily married and intends to keep it that way – or so he says! Let us call more eye candy on the show – Arjun Rampal. Hello and welcome!

Arjun Rampal: Thank you. Hey, Priyanka!

Priyanka Chopra: Hi, Arjun!

Arjun Rampal: Looking gorgeous!

Priyanka Chopra: Thank you.

Karan Johar: Everyone is being so nice with each other. How wonderful! I like it that way.

Priyanka Chopra: You are so mean!

Karan Johar: So you like each other?

Priyanka Chopra: Yes.

Arjun Rampal: Yes.

Karan Johar: You have done two films. I was just congratulating Priyanka on her recent success.

> **If women find me good-looking, I make money – it is good!**
>
> *– Arjun Rampal*

Arjun Rampal: Yeah! She has been brilliant.

Karan Johar: Arjun, as I said, you are Greek-gorgeous and have women going weak in the knees. So does it frustrate you after a point?

Arjun Rampal: It has got nothing to do with me. It is the way I am. If they find me good-looking, I make money. It is good.

Karan Johar: That is wonderful!

THE GOOD TIMES AND THE BAD

Karan Johar: Arjun, box office has eluded you in the recent past. You have done about ten films. You have been performing tremendously. You are good looking, followed by huge female fans. I saw what happened at the overseas shows – when you removed that shirt of yours and the women went wild!

Priyanka Chopra: And the girls went mad!

Karan Johar: What happens when you have had a string of flops? How does that bother you?

Arjun Rampal: Well, it does bother you because you want to make good films. I consciously want to do it. I am very passionate about films – I want the films to work. I work on every film really hard, but it seldom works out that way. I guess you just got to be strong. Even Mr. Bachchan had 10-12 flops before scaling such tremendous heights – there is a man who has rocked even after many flops and disasters.

Karan Johar: Is it not too late?

Arjun Rampal: Not so long as people like you.

Karan Johar: OK. What do you attribute it to? Wrong career moves or decisions?

Arjun Rampal: Well, I do not think so.

Karan Johar: Screenplays that you should dislike?

Arjun Rampal: You cannot help whatever goes wrong.

Karan Johar: Does it go wrong?

> **Even Mr. Bachchan had 10-12 flops before scaling such tremendous heights!**
>
> *–Arjun Rampal*

Arjun Rampal: I have enjoyed working on them. I have learnt a lot. I believe I have grown a lot. Now, I have got to be a little bit careful and choose better subjects. I believe Priyanka's luck shines my way.

THE CASTING COUCH

Karan Johar: Arjun, you have come from the modeling world. There are a lot of people asking about the casting couch for men in the modeling world. Have you been subjected to that couch or denied access? What is your take on it?

Arjun Rampal: I have not seen nor experienced it, but have heard about people who have. People who came from Haryana have been tried. There is this poor guy who is not from the fraternity, but from outside. You know the wheeler-dealer kind of people who like hanging around and who promise you an ad. I remember the guy was really upset about it. I was a senior model, so he told me what happened to him. He was summoned to a hotel room. The guy offered him drinks laced with something. He began feeling faint. The host tried to do something, but that is like a one-off case. I mean, it does not happen like that.

> **I am affirming that the casting couch for men exists in the modeling world!**
>
> *–Arjun Rampal*

Karan Johar: It does not?

Arjun Rampal: There are gay people in the fashion industry. There is nothing wrong in people being gay. They should go and sleep, if they desire to, but....

Karan Johar: Only for pleasure and not for their careers?

Arjun Rampal: Yeah. I am affirming it exists. Some people may want to sleep for their careers, but I am not going to.

Karan Johar: No, of course you are not. Have you ever said no and been hit on by the models?

Arjun Rampal: There are so many gay people around. I think they will do so after a couple of drinks. I think it is the vibe you give. I do not think I look gay from any angle – not at all. Nobody really comes up to me and makes a pass at me.

Karan Johar: All right! Do you say that it exists **but it is** really up to the person if they want to get in?

Arjun Rampal: Yeah. I think that is the way.

Karan Johar: Are you feeling left out on being hit, darling?

Priyanka Chopra: By gay people or otherwise?

Karan Johar: No, not gay. Have you felt the vibe around you ever?

Priyanka Chopra: I have never had to go through the casting couch, but I have felt the vibe of it. I was already Miss World when I was offered my first role.

Karan Johar: Had you never modeled before Miss India?

> **I was already Ms World when I was offered my first role - so people did not take a chance!**
>
> *–Priyanka Chopra*

Priyanka Chopra: I was in 12th standard. I never really got to know the industry without being somebody or having a name. I do not think the people took a chance often.

Karan Johar: Also, you do not give the vibe at all.

Priyanka Chopra: You have got to know how you come across people. Anybody could take advantage of that, but it has not happened with me.

Karan Johar: What about good-looking men hitting on you in the fraternity? Heroes?

Priyanka Chopra: You have to know how to speak to the people when it comes to girls in the profession. Men ascertained whether there was any possibility but failed in their attempts to come on to me.

Karan Johar: So, who has tried?

Priyanka Chopra: I am not naming anyone. Guys think that they are sometimes cool.

Karan Johar: What kind of lines do you get – 'Are you alone tonight' or something like that?

Priyanka Chopra: No, it has never been so strong with me.

Karan Johar: Because you are always with mummy and papa!

Priyanka Chopra: Yeah! They are always around. I am always guarded. 'Listen, dude! My mom's a Punjabi.'

> **When it comes to girls, men ascertain whether there is any possibility.**
>
> *–Priyanka Chopra*

Karan Johar: Like a line – 'a hug that might mean something more!'

> **I am always guarded by my parents. So, it is 'Listen, dude! My mom's a Punjabi!'**
> *- Priyanka Chopra*

Priyanka Chopra: I think this industry has taught me a lot. I now tend to be myself. I was 18 when I came into the industry. Stuff like, 'I have never connected with anybody the way I connect with you' happened.

Karan Johar: 'Go to a shrink and connect!' – that could have been your answer!

RESISTING THE IRRESISTABLE

Karan: Arjun, what happens when you are happily married to a beautiful woman? Everyone knows that Meher is stunning.

Priyanka Chopra: She is pregnant again.

Karan Johar: Meher is pregnant? Congratulations!

Arjun Rampal: Thank you!

Priyanka Chopra: Yeah! Congratulations!

Karan Johar: That is wonderful! How do you stop yourself? You are surrounded by many beautiful women – Priyanka or Lara or Sushmita or Aishwarya. You work with So many stunning women all the time. All four are Miss World or Miss Universe. Beyond them too – everybody else – Kareena or Amisha Patel are beautiful women. You are a man at the end of the day. How does it work for you? How do you stop yourself?

Arjun Rampal: I do not feel anything as I have a beautiful woman at home – my wife!

Karan Johar: Do you control yourself because you want to be morally right?

Arjun Rampal: No. Meher is exceptionally beautiful. We have a wonderful relationship – I dislike disturbing it.

> **I do not feel any attraction as I have a beautiful woman at home – my wife!**
> *–Arjun Rampal*

Karan Johar: All right! You said that you have been through your wild past. Now, it is your marriage, nothing else. It is quite fantastic to see a happy marriage in this era.

Priyanka Chopra: I know it really is!

Karan Johar: I give full credit to your for maintaining a happy marraige.

CONTROVERSIES

Karan Johar: I want to speak about controversies that might surround you. Let us start with Arjun. I read your hilarious quotation in the morning – You kept away from yellow because of the jaundice wave!

Arjun Rampal: Yeah!

Karan Johar: *Rang de Basanti* did not work out. Any problem with Aamir Khan?

> **I am sitting on your show today because these are all the *Rang de Basanti* dates!**
> *–Arjun Rampal*

Arjun Rampal: Well, I think I had a problem with the director. I was signed for the film. I was supposed to do it, but he got a new look designed for the film. I am sitting on your show today because these are all the *Rang de Basanti* dates!

Karan Johar: Perhaps you would have been filming with Rakesh Mehra?

Arjun Rampal: I would have been. I think I became very confused about the director who stopped fairly. Rakesh was very confused about the script. He was very erratic. Sometimes, he felt he should do that character. It was best to say, 'OK, dude, I cannot work with you. Good luck!' It could not work out and I believe I am happier.

Karan Johar: You must have lost out on a fair amount of work for three months.

Arjun Rampal: Right!

Karan Johar: Does that bother you today?

Arjun Rampal: No.

Karan Johar: That was the confusion of somebody else?

Arjun Rampal: No. I think it was definitely unprofessional. I had blocked dates so that people supposed to work could do so. I lost out on work. It is OK – everything happens for the best.

Karan Johar: The best?

Arjun Rampal: And you move on. I am not holding anything against anybody.

> **I lost out on work because of *Rang De Basanti*. It is OK – everything happens for the best.**
> *–Arjun Rampal*

Karan Johar: Nothing against Aamir Khan because it was his baby as well?

Arjun Rampal: Well, I had loved the idea of working with him because he was interested in the film.

Karan Johar: Priyanka! You have been surrounded by controversies of your alleged romance with Akshay Kumar. One has read it through periodicals. You have denied it everywhere. It can have an adverse impact. How do you justify things on a big platform?

Priyanka Chopra: I am really tired to comment upon it. It had been speculated from the *vox populi*. It does not matter to my family or me so long as my parents are fine. They know the truth. My friends are fine. I seldom need to prove anything.

> I seem to be crowned as the 'controversy queen' for some reason!
>
> –*Priyanka Chopra*

Karan Johar: OK. Does it upset you? Sometimes, it could upset your work relationship with a man.

Priyanka Chopra: Of course, it does. Any kind of controversy is not just an alleged affair. People have a tendency to make a mountain out of a molehill. I seem to be crowned as the 'controversy queen' for some reason, which I detest. I just so badly want to be known for my work. I was very happy that people were actually talking about performances and my work. It is really tiring – doing well than anything else!

Karan Johar: For, (a) Akshay is a married man, and (b) it just becomes awkward. You have been working with him in many movies. Does that bother you?

Priyanka Chopra: It does bother me. I have my family. He has his family. It is high time to look at people for what they really are; I wish people would do that.

Karan Johar: Did you ever speak to him? How does one clear the air?

Priyanka Chopra: I did not feel any need to do so.

Karan Johar: All right! You want to say anything to the media who comment on the development?

Priyanka Chopra: Are not you tired of it? I mean it goes on forever! Let us talk about something interesting afresh. Please. It has become stale.

> I have my family. Akshay has his family. It is high time to look at people for what they really are!
>
> –*Priyanka Chopra*

Karan Johar: What happened

to that gentleman who sprang up for no reason? Prakash Jaju – your former secretary who went to the media. What happened there?

Priyanka Chopra: He is just pretty obsessed!

Karan Johar: Do you think he was responsible for creating stories about this affair?

Priyanka Chopra: I really do think so. Whether it was a working relation with a secretary or anybody, every relationship has a ceiling limit. It worsens when you cross the limit. It is dangerous, becomes bad and unhealthy. He was my secretary. He had to stay where he used to, but meddled in others' affairs.

Karan Johar: Was it personal? You have to draw the line somewhere, of course, which is not anybody's business.

Priyanka Chopra: This is nobody's business. 'Are you seeing anybody among the people you work for? Are you single and ready to mingle?' I am sick and tired of it. I just want to work.

Karan Johar: Darling, you are only 21. How can you be sick and tired?

Priyanka Chopra: I have become 22. I remain honest forever! I add years to my own age!

Karan Johar: All right! You do not have any boyfriend on the block?

Priyanka Chopra: No. I do not want to get involved. I just want to work.

Karan Johar: Who is Harman Baweja?

Priyanka Chopra: Oh Lord! He is Harry Baweja's son. I am doing their film called *Karam*. He is a friend and I know Harman from that aspect.

Karan Johar: Nothing had happened?

Priyanka Chopra: No, he is a friend. That is it.

Karan Johar: Good friends. Oh, God! Look at that smirk! Of course, there is a denial here. Well done. You, Arjun, spoke about the controversy with Akshay while working in *Aankhen*. Was it true about your role being cut when you accused Akshay?

Arjun Rampal: A controversy with Akshay and me? Yo dude, I am Arjun Rampal!

That is Priyanka Chopra. The controversy continues with her, but not me.

Karan Johar: Is it true?

Arjun Rampal: No, obviously not. He is a good guy.

Karan Johar: And is Priyanka a good girl?

Arjun Rampal: She has been a wonderful co-star to work with. I know how Priyanka is – she carries herself extremely well. She does not allow anyone to comment. She thinks that I am totally against her, but in reality I am not. She would not do what people accuse her to do. I have seen her on my shootings with a spate of controversies every time. In fact, we were on a world tour and she was really hassled about the rumours. Neither had it affected me, nor her.

Karan Johar: Perhaps the media wrote about that?

Arjun Rampal: Yeah! I think people should take it easy. Akshay is a married man. Let him enjoy his marital life and look after his family. Let Priyanka grow as an actress and do really well.

Karan Johar: She is doing a great job. I mean suddenly, everybody wants to work with Priyanka Chopra.

Arjun Rampal: Yeah!

Karan Johar: Well, wonderful, Arjun! Hold his hand, Priyanka, and say 'Thank You.' He speaks very well of you, I must tell you – maybe behind your back.

Priyanka Chopra: So sweet! That is a better thing to do.

Karan Johar: No controversies with you, Arjun. I looked all over the place. You are a very good boy. That sounds very suspicious. Are there things that we seldom know about?

Priyanka Chopra: The usual suspicions – things that we do not know about!

LOOKS VS TALENT

Karan Johar: Arjun, sometimes do you think your chiseled look is more international than Indian? Do you think that you don't look like a filmy prototype, so to say?

Arjun Rampal: No. I think if somebody comments, 'Oh! That is a good-looking guy,' how long are you going to watch him – say 15 minutes? Perhaps you get bored of it. I have to hold a film for two and a half hours. You have got to hold the story. I hope people look at me as a good actor. I strive for that.

> **I have to hold a film for two-and-a-half hours, not 15 minutes!**
> *–Arjun Rampal*

Karan Johar: Priyanka, how do you perceive Arjun as an actor?

Priyanka Chopra: I think he is very involved. We just did a film called *Yakeen*. It is an interesting story where he has a very pivotal role. I remember my parents watched it and my dad told Arjun that he had grown up as performer as did such a good job in that film. Arjun takes a lot of interest in his work. He gets involved with the director. He does so even post-production for assuaging the publicity.

'CAMP'ING AROUND THE WORLD (TOURS)

Karan Johar: Priyanka, you were on a world tour and met with three interesting personalities. They were, indeed, different kinds of men – Shahrukh Khan, the emperor of the film fraternity; Saif, who has recently reached the pinnacle; and then, there is this hottie – Arjun Rampal. What was your experience with them?

Priyanka Chopra: I knew Arjun the most – we did *Asambhav* together. We had such a rapport! I did not know Saif before performing with him. I found Shahrukh a wonderful guy because he co-produced the show. He was responsible for everything. He really made everyone feel comfortable. I had known him a little from before. He was very nice.

Karan Johar: What happened when things were thrown at you like – 'Priyanka Chopra wants to get into the Shahrukh Khan camp' or 'Priyanka Chopra wants to get into the Rakesh Roshan camp?'

> **During the tour, Shahrukh really made everyone feel comfortable – because he co-produced the show!**
> *–Priyanka Chopra*

Priyanka Chopra: It is annoying. I did not know Rakesh. I met Hrithik maybe once or twice. I have known Sunaina, Hrithik's sister. We have a common friend, so we were acquaintances.

Karan Johar: You signing Rakesh Roshan's film was big news. Yeah! Other heroines were apparently vying for that role.

> **I just have the tendency to live in my ivory tower because I do not have friends in the industry.**
> *–Priyanka Chopra*

Priyanka Chopra: I just have the tendency to live in my ivory tower. I dislike getting into this because I do not have friends in the industry. I prefer just going to work and coming back.

Karan Johar: So you did not pitch for that role at all?

Priyanka Chopra: I did not even know Rakesh. He just called me one day; I met him and he asked me to do the role. We did a photo shoot. Our chemistry worked and the film was completed.

Karan Johar: Don't you feel you were accused that you pitched in for roles with top banners?

Priyanka Chopra: Yeah. It is very annoying. I did a tour with Shahrukh. People went on bashing me with ridiculous epithets. It is very silly, because there is nothing beyond what you know. I wish people would just chill.

Karan Johar: Gangs exist in cinema. Do you think it does so too in Indian cinema?

Arjun Rampal: You tell us. You are from the industry. We are from outside the industry.

Karan Johar: Well, I do not know. I keep hearing about inevitable clicques in the industry. You know there is a Yash Chopra gang.

Arjun Rampal: I heard about this when I came into the industry. They told me why I should not do a movie with Yash Chopra or Dharma Productions or Ram Gopal Verma and such things. I have never gone to any agency as a model or as an actor. Everyone must have seen enough of my films by now to know that. They come to me if I am compatible for any role to be cast. I think it would be great that everybody is making more films. You have been encouraging new talent to come forward and direct a film or whatever, even though they are incapable. I believe new blood is what is being sought after.

Priyanka Chopra: That is a really good thing.

Arjun Rampal: Yes. I think this camp seldom exists.

Karan Johar: Do you feel it is below your dignity to make a call to a filmmaker?

Priyanka Chopra: I shall reply that I may be suitable.

RAPID FIRE

Karan Johar: All right! We have reached the *Rapid Fire Round*. Do you know what that is about?

Priyanka Chopra: Yes.

Arjun Rampal: Yo.

Karan Johar: I throw the volley of questions.

Arjun Rampal: Against Miss World – I have no chance!

Priyanka Chopra: No, we are good. I am diplomatic.

Karan Johar: You have to reply with a pun and lots of fun at fast pace. I am the judge and decide the winner. He/she will get the *Koffee with Karan* coffee hamper. It has become heavier. Are you ready to play this game? Let me commence with Priyanka. The one man from the Hindi film industry, (a) drop dead gorgeous.

Priyanka Chopra: Arjun Rampal!

Karan Johar: All right! (b) arrogant, yet sexy.

Priyanka Chopra: Arjun – definitely arrogant, yet sexy.

Karan Johar: All right! (c) under-rated sex appeal?

Priyanka Chopra: Abhishek Bachchan – but not of my type!

Karan Johar: John Abraham, Salman Khan, Akshay Kumar – the shirtless man that is best eye candy to you?

Priyanka Chopra: I think John.

Karan Johar: A rumour afloat you have believed?

Priyanka Chopra: I was supposed to be at Subhash Ghai's farmhouse during the release of his film *Aitraaz* for the script session!

Karan Johar: The incident never happened. All right. a true rumour about yourself?

Priyanka Chopra: Oh, lord! I was not bonded to Hollywood film where I have already worked.

> I get along with Lara well. She taught me how to do makeup.
> *—Priyanka Chopra*

Karan Johar: Lara and Priyanka are arch rivals. Comment.

Priyanka Chopra: We are not. I get along with Lara well. I looked up to her sweet behaviour during Miss India contest. She taught me how to do makeup.

Karan Johar: Arjun Rampal, John Abraham, Dino Morea – your favourite super model turned actor. Do not say Arjun.

Priyanka Chopra: I have worked with Arjun and John, but I would not like to say anything about them.

Karan Johar: OK. A man with whom you wish you had a torrid affair?

Priyanka Chopra: Dharamji in his youth.

Karan Johar: A woman of substance you admire? You said Mother Teresa in your contest. Lara commented about it.

Priyanka Chopra: No, I admire Sushmita a lot. She is not only a gutsy lady but also carries herself with lot of élan as well. She has been an independent girl since she was young. She has the guts to say what she wants to. I admire her a lot.

Karan Johar: Lara on the show believed in the spirit of Mother Teresa. What do you say?

Priyanka Chopra: I still do when I mean it as a woman.

Karan Johar: That made you win Miss World?

Priyanka Chopra: I do not know what did, actually. I was very naïve to understand that that was not the answer. I would like to stress that she was a lady from another country.

Karan Johar: What would you do if you were forced to share a vanity van with Lara Dutta and Mallika Sherawat?

Priyanka Chopra: I will share it.

Karan Johar: OK. Anything you would like to say about Mallika Sherawat?

Priyanka Chopra: She is daring. I love watching her spicy interviews.

> I love watching Mallika Sherawat's spicy interviews!
> *—Priyanka Chopra*

Karan Johar: All right! What would you do, if you were a plastic surgeon, to (a) Aamir Khan?

Priyanka Chopra: I may change his chubby cheeks.

Karan Johar: Good! (b) Shahrukh Khan?

Priyanka Chopra: Nothing.

Karan Johar: (c) Arjun Rampal?

> **If I were a plastic surgeon, I would change his chubby cheeks!**
> *–Priyanka Chopra*

Priyanka Chopra: You cannot change anything in him. You will rarely get a face like that. I will put on some more fat beneath the tissue.

Karan Johar: OK. Choices. Akshay Kumar or Salman Khan?

Priyanka Chopra: Salman.

Karan Johar: Politically correct. Shahrukh Khan or Hrithik Roshan?

Priyanka Chopra: Oh, Lord! He is not in the run. Pass.

Karan Johar: Aishwarya Rai or Sushmita Sen?

Priyanka Chopra: Sush.

Karan Johar: Yash Chopra or Rakesh Roshan?

Priyanka Chopra: Both.

Karan Johar: Whom do you want to work with – Shahrukh Khan, Hrithik Roshan, Yash Chopra and Rakesh Roshan?

Priyanka Chopra: All of them.

Karan Johar: Farhan Akhtar or Ashutosh Gowariker?

Priyanka Chopra: Farhan.

Karan Johar: Wonderful, Priyanka! Ok, Arjun! What would you say when proposed by a man?

Arjun Rampal: I would say I dislike being on the other side!

Karan Johar: Who would you adjudge as Miss World if Lara, Priyanka, Aishwarya and Sushmita were in the fray?

> **Aishwarya was brilliant in Miss World – hats off to her!**
> *–Arjun Rampal*

Arjun Rampal: I would give it to Ash. I really admire the way she won Miss World. I remember watching that show. She had a lot of pressure. Sush had gone and won Miss Universe. She had beaten her in Miss India. She was brilliant in Miss World. I mean she won it – hats off to her!

Karan Johar: OK. You choose Aishwarya over Priyanka. All right. The worst criticism about your performance and by whom?

Arjun Rampal: 'He is an eye candy.'

Karan Johar: If you were to cheat on Meher, whom would it be with? Angelina Jolie? Miss India?

Arjun Rampal: All of them!

Karan Johar: Best pick-up line used on you?

Arjun Rampal: 'Take off your clothes!'

> *Karan Johar:* **Best pick-up line used on you?**
> *Arjun Rampal:* **'Take off your clothes!'**

Priyanka Chopra: You were hit that directly?!

Karan Johar: Cheesiest dialogue you were ever asked to say onscreen?

Arjun Rampal: See, I am not good at remembering my lines. I cannot recall.

Karan Johar: All right! Whose face would you like to incise when asked - (a) Mallika Sherawat?

Arjun Rampal: Oh, my god! Mallika has got enough surgery done!

Karan Johar: (b) Kareena Kapoor?

Arjun Rampal: Nothing. I think she is fine.

Karan Johar: (c) Priyanka Chopra?

Arjun Rampal: Priyanka is fine too.

Karan Johar: A rumour afloat about yourself you would like?

Arjun Rampal: 'Arjun is in the next Bond!'

Karan: All right. John-Bipasha, Shahid-Kareena, Vivek-Aishwarya – the onscreen pair that looked most uncomfortable and why.

> **Mallika Sherawat has got enough surgery done already!**
> *–Arjun Rampal*

Arjun Rampal: I think Shahid-Kareena. Why? She is taller than him.

Karan Johar: The male physique on Indian celluloid that you envy?

Arjun Rampal: I think Salman has a great body.

Karan Johar: OK. The female physique on Indian celluloid who needs help?

Arjun Rampal: Well, Manisha is a great actress. She needs to care well about her body.

Karan Johar: A Hindi film that comes to your mind when I say - *Wanna be cool.*

Arjun Rampal: The Vivek-Ash one. *Kyun Ho Gaya Na.*

Karan Johar: All right. Sleazy sex model?

Arjun Rampal: Neha Dhupia in *Sheesha.*

Karan Johar: All right. Pretentious?

Arjun Rampal: *Asambhav.*

Karan Johar: Brilliant cinema.

Arjun Rampal: *Black.*

> **Manisha is a great actress, but she needs to care well about her body!**
> *–Arjun Rampal*

Karan Johar: Choose between Sushmita and Aishwarya.

Arjun Rampal: Ash.

Karan: Priyanka or Kareena?

Arjun Rampal: Priyanka.

Karan Johar: Farhan or Ashutosh?

Arjun Rampal: Farhan.

> *Karan Johar:* Sleazy sex model?
> *Arjun Rampal:* Neha Dhupia in *Sheesha!*

Karan Johar: Wild sex or big hits?

Arjun Rampal: Big hits.

Karan Johar: Oh, God! Poor Meher. All right. Saif's comic timing or Hrithik's dance moves?

Arjun Rampal: Hrithik's dance moves.

Karan Johar: All right. I think Arjun fared well.

Priyanka: I definitely think so, too.

Karan Johar: Should I say so? You gave committed answers.

Arjun Rampal: I walked on a tight rope.

Karan Johar: And then, the very politically correct Priyanka!

Priyanka Chopra: I have gone through trauma.

Arjun Rampal: Anyway, I drink coffee; she does not.

Priyanka Chopra: Yeah. I hate coffee.

> *Karan Johar:* Wild sex or big hits?
> *Arjun Rampal:* Big hits.

Karan Johar: All right. There is lot of other stuff. She drinks *lassi.* Well done, Arjun. Thank you. We shall share.

Arjun Rampal: Of course, we shall share it. Finally, I win something!

CHILLING OUT

Karan Johar: We have photographs taken by the very talented cameraman, Subi Samuel. They are really wacky photographs. Tell me, what the stars conceive? You have to come up with some fun or wit. We shall display the photographs on the monitor. Tell us what the stars conceived during their pose?

Arjun Rampal: We cannot be sued for comments, can we?

Karan Johar: No. I would not sue; I do not know about others. They might be very catty, and very witty.

Arjun Rampal: We shall try.

Karan Johar: You do not get a hamper, but will get applause on your performance. Let me commence with Arjun. The first photograph on the monitor....

Arjun Rampal: 'A good hair day after *Lakshya*.'

Karan Johar: Well done. Photograph two. Aftab.

Arjun Rampal: Oh, My God! 'A bad drug day.'

Karan Johar: All right!

Priyanka Chopra: I am definitely not getting the applause.

Karan Johar: Photograph three. Urmila.

Arjun Rampal: 'Ramu, where did you bring this bread from?'

Karan Johar: Photograph four. John.

Arjun Rampal: 'Why am I not in *Dhoom* 2?'

Karan Johar: All right. That is Priyanka with a *belan*.

Arjun Rampal: 'Karan, sign me now, or else!'

Karan Johar: Fardeen in the pool.

Arjun Rampal: 'Is the party over? Am I the only one in the pool?'

Karan Johar: All right.

Arjun Rampal: Oh, My God! Bipasha *Hunterwali*. 'Stay away from John!'

Karan Johar: All right. The last one.

Arjun Rampal: 'I told you that size matters!'

Karan Johar: All right, Arjun. Very well done in this round. Where were those replies in my *Rapid Fire Round*?

Arjun Rampal: Your questions!

Karan Johar: You did better here. All right. Brace ahead, Priyanka. Watch these photographs. Here you go. Hrithik.

Priyanka Chopra: '*Koi Mil Gaya.*'

Karan Johar: Is that what he conceived?

Priyanka Chopra: I think so.

Karan Johar: OK, second.

Priyanka Chopra: 'I bought my own ring.'

Karan Johar: All right. Well done. Vivek?

Priyanka Chopra: 'This is what they did to me after my first press conference!'

Karan Johar: All right. Well done! Namrata.

Priyanka Chopra: 'My plastic surgeon was squint!'

Karan Johar: Yes. Arjun.

Priyanka Chopra: 'Some day, I will reach the top.' See, I was so nice!

Karan Johar: Very sweet. And that is Shilpa.

Priyanka Chopra: 'It is I – notice me! I am right here. Please.'

Karan Johar: Wonder what that meant? Here is Abhishek.

Priyanka Chopra: 'I could blow my own trumpet!'

Karan Johar: Well done. Rani.

Priyanka Chopra: 'Black hair day.'

Karan Johar: All right. Well done, Priyanka. Thank you. You gave some good answers. You are very witty. What happened to you in my *Rapid Fire* round?

Priyanka Chopra: Your questions!

Arjun Rampal: Now we want to ask you one question.

Karan Johar: Me? OK.

Arjun Rampal: What is the thing of you being chucked out of movie trials these days?

Karan Johar: I got thrown out with Gauri. Rangita Nandy didn't like us. She asked us to leave. We left. Why? She didn't want us to see *Shabd!*

Priyanka Chopra: Why?

Karan Johar: I think she did us a favour. Nobody could say anything else, but there is a photograph of mine. You could comment on it. Arjun, tell me; I do not know what I am doing.

Arjun Rampal: Koffee *mein kuch kala hai!*

Karan Johar: Yes. Priyanka! Do you want to give it a shoot?

Priyanka Chopra: 'How else can I shoot sitting ducks?'

Karan Johar: All right!

CONCLUSION

Karan Johar: Thank you, Arjun. Thank you, Priyanka. Thank you for being on the show. You have been wonderful. I had a great time in the last round. I must say that the lines were very witty. I have a mug next to you which you have to sign, Arjun. Remember, this personally autographed mug could be yours only if you take part in the *koffee quest contest.* Thank you, Arjun. Thank you, Priyanka.

Priyanka Chopra: Thank you.

Arjun Rampal: Thank you, Karan.

Karan Johar: Are you happy that the show is over? Yeah! It has been wonderful to be with you.

Arjun Rampal: It is wonderful.

Karan Johar: Let us walk with that mug to the coffee wall. You have seen the show. You know the drill.

Priyanka Chopra: Yes, we do. Shall we go? Let us go.

Karan Johar: All right. Thank you.

● ● ●

18

Vivek Oberoi & John Abraham
Tango and Cash

His performance in films *Saathiya* and *Company* announced the arrival of a dynamic star. Vivek Oberoi emerged as a star with unconventional appeal and tremendous intensity. The year 2002 truly belonged to him. Some controversies were justified through press conferences, followed by the media bashing. Today, he wants to fight back with a will to survive. He has the support of the most beautiful woman in the world, Aishwarya Rai. Let us find out what makes Vivek Oberoi chime with vagaries of time.

Karan Johar: Hello! Good evening.

Vivek Oberoi: Hi, Karan!

Karan Johar: Welcome to *Koffee with Karan*.

Vivek Oberoi: It is my pleasure.

Karan Johar: Yeah. How do you feel to be on my show?

Vivek Oberoi: I feel rather scared.

Karan Johar: Are you scared? Why?

Vivek Oberoi: I am worried. I find lots of hoardings and signboards displaying 'Beware' everywhere...

Karan Johar: Beware?

Vivek Oberoi: Of *Koffee with Karan*. It is everywhere.

Karan Johar: No. Trust me. I am going to be extremely polite. I will present myself nicely. You will find me a good boy.

Vivek Oberoi: Really? It will not be fun.

EVERYTHING IS FAIR IN LOVE AND WAR

Karan Johar: All right. I do not beat around the bush. I will attack. Are you seeing Aishwarya Rai?

Vivek Oberoi: Yes.

Karan Johar: Wonderful. Why does she never admit it?

Vivek Oberoi: I do not think you have asked her.

> I am really grateful to Heavens to have such a wonderful woman in my life.
> –*Vivek Oberoi*

Karan Johar: Of course I have.

Vivek Oberoi: Did you ask her on the show?

Karan Johar: Well, I know Ash is always very politically correct. She never commented about her personal life. I can understand that. I just wanted to hear it from you.

Vivek Oberoi: Yeah. I am really grateful to Heavens to have such a wonderful woman in my life.

Karan Johar: She has extended her support to you as well.

Vivek Oberoi: Amazing! She is really wonderful.

Karan Johar: You have been through this entire roller coaster ride. You came in 2002 with films like *Company* and *Saathiya*. I believe you took a U-turn in your career, mostly about decisions.

Vivek Oberoi: Yeah.

Karan Johar: I believe there were a few press conferences. There were down swings with media bashings here and there. What was the outcome?

Vivek Oberoi: I believe that it was something I had to do.

> **Salman Khan has been quite interesting whenever we have met.**
> *–Vivek Oberoi*

Karan Johar: OK.

Vivek Oberoi: I stand by it. The decisions have had some repercussions in personal life. I have had lot of media bashing. The entire film industry turned around. It led to a lot of unpleasant developments. I did it to haul the spate of disturbances within my life. Karan! Come on! You have better general knowledge about that.

Karan Johar: All right. You have not interpreted it. I shall say that the troublemaker obviously was Salman Khan. That is what you were referring to.

> **To protect the lady in my life, I did what I thought was right.**
> *–Vivek Oberoi*

Vivek Oberoi: I did not have anything offensive against Salman at the beginning of my career.

Karan Johar: Of course.

Vivek Oberoi: I liked the guy, had nothing personally against him. Moreover, he has been quite interesting whenever we have met. To protect the lady in my life, I did what I thought was right. I got lots of reaction. I stood by that decision and I still do.

Karan Johar: I believe you would do the same if something happens to you. Won't you protect your lady or someone you love? I am sure one would do what you have done.

Vivek Oberoi: We actually operate within a family. It is not so much of a fraternity as it is a family. We sort out our differences within ourselves.

THE OFFICE

Karan Johar: You might have revealed to the world outside probably that this girl (Aishwarya) who was in the fraternity, for about 8-9 years......

Vivek Oberoi: Yes. Members of the fraternity could have solved the problems. The heavyweights in the industry could have helped, but things remained frozen.

Karan Johar: OK.

Vivek Oberoi: So, nobody stepped in and resolved the issue. I had to solve it ~~for~~ being the man in her life. I had to take some stand. I was not big enough in the industry to advise the fraternity and get ~~the~~ things ~~in~~ sorted out. I mean, that is all good to say.

> Aishwarya had been boycotted from different quarters within the industry.
>
> –*Vivek Oberoi*

Karan Johar: Yeah.

Vivek Oberoi: We see quite often that nothing really happens.

Karan Johar: Has she received any support? You might have thought of your importance in her life to lead.

Vivek Oberoi: Yeah. There were situations where she lost work for no fault of hers. She had been boycotted from different quarters within the industry. I often thought about the unfair attitude of the industry.

Karan Johar: OK.

Vivek Oberoi: I thought about weeding out the opposition. Why did the fraternity oppose her instead of supporting her career? I never thought about the modus operandi of the fraternity.

CAREER FAUX PAS

Karan Johar: Well, it is a part of the past. You took erroneous career decisions in your life. You rejected the offer to work in the popular title *Hum Tum*.

Vivek Oberoi: Yeah.

Karan Johar: You might have been annoyed by the people or the brand names...

Vivek Oberoi: I believe refusing to work for *Hum Tum* was probably the biggest mistake of my career. What was even disheartening was the manner in which I refused to do so. I think it was completely unbecoming in terms of my behaviour. There was a complete change in my life thereafter. It was just too much for a kid like me to handle. I told myself that I was a kid. I was just 27-28 years at that time. I was new to the industry and did not know how to work. Lots of people influenced me to remain indifferent.

Karan Johar: Yeah!

Vivek Oberoi: I got carried away in a tumultuous wave of commotion.

I have had peace with many people due to the correct decisions I took. I have reached out and have apologized to the concerned

> I believe refusing to work for *Hum Tum* was probably the biggest mistake of my career.
> –*Vivek Oberoi*

people whenever it was necessary. Kunal, a good friend, extended support during the bad days. What peeved me more was losing a good friend in Kunal than *Hum Tum*.

Karan Johar: OK. Well, that is a part of one's past deeds. I think you should have admitted your mistake with a firm will.

Vivek Oberoi: I think I have been forgiven.

JOHN ABRAHAM

Karan Johar: I will introduce my next guest. You know who he is.

Vivek Oberoi: Yes, I do.

Karan Johar: All right.

Vivek Oberoi: The strange guy on earth with weird reasons who refuses to call me anything else but *Kaju barfi*. Why does he call me so? I have no idea. Please call and ask him.

Karan Johar: OK. We will ask him right now. Hold that thought. He will be the ambassador of girlfriend Bipasha Basu, who has been the ambassador of sensuality in Indian cinema. Today, most women, mostly girls, or chicks like guys on bike. He belongs exactly to that category. Moreover, he is ever ready to ride the bike. Let us call the hottest hunk in Indian cinema. Women love him. As for Most of them balk under his shadow. He is eye candy for them. Yes, he is John Abraham.

John Abraham: How are you doing?

Karan Johar: Good evening. Welcome to *Koffee with Karan*. Thank you. You have to hug me.

Vivek Oberoi: Hi!

JOHN – THE EYECANDY (KAJU BARFI EFFECT)

Karan Johar: Okay. Sit down. Get comfortable.

John Abraham: One second... let me just... I am not used to wearing suits.

Karan Johar: Are you taking off your clothes already?

John Abraham: I am just unbuttoning so that I can be comfortable.

Karan Johar: OK, girls! It is your lucky day. He removed his shirt. I have told good things about you in the introduction —the hottest hunk and what not!

John Abraham: Thanks.

> **Between bikes and me, I think the bike is sexy!**
> *–John Abraham*

Karan Johar: Sexy on a bike. You agree?

John Abraham: I think the bike is sexy, to be very honest.

Karan Johar: OK! The bike is sexy, and then you are?

John Abraham: Absolutely.

Karan Johar: OK.

John Abraham: Everybody looks at me and says 'Hibuza.'

Karan Johar: They call you 'Hibuza?'

John Abraham: They do not say John Abraham. They say 'Hibuza, Hibuza. Where is Hibuza's bike?' That is all they say.

Karan Johar: Oh God! That is not a compliment.

Karan Johar: All right. We want to know why you call him *Kaju barfi*.

John Abraham: Vivek and I have just finished a movie. It is called *Kaal*. Vivek was directly above me. I thought as a co-star, I should take care of him. So I used to feed him *Kaju barfi*.

> **My mom wanted to get me married to a sweet maker as I loved *Kaju barfi*.**
> *–John Abraham*

Vivek Oberoi: Oh God! He fed me *Kaju barfi* for thirty days... is this where it comes from?

Karan Johar: You just wanted him to put on weight.

Vivek Oberoi: Yeah. This is sabotage. Now you understand why I look fat in the film. And he looks like that.

Karan Johar: Because he got you all fed up and bloated.

Vivek Oberoi: It was just because of my splendid physique and super model looks that the film cashed me in.

Karan Johar: Oh, I vouch for that thing. You do not have any *Kaju barfi*. It is evident from your looks.

John Abraham: I swear on you, I eat a lot. You can ask Vivek about the habit.

> **I eat a lot!**
> *–John Abraham*

Vivek Oberoi: He is the worst guy. Sorry, John.

Karan Johar: I have heard about you endorsing heroes to become fat to ensure your looks.

Vivek Oberoi: Did Abhishek and Uday tell you?

Karan Johar: Abhishek, Uday, Vivek – I have been told by all.

John Abraham: No.

Karan Johar: It is all part of a conspiracy.

Vivek Oberoi: Chocolates, sweets - everything reaches your room.

John Abraham: I eat a lot. When I was small, my mom wanted to get me married to a sweet maker as I loved *Kaju barfi*. I just feed that to everybody.

Karan Johar: Sweet maker? John! What about the criticism on your looks, physique, and performance?

John Abraham: Yeah. Now that may be changing.

LOOKS VS TALENT

Karan Johar: Initially, the perception was — use John for his looks and nothing else.

> People came to see Bipasha Basu in Jism; no one came to see me.
>
> *–John Abraham*

John Abraham: I completely agree with you. That was the initial perception. People came to see Bipasha Basu in *Jism*. No one came to see me. Even the hoardings, to be frank, carried Bipasha Basu. So presuming not to have performed in that movie, I would not have sat in front of you. I would not have enacted in *Dhoom*. Aditya chose me because he liked me in *Jism*. He told me that I had enacted better than I looked. So it was the initial inertia that got me by.

Karan Johar: So do you think that whole thought process is changing now?

John Abraham: Hopefully, yeah. I am still very new in comparison to the established actors. I have been learning how to be in demand of big producers. I have not entered the movies directed by you and Aditya. I may get in there any time. I will make the A-list by the grace of God.

ON BIPASHA BASU

Karan Johar: All right. Aishwarya Rai and Bipasha Basu cannot perform without Vivek

> I feel complimented by the fact that people find Bipasha sexy.
> *–John Abraham*

Oberoi and John Abraham. What happens, John? So many boys have been lusting for Bipasha. They find her the sexiest woman ever. Does that make you feel insecure?

John Abraham: On the contrary, you feel complimented. People turn aggressive when we participate in public places. The crowd swells out disproportionately and turns aggressive. It warrants you to discipline them. Bipasha told me, 'John! Most of the men who ogle at me are shorter than me, so I can handle the scene myself. You come into the picture when I find taller guys.'

Karan Johar: So that is when you arrive.

John Abraham: Yeah.

Karan Johar: You say 'discipline them,' which is a very polite way of saying you must be hitting them.

John Abraham: No, I do not hurt anyone. Somebody told once that I became a He-man during the shooting of *Rain*. Yeah. Someone tried to grab Bipasha. To be honest, I wanted to do something had he grabbed anyone – probably, I would have disciplined them. That was not much.

Karan Johar: I believe you use the word *discipline,* but not those like jealous, envious, irritating moments in building up a relation.

> Bipasha and my arguments are always constructive.
> *–John Abraham*

John Abraham: Yeah. We argue about different things. It is always a constructive argument. Work does not permit us to spend much time together. See how Bipasha has lost weight. She has to work more. Whatever little time we get to spend together proves to be qualitative. Let us talk about nicer things.

Vivek Oberoi: Bipasha told me that it was really funny when they partied together because he stood around looking at the dancer when she danced.

Karan Johar: What do you look like when you stand around Aishwarya?

Vivek Oberoi: Nothing. I have not faced such problem.

John Abraham: Big bouncer.

Karan Johar: Big what? Big bouncer. OK.

CHIVALROUS VIVEK

Vivek Oberoi: I am aggressively protective about any lady around me. I have been so since my childhood. That is why I identify and agree with John. And there was a stupid thing in between when they said that Bipasha should watch the way she dresses and blah blah blah. I think that that was really

> **I can behave a little uncivilized when my girlfriend is not in town.**
> –*Vivek Oberoi*

uncivilized and stupid, and backwards to talk like that. I think she is a wonderful girl. I have interacted with her. She is in her place to wear what she likes and do what she wants freely.

John Abraham: She is very civilized in her dressing.

Karan Johar: We will speak about Aishwarya. Why are you starting on Bipasha?

John Abraham: She dresses in an extremely civilized manner. What is this? His buttons are open till there. See, the cleavage is showing. Bipasha is very civilized.

Vivek Oberoi: My girlfriend is not in town. So I can behave a little uncivilized.

LOVE VS EGO

Karan Johar: OK. What happens when your girlfriend grabs ~~the~~ attention? Forget about men in general. What do you feel when she is on the cover of an international magazine and social platforms? People say that she is the face of Indian cinema. Do you ~~find~~feel jealousy and insecurity?

Vivek Oberoi: Not really. I have come from a stage where I was her fan. I am in her life today.

Karan Johar: So you are dating a star of whom ~~that~~ you were a fan ~~of~~.

Vivek Oberoi: Yeah, I have been a fan of her work. I think she was brilliant in *Hum Dil* ... I thought she was brilliant in *Taal, Devdas* and I presume to be so in *Raincoat* and *Choker Bali*. She was highly underrated as an actress.

> **Aishwarya was brilliant in *Hum Dil De Chuke Sanam!***
> –*Vivek Oberoi*

Karan Johar: OK.

Vivek Oberoi: She gets the accolades she deserves. I believe unless you are really insecure about who you are and what your potential is, you should not have any problem with your successful spouse or partner. You should be able to celebrate that. I believe in celebrating.

Karan Johar: If you can manage to do that, then that will be amazing.

Vivek Oberoi: I think that is one thing. We have been very supportive of each other. I am happy to see that she has grown in leaps and bounds. She has done brilliantly.

Karan Johar: What happens when people comment on what Vivek Oberoi is doing in the Cannes festival? What was he doing while hanging around Aishwarya Rai? How do you take that kind of criticism?

> **Very few people know that Aishwarya is just amazing.**
> *–Vivek Oberoi*

Vivek Oberoi: I do not think it was anybody's business. You have to measure the pros and cons when you are with the most wonderful woman in the world.

Karan Johar: Yeah.

Vivek Oberoi: I am not commenting on Aishwarya Rai, the actress or the starlet. I am speaking about the simple girl behind that make-up. Very few people know that she is just amazing. The way she touched my life and changed my personality as an individual is amazing.

Bygone Relationships

Karan Johar: Well done. How do you deal with her former boyfriends?

Vivek Oberoi: I do not want to.

Karan Johar: And you have former girlfriends. How does she deal with them?

Vivek Oberoi: We do not (deal).

Karan Johar: For many years, she has been with Dino Morea!

John Abraham: Yeah.

Karan Johar: And before that, there have been other relations. So does that come in your way?

John Abraham: Not really.

Karan Johar: So you just leave the past out of the way?

John Abraham: Yeah. I guess so. It is better that way.

> **Bipasha and I don't deal with our past relationships.**
> *–John Abraham*

Karan Johar: OK. Not to allow it to affect the present.

John Abraham: Yeah.

Karan Johar: The same with you?

Vivek Oberoi: Not exactly. I have not dealt the way he has. I think it is just part of life to cash in on jokes.

Karan Johar: Do you know what is he talking about?

John Abraham: Yeah. I have read about it.

Vivek Oberoi: He has proved to be a good buddy.

Karan Johar: Oh! Would you have done the same in that situation?

John Abraham: No. I would have sorted it out in a disciplined manner without meeting the press. I would have done a bit from my side. Each one of us has to resort to his own methods.

ON RUMOURS AND LINK-UPS

Karan Johar: What happens about the rumours afloat across the place? Like your supposed link-up with Lara Dutta. Does that affect your relation or bother you?

John Abraham: No. See, he is laughing.

Karan Johar: Laughter means what I do not know.

Vivek Oberoi: I was there for 45 days during the shooting of *Kaal*.

Karan Johar: You want to share something with us?

Vivek Oberoi: Oh my God! You know things about Lara - those girls and actresses are such a hoax. Nobody knows the real thing. He was crazy about Vaishali, who lived right behind us. He used to frolic with her. Our association started around her.

Karan Johar: Did you partake in that affair?

Vivek Oberoi: I broke down as I was emotionally connected to Vaishali.

> **John was crazy about Vaishali during the shooting of *Kaal***
> *–Vivek Oberoi*

Karan Johar: What! Let's talk about Lara Dutta. I do not want to talk about any washerwoman. How did that rumour start?

John Abraham: It commenced from the movie we have made. Lara and Bipasha knew each other. It does not really make any difference to me

Karan Johar: Meaning?

John Abraham: I am just doing my work. I read about selective distortion. You will exercise the option either on selecting or hearing something. You keep away from the things you dislike to hear. Nothing really affects me negatively or positively.

> **Nothing really affects me negatively or positively about rumours.**
>
> *–John Abraham*

John Abraham: The better option left with me is to continue working.

Karan Johar: OK.

John Abraham: Right, now?

Karan Johar: Yeah, right of course. You don't let it affect you or bother you?

John Abraham: Not at all?

Vivek Oberoi: It seldom affects him whether he has had any affair.

Karan Johar: Yeah. I am still not getting it right. You are not denying it.

John Abraham: He spoke about Vaishali, the washerwoman.

Karan Johar: You are not denying the affair. I do not want to know more about the affair.

John Abraham: I am denying the affair very honestly.

Karan Johar: Are you?

John Abraham: Yeah. I assert that I have nothing to do with Lara.

> **It seldom affects John whether he has had any affair.**
>
> *–Vivek Oberoi*

Karan Johar: Is it so?

John Abraham: No.

Vivek Oberoi: Kelly will be so happy.

Karan Johar: OK! You have not been naughty at all.

Vivek Oberoi: I am a good boy.

Karan Johar: Has he seen anything?

John Abraham: On the sets...

Vivek Oberoi: I will kill you, John, if you talk rubbish.

John Abraham: No. We hung around with more boys on the sets, played table tennis and roamed around while on the set of *Kaal*. It was a healthy atmosphere. Ajay was there.

Karan Johar: So, you have not seen Vivek doing something that he should not have been?

On Rani Mukherjee

John Abraham: I do not know whether he has a bodyguard up there. What really materialized was a professional relationship with Rani Mukherjee. Of course, she dislikes commenting on you.

Karan Johar: Anything went wrong?

Vivek Oberoi: I have shared a wonderful relation with Rani. It meant a lot more to me than the professional one. I reached out to her personally as a friend. Something went wrong. It is an industry where people talk with a tendency to divide the shades of opinion. I believe life is long. We are sure to work with each other. I have great regards for her professionally. I am sure it will clear out when we work together.

Karan Johar: She does not look eye-to-eye with you.

Vivek Oberoi: It should be sorted out. She is too wonderful as an actress for me not to work with. They have been wonderful people, extending warmth and affection.

> My relationship with Rani (Mukherjee) meant a lot more than the professional one.
> *–Vivek Oberoi*

John Abraham: Mr. India.

Karan Johar: He takes a politically correct stand. Rani, of course, adores you, John.

John Abraham: Yeah, I also adore her a lot.

Karan Johar: Yes.

Vivek Oberoi: John has a thing for Bengalis, in case you did not know.

Karan Johar: Yes, I know.

John Abraham: Rani is damn cute.

Karan Johar: All right. Rani Mukherjee ignores Vivek Oberoi, but adores John Abraham.

'Arrogant' Vivek and 'looker' John

John Abraham: Do you want to see Vivek on the set? I do not know what is acting all about. My father saw *Dhoom* and *Jism,* and wondered the way I did not act. So, I really do not know. I remember there was a scene. Vivek is an arrogant guy in the movie *Kaal.*

Vivek Oberoi: Don't make it up John.

John Abraham: The director Soham told him, 'Listen Vivek, you're getting arrogant. You found my level (of arrogance) either at 2 or 7 on the set. I am ready for the shot. Let me know exactly at what level you want to cast me?

Vivek Oberoi: Oh, this is such a...

> My father saw *Dhoom* and *Jism,* and wondered the way I did not act.
>
> *–John Abraham*

Karan Johar: Levels of arrogance?

John Abraham: Yeah.

Vivek Oberoi: In real life?

Karan Johar: Show me how you did it?

John Abraham: You know, Vivek does something like this – whenever he stands up, puts his hair down and gets ready for the shot, he says, 'Soham, I am ready for the shot. Tell me what to do.' 'OK! Soham I am ready. Come on, get ready to roll.' He always moves his body around like this. I can do more. I will not do it right now on the show.

Karan Johar: You have anything to portray about John?

Vivek Oberoi: John has this tendency of, you know, doing two things. He kills people with one liners and comments. He looks very nice and simple as a good boy. He attacks people in an innocent manner.

Karan Johar: Innocent?

Vivek Oberoi: Innocent about it.

Karan Johar: So I figured.

Vivek Oberoi: Like what he is doing right now. He is gutting me by remaining

> John kills people with one liners and comments.
>
> *–Vivek Oberoi*

innocent. He has the tendency of doing everything. He looks in the mirror and puts strands of hair behind his head. He always looks at his chest and arms, and applies this whole lotion and colour. He does every shot after the bronzer. Ask anybody from the cast and crew. We wait for John to give the shot. He looks around and says, 'Nice, good, uh-huh.' He keeps doing what he needs to. He is cut off from you and thinks about bikes, Bipasha, etc.

Karan Johar: Really.

John Abraham: I put on the bronze colour because I sweat so much. I have to describe an incident, which is really funny.

Karan Johar: Yes, please tell.

John Abraham: We had a running sequence in the movie.

Karan Johar: I know that.

John Abraham: Vivek and Lara ran in front of me. After the first run, Vivek was exhausted.. So action director Allen demanded what happened. I comforted Vivek and I told him to wait, just relax, everything is fine. He said okay. He came back and sat there. I told him that I would go for one more run. I ran and returned since Vivek and Lara sat. From then on Vivek identified me as a cross country racer.

Vivek Oberoi: Runner.

> **There is some level of arrogance in Vivek.**
> *–John Abraham*

John Abraham: So, I'm like OK.

Vivek Oberoi: Ask him what happened after that.

Karan Johar: What happened after that?

Vivek Oberoi: Allen tried to create hurdles in the middle of the shot over one branch. He sent me landing with my knees out.

THE TANGO AND CASH EFFECT

Karan Johar: I wonder about such tremendous love that exists between you. Do you like Vivek?

Vivek Oberoi: Yeah. He is a sweet and nice guy. Once, he was subjected to diarrhea.

> **John is very intelligent compared to what he looks like.**
> *–Vivek Oberoi*

Karan Johar: He is just humane.

John Abraham: A nice boy.

Karan Johar: What about you?

Vivek Oberoi: John is a wonderful guy.

Karan Johar: Stop your speech. What do you mean? It was a wonderful time working with him?

Vivek Oberoi: I had a very good time. He is very intelligent compared to what he looks like. You know, his body.

Karan Johar: OK. It was contrary to popular belief.

Vivek Oberoi: Very smart, very mature.

Karan Johar: What happens when Vivek is a boy? And so everyone loves to hate him in the fraternity. Do you hear things like that? How do you evaluate things?

John Abraham: Well, I had heard a lot about Vivek before I came to shoot. There is some level of arrogance. And there is —

Vivek Oberoi: Level 2 or 7?

John Abraham: Whatever. Maybe it was 11, I do not know.

Karan Johar: Well done.

John Abraham: I heard something about the way Vivek is and how he. But He has been a lovely co-star. He has given cues even

> **Vivek has verbal diarrhea – he speaks continuously about something or the other.**
> *–John Abraham*

when he was not on camera. He has been fun-loving, nice and very helpful. I have had a great experience, a lovely experience.

Karan Johar: He just has verbal diarrhea, as you said.

John Abraham: Yeah. You speak continuously about something or the other.

Karan Johar: Is that you Vivek?

Vivek Oberoi: I do not know...

PERCEPTION VS REALITY

Karan Johar: Initially, when you came in. They said, 'Oh! Vivek has an opinion on the shot, on the scene and everything.' Did that harm your commercial prospects subsequently? Do you think that that was an unnecessary perception - that Vivek interferes creatively? Was that true?

Vivek Oberoi: Yeah. It must have been true. There must be something real about for people to have made their observation. I believe that life is about living, learning and moving on. I have learnt and made conscious efforts when I really became enthusiastic about something. Sometimes, enthusiasm is misinterpreted as interference.

Karan Johar: There is a thin line between passion and interference.

Vivek Oberoi: Absolutely.

Karan Johar: Often, you may have crossed that without realisation.

> **I have crossed the line between passion and interference many times.**
> *–Vivek Oberoi*

Vivek Oberoi: I must have crossed it many times. That is the reason why a lot of people have felt it. There must be some truth in it.

Karan Johar: What about you, John, on the set? I mean, do you look beyond the mirror?

John Abraham: No.

Karan Johar: Do you get into the scene, into the structure of the film? Or do you think you are completely the actor of a director? Do you come blank on the sets?

John Abraham: I will listen to the director when he calls for something. I shall follow whatever instructions he gives.

Karan Johar: All right. Totally?

John Abraham: Yeah.

> **I am completely a director's actor.**
> *–John Abraham*

Karan Johar: So you would say that you're a director's actor?

John Abraham: Completely. I try my level best and remain honest to my shot. I will try to remain safe, if I cannot do more than that.

Karan Johar: No, but your effort is evident. Everyone believes that you develop with every passing film. I believe it with confidence.

K3G AND KARAN

John Abraham: It will be so from the first film that you offered me. Karan! Do you remember *K3G*?

Karan Johar: Look, don't get into that.

John Abraham: You offered me the role of Rocky who was Kareena's boyfriend.

Karan Johar: Robby, on the bike, like that. He had one line and one scene in the whole movie.

John Abraham: Karan offered it to me so sincerely. I said, 'John, it is a lovely role. I really do not want to do it.'

Karan Johar: I want to tell you that I was one of the judges when he was crowned.

John Abraham: Gladrags.

Karan Johar: Not crowned. Sorry. He was strapped.

John Abraham: I was stripped and then strapped.

> **Karan offered me the role of Robby who was Kareena's boyfriend in K3G!**
> *–John Abraham*

Karan Johar: Stripped and strapped. Right. He came to me. I said, 'Poor fellow, why does he wants to become a hero?' He is the kind of model who would be great on the ramp – but definitively never on the screen.

John Abraham: Yeah.

Karan Johar: I told him when he came to me, 'Look! You should weigh your options, do other stuff.'

John Abraham: I came to you, Karan, because I asked you for a lot of advice. I was offered X Y Z movies. What could I do?

Vivek Oberoi: Robby.

John Abraham: Robby. I was searching for Robby in the movie. 'Where's Robby, where's Robby?' And I couldn't see Robby.

Karan Johar: I am sorry about that.

John Abraham: I have traveled a long way..

Karan Johar: To become the poster boy of one of my films?

John Abraham: One of your films.

> It is like having pizzas and burgers in the house with a name like John Abraham.
> —*John Abraham*

Karan Johar: Well done. I am sorry. I never thought you would reach that stage.

John Abraham: I know. No one ever thought.

Vivek Oberoi: That is something that he always says.

John Abraham: Yeah. It is like having pizzas and burgers in the house with a name like John Abraham, and what would happen? So, I would understand.

ON TIGERS AND BRAVENESS

Karan Johar: What happened when you were shooting for 'Kaal' with tigers?

John Abraham: Yeah. We were in front of the tiger. Soham said, 'Turn back and I will give you the cues. Relax, relax.' But the minute Sher Khan, Tara and Titan, the three tigers were in front of us and they were looking at us, both of us were like statues. There was no movement.

Karan Johar: The news report justified that he was rather brave.

John Abraham: He tells lies.

Vivek Oberoi: I think...

Karan Johar: Was he not brave?

John Abraham: We were all scared.

> The day after we finished shooting *Kaal*, the trainer was attacked by his own tiger.
> —*Vivek Oberoi*

Vivek Oberoi: It was really brave from the entire cast point. Everybody – John, me, even the girls. They were so close to real roaring tigers. The felines could have attacked. We finished shooting the day after which the trainer was attacked by his own tiger. A real act of courage, indeed, since we had nothing between the tigers and us.

Karan Johar: You dared to face while others did not?

John Abraham: Yeah. I was scared.

Vivek Oberoi: We were scared.

Karan Johar: Vivek was naughty?

John Abraham: Vivek is Mr. India.

> **Tara (the tigress in *Kaal*) hit on me. Not Lara, Tara. Lara is that (John's) side!**
> *—Vivek Oberoi*

Vivek Oberoi: I am a tiger by myself. I growled right back. Tara hit on me. Not Lara, Tara. Lara is that side.

Karan Johar: All right.

Vivek Oberoi: Sorry, I mean in terms of our link-ups.

RAPID FIRE

Karan Johar: I will have fun in what I will do next – my rapid fire round!

Vivek Oberoi: Yeah!

Karan Johar: Do you know what it is?

Vivek Oberoi: I love that.

Karan Johar: Do you know the rapid fire?

Vivek Oberoi: Yeah. I love rapid fire.

Karan Johar: I throw a volley of questions. You have to answer them quickly. I will decide who is better, you or Vivek. If you're better, you will win the *Koffee with Karan koffee hamper.*

Vivek Oberoi: Amazing!

John Abraham: Yeah.

Karan Johar: Are you ready to rock the rapid fire round?

John Abraham: Whom are you starting with? Him or me?

JOHN UNDER (RAPID) FIRE

Karan Johar: John. What is the sexiest part of Bipasha?

John Abraham: Her voice.

Karan Johar: OK.

John Abraham: Body.

Karan Johar: Better.

> **The sexiest part of Bipasha is her voice!**
> *—John Abraham*

John Abraham: Face.

Karan Johar: Much better. OK. Women find John Abraham sexy because...

John Abraham: He is honest.

Karan Johar: You think they like you because of your honesty and not for your body?

John Abraham: I think it is more honesty on the camera, unassuming.

Karan Johar: Body building tips to.... (A) Vivek Oberoi?

John Abraham: Stop eating *Kaju barfi.*

Vivek Oberoi: Yes.

John Abraham: Stop having *Malai Kofta,* mayonnaise, and stealing my chocolates.

Karan Johar: All right.

Vivek Oberoi: Stealing!

> **Shahid Kapoor should reduce his biceps slightly to have a proportionate look.**
>
> *–John Abraham*

Karan Johar: ....(B) Shahid Kapoor?

John Abraham: Shahid Kapoor, reduce slightly. He is a sweet looking boy. Reduce your biceps slightly to have a proportionate look.

Karan Johar: OK. Well done..... (C) Aamir Khan?

John Abraham: Aamir Khan is perfect the way he is. He is superb. He does not need anything. He is just right.

Karan Johar: All right. ..... (D) Shahrukh Khan?

John Abraham: He should be giving tips to me, but I am giving them now.

Karan Johar: All right. Akshay Kumar, Salman Khan, Arjun Rampal and Sanjay Dutt. Please rate them in the order of their physical fitness.

John Abraham: Salman Khan, Akshay Kumar, Arjun Rampal and Sanjay Dutt.

Karan Johar: If you were forced to give advice to Vivek, what would it be?

John Abraham: Talk less. Honestly. A good boy. He needs to talk less.

Karan Johar:. A Hollywood actress you love to commit *Paap* with?

John Abrham: Nicole Kidman.

Karan Johar: Which of the following statements are true? 1. Models cannot act.

John Abrham: Untrue.

Karan Johar: Only sex and SRK sell.

John Abrham: False.

Karan Johar: What else sells?

John Abraham: Good films.

Karan Johar: Off screen couples seldom work on screen.

John Abraham: Untrue. It works if your movie is good. Whether you're onscreen or off-screen, nothing will help you if you are in a bad movie. It will seldom work if you are bad.

Karan Johar: Okay. The onscreen moment between you and Bipasha that really turned you on?

John Abraham: I guess the number *Jadoo Hai Nasha Hai* in the film *Jism*.

Karan Johar: Comment why the off-screen chemistry does not translate into the onscreen variety.

John Abraham: True. You could be the best of buddies off screen. You might have a great sensual or sexual or love relationship. But that seldom translates onscreen. That is primarily so because you are the director.

Karan Johar: Alright.

John Abraham: Of your own little movie.

Karan Johar: Okay. Well done. The best part about being in relationship with an actress is?

John Abraham: You were the boyfriend of an actress.

Karan Johar: Okay. The worst part?

John Abraham: You have a lot of actors indirectly to compete with you.

Vivek Oberoi: Yeah!

Karan Johar: All right. If you were stranded in a tiger infested jungle with Kareena and Amisha, you would...

John Abraham: I would love to be with the tigers.

Karan Johar: So you prefer the tigers to poor Kareena and Amisha! The cast of *Dhoom 2* would be...

John Abraham: I guess the way it is right now. Adi knows exactly what he is doing.

Karan Johar: Very quickly, choices then. Bikes or babes?

John Abraham: Bikes.

Karan Johar: Lara or Priyanka?

John Abraham: Priyanka.

Karan Johar: Ashutosh or Farhan?

John Abraham: Farhan.

Karan Johar: Vivek on the sets or Vivek off the sets.

John Abraham: Both.

Karan Johar: Working out or making out?

John Abraham: Working out while making out.

Vivek Oberoi: Pretty good.

> **If I was stranded in a tiger infested jungle with Kareena and Amisha, I would love to be with the tigers!**
>
> *–John Abraham*

> *Karan Johar:* Working out or making out?
>
> *John Abraham:* Working out while making out.

Karan Johar: Very good.

Vivek Oberoi: Now you know how he is so fit.

Karan Johar: Abhishek or Uday?

John Abraham: I guess both of them. They are both darlings, sweethearts.

Karan Johar: All right. Well done, John; answered very well. Congratulations!

John Abraham: Thanks.

Karan Johar: Now, I have to turn left.

Vivek Oberoi: Hello.

Karan Johar: I have one more person you have to compete with.

Vivek Oberoi: Hamper is mine.

John Abraham: Hamper is mine.

VIVEK UNDER (RAPID) FIRE

Karan Johar: Are you ready?

Vivek Oberoi: Ready.

Karan Johar: All right. The worst part about having an actress as a girlfriend is...

Vivek Oberoi: The lack of time with each other.

Karan Johar: Your worst error of judgment ——*Road, Kisna* or *Kyon, Ho Gaya Na?*

Vivek Oberoi: *Kyon, Ho Gaya Na?*

Karan Johar: Why would that be?

Vivek Oberoi: Was there any script? I was just carried away by working with a friend.

Karan Johar: What will you do if you get stuck in an elevator with Salman Khan?

> **My worst error of judgment was *Kyon, Ho Gaya Na?* Was there any script?**
>
> *–Vivek Oberoi*

Vivek Oberoi: I think I will talk it out to clear the misunderstandingsit.

Karan Johar: Your take on the following. Press conferences? Quickly.

Vivek Oberoi: Bad idea.

Karan Johar: OK. So what you did was bad?

Vivek Oberoi: No, just joking.

Karan Johar: All right. Mobile phones, cameras?

Vivek Oberoi: Dangerous.

Karan Johar: Film critics?

Vivek Oberoi: Great! Sometimes pain in the back, but mostly great.

Karan Johar: Who is the Hollywood actress with whom you would love to have fun?

Vivek Oberoi: Salma Hayek.

Karan Johar: Vivek Oberoi is misunderstood because… complete the sentence.

> **I am misunderstood because I commit too many mistakes.**
>
> *–Vivek Oberoi*

Vivek Oberoi: He commits too many mistakes.

Karan Johar: If you were stuck in a tiger infested jungle with Sushmita Sen, you would...

Vivek Oberoi: I would stick with the tigers.

John Abraham: Give me the hamper now.

Karan Johar: Is that so?

Vivek Oberoi: A tigress would wait back home.

Karan Johar: All right. Rate yourself on a scale of 1 to 10 as an actor.

Vivek Oberoi: 3.

Karan Johar: Boyfriend.

Vivek Oberoi: 9.

Karan Johar: Social worker.

Vivek Oberoi: 6.

> I think Bipasha is one of the sexiest on screen.
> *–Vivek Oberoi*

Karan Johar: Your comment when asked about Rani Mukherjee?

Vivek Oberoi: Wonderful actress. Very warm person.

Karan Johar: Is that all?

Vivek Oberoi: She is hot.

Karan Johar: A current Hindi film heroine who has turned you on. Please don't say, 'Aishwarya Rai.'

Vivek Oberoi: I think Bipasha is one of the sexiest on screen.

Karan Johar: OK. Somebody you would like to apologize on camera?

Vivek Oberoi: Aditya Chopra and Kunal Kohli.

> *Karan Johar:* Yash Chopra or Sanjay Bhansali?
> *Vivek Oberoi:* Yash Chopra. I like colour movies rather than black or white.

Karan Johar: What would you say when accused of being a me-too of Shahrukh Khan?

Vivek Oberoi: Oh, my God! That's like a huge compliment, man. Shahrukh Khan is like God.

Karan Johar: Aishwarya in Hollywood or in Bollywood?

Vivek Oberoi: Aishwarya in my arms.

John Abraham: That's a nice answer.

Karan Johar: Ram Gopal Verma or Mani Ratnam?

Vivek Oberoi: A bit of both.

Karan Johar: Yash Chopra or Sanjay Bhansali?

Vivek Oberoi: Yash Chopra. I like colour movies rather than black or white.

Karan Johar: Well done. *Company* or *Saathiya*?

Vivek Oberoi: *Saathiya*.

Karan Johar: Hrithik Roshan or Aamir Khan?

Vivek Oberoi: One is a great buddy. Another is a brilliant actor.

No Losers

Karan Johar: That brings us to the end of my rapid fire round. You have done very well. Both of you deserve the hamper.

John Abraham: Thank you.

Karan Johar: So, we have two hampers for the first time. Actually, two men have won. Earlier, Shobha De and Shabana Azmi won it together. For the first time, we have two men who won the coffee hampers. I could not decide. Congratulations on winning the *koffee hampers,* both of you!

Vivek Oberoi: Thank you.

John Abraham: Thank you.

Karan Johar: How does it feel to win the *koffee hamper?*

John Abraham: Is there Kaju in it?

Karan Johar: You can feed it to Vivek.

John Abraham: OK.

Karan Johar: OK. Now we do something fun in our final segment. We asked people about our guests in a survey. We went to some women to find out (A) Who is better between Vivek Oberoi and John Abraham? (B) Who is sexier amongst them? Would you like to see it? Watch the glamorous women talk about you.

Vivek Oberoi: Oh my God! That is a long one.

On John Abraham

Preity Zinta: Vavavooooom.

Rani Mukherjee: He's hot.

Farah Khan: He is a good Parsi boy.

Lara Dutta: Sex symbol.

Priyanka Chopra: He is a very good soul.

Neha Dhupia: Tall, dark and handsome.

Malaika Arora: Is very James Deans.

On Vivek Oberoi

Lara Dutta: First thing that comes to your mind when you say Vivek...

Farah Khan: Press, camera, photographer.

Malaika Arora: Quite sincere.

Kareena Kapoor: He is very sweet.

Lara Dutta: Talkative.

Kareena Kapoor: Very well-mannered.

Lara Dutta: Fun.

Bipasha and John

> **They have this very animal PETA to look them.**
> *–Farah Khan*

Farah Khan: They are very smoldering. They have this very animal PETA to look them. Sorry, John.

Rani Mukherjee: Both of them compliment each other. Bipasha is hot and so is John.

Malaika Arora: They were really hot and totally burned the screen in *Jism*.

Kareena Kapoor: They had great chemistry in *Jism's* number *Jadoo Hai Nasha Hai*.

Neha Dhupia: They flatter each other.

VIVEK AND AISHWARYA

Farah Khan: Vivek and Ash are hot on screen. They make a really sexy couple.

Malaika Arora: I do not think so. I think they were very *thanda* onscreen.

Lara Dutta: They make an unlikely sort of pairing couple. Opposites attract when looks are concerned.

Kareena Kapoor: I have seen *Kyon, Ho Gaya Na*? I think I will make a better pair with him.

> **I think I will make a better pair with him than Bipasha!**
> *–Kareena Kapoor*

Neha Dhupia: Great.

JOHN THE ACTOR

> **I was quite shocked to see John act so well!**
> *–Farah Khan*

Farah Khan: I really liked John a lot in *Jism*. In fact, I was quite shocked to see him act so well.

Lara Dutta: Yes. I would say he has the potential as an actor. But he is not there yet.

Malaika Arora: He has loads of scope to improve.

Rani Mukerjee: His presence in *Dhoom* was definitely something that added on to the film.

Kareena Kapoor: *Dhoom* was not really a performance driven role as such. It was more of a biking look that worked.

Priyanka Chopra: He is one of those complete actors who can act, dance, as well as look great.

VIVEK THE ACTOR

> **Sometimes, Vivek gets carried away by wanting to be a hero on screen rather than an actor.**
> *–Lara Dutta*

Preity Zinta: I only saw bits of *Company*. I thought he was very good.

Lara Dutta: Vivek is a very good actor. Sometimes, he gets carried away by wanting to be a hero on screen rather than an actor.

Kareena Kapoor: He is very natural. I have seen *Company*, *Sathiya*. and *Yuva*.

Malaika Arora: I see him more like some bad boy.

Farah Khan: I think Vivek is a tremendous actor. I was really shocked when I saw *Sathiya*.

GRADES ON ACTING

Malaika Arora: Vivek will lie between 6 and 7 as an actor on a scale of 1-10. I would give John 5.

Lara Dutta: John will get 5 on 10. I would give Vivek at least 8.

Farah Khan: John as an actor is 9 on 10. Vivek as an actor is 8 on 10.

Priyanka Chopra: John will get 7 on 10 and Vivek as 8 on 10 as an actor.

Kareena Kapoor: I have only seen John's role in *Dhoom*; I will give him 5 and Vivek 8.

Neha Dhupia: I would give John 7 on 10 as far as his acting abilities and Vivek 8-1/2 out of 10.

Preity Zinta: I have seen only one film of John, *Jism*. He was pretty good. I will give him 7 on 10, while Vivek will score 9 on 10 as an actor.

SEX APPEAL

JOHN ABRAHAM

Lara Dutta: John's sex appeal lies on being a hot Parsi with long hair.

Rani Mukherjee: His face, his smile, his eyes.

Kareena Kapoor: I do not think he is really sexy. But he's good looking.

Farah Khan: He has this macho image and very renegade, rebel kind of dressing and looks. He is a very good mama's boy. He is soft spoken and well-mannered.

Lara Dutta: He has a great body. He works out. He knows bikes. He does things fast and furious; that ticks him out.

Neha Dhupia: He has got a certain kind of casualness that he works on a lot. Like the whole *ganji* and jeans.

Preity Zinta: John without a shirt is almost perfect. He has washboard ads; he has got a great body.

Farah Khan: You do not have to imagine John shirtless. John is shirtless most of the times.

Kareena Kapoor: The only screen actor in the industry that looks hot shirtless is Salman Khan.

VIVEK OBEROI

Lara Dutta: I don't consider Vivek to be my sexy type. I think he has a boyish charm, which is really good.

Malaika Arora: No offence to Vivek. Vivek is not my kind of hot.

Neha Dhupia: He is not perfect looking. Sorry.

Priyanka Chopra: He has those puppy dogs' eyes, which are not sexy but very endearing.

Neha Dhupia: He is more reliable to appear normal.

Kareena Kapoor: He has very unconventional looks. Something nice about him is that he will not look the best.

> Something nice about Vivek is that he will not look the best.
> –*Kareena Kapoor*

Farah Khan: Yeah. I guess some people would find him sexy. Aishwarya Rai does.

GRADES ON SEX APPEAL

Lara Dutta: I would give John 10 on 10 for sex appeal. Vivek on sex appeal, I would say just 7 on 10.

Farah Khan: John on sex appeal would fetch 8 out of 10. Vivek gets 10 out of 10.

Malaika Arora: John overrates with 7.

Kareena Kapoor: John in sex appeal gets 6; Vivek 6.

Priyanka Chopra: John gets 9 on 10 and Vivek 6 on 10 for sex appeal.

Priety Zinta: John and Vivek will get 9 and 7 on 10 respectively for sex appeal.

Neha Dhupia: John will get 8 and Vivek 7 on 10 for sex appeal.

Vivek Oberoi: I am surprised.

ACTING VS SEX APPEAL

Lara Dutta: John is sexier than Vivek. Vivek is a better actor than John.

Farah: Vivek Oberoi is sexier than John. John is a better actor than Vivek but.....

Kareena Kapoor: John, do not feel that I have been partial to Vivek and vice-versa. You are really nice guys.

Priyanka Chopra: I am sorry if I have said anything wrong. Good luck for you in whatever you do.

Lara Dutta: I really adore you guys. I adore you for totally different reasons. You are fantastic co-stars. I really wish you all the very, very best in your career. You are definitely going to achieve it.

REACTING TO REACTIONS

Vivek Oberoi: How sweet!

John Abraham: Very nice.

Karan Johar: OK. That was our little survey. John Abraham, the sexier one. Vivek, the better actor. You have scored very high points even in the vice-versa department.

Vivek Oberoi: I think as far as the sex appeal was concerned, they were being really polite to me. I never consider myself as sexy, either.

> They were being really polite to me – I never consider myself as sexy, either.
>
> –Vivek Oberoi

Karan Johar: OK. Do you think they were polite?

John Abraham: No. they have been kind to us. It is very positive.

Vivek Oberoi: Yeah.

Karan Johar: Yeah. What do you think about Kareena's opinion?

John Abraham: She has an opinion. She is a nice girl. I do not have any problem with her. I have met her twice or thrice.

Vivek Oberoi: I thought we would gang you.

John Abraham: I have been honest. I still stand by what I said.

Karan Johar: All right. She was good to you.

Vivek Oberoi: She is wonderful. They are wonderful. Farah was adorable. I had a great time working with Kareena.

Karan Johar: Do you want to say anything to them?

John Abraham: Yeah. I am not a bad actor.

> *Vivek Oberoi:* I am trying to get John's diet!
>
> *John Abraham:* I am going to get my acting abilities like Vivek!

Vivek Oberoi: I am going to work really hard. I am trying to get John's diet and everything.

John Abraham: I am going to get my acting abilities like Vivek Oberoi.

CONCLUSION

Karan Johar: All right. Thank you. There's a mug right next to you.

John Abraham: Yeah.

Karan Johar: Pick up and sign it for me. Please remember that this personally autographed mug could be yours only if you partake in the *Koffee with Karan* quiz contest. John, thank you so much for being on *Koffee with Karan*. It was absolutely wonderful talking to you. I hope you had fun without me being nasty either. Was I?

Vivek Oberoi: No.

John Abraham: Not at all.

Karan Johar: I was very good.

John Abraham: You are very nice.

Karan Johar: It was fun. Did you have fun?

John Abraham: Yeah.

Vivek Oberoi: Did you have fun, too?

Karan Johar: I had a great time.

John Abraham: Give the lie-o-meter.

Karan Johar: Can we walk down the *koffee wall*? Can you walk with me?

Vivek Oberoi: Sure.

Karan Johar: All right, let us go to the *koffee wall*. Thank you.

●●●

19

Malaika & Amrita Arora
The Indian Hilton Sisters

Malaika is the hottest young mother in India. She has danced around a pole, on a train and right into your hearts. She had been a successful model, a successful VJ, a successful sexy story. She shares her features and characteristics with Jennifer Lopez. Welcome Malaika Arora Khan.

MALAIKA ARORA

Karan Johar: Hello, darling!

Malaika Arora: Thank you. Jennifer Lopez? You have been sliding the eye and having a peak at me!

Karan Johar: I am sure your husband would not mind!

SHE'S GOT THE LOOK

Karan Johar: When men make their remarks, does it feel good?

Malaika Arora: I would be lying if I replied in the negative. Any compliment is a good compliment! I guess any fairly attractive girl down the street gets whistles and compliments galore. So yes, I guess.

Karan Johar: There is this part of your figure that is always spoken about everywhere.

Malaika Arora: Ah! It feels good. Every time somebody says something, I have to look over my shoulder to see whether it looks good or not!

Karan Johar: Oh God! So, that is the one thing that you are really conscious about. All right. So much talk about your sex appeal, your sensuality – do you feel it is away from the woman inside you?

Malaika Arora: Sometimes, I ask myself whether it will dilute my personality. It means something also to the person who pays you a compliment. It does not deprive you of your actual personality if somebody rates you as sexy.

Karan Johar: No, it does not.

Malaika Arora: I still continue to be the same boring Malaika that you see!

Karan Johar: Boring Malaika? I do not think you are boring from any angle.

Malaika Arora: That is what you see from the outside.

Karan Johar: So, you are a simple girl; it does not bother you. There's only talk about sex appeal. Nobody knows the real Malaika except close family and friends – and we are not interested in it at all! I don't want to know the reality of yours – I want to know what lies outside. It's about being artificial and selling that in the real world!

MARRIED LIFE

Karan Johar: You have been married to Arbaaz – how many years have been married?

Malaika Arora: The seventh year itch is on actually.

Karan Johar: OK. You are married into a fairly conservative family. The Khan family has been active in the world of cinema for years.

> I always saw Sohail sitting in a pair of really tiny denim cut-offs – this is totally my kind of a home!
>
> –*Malaika Arora*

Malaika Arora: I always saw Sohail sitting in a pair of really tiny denim shorts, bare chested, blonde haired on the balcony taking a sunbath. I liked the development – totally my kind of a home! Things just fell wonderfully into place. My in-laws don't really condition you to follow certain norms – it had been an open arms welcome into the home. That state of development persists irrespective of whosoever comes into the house.

Karan Johar: It is amazing to look at the way you carry yourselves at public places. It is wonderful, great, and it is a modern way of thinking.

> My biggest fan continues to be my mother-in-law; she always pulls me aside to applaud my performance!
>
> –*Malaika Arora*

Malaika Arora: I totally agree. My biggest fan continues to be my mother-in-law. Whenever she flips through magazines or watches me on television, she always pulls me aside to applaud my performance. My father-in-law always behaves like a child.

Karan Johar: Indeed, they are model in-laws. I hope other in-laws in India emulate them.

LOVE ACTUALLY

Karan Johar: Arbaaz Khan, the truly modern husband, should get a crown. What was his response to your sensuality?

Malaika Arora: I think he is quite confident about himself. If you have the confidence from within, it transcends into something that seldom bothers you. Arbaaz is very understanding, and very confident and very comfortable with himself. I should take credit for that!

Karan Johar: Why? Wasn't he like this before? Under what circumstances did Arbaaz and you meet?

Malaika Arora: We met over an ad. It was one of those ads, where we had to be really close and hot – well, act the suggestions of making love. The circumstances made us hot, happening and dynamic. Obviously, it was like that brewing cup kept there!

> Arbaaz and I met over a coffee ad – we were like that brewing cup kept there!
> –*Malaika Arora*

Karan Johar: All right. How does he react to the state of developments?

Malaika Arora: Many people have questioned our marraige - 'I don't know how Arbaaz accepts Malaika' – in a very derogatory way – and it's been mostly women. Is not it strange? Eventually, he brushed it off by mentioning what was necessary.

Karan Johar: Yeah. He is confident, and cool about you. You have a great marriage. I am sure it will not stay like other marriages. People's relationships go on changing.

You are closer to your sister in the nuclear family. Do you know she is our next guest?

Malaika Arora: Am I supposed to act surprised?

Karan Johar: Yes, you are. Let me give her a sexy introduction.

AMRITA ARORA

Karan Johar: Malaika's sister, Amrita Arora. We have heard about her performances. She is hot, always active, representing the Gen X. She had many boyfriends and *girlfriends*. Let us bring her on to the show. Welcome.

Amrita Arora: We were actually called the Pointer sisters!

> We were actually called the Pointer sisters!
> –*Amrita Arora*

Karan Johar: OK. I like the visual of these two sisters – it is all leg and everything else. You look hot and happening. Are you comfortable?

Amrita Arora: Yes. I finally get to sit on this couch!

BRICKBATS AND BOUQUETS

Karan Johar: We shall talk about your boyfriends and a *girlfriend* on celluloid. So, was that fun?

Amrita Arora: No. I am not someone who regrets things but if I could go back and change something, I would change that.

Karan Johar: But why is that?

Amrita Arora: It was something, which I just did not enjoy. I do not blame anyone except myself because of my misconeptions of being progressive; instead, it catered to the sleaze going around. I found my parents upset when they watched my film. Everybody was uncomfortable. I heard my sister commenting that our parents disliked my performance.

Karan Johar: What did you say, Malaika?

Malaika Arora: 'What were you thinking?'

Amrita Arora: Everybody in the family got disappointed, but not ashamed or hurt. I just walked out and said, 'OK! Forget it! Mistakes will happen which need to be forgotten!

Karan Johar: So, it was the way it was packaged but not the portrayal of lesbian love?

Amrita Arora: Yeah. I thought it was quite progressive. It ended up sleazy when I saw the film.

> *Girlfriend* **ended up being a sleaze film!**
>
> *–Amrita Arora*

Karan Johar: Isha Koppikar, your *girlfriend*, went on record saying she was more comfortable with you than she had been with any man. That sounded very suspicious. I don't know what she meant by that!

Malaika Arora: That is interesting to think about!

GROWING UP

Amrita Arora: Karan! I was young, someone whispered, 'Find Mr. Right!' When I grew up, I remained the tattletale sister. I was the geek when Malaika was attracted to male personalities. I would be like her agitated mom, whenever a guy spoke to Malaika near the bus stop!

Malaika Arora: She was painful. She would never even let me talk to a guy in peace.

Amrita Arora: I wanted to become a nun, Karan!

Karan Johar: A nun! Let us be specific. There was a rumour afloat linking you with Fardeen at some stage. Did that ever happen or was it just a friendship? I have my lie-o-meter. You feel that I should use the instrument?

> **Amrita was painful – she would never even let me talk to a guy in peace!**
>
> *–Malaika Arora*

Amrita Arora: No, I am telling the truth. It was just a

friendship. At MTV, everyone has freedom. I used to call him up or meet in his vehicle if I wanted to speak to my co-star. I went and gave an interview to the print media and said I thought him to be the hottest. The media misinterpreted the issue by blowing things out of proportion. I did not know how to play hide-and-seek with the media. A good friendship turned sour because of rumours and people talking rubbish. He is a great guy and one of my best co-stars. I enjoyed working with him. I always thought he was good looking.

> **I wanted to become a nun!**
> *–Amrita Arora*

Karan Johar: You are absolutely right – he is a sweet person.

LOOKING FOR LOVE

Karan Johar: You were the victim of the media. You got the shoulder to cry on. The poor thing was so victimized that she jumped onto another man immediately! The long relationship with Ashmit Patel, the brother of Amisha Patel, lasted one year plus a day. That was true love there.

Amrita Arora: I always got into relationship that seemed to go the highway! Karan! My mother and sister are to be blamed for the relationship.

Karan Johar: So she did not approve of Ashmit?

Amrita Arora: No. She did not.

Karan Johar: You did not think Ashmit was Mr. Right?

Amrita Arora: No, I did not.

Karan Johar: Then, the poor child found London boy Upen. The relationship lasted for a while.

Amrita Arora: I always desired my relation to last but somewhere along the way something happened – genuine things seldom work out.

Karan Johar: That seemed you were going to stay with each other for a while. Malaika, you and Arbaaz became friendly with Upen. You approved of Upen?

Malaika Arora: I did not really approve – I just thought he was really a nice guy; that it might be given a shot and we would see where this goes.

> **Poor Amrita was so victimized that she jumped onto another man immediately!**
> *–Karan Johar*

Karan Johar: Did it go anywhere?

Amrita Arora: No. Things did not work. I wanted to compromise, but could not. It failed to work, making me unhappy. It was time to move on.

Karan Johar: So, who dumped who?

Amrita Arora: Well, both of us dumped each other!

Karan Johar: Malaika, I do not know whether you know about this incident – I got an invitation from Amrita once for a party. She told Upen about the party but she was not there!

Malaika Arora: Yeah! 10,000 other people asked me the same question – where the hell was Amrita? She did not show up!

Amrita Arora: Things could not work as planned.

Karan Johar: So you ran to London in despair and found another man. Malaika, tell us about her current boyfriend.

Malaika Arora: Well, I do not know Usman well. He plays cricket for the England team. I met him very briefly. That is how Amrita met Usman – through Arbaaz and me. It is in that phase where things are still very rosy and looking up.

Amrita Arora: Let me just quote Britney Spears to set the records straight. She said she had to kiss a lot of frogs to ascertain who was her charming prince! The quote, I think, with regard to Usman is completely true.

Karan Johar: OK. Ah! So, he is the last frog in the line, isn't he?

Amrita Arora: He is a frog who turns into a prince!

Karan Johar: All is well that ends well. So are you happy?

Amrita Arora: I am. He just lets me be. I needed someone who was just an extension of me, giving me secure space, respecting my work.

Malaika Arora: Someone like Arbaaz, basically.

Karan Johar: Are you looking for someone like Arbaaz?

Amrita Arora: Yeah! I always thought Arbaaz to be the ideal husband and the ideal brother. Every time, people would say about my ideal man, I would reply about his

> **I always thought Arbaaz to be the ideal husband and the ideal brother –I needed someone just like him!**
>
> –Amrita Arora

qualities. Usman does have these qualities. He is a very mature adult man, even though he is only 27. He is someone who respects himself, is hardworking and ambitious, and just lets me be.

Malaika Arora: We will keep our fingers crossed!

Amrita Arora: All former boyfriends were great guys who shaped my personality.

Karan Johar: Well, Amrita Arora is trying to be diplomatic. Let us call a sexy boy to pep up the scene.

Amrita Arora: Well, I hope it is no blast from the past!

Karan Johar: Ah! Darling it was very difficult for you to avoid men. We will have someone involved with modeling and film world.

DINO MOREA

Karan Johar: Our next guest is a successful supermodel. He is also an actor whom women consider extremely hot. Let us call Dino Morea, the Italian stud of the film industry. Welcome, Dino, to *Koffee with Karan*. Meet the beautiful women!

Malaika Arora: Wow! This is a good surprise.

> **I'm on TV – I think, Malaika, you're very beautiful!**
>
> –Dino Morea

Karan Johar: We have to talk about the two lovely ladies. You have worked with Malaika, modeled with her and walked the ramp together. How do you perceive Malaika, Dino?

Dino Morea: I think, Malaika, you're very beautiful.

Malaika Arora: Thank you! You've never ever said that all through our modeling days!

Dino Morea: I am on TV!

Malaika Arora: He barely ever spoke to me all through. I thought he was very shy!

Dino Morea: I was very shy! Every time Malaika stood next to me, I would look down, be really shy. She has an overpowering personality.

Karan Johar: What about Amrita?

Dino Morea: She looks beautiful and is quite stunning. We are doing a film together. I feel honoured acting with her. When you have a co-star like her, the chemistry sparks! So it's nice to act with Amrita. Have I said enough?

Malaika Arora: Yeah! We are happy.

Karan Johar: Amrita is dating an English cricketer while Malaika is married. Dino! Are you dating anybody? I believe you are single.

Dino Morea: It may sound clichéd, but I am really concentrating on my career and work. So honestly, to give time to both a relationships and work will be a bit tough right now.

DRAWING THE LINE

Karan Johar: Malaika, we have done a song together, where you look super hot and it was all very aesthetic. People keep pointing fingers about your clothes. You can give any actress, any model, any socialite a run for their money. I mean no one can look half as good as you are.

Amrita Arora: I think we should retire if we can't look half as good as her after having a child.

> I think we should retire if we can't look half as good as her after having a child.
> *—Amrita Arora*

Karan Johar: Malaika, do you draw a line somewhere?

Malaika Arora: Of course, I do. I know there are people whom I care about at home. I have got to keep a lot of things in mind – that I am a daughter-in-law, daughter and wife to respective persons. I have to account for these parameters while in public. I am somebody who knows what is good

> I know that I am a daughter-in-law, daughter and wife to respective persons – I have to draw a line somewhere.
> *—Malaika Arora*

between right and wrong – I can differentiate. I do not think anybody could say, 'She slipped somewhere'.

Karan Johar: And Amrita, do you draw the line?

Amrita Arora: Karan, I drew certain lines. I do not feel I am sexy enough to pull off anything. I wear a pair of shorts if I am comfortable. It has nothing to do to with drawing certain lines about the clothes. I wear for the scenes I enact. I shall proceed if I am absolutely convinced about that. You could look horrible fully clad in just the way it was done. I would dislike enacting a lovemaking scene – I know my mom will be watching it.

Karan Johar: And kissing? What about kissing?

Amrita Arora: I have never kissed onscreen. My director forced me to kiss Dino onscreen, which I am kind of pondering over.

Karan Johar: Dino, you don't have mummy and in-laws to answer to. So where do you draw the line? You did an underwear ad.

Dino Morea: Yeah. I have already done an underwear ad. It became a big controversy. It had me biting Bipasha's underwear, which became the huge uproar among people. There is a fine line between vulgarity and something aesthetic.

Karan Johar: An aesthetically shot film like *Murder* really did well. Of course, Mallika Sherawat was the woman in question but as a man, would you commit to the lovemaking scene?

Dino Morea: I will not endorse the fully frontal nudity. I would probably agree to do something sought in the script, if my director shoots the part nicely or makes it aesthetic rather than promoting vulgarity, leaving the people to malign my image. I think that the sentiments of Indian audience have to be kept in mind – but I have no qualms about shedding my clothes.

Malaika Arora: They paid you extra amount of money to drop your pants!

LETS TALK ABOUT SEX

Karan Johar: All right. Let us talk about sex, baby. Dino Morea, Malaika Arora Khan and Amrita Arora. Okay. We have heard of the casting couch. How did you feel when you heard about the recent escapade?

Dino Morea: I am in receipt of messages from a Delhi girl. She asserts to be beautiful and needs my help in becoming a starlet. She claims to belong to some family. I have saved the messages but have not answered yet.

Karan Johar: It would not be fair.

Malaika Arora: It is ridiculous. It is nothing but invading someone's privacy.

Karan Johar: You cannot have your camera everywhere.

Amrita Arora: You cannot set someone up. It will be fine naturally, if it happens. You cannot set someone up.

Karan Johar: I dislike the way things happen. Let us revert to sex. We surveyed about the sex boom in the film fraternity. Do you want to watch?

Dino Morea: Yummy.

Karan Johar: Let us watch.

DOES SEX SELL IN INDIA?

Dino Morea: I think sex sells definitely.

Fardeen Khan: I think it will always sell.

Smriti Irani: Otherwise, how would you explain the presence of Mallika Sherawat and her popularity?

Kareena Kapoor: No. I disagree.

Sunil Shetty: It sells by genuinely believable subjects.

Kareena Kapoor: It is the script.. It will work if sex is part of the story.

Neha Dhupia: I think anything afresh sells in Hindi cinema.

Farah Khan: Sex sells to a certain degree – it will depend on who is selling and how much of sex images you show.

Neha Dhupia: The images used to sell some eight months ago. Now, you will see everybody stripping off clothes and doing almost the same thing.

Dino Morea: Everybody loves to see a lot of the body bare. Why not show the good body you have?

Smriti Irani: It is sad to sell the images. It will be so, if you are not sure of your creativity or your talent. You have to depend on certain gimmicks.

Fardeen Khan: Everyone seems to run away from sex in our country. It seems to be a subject of taboo. Look at our population, man!

Neha Dhupia: Are we making a big deal out of nothing?

Farah Khan: I think sex is an important part of life. The songs picturised, to some extent, are a substitute for sex scenes. You are not allowed to show sex so you have women draped in a sari amidst heavy downpour.

Dino Morea: I take my shirt off when a sexy song is picturised. I feel rather comfortable and I have a good physique. Women love to see my bare chest. So why should not I show them what they want to see?

Neha Dhupia: Sex is really overrated in our country. I am bored of seeing myself doing steamy scenes!

Lara Dutta: I definitely would have my boundaries, when it came to sex on cinema. I do not think I am ready to walk naked around the sets.

Fardeen Khan: I do not personally feel anything wrong in picturising a lovemaking scene. I would mind doing it unless it is aesthetically shot.

Kareena Kapoor: Even kissing on screen; I have done it in *Dev* and *Main Prem Ki Diwani Hoon.* It will be fine if required by the script. Else, I shall put my foot down.

Arjun Rampal: I am very uncomfortable with doing a sex scene. I do not think I shall do anything so – unless you get me Angelina Jolie!

Fardeen Khan: The way sex is projected in our cinema glorifies women. It if you are selling sex, you are selling it to a man.

Suniel Shetty: I do not think the product will sell when a woman of your choice is being stripped.

Kareena Kapoor: I think Sri Devi and Madhuri were completely sexy. The way they draped a sari or danced – nobody else could be as sexy and sensual!

Fardeen Khan: What Zeenat Aman portrayed in *Qurbani* is one such example; when she comes out of the beach.

Lara Dutta: *Jism* was not portrayed beautifully.

Neha Dhupia: I would probably be the happiest actress if sexuality were treated casually in Indian cinema.

Fardeen Khan: Sex is the inherent part of our existence. I am not ashamed of its portrayal. I do not see anything wrong in its exhibition.

Lara Dutta: I am really glad to arrive at something normal onscreen; it will change the mindset of the audience.

> *Jism* **was not portrayed beautifully.**
> –*Lara Dutta*

Karan Johar: All right. Sex sells. It is universal.

Malaika Arora: I uphold the opinion of Lara where she endorses its portrayal. You have to draw a line.

Karan Johar: You have to set the basic parameters.

Malaika Arora: It needs to be blended well with the subject of the film.

Dino Morea: Sex is considered taboo in our society. People look at it in a different way. People shall perceive it as normal if you expose them to it..

Karan Johar: The removal of restrictions will condition things to proceed in an aesthetic manner.

Karan Johar: All right. Goodbye Dino.

Malaika Arora: Bye, Dino. See you.

RAPID FIRE

Karan Johar: I hope you are ready for the rocking *Rapid Fire round*. I throw questions at you. You should answer abruptly. The prize is, of course, nobody's guess.

Amrita Arora: The much-wanted hamper!

Karan Johar: Let us see which one of you hotties wins the koffee hamper.

Amrita Arora: Yes, with whom the *koffee hamper* gets to go home with!

Karan Johar: Well done, Amrita. Go ahead. Any man should be capable of such qualities – grade them according to their importance.

Amrita Arora: Great shoes, great footwear, good smelling man and nice hands.

Karan Johar: Rank the following non-film people in terms of sex appeal like sizzling, hot, lukewarm or ice cold – let us start with Upen Patel.

> **Lets see whom the *koffee hamper* gets lucky to go home with!**
> –*Amrita Arora*

Amrita Arora: Hot.

Karan Johar: Rahul Gandhi.

Amrita Arora: Sizzling hot.

Karan Johar: Irfan Pathan.

Amrita Arora: Cold.

Karan Johar: Vijay Mallya.

Amrita Arora: Ice cold.

Karan Johar: Usman Afzal.

Amrita Arora: Sizzling hot as on a sizzler!

> **Karan Johar:** Usman Afzal.
> *Amrita Arora:* Sizzling hot as on a sizzler!

Karan Johar: How would you handle yourself as an attractive young woman if a man checks you out while talking to you?

Amrita Arora: I will check him out.

Karan Johar: What would you say if a director summons you to his farmhouse for a script reading?

Amrita Arora: Well, I shall take him to a farm and make him graze around with the cows!

Karan Johar: If a co-star said you are very naughty?

Amrita Arora: Good girls go to heaven; naughty girls go everywhere – so decide!

Karan Johar: Well done! A tattoo you would love to have?

Amrita Arora: 'I seldom forget to wake him up' – whomsoever I shall marry.

Karan Johar: Cricketers are sexy because?

Amrita Arora: They play on the field and sweat it out – they are not city boys who go to straighten their hair!

Karan Johar: The best way to seduce Amrita Arora?

Amrita Arora: Take her for a good meal.

Karan Johar: Whom would you dedicate the following songs to – *Ice, ice baby?*

Amrita Arora: Ashmit.

Karan Johar: *I am too sexy for my shirt?*

Amrita Arora: Myself.

> **Good girls go to heaven; naughty girls go everywhere – so decide!**
>
> *–Amrita Arora*

Karan Johar: *Man, you make me feel like a woman?*

Amrita Arora: Usman.

Karan Johar: The most absurd thing you have been

asked to do on screen by a director?

Amrita Arora: Feel up Isha Koppikar.

Karan Johar: Whom do you prefer to tie rakhi to become the sister – John Abraham, Abhishek Bachchan, Zayed Khan or Shahid Kapoor?

Karan Johar: The most absurd thing you have done onscreen?

Amrita Arora: Feel up Isha Koppikar!

Amrita Arora: Shahid. He is the boyfriend of my good friend.

Karan Johar: Okay. Very quickly then – Aishwarya Rai or Sushmita Sen?

Amrita Arora: None.

Karan Johar: Business tycoon or cricket icon – your choice for marriage?

Amrita Arora: Cricket icon.

Karan Johar: Rekha, Hema Malini, Sharmila Tagore – the woman like whom you prefer to grow older.

Amrita Arora: I have to choose between Hema Malini and Sharmila – they are absolutely beautiful and gorgeous. My jaw drops every time I look at them. They are stunning.

Karan Johar: Choose your best visual – Akshay Kumar, John Abraham, Arjun Rampal.

Amrita Arora: John Abraham.

Karan Johar: Very well done, Amrita. Clap to yourself! So Malaika, are you ready?

Karan Johar: Aishwarya Rai or Sushmita Sen?

Amrita Arora: None!

Malaika Arora: Ready!

Karan Johar: One irresistible quality in Arbaaz – don't say his smile; I know that.

Malaika Arora: His self-confidence.

Karan Johar: One habit in Arbaaz you wish to change.

Malaika Arora: Twirling his hair; he just keeps doing that.

Karan Johar: Shahrukh and Gauri, Hrithik Roshan and Suzanne, Ajay Devgan and Kajol – the film industry couple that comes closest to your ideal love marriage?

Malaika Arora: Shahrukh and Gauri – a great chemistry makes them compatible. They look like they are raring to go.

Karan Johar: Why would you recommend marriage to Amrita?

Malaika Arora: Babies. I recommend marriage for this reason.

Karan Johar: Why marriage may not be such a good idea for Amrita?

Malaika Arora: It ties you down. Are you sure you are ready for that? Think long and hard before you get married.

Malaika Arora: Amrita, think long and hard before you get married.

Amrita Arora: Okay mom!

Amrita Arora: Okay mom!

Karan Johar: What does the man mean when he says 'Trust me; I know what I am doing.'

Malaika Arora: He never knows it. The biggest lie!

Karan Johar: All right. Who would you dedicate the following songs – 'Can't live with or without you?'

Malaika Arora: My sister.

Karan Johar: 'Black magic woman?'

Malaika Arora: I think Rekha.

Karan Johar: 'Said I loved you but I lied?'

Malaika Arora: You know, Arbaaz dedicated once that song to me. I wept I heard it for the first time – it has a beautiful line later.

Amrita Arora: 'Said I loved you but I lied because this is more...

Malaika Arora: ..than love I feel inside.' That's what it is. And he told me that. So I did not catch the second line. Much later after weeping, I heard the song!

Karan Johar: All right. This song I am sure is much easy – 'the most beautiful girl in the world?'

Malaika Arora: My mom; that's for sure.

Karan Johar: Your take on the facial hair of the guy in question?

Malaika Arora: Totally unwanted!

Karan Johar: Pubs?

Malaika Arora: Etiquette classes, maybe.

Karan Johar: Your take on the statement – size does matter.

Malaika Arora: But it does!

Karan Johar: Obsession with biceps?

Malaika Arora: Turn off totally.

Karan Johar: All right. Your take on the statement – size does matter.

Karan Johar: If you could have a harem of Bollywood heroes?
Malaika Arora: Sanjay Dutt, a bit of Salman Khan, a dash of Arbaaz, sure Shahrukh. Bachchan will be the cherry on the cake!

Malaika Arora: But it does!
Karan Johar: If you could have a harem of Bollywood heroes?
Malaika Arora: Sanjay Dutt, a bit of Salman Khan definitely a dash of Arbaaz, sure Shahrukh. Bachchan will be the cherry on the cake!

Karan Johar: All right. John, Shahid, Zayed, Abhishek – the future.

Malaika Arora: I think John.

Karan Johar: A tattoo you possess?

Malaika Arora: 'She's naughty and nice.'

Karan Johar: The sexiest thing any man has ever said?

Malaika Arora: 'You turn me on.'

Karan Johar: The best pick-up line ever used on you?

Malaika Arora: I hate pick-up lines – cheesy things like 'your place or mine?'

Karan Johar: All right. Very quickly then – pole dancing in *Kaante* or train dancing in *Dil Se*.

Malaika Arora: Train dancing.

Karan Johar: Salman or Sohail?

Malaika Arora: Sohail.

Karan Johar: OK. Better shirt, less visual – John Abraham, Akshay Kumar or Arjun Rampal?

Malaika Arora: Arjun.

Karan Johar: In bed or in love?

Malaika Arora: Both.

Karan Johar: In bed or in love?
Malaika Arora: Both!

Karan Johar: All right. Well done, girls. I think that was really the rocking rapid fire.

Malaika Arora: Flummoxed! Pondering! Need some help?

Karan Johar: Yes. Malaika, do you think it is you or Amrita?

Malaika Arora: I know she is wearing my shoes. I shall forgive her and give it to her.

Karan Johar: All right. I agree. Let us give it to Amrita. Well done, Amrita! You had the endorsement by your sis. This is your coffee hamper.

Amrita Arora: Thank you!

CONCLUSION

Karan Johar: Thank you for being on the show.

Malaika Arora: Thank you, Karan. We had a wonderful time.

Karan Johar: I had an absolutely wonderful time. In fact I had a blast. I think you girls were absolutely fantastic. This has truly been one of my better shows. You have to sign the koffee mug next to you, Amrita. It is right next to you and then to Malaika. Please remember – this personally autographed mug can be yours only if you participate in the *Koffee Quest Contest.* Thank you again, Amrita. Thank you, Malaika.

Malaika Arora: Thank you Karan.

● ● ●

Neetu Singh & Rishi Kapoor
Ek Main Aur Ek Tu

Tonight is extremely special to me. It will be my favourite episode. We have one of the hottest off screen and on screen couples of Indian cinema. He had been the king of romance. She used to be the teen queen. And together they have made a love story resembling a fairytale. He is one of my favourite actors ever. He has been the main proponent of natural acting. We are so honoured to have her first appearance on camera after 25 years. Let us welcome the heartthrob of 1970s on the Indian television. Neetu and Rishi Kapoor. !

NEETU SINGH

Karan Johar: I am so excited to have you on the show.

Neetu Singh: And I am so nervous!

Karan Johar: You are nervous? You look rather stunning!

Neetu Singh: Thank you. 25 years have rolled out. I do not know what I am going to do!

Karan Johar: We used to play *Ek Main Aur Ek Tu* number everyday. Indeed, it was a practical game in our life.

> Good marriages are like dinosaurs– they seldom exist!
>
> *–Karan Johar*

Rishi Kapoor: We shot that song in this studio.

Karan Johar: In this studio? What are you saying?

Neetu Singh: Oh! Yeah.

Karan Johar: So this will be quite nostalgic. Just the other day, I realized how 25 years have rolled out in association of marriage.

Neetu Singh: And five years before. So, I know him for 30 years.

Karan Johar: So good marriages are like dinosaurs – they seldom exist! How does it feel? Really 25 long years, my God! Sir, you tell me.

Rishi Kapoor: Well, I am a difficult man, she is..

Neetu Singh: He has admitted anyhow. Thank God!

Rishi Kapoor: We have had our ups and downs. And we have sailed through.

> Today, on April 13, we were engaged 26 years ago!
>
> *–Rishi Kapoor*

Neetu Singh: You got to present yourself as good human being. Everybody has their ups and downs.

Rishi Kapoor: We knew each other. We dated for five years. We found that we gelled together. It just happened, my friend! Today is April 13. We were engaged 26 years back.

THE LOVE STORY

Karan Johar: Oh my God! It has so much nostalgia. I must admit millions of would-be couples including me will initiate a love story. What happened at the initial stage between you?

Neetu Singh: I was just his friend. I was just his confidante.

Karan Johar: You were just 13 or 14 at that time?

Neetu Singh: He used to fight with me with arguments. I was barely 13 and was unexposed to such fights. I was his confidante and he used to have girlfriends. I gave him just a shoulder to cry on. And he used to always say, 'Oh I like this one! I like that one and this one needs to be broken off!' He eventually said, 'I miss you when you are not around.' And it was just one of those things.

> **Initially, I was his confidante and he used to have girlfriends!**
>
> – *Neetu Singh*

Rishi Kapoor: We were shooting for *Kabhi Kabhi* in Kashmir. I had to leave for Chakida's film *Babul* that we shot in Paris. We worked quite regularly. When I was alone in Kashmir, I had the opportunity to share a lot with her.

Karan Johar: Yashji's unit is always very interactive.

Rishi Kapoor: So, when I went to alien soil, everybody knew I was quite indifferent. I received plenty of telegrams but no phone calls in the evening. I sent a telegram saying that I miss the Sikh lady very much.

Karan Johar: Very nice!

Neetu Singh: And that telegram, Karan, was all over the place! I was looking for Pam aunty!

Neetu Singh: Pam aunty just saw what he wrote. I was equally excited.

Karan Johar: So, you are truly the son of Raj Kapoor. A film man only could write such things. This is true filmy romance – 'I have miss the Sikh woman very much.' How did you feel?

Neetu Singh: I went jumping to Pam aunty. She showed everybody what Rishi had written in the telegram.

Karan Johar: So that means that you always loved him?

Neetu Singh: Yeah, I did. I was more like a friend to him. I never realized he cared for me. It was like a shock.

Karan Johar: Were you dating someone at that time?

> **I sent her a telegram saying that I miss the Sikh lady very much.**
>
> – *Rishi Kapoor*

Rishi Kapoor: Could you ask me later?

Karan Johar: Okay!

Rishi Kapoor: When she is not around!

Neetu Singh: No. I knew all his girlfriends. He used to call her indirectly, telling me to call her up. I used to do that for him.

Rishi Kapoor: Come on! You never did that for me!

Neetu Singh: She broke off. She was very artificial.

Karan Johar: Lots of names, but you are not giving me any!

> He would say, 'I will never get married to you. I am dating you!'
>
> – Neetu Singh

Neetu Singh: No. But not filmy girls although he had plenty of girlfriends. I was his best friend.

Karan Johar: So you were the true friend?

Neetu Singh: I went on perceiving him on being conscious.

Karan Johar: Did you date seriously for five years?

Neetu Singh: 5 years? No. Seriously was 4 years.

Rishi Kapoor: Yes, probably.

Karan Johar: I heard about your commitment phobia. You were scared to commit yourself and get married.

Neetu Singh: Yeah. He would say, 'I will never get married to you. I am dating you.'

Karan Johar: So, what did you want?

Rishi Kapoor: I really do not remember. I did when my sister got me engaged this day, 26 years ago. It was not planned. I went to Delhi for the engagement of someone else. Whatever is destined will happen certainly. People say marriages are made in heaven. And it so happened when my sister took me into confidence.

Neetu Singh: She knew what was going on between us.

Rishi Kapoor: She secretly got Neetu and my mother-in-law into Delhi with my parents. I had a producer friend who had just released the film *Jhoota Kahin Ka*. He used to wear a gold ring with the alphabet '*R*'. I did not even have a ring to reciprocate my engagement.

> We had gone to Delhi for an engagement party and instead got engaged!
>
> –*Rishi Kapoor*

That ring was given to Neetu to wear it on me whereas I gave her my sister's ring.

Karan Johar: You put on your sister's ring?

Rishi Kapoor: It was not pre-planned in any way.

Karan Johar: It happened abruptly?

Rishi Kapoor: If it is inevitable, it shall happen.

Neetu Singh: I was draped in a gold sari with corals. We were so excited. It happened some 26 years back in 1979.

WORK VS FAMILY

Karan Johar: So, it happened swiftly. You gave it all up in one stroke?

> It was her decision not to work in films, not mine.
>
> *–Rishi Kapoor*

Neetu Singh: Yeah. I handed over a couple of letters with warnings to my producers. That was my last day.

Rishi Kapoor: And please, once and for all, I want to make it very clear. I had nothing to do with this. People keep blaming me that Rishi Kapoor is the one who was responsible for Neetu Singh not working in films. But it was her decision.

Neetu Singh: I was obsessed, dear. I began working when I was just five. I had worked a lot for 15 years when I was 21. I do not believe to have enjoyed my childhood. Neither had I had a life of my own. I looked forward to getting married, but not engaged to enact or get into shooting.

Karan Johar: You might have been liberated then. Nothing could change your mind?

Rishi Kapoor: The whole fraternity blamed me. I was squarely responsible. I became the male chauvinist pig. And it was her decision!

Karan Johar: It was this whole story that the Kapoors' daughters-in-law will not act. I mean, the Kapoor family women will not act.

Neetu Singh: Everyone has been acting.

Rishi Kapoor: So have the daughters-in-law. My aunts, my nieces, and she.

Karan Johar: Where does the story then come from?

Rishi Kapoor: Well, there must be some iota of truth. I may have been a little wary of the state. Priorities change as time rolls by. Everything changes.

Karan Johar: Did you find your father OK about the situation?

Rishi Kapoor: He was. Why not?

Karan Johar: He would have been fine?

Rishi Kapoor: Yeah.

Neetu Singh: He was such a sweetheart. He was a lovely human being and welcomed my decision.

Karan Johar: So, you got a warm welcome away from home?

> **My father-in-law was a lovely human being.**
>
> *–Neetu Singh*

Rishi Kapoor: Oh yes! I still remember we reached the hotel in Delhi. Papa came in a kurta in our room. He spread out his kurta and said 'Put my daughter into my jholi' She did not know what to say. She said 'Thank You'.

Karan Johar: That was all?

Neetu Singh: I did not know what to reply. I said, 'Thank You'.

Karan Johar: Probably, she must have been so moved......

Rishi Kapoor: She was taken aback and tears rolling down and, 'Thank You.'

LIFE AFTER MARRIAGE

Karan Johar: That was fantastic. Everyone was rather excited to hear the development. Ups and downs are a part of every marriage. One should read between the lines to patch up.

Rishi Kapoor: Yeah. It happens in every marriage. We also went through those patches in our marriage.

Karan Johar: Was it not a difficult phase?

Rishi Kapoor: Indeed. What you call shock absorbers! Really absorbed my jerks in life!

Karan Johar: No, but did you tide through easily?

Neetu Singh: Oh! Yes. I was very strong. I was immovable. I knew what I wanted from him – children and everything else. I was very strong. It seldom bothered me.

Karan Johar: You have tided through easily. And your children?

Neetu Singh: He is a wonderful husband and a wonderful father. He was the most pathetic boyfriend. Karan, perhaps, you have no idea what he made me sail across.

> **I knew what I wanted from him. Rough patches seldom bothered me.**
>
> *–Neetu Singh*

Karan Johar: Was he jealous, possessive?

Neetu Singh: It was just that he was a brat. I used to do my own makeup before schedule.

I used to enact on the sets besides sing the song as in *Amar Akbar Anthony* (on the train). Rishi used to come into my room, take my eyeliner and spread it over my face.

Karan Johar: But why? My God!

Neetu Singh: Just like that. And Mr. Mann used to tell him Chintu, 'Why do you do this?'

> **Rishi used to come into my room, take my eyeliner and spread it over my face!**
>
> *–Neetu Singh*

Karan Johar: Just being bratty for no rhyme or reason?

Neetu Singh: Or he would just empty my bag on the road.

Rishi Kapoor: Yes. I do remember that.

Neetu Singh: He used to do similar things.

Karan Johar: Did it bother him that you worked with other heroes? Was he envious or jealous?

Neetu Singh: There was a thing like you cannot shoot after certain time.

Rishi Kapoor: See, I used to pack up by 8.30 pm..

Karan Johar: There was a ceiling limit.

Rishi Kapoor: I wanted to meet my girlfriend. I felt it as a dictate.

Neetu Singh: He told me not to upset it. So, I used to meet him sharp by 8.30 pm.

Rishi Kapoor: She did not want to work after 8.30 pm.

Karan Johar: I think she had constantly used you. Is that what are you trying to say?

Neetu Singh: Or he has used me.

Karan Johar: And then at 8:30, you were very happy packing up, I think.

> **I used to meet him sharp by 8.30 pm.**
>
> *–Neetu Singh*

Neetu Singh: I still remember there was a number *Dhoom Mache Dhoom* for Mr. Yash to be shot by 9.00 pm. I was to return home by 9.30. There were heavyweight actors like Amitabh Bachchan, Parveen (God bless her), Rakhi, Shashi uncle and everybody. It was my number to be sung. And Mr. Yash knew my problem. He always supported me. My sweetie pie!

Karan Johar: He is another one who loves romance. So, he might have foreseen your love scene.

Neetu Singh: What could I do? It was shooting in the night. We commenced at 7

> **I am not so bad!**
> –*Rishi Kapoor*

pm. It was an outdoor event. I had to return home by 9.30 pm. I was through my shots. One day, I got stuck in a shot. I called up my maid and told her to put off the phone receiver. I rushed home with jewellery et al after the enactment. I reached home and put the phone receiver on the hook. My maid said, 'You asked me to keep the phone down.' I asked her, 'Did Sir call up?' She replied, 'No, he did not.' I said, 'Thank God!'

Karan Johar: You were probably lucky that night?

Neetu Singh: Yes!

Rishi Kapoor: She paints such an ugly scene! I am not so bad!

Karan Johar: Of course, those were the days of fun. I believe it increases the responsibility on being married to an actor.

Rishi Kapoor: Yes, there will be an understanding between actors after marriage.

Affairs of the Heart

Karan Johar: Did you think something was going on between your husband and other heroines?

Neetu Singh: I never suspected him.

Rishi Kapoor: Communication gap creates problem. Actors have a different lifestyle.

> **I never suspected my husband of having affairs.**
> –*Neetu Singh*

Karan Johar: Do you mean in terms of timing and similar parameters?

Rishi Kapoor: Yeah. There were irregular timings. Your better half should understand the problems you come across. I used to work one shift every day between 10.30 am and 08.30 pm. She used to live in Pali Hills and me in Chembur. So I used to visit her on the sets.

Neetu Singh: I wanted to be with him. So, I also did my thing.

Rishi Kapoor: There was no other reason.

Karan Johar: No. Of course, everything was understandable. You were one of the couples meeting each other for a longer period.

Neetu Singh: We never went out alone. My mother used to send a person with us. We used to drop him on our way for dinner, pick him up and then return home.

Karan Johar: Who was that chaperone?

We used to drop our chaperone on our way to dinner, later pick him up and then return home!
–Neetu Singh

Neetu Singh: My cousin.

Karan Johar: Poor fellow!

Neetu Singh: She used to say that we could not go alone.

Karan Johar: Someone had to accompany you. He did not mind on being your chaperone?

Neetu Singh: He knew. He was of my age. So, it was okay.

Karan Johar: I mean you know the write-ups one reads and does research. Most heroes were involved in some link-up, gossip, and controversy. I hope nothing emerged from your link.

Neetu Singh: He did not let it happen. He was very smart.

Karan Johar: He hid some facts?

Neetu Singh: Oh yes! Lots!

Rishi Kapoor: I was an open book!

Karan Johar: Do you believe that?

Neetu Singh: I do, actually. I cannot believe him having an affair. Let him do such a thing openly. If some girl comes and says, 'I love you' he would say, 'What is it?' He used to push the girl away!

Karan Johar: He has worked with many young girls, say some 25 or 26.

Rishi Kapoor: 23.

Neetu Singh: Nobody appeased him. He was so young when he was in the movies. Everybody was senior to him – Hema, Rekha, Zeenat, et al. Nobody befitted him except me. I enacted with him in 11 movies. He introduced like 25 girls.

Karan Johar: Probably, you might have been challenged by varieties of women. You might have been the heartthrob of romance.

Rishi Kapoor: I am very grateful to my leading ladies. They played a very big part in my career. The year 1973, I was with a new girl and the year 1991 kept me busy with another.

If some girl came and said, 'I love you,' he would push the girl

Karan Johar: Yeah. You have worked with Divya Bharti in *Deewana*. I believe you were right up there.

> **It was quite amazing – I have worked with 23 new heroines!**
> *–Rishi Kapoor*

Rishi Kapoor: There were many of them – so many young girls. It was quite amazing. 23 new heroines! She had worked in one film. Everybody knew about it.

Karan Johar: Neither was there any link nor affair? A very good boy!

Rishi Kapoor: This is the irony.

Karan Johar: Do you feel guilty when you look back?

Neetu Singh: When he returned home, he wanted his wife and kids to be there. He inquired where Mushki was. Mushki is my daughter. Where was Guddo, our dog? He wanted everybody to be present before him. He likes a good house and is proud to be a family-oriented man. He is very much into that. So, I think he never wanted to risk that part of him.

Karan Johar: You admit his role, of course.

Neetu Singh: I am a part of his life. He did not need to have an affair.

Karan Johar: Why should any man have an affair if he is getting married to you? You have acknowledged your arrogance!

Rishi Kapoor: Can anybody get a more patient husband than this? She acknowledges it herself!

Karan Johar: OK. Is she lying?

Neetu Singh: Karan, I was extremely innocent when I got married. I was barely 22. I was a young bride. Imagine! At 22, people come into the movies. I was married to Rishi. I begot a kid. He used to bully me with big words!

Karan Johar: Like what?

> **At 22, people come into the movies. I was married to Rishi!**
> *–Neetu Singh*

Neetu Singh: He is very good at scrabble. I was not that much educated. I have passed just 8th grade. He used to move with his friends. I escorted them for about 5 times. I was rather bored and gave up on accompanying them. He used to come home very late every day. He opened the door after we returned after 5 days. He told me, 'Look, I cannot lead the life in duress.' Karan, I forgot my anger and went on combing the meaning, *under duress* through a dictionary!

Karan Johar: Had he used any other big words?

Neetu Singh: We went for a wedding with his sister Reema. There was heavy downpour. We could not reach on time. We stopped at some stage. We did not have mobiles in those days.

> **He used to bully me with big words!**
> –Neetu Singh

Neetu Singh: He went to a gas station. He rang up the hosts and informed about the 'torrential rain.' So, his sister Reema uses the word 'torrential'.

Karan Johar: So, you use the biggest unfamiliar words and relieve off the unease.

Rishi Kapoor: Confuse the other person!

Neetu Singh: I got totally confused!

Rishi Kapoor: It works with her. Some days, it doesn't work with somebody.

Neetu Singh: I now use bigger words, which he acknowledges.

Saying 'No' to Lead Roles

Karan Johar: All right. You have abandoned sweaters. You gave up even dancing.

Rishi Kapoor: Well, you know that. See, once I got obsessed with repetition, I went on putting weight on quitting the film industry. The boys like Salman, Shahrukhkh, and Aamir came to me and told I was behind by 25 years. I am so grateful to God for leading a romantic life for 25 years. I have worked with such macho men. I found myself misfit on the screen and decided not to work with anybody. And decided to look good on the screen.

Karan Johar: So you made up your mind consciously?

Rishi Kapoor: No. I just did not want to do films. I was bored. I recollect not naming anybody. Producers used to come home and inquire about my wardrobe for those jerseys! They labeled me as the South African jersey man. They nicknamed me the jersey man.

Karan Johar: Because of the jerseys you wore!

Rishi Kapoor: Exactly! You get into one thing. They wanted you to wear the same thing again and again. I was so peeved to repeat them and looked back to remain happy.

Neetu Singh: I think he has done some amazing work!

Rishi Kapoor: I like fun. I have great fun working in films. It was not so in the past couple of years. But, now it has been.

> **They labeled me as the South African jersey man because of the jerseys I wore!**
> *–Rishi Kapoor*

Karan Johar: Was there any kind of frustration and insecurity, which compelled you to abandon everything?

Rishi Kapoor: No. I recollect that one time I did not shoot for 15-20 days. Ranjita fell or something. I have worked continuously for 25 years. You know, certain actors have a lull; they have a break for 2 years. They have ups and downs, but mine was no great shake. It was rather satisfying.

Karan Johar: Did you feel when you were at home that everything was over?

Neetu Singh: I wanted him to just go out. I couldn't take it. I said, 'Bob, why you don't go to RK? Go and help Daboo. Go and help your brothers.' Just go there, you know!

Karan Johar: He was at home very much.

Neetu Singh: I could not take it. He was very lovable. I missed him for ten days. I wanted him to go. When he was at home for too long, I could not take him. He was always up to something. 'We shall do this.' Finicky. I said, 'Bob, please calm down.'

Karan Johar: I think he admitted that he was difficult.

Rishi Kapoor: I told her on the very first day that it would be very difficult. I said kudos to her when you asked whether she stood by me.

> **When he was at home, I could not take it! I wanted him to go out!**
> *–Neetu Singh*

Karan Johar: You told her any other women might have run off?

Rishi Kapoor: No chance. No way.

Neetu Singh: Your mom says that you should always say 'thank you.'

Rishi Kapoor: She says Neetu should get a medal. My family members repeat it.

Neetu Singh: They should give me the medal.

Rishi Kapoor: They used to see the medal whenever I had a row with my siblings or mother. You need to give her a medal!

Neetu Singh: Ritu calls me Only Vimal because only I could handle him.

Karan Johar: Only Vimal! And who calls you mother Teresa?

Neetu Singh: Daboo. He says you are Mother Teresa, the punching bag. I don't know what all they used to call me. But, I am so no longer.

> **My mom says Neetu should get a medal for handling me!**
> *–Rishi Kapoor*

Karan Johar: Are you fighting back?

Neetu Singh: He is an adult with a unique identity. He has calmed down to have better relations.

WIFE AND MOTHER

Rishi Kapoor: You should inquire how she lost so much weight?

Karan Johar: Everybody just loves the way she looks. You should ask how she looks so beautiful. Why are not you in cinema? I mean you refused me. But, I had to bring you back. I just told Neetuji that your return should correlate with me in one way or the other.

Neetu Singh: I think it is just my nature. I am a Cancerian. I am a housewife. I spoil my family. I want to be around them. My kids cannot do without me. My husband cannot do without me. I never want to be alone.

Karan Johar: OK. You might be giving more importance to yourself. They are doing very well.

Neetu Singh: When I am not around this guy, he wants me to be around. It is not that he will be insecure with wherever I am. It is just that he feels lonely. He wants everybody to be there.

Karan Johar: Would you be averse, Sir, if she worked in a film?

Rishi Kapoor: No way. I said that she must do a film when you approached her. I cannot imagine myself if she had to be 'outdoors' – on location.

> **I prefer locations when my family is not with me.**
> *–Neetu Singh*

Neetu Singh: I prefer locations when my family is not with me.

Karan Johar: You don't miss it at all?

Neetu Singh: Not at all.

Karan Johar: Today, you have enveloped yourself with make-up. Don't you think of doing that more eventually? You look amazing!

Neetu Singh: I do not know. I may do it after a few years when my kids are on their way.

Karan Johar: Would you like to play a mother to Ranbir?

> **I am just more of a homebody.**
> –Neetu Singh

Neetu Singh: May be. I don't know.

Karan Johar: I am just putting the options out for filmmakers who are watching this show.

Neetu Singh: No. I just want my daughter, my son to be on their way. They don't need me. I am on my own.

Rishi Kapoor: What happens to me? Am I also on my own?

Neetu Singh: He found his family with literati. They scramble for incomplete information. So, I want my kids to acquaint with such skills on their own. I think about it, but I am just more of a homebody. Basically that's my problem.

Karan Johar: Well, I hope some day, someone convinces you. And I hope that someone is me. You are full of amazing things. You are so candid in your interviews. You know booze and food has been Neetu's biggest co-wives. Booze I can understand, but why the food?

Neetu Singh: Food because I can't control him. You know, people say fat is genetic. I do not think so. It is a lifestyle syndrome. You develop that style with your parents.

Karan Johar: Good eating is part of the Punjabi habit. We cannot help it! It is inherently within us. What do you have to say? Where did that comment come from?

Neetu Singh: I cannot control his food habits. He was used to having rich food throughout which I have resisted.

Karan Johar: And what about the booze? What happens there?

Rishi Kapoor: I do not mobilize him to do so. People comment on his food habits.

Karan Johar: Do you find yourself entertaining when you are drunk?

> **Being fat is a lifestyle syndrome, not genetic. You develop that style with your parents.**
> –Neetu Singh

Rishi Kapoor: I go euphoric!

Neetu Singh: He is very entertaining when he throws up himself.

Rishi Kapoor: I feel nice when I get my quota of whisky. I work the whole day like a donkey – I feel that I must have a drink.

Neetu Singh: He walks a lot. He does a lot of things and then it's okay.

RAPID FIRE

Karan Johar: We shall put across a volley of questions. Answers should be racy. Delay is not allowed. The rapid fire round is on.

Neetu Singh: This hamper will come on my way.

Karan Johar: It has to go home.

Neetu Singh: Does not matter; that will happen even if I went mute!

Karan Johar: But I don't want you to be so.

Neetu Singh: I am not going to say anything.

Karan Johar: All right. It is me who decide who the winner is. The winner takes home the *Koffee with Karan Koffee hamper.*

Rishi Kapoor: Well, give her the koffee. Is there no liquor hamper?

Karan Johar: That was the line of the show!

Rishi Kapoor: Give her the koffee.

Karan Johar: And you take home the liquor then! All right. Ladies first.

Rishi Kapoor: Sure!

Karan Johar: Which contemporary actress reminds you most of yourself on the screen?

Neetu Singh: Should I give myself a compliment?

Karan Johar: Yes.

Neetu Singh: Rani.

> **Is there no liquor hamper?**
> –*Rishi Kapoor*

Karan Johar: Of course, Rani. All right. Your favourite co-star after Rishi Kapoor and why? Amitabh Bachchan, Rajesh Khanna, Vinod Khanna.

Neetu Singh: Amitabh Bachchan. He was too funny.

Karan Johar: Good to hear that.

Neetu Singh: The world knows he is great actor. He was the funniest.

Karan Johar: Sanjay Bhansali, Aditya Chopra, Farhan Akthar, Farha Khan – which director you would have liked to work with in your prime?

Neetu Singh: All of them.

Karan Johar: The biggest advantage of being married to an actor is?

> **My favourite costar was Amitabh Bachchan – he was the funniest!**
>
> –*Neetu Singh*

Neetu Singh: You do not leave the movies. You are still there. The glamour is still there. You are still a part of it. You have not left completely.

Rishi Kapoor: You have left the scenario, but you are still connected.

Karan Johar: All right. The biggest disadvantage of being married to an actor is?

Neetu Singh: I don't think there is any really. If he is basically a good guy, it is okay.

Karan Johar: The off screen couple who has the least onscreen chemistry – Shahid-Kareena, John-Bipasha, Vivek-Aishwarya.

Neetu Singh: Vivek-Aishwarya.

Karan Johar: All right. The hero you have worked with whom your husband was jealous of?

Neetu Singh: No one. They never flirted with me. They were his friends and scared.

Karan Johar: Are they scared of Rishi Kapoor?

Neetu Singh: His girlfriend.

Karan Johar: OK. Which young actors/actress would be well cast in *Naukar Biwi Ka*?

Neetu Singh: I don't know.

Karan Johar: There's no servant with any wife.

Neetu Singh: No. Not really.

Karan Johar: All right. OK. *Loafer.*

Rishi Kapoor: Rishi Kapoor.

Neetu Singh: Not at all. No way. Salman.

Karan Johar: *Junglee.*

Neetu Singh: Vivek.

Karan Johar: Okay. *Rangeela Ratan.*

> **Karan Johar:** The off screen couple who has the least onscreen chemistry?
>
> **Neetu Singh:** Vivek-Aishwarya.

Neetu Singh: Shahrukh.

Karan Johar: OK. Hema Malini, Dimple Kapadia, Rekha, Sharmila – the actress who looks best on screen today.

Neetu Singh: They all look gorgeous.

Karan Johar: Give one name.

Neetu Singh: I don't know. I think Dimple.

Karan Johar: One hero you don't mind playing mother to and don't say Ranbir.

Neetu Singh: Ranbir.

Rishi Kapoor: He is not a hero.

Neetu Singh: Well, whenever.

Karan Johar: Only him? No one else?

Neetu Singh: I don't know. May be.

Karan Johar: OK. If you could change one thing about Rishi Kapoor, you would change?

Neetu Singh: His drinking.

Karan Johar: Rishi Kapoor in *Bobby* or in *Karz*?

Neetu Singh: Rishi in *Karz*.

Karan Johar: OK. Your two brothers-in-law, Randhir Kapoor or Rajeev Kapoor?

Neetu Singh: Both are cute. I am closer to Chimpu.

Karan Johar: Rajeev Kapoor. OK. Actresses – Karishma or Kareena?

Neetu Singh: Both are fantastic. Karishma has done whatever she had to do. But Kareena needs time. But both are fantastic.

Karan Johar: All right. Husband or Son?

Neetu Singh: Both are my life.

Karan Johar: All right. Rani, Preiti, Aishwarya – who rules Bollywood?

Neetu Singh: Rani.

Karan Johar: Shahrukh, Salman, Aamir – the most romantic Khan.

Neetu Singh: I think Shahrukh is God. Salman remains the cutie pie.

Karan Johar: That was your rapid fire. Not too bad.

Neetu Singh: Not too bad?

Karan Johar: I think you answered very well. We will see whether you are the potential winner. We have great competition right next to you. So are you ready, sir? All right. Abhishek, Shahid, Vivek, John – the upcoming hero. Who has the best future?

> My marriage advice would be, 'Just be under your wife's shadow!'
>
> –*Rishi Kapoor*

Rishi Kapoor: Abhishek Bachchan.

Karan Johar: A piece of marriage advice you would like to pass on would be?

Rishi Kapoor: Just be under your wife's shadow.

Karan Johar: And you'll manage really well!

Neetu Singh: No. Be patient.

Karan Johar: OK. After 25 years of marriage, what does a wife mean when she says the following. 'How much do you love me?'

Rishi Kapoor: 'You are drinking too much.'

Karan Johar: 'Nothing is wrong.'

Rishi Kapoor: Well, nothing must be really wrong. That is why she is saying so.

Karan Johar: 'We need to talk.'

Rishi Kapoor: There is a serious problem.

Karan Johar: OK. A piece of career advice to Ranbir would be?

Rishi Kapoor: See, we are living in an industry where you know failure is a must. Every film cannot not succeed. You know that for that one odd film, success comes very occasionally. An actor should preserve whatever he comes across. I always feel this out of my own experience. I have told him many times that never take failures to your heart and never let the success go to your head. These are the two sides of the same coin. Give it your better shot to be a good actor. Leave the rest and work well.

Karan Johar: Bipasha, Priyanka, Lara, Mallika – the heroine with the maximum oomph?

Rishi Kapoor: I like Bipasha.

Neetu Singh: Hello!

Karan Johar: Did you know that? I did not. OK. Rani, Kajol, Aishwarya, Preeti – the contemporary actress you would have loved to work with in your prime?

Rishi Kapoor: I would love to work with Preiti.

Karan Johar: Which young actor/actress would be the perfect choice for the title role in the following remixes? *Sharmeelee.*

Rishi Kapoor: This generation is not of shy people.

Karan Johar: There is no shame. OK. *Hunterwali?*

Neetu Singh: I think Mallika Sherawat.

Rishi Kapoor: Mallika Sherawat.

Karan Johar: *Bluff master?*

> **I would love to work with Preiti.**
> *–Rishi Kapoor*

Rishi Kapoor: Govinda would make it.

Karan Johar: Govinda. OK. The biggest problem Aishwarya will face in Hollywood is?

Rishi Kapoor: Is? Sorry, I just asked – is?

Neetu Singh: Oh! He is being you know what?

Karan Johar: Okay. The Hollywood actress you would love to get naughty with?

> **I would love to get naughty with Salma Hayek!**
> *–Rishi Kapoor*

Neetu Singh: Salma Hayek.

Rishi Kapoor: Salma Hayek.

Karan Johar: A song which best describes your relation with your wife?

Rishi Kapoor: *Ek Main Aur Ek Tu.*

Karan Johar: Salman, Aamir, Shahrukh – who according to you is the most rocking Khan and why?

Rishi Kapoor: All three are friends. I have worked with only two of them. So, I look forward to working with Aamir.

Karan Johar: Do you find an underrated actor?

Rishi Kapoor: I have seen Salman doing some good work in a film with me. I always felt why does not he deserve his due? No doubt, he is a big star, but an underrated one.

Karan Johar: Very quickly, choices. Amitabh Bachchan, Shashi Kapoor, Daboo Kapoor – who do you think Neetu makes the best onscreen pair with besides you?

Rishi Kapoor: Shashi Kapoor.

Karan Johar: Dimple or Sri Devi?

Rishi Kapoor: Dimple.

Karan Johar: All right. Sanjay Bhansali or Yash Chopra?

> **No doubt Salman is a big star, but an underrated one.**
> *–Rishi Kapoor*

Rishi Kapoor: Yash Chopra.

Karan Johar: Shammi Kapoor or Shashi Kapoor?

Rishi Kapoor: Both.

Neetu Singh: They are his uncles.

Karan Johar: Madhuri or Juhi?

Rishi Kapoor: Juhi.

Karan Johar: Shah Rukh or Aamir?

Rishi Kapoor: I will say Shahrukh because I have pleasant memories of working with him at one stage when he was new to Bollywood.

Karan Johar: OK. Well done. That was your rapid fire round. The winner is your husband.

Neetu Singh: Okay. It is coming to me anyway.

Karan Johar: I am giving you the coffee hamper. My honour.

Rishi Kapoor: Thank you.

Karan Johar: And your sentiments on losing?

Neetu Singh: It has come to me anyway!

Karan Johar: You are the winner.

Neetu Singh: I am the winner.

Karan Johar: All right. That is wonderful. We have spoken much about everything. I have not asked about the interesting thing you do today. I believe you are doing this film for which you have been shooting in England. The press reports about this completely crossover film that is very exciting. What are your feelings?

Rishi Kapoor: It is an English film. The film speaks about music. Music happens to be the hub of England. Rappers have come in. The *Bhangra* and all of that. The film is based on that kind of issue.

Karan Johar: English language. So, the big words you have in your dictionary have come out!

Neetu Singh: The really interesting movie was *Pal Tham Gaya* where he enacted with Dimple.

Karan Johar: Bobby's romance is back.

Neetu Singh: He acted in 73 as a teenager, then there was *Sagar* as an adult, and now in 2005 this as mature guys. So, the three movies it is some kind of a record, Karan. For thirty years, this pair is together.

Karan Johar: Do you feel different when working with Dimple after so many years?

Rishi Kapoor: Yes. I always felt after *Bobby, Sagar* the transition has been towards maturity, understanding and experience. Dimple has really scaled heights and is really fabulous as an actress. I don't know – I would like to check this factor, whether any pair has worked for 32 years in love stories.

> **For thirty years, the onscreen pair of Dimple and Rishi is together!**
> –*Neetu Singh*

Karan Johar: This is a record!

Neetu Singh: It reminds you a lot of Prince Charles and Camilla Parker Bowles.

Karan Johar: The very topic is romantic.

Neetu Singh: It is a romantic movie

Rishi Kapoor: It's not really a romantic film. It is an issue-based venture. We play 50 plus when we decide to get married. There could be romance in it. It does when you ask questions. Why has Prince Charles married Camilla right now at this age? Obviously, he is not starting a family. It is about some companionship. The film is based on companionship at a certain age.

Karan Johar: It will not relate to the physical aspect.

Rishi Kapoor: Exactly. That's where you need some companionship. I personally feel it makes good viewing.

Karan Johar: The whole record is quite interesting. You will have varieties of record.

Neetu Singh: Oh yes!

Yeh Jo Public Hai

Karan Johar: 25 years of happy marriage is a record in itself. You are enacting in a film again with Dimple. I think you are coupling with her. The marriage and onscreen presence is truly nostalgic, aesthetic and blessed. We have so many people who have said so many things about this when we surveyed. Would like to see it for yourself?

Neetu Singh: That is so sweet!

Karan Johar: Neetu Singh and Rishi Kapoor have proved to be good couple – a very good pair. They are always bubbly, chirpy, cheerful, full of energy. They have retained these characteristics before and after marriage. They look as if they are made for each other and remained the symbol of seventies romance. We remember them as a very cute and adorable couple. I think they look amazing together.

- Rocking. Rocking couple.
- I think they compliment each other.
- He is so jovial. She is so refined. That makes a great couple.
- They are very buoyant and lively people. They translate their skills into reality onscreen.
- We really remember the movies they have enacted together. Youngsters used to see their movies not only once but five to six times. They are the most beautiful pair onscreen and off screen. Their screen presence was phenomenal and fantastic.
- We will love openly that very nice song.
- They really look as if they are made for each other in the song in *Rafu Chakkar,* the comedy and *Kabhi Kabhi*, wherein they enact as a young couple. The second generation movie *Khel Khel Mein* brings back their memories.
- I used to watch their movies even when they were not married. And I liked them very much.
- Neetu Singh, as usual, is a very amazing girl. She is adorable with dignified look. Neetu Singh should not have retired from film world. I think we should see more of Neetu Singh.
- Neetu Singh is my favorite heroine. I would like to see her again.
- Rishi Kapoor starting with *Bobby* was phenomenal. He was damn handsome during that point. Rishi Kapoor's dancing is very good. He is very spontaneous in acting. I love the way he dances. I think he is rather cute.
- Rishi was handsome. Neetu was beautiful. The charm was seen in Rishi and Neetu's pair during our times. They have managed to still retain that charm. They presented a very romantic image that lingers on. It has stayed with us even after 20 or 30 years, always younger than their age. I think probably they could strike a very good chord with youngsters when they watch the movie. I was a teenager and believe age doesn't matter when both of them are concerned. They look young. I would definitely like to see again *'the wonderful couple'*.

- We will be very happy to see Rishi and Neetu Kapoor performing onscreen together. The whole public would like to see Neetu back. So, please come back. We want to see you again. *Ek main aur ek tu, dono mile is tarah* – I am a very big fan of yours. I have seen many films of yours. I want you both to remain like this forever.
- Rishi, you are one of my favorite stars. Neetu, you are more than that. I wish both of you, longer life! And that your children also may act better than you and bring fame to the Kapoor family.

Rishi Kapoor: I thank all of you!

Neetu Singh: That was so wonderful! Thank you so much. It was so touching.

Karan Johar: What do you feel when they all say that you should come back as a couple?

Neetu Singh: We will have to do it now.

Karan Johar: I see so much love out there.

Rishi Kapoor: This is what you have gained all these years.

Karan Johar: I think truly as he said – blessed.

Neetu Singh: This is my achievement. I know people still love me.

Rishi Kapoor: They still love us rather. And that's something gratifying.

Karan Johar: Well, I think there is an amazing feeling. I was just watching it. It should make you feel so wonderful.

Neetu Singh: I was really touched.

Rishi Kapoor: This is the real treasure – to have this kind of relationship with your fans.

Karan Johar: There is a deep connectivity, which exists even today. So now you are going to think of what we said?

Neetu Singh: Think about it, definitely.

Karan Johar: When you go home with these thoughts. Hopefully, they have convinced you.

Neetu Singh: I hope so.

Karan Johar: I just want to say I had the best time. Thank you so much for taking the time out and coming on *Koffee with Karan*. The show could not have been complete without you. I am so glad you managed.

Rishi Kapoor: And Karan, we remember Mr. Yash today a lot. I have worked with him. God bless him as well.

> Yash Johar and I used to call each other 'Maalik!'
> —*Rishi Kapoor*

Karan Johar: Thank you. He was always exceptionally fond of you.

Neetu Singh: Do you know what they used to call each other?

Rishi Kapoor: Maalik!

Neetu Singh: I didn't know what this Maalik was. Whenever they met – 'Maalik!'

Karan Johar: Thank you again. Thank you so much. Truly, we are much honored to have you.

Rishi Kapoor: Thank you.

Neetu Singh: Thank you for calling us.

Karan Johar: I am not going to let you go so easily. There is a cup right next to you with a silver pen. I want you to sign it. Please remember that this personally autographed mug can be yours only if you take part in the *koffee quest* contest.

Let us walk towards the *koffee* wall. We shall place the cup there. Thank you so much.

● ● ●

21

Esha Deol & Shahid Kapoor
The New Kids on the Block

This poor girl was truly burdened with heavy expectations. Dharmendra and Hema Malani's daughter had a rough ride. *Dhoom* really did it with the right bike ride that came along. The title song became a national rage. Esha Deol has announced her arrival. What does the future hold for her? Esha Deol, the daughter of yesteryear's Dream Girl.

ESHA DEOL

Karan Johar: Hello! Welcome to *Koffee with Karan*.

Esha Deol: Hello!

Karan Johar: You are looking lovely! So Esha, how does it feel to be on *Koffee with Karan?*

Esha Deol: I feel great!

THE SILVER SPOON

Karan Johar: I believe your father will watch this show and you are scared of wearing a western outfit.

> **I am wearing an Indian outfit today because I am scared of my father who will be watching me!**
> *–Esha Deol*

Esha Deol: That's the best excuse I could give you, Karan.

Karan Johar: Oh, that will be an excuse! I believe Esha is extremely scared. She must look very Indian because her pa Dharmendra is watching the show.

Esha Deol: I don't know. It is just me in here, anyway. I like wearing Indian costumes.

Karan Johar: That is not the impression you gave, my dear.

Esha Deol: Yes, I know after *Dhoom*.

Karan Johar: Yes. Had it been difficult initially in your career for being the daughter of Hema Malini and Dharmendra?

Esha Deol: People have this whole thing that star kids get it very easy. Usually, people come and give you offers just because you are so and so's daughter. Your introduction becomes really hot for the producer. I realized through my experience that everything will rest on you – if the first three films flop, nobody will give you a second look. You have to work hard on your own. Then only you will emerge as Esha Deol.

Karan Johar: So, did you feel the whole perception change when the euphoria died? You gave a few flops in your earlier ventures. Do you think that Esha Deol suffers from lack of confidence?

Esha Deol: I was dissociated from the industry before landing there. I felt nothing worked out due to articles appearing in the media. I believed that I would be consigned to the back seat

> **If the first three films flop, nobody will give you a second look. You have to work hard on your own.**
> *–Esha Deol*

because luck would not push me ahead. I met Adi by sheer luck. He told me in good confidence that I had to pull up my socks. Otherwise, I would not have been sitting in front of you today.

Karan Johar: The industry felt en masse that Esha was not concerned about her work. Was it true?

Esha Deol: See, I have been cherishing movies ever since I knew about them. I always wanted to be an actress. Not for glam but because I plainly love acting. I want to be loved in front of the camera – act as a heroine. I have seen mom doing it since I was kid. I must have given the impression that I am not that serious. I commenced acting when I was barely 18 years of age. To say in confidence, I was lifted literally from football ground.

> **I was lifted literally from football ground!**
> *–Esha Deol*

I was made to pose before the camera. I believed that I should have taken some time before entering the industry and groomed myself as a better product – although I think it is never too late.

Karan Johar: Of course, it is not and the film *Dhoom* happened. The song picturised became a national rage. It is like the national anthem even today. In ringtones, I felt the pulse of a *Dhoom* girl wherever I travelled. So, you should feel great for the public opinion.

Esha Deol: Yes, I feel nice.

Karan Johar: Well, I always say that you project the new brand of genes in Bollywood. Our next representative tonight is also a true copy.

Esha Deol: Yes.

SHAHID KAPOOR

Karan Johar: He is a teenage heartthrob. Girls between six and sixteen years of age adore him as an angel. I have come across a girl little older who has glorified him. Yes, he is Kareena Kapoor's love interest. The nation is aware of that. He is on the anvil of an extremely interesting career. Let us find what makes him tick. Let us call him. Shahid Kapoor, Come on!

Shahid Kapoor: Hello!

Karan Johar: Hello! Welcome to *Koffee with Karan*.

Shahid Kapoor: Finally!

Karan Johar: We coordinated for the dates for a while. Why have you been busy?

Shahid Kapoor: Well, I was out of the country. I apologize profusely.

Karan Johar: Shahid Kapoor has no dates for me. I told Esha about her arrival with *Dhoom*. The song became a national rage. I would say it was easier for her. She did not have to struggle.

Esha Deol: Star kid.

Karan Johar: Of course, Pankaj Kapoor is such a great actor. I am sure you are just honoured to share the film world with him.

Shahid Kapoor: Right.

IN THE BIG LEAGUE

Karan Johar: *Ishq Vishq* was an immediate success related to the whims and fancies of youth. Indeed, there was not much struggle. How did you feel when it happened?

Shahid Kapoor: It was overwhelming. The whole film had appreciable number of actors and actresses.

Karan Johar: Yes.

Shahid Kapoor: It wasn't the biggest launch of the year. It had lots of new artists who tried to do something anew. The producers

> I was only 21 when I did *Ishq Vishq*. The experience was rather intense.
> – *Shahid Kapoor*

portrayed something new, which worked out. Most of us were overwhelmed with the overall response, because we did not know what went on. I was barely 21 when I ventured out. I felt the experience was rather intense.

Karan Johar: You heard how Esha could not concentrate on her career?

Shahid Kapoor: Yes.

APTITUDE VS ATTITUDE

Karan Johar: Common perception is that you have an attitude on the sets. May it was because of abrupt success, Shahid?

Shahid Kapoor: Right.

Karan Johar: Do you want to correct the stories afloat?

Shahid Kapoor: Well, I don't know where they came from.

Karan Johar: The universal adage focus on the fire and not on the smoke is pointless. One is always pensive when rumours like these afloat.

Shahid Kapoor: I never really thought much about it. I am moulded my own personality. I always do what I feel is right.

> **I am very comfortable with myself as a person.**
> – *Shahid Kapoor*

I am always instinctive about my decisions. I am very comfortable with myself as a person. Work has been my focus. So long as I am punctual, disciplined and remain professional, these things won't disqualify my skills.

Karan Johar: You do not know why and where that happened?

Esha Deol: No, I do not know. Whether it due to too many people or you were trying to remain selective.

Shahid Kapoor: Well, I guess every body says no to people. The reality of easy escape comes to anyone who seldom says no to any work. So, it would be really easy escape to say it was only because I was saying no to people. Maybe I was young, impulsive and I came across too strongly to some people in the industry.

> **The reality of easy escape comes to anyone who seldom says no to any work.**
> – *Shahid Kapoor*

THE 'K' FACTOR

Karan Johar: People talk of your relation with Kareena. That seems to be their focus. Do you feel this would usurp your unique personality (and individuality)? Initially, when it started, people got to know about you.

Shahid Kapoor: It became a public knowledge that we saw each other. It was rather blown out of proportion. I suddenly realized that things were written more about my personal life than my work for a certain amount of time. And somewhere, it was uncomfortable.

Karan Johar: All right.

Shahid Kapoor: I am a very private person. I have never felt the need for us to hide our relationship. We realized that the media never drew a line.

> **I suddenly realized that things were written more about my personal life than my work!**
> –*Shahid Kapoor*

Karan Johar: Did they blow it out of proportion?

Shahid Kapoor: Yes. It is up to the individual to draw the line. I decided to take that decision. I have become a lot more private about my personal life. Whenever you are outside, you represent somebody whom they see onscreen. So, whatever little time you have, you can utilize it properly.

MY CO-STAR

Karan Johar: All right. Let's find out whether Kareena and Esha are friends. So, what happened? Has the big friendship gone? Let us talk about Kareena.

Esha Deol: You know, Karan, I can never be uncomfortable about it. Bebo and I both are equally honest. We are very brutal and brash.

Karan Johar: OK. I have this lie-o-meter. Tell me the truth about yourselves. I have heard that there was a rough ride in between.

Esha Deol: See, Bebo and I know each other from our school days. We were in the same school and ended up in the same career. Initially, we used to hang out and spend time. I was not that busy when I started out. Bebo was already full fledged in it.

> **Bebo and I have just decided to let each other do our own things.**
> – Esha Deol

So I used to meet her on the sets. We were very open about our friendship. We were slightly off to a point, unaware of how things went wrong in between.

Karan Johar: What went wrong?

Esha Deol: Nothing. We have just decided to let each other do our own things. I am sure neither she nor I have changed as a person. The things around us have changed. Everything else changed. You have to grow and change accordingly.

Karan Johar: Yes.

Esha Deol: I believe things moved in quite a complicated manner.

Karan Johar: Do you believe two actresses can be friends? I have asked this question to all actresses.

Esha Deol: I am a good friend of Lara. I am good friends with Celina and Bebo, who is friendly with every other lot. She has the right to swerve from certain people, who rub us the wrong way. There is nothing wrong in that.

Karan Johar: And who is that according to you?

Esha Deol: I don't know. Don't ask me such things.

Karan Johar: But your status with Kareena is that you are friends?

> Bebo shared with me that she had been dating Shahid in anticipation of me getting somebody I would love!
>
> *–Esha Deol*

Esha Deol: Yes. We obviously like when we meet each other.

Karan Johar: Did she initially speak about Shahid to ascertain what happened?

Esha Deol: She told me that she had dated someone. And later Bebo shared with me that she had been dating Shahid in anticipation of me getting somebody I would love.

Karan Johar: How sweet! Let us settle at that at this point.

DOUBLE TROUBLE

Karan Johar: What happened between Fardeen and Kareena?

Shahid Kapoor: I am not dating him – honestly!

Karan Johar: You want me to explain the position? Fardeen says he was misquoted by a magazine – 'Shahid has an attitude problem.' Apparently, you experienced some stress on the sets of *Fida*.

Shahid Kapoor: I have no issues with him. Whatever happened was from his side.

Karan Johar: OK. So you feel something brewed on his side?

Shahid Kapoor: He spoke about the matter at few places. So I am sure there was something. I had no issues working with him. It was purely a professional relationship. I went on my sets. I did my job and slept at home. I resumed work on the sets the next day. I really do not know how he felt I was rude.

Karan Johar: So you don't remember the incident?

Shahid Kapoor: No, I am never rude to any of my co-stars. I don't know what problems he had. He could have just given me a call and spoken about it. We met on the sets everyday. I guess he prefers to go into print media and explain.

> I have no issues with Fardeen – whatever happened was from his side.
>
> *–Shahid Kapoor*

Karan Johar: I like the way he (Shahid) puts things across! You deny the position?

Shahid Kapoor: I have no issues with him. If he had, it

Me, controversies? I am the most boring person!

–Shahid Kapoor

would be pretty bad to speak about them to somebody else.

Karan Johar: All right. I am only clearing the controversy.

Shahid Kapoor: Me, controversies? I am the most boring person.

Karan Johar: See how he is sharing his innocence?

Shahid Kapoor: But I am. What to do?

Karan Johar: Much has been said about your alleged link up with Zayed, Esha. I remember it while confronting him on the show.

Esha Deol: Oh God! I have already spoken about it.

Karan Johar: Yes. Suddenly, I just threw it at Zayed when he was here. He denied it on my show. Do you get obsessed on hearing the topic?

Esha Deol: I think it's over, done. I never answered everything.

A SUITABLE BOY

Karan Johar: Is there any relation you admit in the fraternity so far?

Esha Deol: No, Karan. My mom and dad are looking for someone for me. I did not find anybody interesting. I don't know what is wrong with me.

Karan Johar: Are you not attracted to any of the young boys in Bollywood?

Esha Deol: No. They are nice looking and attractive, and I have other parameters. I am very choosy. I want to be with someone for keepsake.

Karan Johar: Are you looking for Mr. Right?

Esha Deol: Not at all, but if he is around, he could have a cup of coffee with me!

Karan Johar: All right. I read some quite interesting facts – your mom wanted you to enter into a relation with somebody. She wants to proceed ahead but you were found drifting from that path.

Esha Deol: I won't deny the fact. I used to crash with any guy during my school days. My mom wants me to choose someone from among friends visiting our home. So she is just like other matured moms – 'Why don't you see someone?'

My mom and dad are looking for someone for me!

–Esha Deol

Karan Johar: That's so cool. She tells that Esha should find somebody.

Esha Deol: Yes, she really wants me to see someone, but I am in no hurry. I know how difficult it is because you have to sit comfortably and send the message. I should also be ready to fight along. I don't want to get there.

> **I do not find anybody interesting – I don't know what is wrong with me!**
> –*Esha Deol*

THE BUGGING BUGS

Karan Johar: All right. A message reminded some big thing to have happened between you, Shahid, and Bebo. Might have been a paparazzi attack. I have spoken about that at many places. How do you reciprocate?

Shahid Kapoor: It really affected me, and Bebo's- anyways also, my family. When you invade somebody's privacy, you will find a spectrum of emotions. Where will you draw the line? Are you going to hide a camera in their bathroom

> **Where will you draw the line as far as the paparazzi is concerned?**
> – *Shahid Kapoor*

or bedroom? I have decided to draw the line with the official media. I knew this young boy who came my way. I spoke to people at face value. I was very open. The incident shook me up and made me realize something similar can happen.

Karan Johar: I believe you have the support from the fraternity in the industry and Bebo. Everybody went on calling you.

Shahid Kapoor: Yes. Appreciable part of the media stood by us and reacted to the incident. The development made Bebo and me come closer.

Karan Johar: Closer. So, the outcome was positive.

Shahid Kapoor: That was really the first traumatic experience that cemented our relationship. We supported each other. It was something painful for my family and me. So, we bore the anguish.

Karan Johar: Did you see it at all?

Shahid Kapoor: I did not know about it for three days.

> **The MMS incident was really the first traumatic experience that cemented our relationship.**
> –*Shahid Kapoor*

Karan Johar: As usual.

Shahid Kapoor: I have not seen the guy at all.

Esha Deol: I don't want or intend to talk about such things but I consider it a complete invasion of your privacy.

THE OOMPH METER

Karan Johar: A new wave in cinema bursts out with sex. It is mere skin show. Did you feel, Esha, to have changed your image to vagaries of time? *Dhoom* suddenly saw something about your actions.

Esha Deol: Adi convinced me about the outcome. I knew the Chopras on the culture. There was no way I could look cheap in a bikini shot.

Karan Johar: So, do you think other girls looked cheap?

Esha Deol: No. I am not interested in involving myself with other girls. It took some time for me to ponder and adjust to the sequence on the sets.

> With the Chopras, I knew I could not look cheap in a bikini shot in *Dhoom*.
>
> *–Esha Deol*

Karan Johar: I believe you have put effort on creating an aesthetic look.

Esha Deol: Thank you.

Karan Johar: You might have felt the need to change your image.

Esha Deol: I often wanted to shape my body up. The trend is obviously new. Everyone wears lesser clothes and enters the gym. You have to do certain things to be in the rat race.

Karan Johar: We don't need to ask Shahid what he thinks about the concept of sex selling or not.

Shahid Kapoor: This is what I am. I am very comfortable.

Karan Johar: All right. You are comfortable. What do you think? Where will you draw the line?

Shahid Kapoor: Well, I have not started exposing. I think it is very personal. It depends on an individual, provided the audience and the model feel mutually comfortable.

Karan Johar: Yes.

Shahid Kapoor: I am not somebody to do things on somebody's instruction. Neither have I attempted for such an image.

> You have to do certain things to be in the rat race – like wearing lesser clothes and entering a gym!
>
> *–Esha Deol*

Karan Johar: It is always the girls who are ready to respond to a kissing scene. What do you make of the big deal of heroes avoiding to kiss heroines on the camera? I think the married ones object to kiss.

Shahid Kapoor: Well, you have answered the question. I don't know; I never thought about it. If a film comes across, I'll think about it.

Karan Johar: All right. Do you think sex and cinema are being much talked about for no rhyme or reason?

Shahid Kapoor: People comment about unpleasant things. Anything that seems to work has proved to be a trend. The fad disappears quite early. It appeals to a certain section of the audience depedning on the aesthetic values. It is not a breakthrough of visionary things. You have seen the concept in Hollywood. It depends on the mode.

MEET THE PARENTS

Karan Johar: Did your conservative dad uphold your act in *Dhoom*? Has he seen *Dhoom* at all?

Esha Deol: No.

Karan Johar: How would he react as he belongs to the industry?

Esha Deol: He had seen certain promos. Everybody is happy. No one has complained so far.

Karan Johar: You have done really well. I am sure he is proud of you in every other way. Are you scared of him?

Esha Deol: I am. I just love him.

Karan Johar: He is senior and veteran actor. I can imagine about my scary nature. You just feel so small when you stand in front of him.

Esha Deol: My dad looks big. He is wonderful, soft and gets hurt very easily. So, I am quite scared of him. He is a very strong man and short tempered. We want to see the father-side of his personality. I respect and love him so much.

Karan Johar: You are very scared, you and I both. Your relationship with your mother obviously is like buddies. Explain your relation with your mother.

Esha Deol: She used to admonish me when I was in school about my homework and routine. I used to look at her as a mother. She is a typical mom. She made me sleep early and meet the deadlines. She made me adapt to everything possible. I used to wonder when she would be chilled out. Today, she is quite relaxed about me.

Karan Johar: Is she?

Esha Deol: Yes. She looks much better. My sister and I are not stressing her out that much.

> **My co-stars and I like to have such a hot mother as mine!**
> *–Esha Deol*

Karan Johar: She looks beautiful and stunning. I think she is the most beautiful and graceful woman forever!

Esha Deol: My co-stars and I like to have such a hot mother!

Karan Johar: Shahid, your father has accomplished great work in Indian cinema. What is his take on the kind of your work? What does he say? Tell me one mean thing he has told you recently.

Shahid Kapoor: He told me I should not have begun my career like I did. He was extremely critical. You need such a person to advice you about really bad things. That will certainly help you improve and understand mistakes.

Karan Johar: Yes.

Shahid Kapoor: My dad is a good actor himself. He applauds or criticizes me according to circumstances. He keeps me rooted to the ground. He gives me a reality check. Every youngster needs a father to condition his actions.

Karan Johar: All right. That is wonderful. The nicest thing you heard from your parents about your film work, Esha?

Esha Deol: It has yet to come, Karan. My mom admonishes me and so does dad. I think they have been in this industry so know about the developments quite well. My parents give normal response but dislike pretending.

> **My father was extremely critical about Ishq Vishq!**
> *–Shahid Kapoor*

Karan Johar: Do you think *chamchagiri* never happens?

Esha Deol: No.

Karan Johar: It is wonderful. You will have response at home as per your requirements.

Esha Deol: Exactly.

INDIVIDUALLY TOGETHER

Karan Johar: Does Kareena respond the same way or is she totally smitten? Is she critical of the work you do? Or she is like everything Shahid does is fantastic.

> **Shahid Kapoor: I would not take Kareena's opinion about my performance so seriously because she is always a little partial!**

Shahid Kapoor: She is, but I would not take her opinion so seriously because she is always a little partial – and so am I.

Karan Johar: What about you? Do you think she has erred instead of timely advice?

Shahid Kapoor: I am rather inexperienced about the career mistakes – I am only three films old.

Karan Johar: Could you and do you persuade her?

Shahid Kapoor: We are from the same profession. So obviously, it will lead to talk about our related works. I think the decisions about your career are strictly individual.

Karan Johar: So you like to keep that divide.

Shahid Kapoor: Yes, each individual decides self-destiny for himself beyond the threshold. I don't have any rights to interfere in her career. We could fight about our wants personally, but professionally, I think it is completely her choice.

Karan Johar: Do you think she has been misunderstood?

Shahid Kapoor: Most of the time.

Karan Johar: She is rather busy gauging people. Some accuse her of misunderstanding. She remains a lovely girl at heart.

Shahid Kapoor: She is. I am a little partial to her, so I am only going to praise her. She is wonderful and outspoken. She

> **I don't have any rights to interfere in her career.**
> *–Shahid Kapoor*

tells you what she feels. She says it at your face if she likes somebody. She is the most loyal friend and lover you could cash in on. She will be as honest about it if she dislikes somebody. The profession has such mediocre people who say nice things in front of you and the opposite behind. She is very much her own person.

And I love her for that character.

> **Kareena is wonderful and outspoken – and I love her for that!**
> –*Shahid Kapoor*

Karan Johar: OK. Shahid Kapoor hooked, booked and cooked. Esha Deol still looking for Mr. Right. That's true, isn't it?

Esha Deol: Yes. I am looking for the rapid fire round.

RAPID FIRE

Karan Johar: Thank you for the introduction. That's what we do next, rapid fire. Now, you guys know about it. Shahid, your girlfriend won the hamper. This is what happens. I throw these questions at you and you have to give me quick answers and I decide who the best is and then you win the coffee hamper. It's the *Koffee with Karan koffee hamper* and I am sure both of you are yearning to win this. Esha, I will begin with you. Brace yourself. Your mother will be happy to see you with Abhishek, Zayed, John, Vivek the bachelor?

Esha Deol: Oh my God! Vivek. He is very religious, goes to temples. He prays, does lot of official work with everything. Who wouldn't want her daughter to have nice boy like that at home?

Karan Johar: Good. The most mean critical comment about your early performance.

Esha Deol: Baby fat, baby fat, baby fat!

Karan Johar: If the following superhero films were remade in Hindi, which actor should play and why? Superman.

Esha Deol: Shahid.

Karan Johar: All right. Hulk.

Esha Deol: John.

Karan Johar: All right. Batman?

Esha Deol: Zayed.

Karan Johar: OK. Catwoman.

> **My mother will be happy to see me with Vivek – he is very religious, goes to temple, does lots of official work!**
> – *Esha Deol*

Esha Deol: Me.

Karan Johar: Well done! The body part you wish you could change?

Esha Deol: I have changed

a lot; I don't want to now. Oh God! Medically, hopefully nothing.

Karan Johar: All right. Identify with a comic book character and say why you do so.

Esha Deol: I think Bugs Bunny. I had buckteeth during school days; I still have them!

Karan Johar: Shahrukh Khan, Aamir Khan, Salman Khan. Who is the rocking Khan?

Esha Deol: Salman Khan.

Karan Johar: The Bollywood man you associate with following terms: Wild and wacky.

Esha Deol: Fardeen.

Karan Johar: Sex on toes.

Esha Deol: Akshay Kumar.

Karan Johar: Bedroom eyes.

Esha Deol: My dad.

Karan Johar: Drop dead gorgeous.

Esha Deol: Still to enter the industry.

> *Karan Johar:* **Identify with a comic book character and say why you do so.**
> *Esha Deol:* **I think bugs bunny – I had buckteeth during school days; I still have them!**

Karan Johar: The best Dhamendra-Hema Malini romantic moment on celluloid?

Esha Deol: *Sholay* – when he tried to help my mom shoot the rifle. He tried to touch her and do the whole thing. That was really sweet.

Karan Johar: Cool. Name two heroines not to be stranded in a desert.

Esha Deol: Mallika Sherawat. She definitely has a better body than mine.

Karan Johar: You have no second option?

Esha Deol: No.

Karan Johar: Just Mallika. All right. React in word to the following people. Amisha Patel.

Esha Deol: Blonde.

Karan Johar: John Abraham.

Esha Deol: Hot.

Karan Johar: Abhishek Bachchan.

Esha Deol: Lovely boy.

> *Karan Johar:* **Sex on toes?**
> *Esha Deol:* **Akshay Kumar!**

> **Aishwarya Rai?**
> **Untouchable cold beauty –**
> **very much like you!**
> — *Esha Deol*

Karan Johar: Aishwarya Rai.

Esha Deol: Cold beauty. She is very much like you – untouchable cold beauty!

Karan Johar: Sushmita Sen.

Esha Deol: She is hot and spicy.

Karan Johar: OK. A piece of advice for Shahid?

Esha Deol: Why did you not get braces when you were younger when I was the only one who went through that crap?

Shahid Kapoor: That's rubbish!

Karan Johar: All right. If you were stuck between a tiger and Vivek Oberoi?

Esha Deol: I would run away astride the tiger.

Karan Johar: Choices. Be quick. Mom or dad in *Sholay*?

Esha Deol: Dad.

Karan Johar: Sanjay Bhansali or Yash Chopra?

Esha Deol: Uncle Yash. I have worked with him.

Karan Johar: All right. Hrithik Roshan or Shahrukh Khan?

Esha Deol: I have worked with Hrithik, so Hrithik Roshan.

Karan Johar: All right. As actresses, Kareena or Rani?

Esha Deol: Oh God! I think Kareena.

Karan Johar: John Abhraham or Abhishek Bachchan?

Esha Deol: Why are you doing this? Abhishek.

Karan Johar: All right. Well done, Esha! Lot of good answers. This was not like rapid fire round. She took her time.

Esha Deol: You have to learn how to do things.

Karan Johar: All right. Well done. I thought you performed really well. You gave spontaneous answers. Shahid, your turn. Your biggest turn on in a woman.

> **Your biggest turn off in a woman.**
> –*Karan Johar*

Shahid Kapoor: Eyes.

Karan Johar: OK. Your biggest turn off in a woman.

Shahid Kapoor: Smell.

Shahid Kapoor: Smell

Karan Johar: All right. Rank the following dancers – Hrithik, Akshay Kumar, Govinda, Prabhu Deva.

Shahid Kapoor: Govinda, Hrithik, Prabhu Deva, Akshay.

Karan Johar: 'Shahid tends to imitate Shahrukh.' Your clarification would be?

Shahid Kapoor: I don't care. It is a compliment. He is the biggest superstar of the country.

Karan Johar: All right. Which contemporaries would you dedicate oldie number *O haseena zulfo wali?*

Shahid Kapoor: I wanted it for myself!

Karan Johar: *Chahe koi mujhe junglee kahe?*

Shahid Kapoor: Vivek Oberoi.

Karan Johar: He will do it well. *Nakhrewali?*

Shahid Kapoor: Abhishek.

Karan Johar: *Khambe jaisi khadi hain?*

Shahid Kapoor: Sushmita, because she is really tall.

Karan Johar: *Yeh dosti hum nahin chodenge.*

Shahid Kapoor: I don't know. I lost the hamper, man!

Karan Johar: React in a word. Priety Zinta.

Shahid Kapoor: Cute.

Karan Johar: Rani Mukherjee.

Shahid Kapoor: Very good actress. I will get into trouble at home!

Karan Johar: Hrithik Roshan.

Shahid Kapoor: Best debut in the last 10 years.

Karan Johar: Longest word for Fardeen Khan.

Shahid Kapoor: Pass.

Karan Johar: Vivek Oberoi.

Shahid Kapoor: Very talented.

Karan Johar: If you propose to Kareena, you would?

Shahid Kapoor: I already have – about seeing each other.

Karan Johar: All right. What would you like to change in Kareena?

Shahid Kapoor: I am pretty happy.

> *Karan Johar:* **Rani Mukherjee.**
> *Shahid Kapoor:* **Very good actress. I will get into trouble at home!**

Karan Johar: All right. A rumour afloat that was believed?

Shahid Kapoor: I don't listen. I have lost the hamper, man!

Karan Johar: A piece of advice for Esha?

Shahid Kapoor: Just enjoy the coffee.

Karan Johar: All right. The film industry woman that enters your mind when I say – too hot to handle.

Shahid Kapoor: Sushmita.

Karan Johar: All body no soul.

Shahid Kapoor: I would not answer.

> **Karan Johar: Too hot to handle?**
> **Shahid Kapoor: Sushmita!**

Karan Johar: Over the top.

Shahid Kapoor: Listen, you cannot ask such questions. I will not talk. Over the top, I don't know.

Karan Johar: Beauty and brain.

Shahid Kapoor: Meena Kumari.

Karan Johar: All right. A contemporary hero you consider in competition.

Shahid Kapoor: All of them are in competition, more or less.

Karan Johar: One hero, whom you consider is really good.

Shahid Kapoor: As of now, Abhishek.

Karan Johar: Shahrukh Khan and Aamir Khan.

Shahid Kapoor: Aamir.

Karan Johar: Rani, Priety or Aishwarya? I am sorry I didn't include Kareena in the series.

Shahid Kapoor: Thank you. Rani.

Karan Johar: Rani, Aishwarya or Sushmita?

Shahid Kapoor: Aishwarya.

Karan Johar: Sanjay Dutt or Salman Khan?

Esha Deol: What a choice! You can't choose; both are cool.

Karan Johar: OK. *Fida* or *Ishq Vishq*?

Shahid Kapoor: *Fida.*

> *Karan Johar:* **Rani, Aishwarya or Sushmita?**
> *Shahid Kapoor:* **Aishwarya.**

Karan Johar: All right; both are Ken Ghosh films, so you felt safe. All right. I will announce the winner. The winner of the *Rapid Fire Round* is Esha Deol. Clap for your colleague. Well done, darling!

Shahid Kapoor: Stay up to sip the coffee!

Esha Deol: Thank you.

Karan Johar: Are you happy that you have won the *koffee hamper*?

Esha Deol: Yes. Something to take back home.

> **I had sleepless nights due to uncertainty about the *koffee hamper*!**
> – Esha Deol

Karan Johar: Did you believe you would win?

Esha Deol: No. I had sleepless nights due to uncertainty.

Karan Johar: You have won. Would you like to thank anyone? Do you want to thank your mom?

Esha Deol: I want to thank her. I would like to give her a film.

Karan Johar: Shahid! Are you upset you lost? Eventually, it happens if you are politically correct.

Shahid Kapoor: May be next time.

SURVEY TIME

Karan Johar: All right. Let us have some fun. We went and asked the people about (a) About your relation with Kareena and what they think about it? (b) What kind of man suits you, Esha? Do you want to know what people commented?

Shahid Kapoor: It is a scary part.

Karan Johar: No. Not really. It is good fun.

ESHA DEOL

M: Esha Deol is damn hot. Esha Deol is a rising star.

F: She has lost weight. She looks good now. She appeared completely changed in *Dhoom*. She looks pretty good.

M: Esha Deol in her new look seems to be a bomb. Esha in *Dhoom* was really rocking. She is damn cool. She has an athletic body and is damn good. Esha Deol appeals to me as well to any other guy. She is really good and hot.

> **Esha Deol in her new look seems to be a bomb.**
> –Male

F: She has improved a lot after *Dhoom*.

M: Now, she really looks good; very hot.

M: I like Esha Deol. She is a very good actress. I do not think she has been given her due.

SHAHID KAPOOR

F: Shahid Kapoor is a great actor. I like his smile. He looks really cute.

M: Shahid Kapoor is a very talented guy. He has worked very hard for what he has achieved.

F: Shahid is kiddish.

> **Shahid is the best dancer after Hrithik.**
> – Male

M: Shahid Kapoor is the new kid on the block. He is in the industry with a bang.

F: Baby boy kind of look, very hot.

M: He has wonderful physique. He is the best dancer after Hrithik.

F: Shahid Kapoor has a lot of girls chasing him. He is a fabulous dancer.

M: Lucky guy. He has got Kareena.

SHAHID AND KAREENA

F: Shahid and Kareena make a good pair. They are meant to be like that. They look really cute and are made for each other.

F: Kareena looks older to Shahid. Shahid and Priyanka Chopra pair well.

M: Shahid and Kareena pair OK – not too good.

F: They would not make a good couple. Individually, they are good.

> **Kareena looks older to Shahid!**
> – Female

F: They love each other.

M: I used to hate Shahid because Kareena was my star.

F: They really look cute (together).

ONSCREEN PAIRING

M: Shahid Kapoor pairs well with Esha Deol. She is also a good dancer. They compliment each other.

F: Shahid Kapoor looks good with Amrita Rao.

M: Shahid would work very well with Esha Deol. He looks better with Aisha Takia. He looks cute enough to be with Kareena, but not hot enough!

F: They are poles apart. That makes them look really cute together like opposite poles attract.

F: Esha Deol and Tushar Kapoor pair well. She looks great with John Abraham. Esha Deol looks good with Aftab.

M: She makes a very good pair with John Abraham. Yes, they look good on screen together.

F: Esha Deol looks good with Zayed Khan. She will make good pair with Ajay Devgan, I think. I think Esha and Abhishek Bachchan will make a good pair. Esha makes a good pair with Tushar Kapoor. She looks good on screen with Zayed Khan. Probably, Esha would look good with Vivek Oberoi. Esha Deol and Shahid Kapoor would look good together. They are very cute. John and Esha look good.

M: John Abraham and no one else. He is the Bollywood hunk. Esha pairs well with him. Oh! You guys rock! You will mould the future of the industry. Keep working without disenchantment.

> **John and I look very nice together – he makes me look smaller and delicate!**
> *–Esha Deol*

F: Well, Shahid, I like your dance. Esha, you too, dance well.

Karan Johar: Have you enjoyed our little survey?

Shahid Kapoor: Yes.

Karan Johar: How do you evaluate the rocking pair — John Abraham and you? I am really enthused with him. What you have to say about John being the survey's winner?

Esha Deol: Best of Luck!

Karan Johar: I like your appreciation. He is already hooked, booked and cooked. He has Bipasha.

Esha Deol: John and I look very nice together. He makes me look smaller and delicate. He is so big.

Karan Johar: Shahid, what about you and their observations about Kareena and you?

Shahid Kapoor: Well, some of them like us, others don't. You look really good together at times and not on other times. Did they comment about us onscreen?

Karan Johar: I think a bit of both. Esha, you like their coupling?

Esha Deol: Yes. I will watch your movies hereafter.

CONCLUSION

Karan Johar: This is the final segment.

Shahid Kapoor: I don't have anything to take home.

Karan Johar: No. You will get nothing.

Esha Deol: You got the compliments from people.

Karan Johar: Yes. Thank you so much. Thank you, Shahid. Thank you for sparing time for my show. Thank you, Esha. Thank you for wearing a beautiful white Indian costume so that papa will be proud of you. Thank you for coming.

Esha Deol: Thank you.

Karan Johar: Any last minutes thoughts on being *Koffee with Karan?*

Esha Deol: I just had a great time. I would like to thank everyone for wonderful compliments and comments. I look forward to *Kaal* with John.

Karan Johar: All right. Any last minute thoughts, Shahid?

Shahid Kapoor: Well, it was really fun. I have enjoyed myself. It was a pleasure to be with Esha and Karan.

Karan Johar: That is my line! See, there is a cup next to you. Please sign on it. Remember, this personally autographed mug could be yours only if you participate in the *Koffee Quest Contest.* Thank you again. Can you hold that cup please? We shall walk towards what I call the coffee wall.

● ● ●

22

Hema Malini & Zeenat Aman
Never Say Never Again!..

Not everyone can make heads turn at the drop of a hat. Not everyone can cause hearts to flutter with a quiver of her eyelash. Not everyone can turn conventional notions of glamour and allure on its head.

But that's the kind of effect the incredible, eternal, and, of course, drop-dead gorgeous Hema Malini used to have on silver-screens worldwide in the 70's and early 80's. Meet her in person, and that's the kind of effect she has on you, even today.

Bold, beautiful and very, very professional, here is the actress who forced audiences to sit up, and take a second look. At how substance ought to be presented on screen: In regal style, nothing less.

No, you touch her. You can't ape her either. Nobody ever could. But here on the show today, you can certainly look forward. To a once-in-a-lifetime tele-a-tele with the one and only Hema Malini as she bares her heart with me.

Believe you me, not everyone has the near superhuman ability to turn on the magic for a full hour on-the-trot, without letting you feel the time fly. But that's exactly what is going to happen today! Maybe it's the look.. Maybe it's the indefinable, uncanny charm. But then again, not everyone is Hema Malini..!

Ladies and Gentlemen, it is my deep, deep pleasure to introduce to you India's original glam-doll and the country's first dream-girl..

HEMA MALINI

Hema Malini: Hello!

Karan Johar: Very nice to have you on our show. Alright. I cannot tell you how excited I am to have you on my show.

Hema Malini: The same here.

Karan Johar: To finally have you on *Koffee with Karan Johar!* What does it feel like to be on this show?

Hema Malini: It is nice. I feel wonderful.

Karan Johar: You do! Thank you for sparing your valuable time amidst a busy schedule. All hail to thee! You are a danseuse, actress-turned-Member of Parliament, an amiable mother, obedient wife, an affectionate mother, *et al.* You have assumed so many roles, but you are one indelible icon to remember. How do you cope with routine chores?

> **I do everything on time, dear!**
> *–Hema Malini*

Hema Malini: I think it is time management. I do everything on time, dear!

Karan Johar: OK!

Hema Malini: And I love doing all chores myself.

Karan Johar: Any order of preference? What do you enjoy doing the most?

Hema Malini: I enjoy Bharatanatyam the most!

Karan Johar: You would do that.

Hema Malini: Yes. I love that.

Karan Johar: Alright. Have you enjoyed your foray into politics?

Hema Malini: Yeah. I have started slowly aligning myself with the state of things in politics. Initially, I was a little uncomfortable. I was just campaigning for the political party. Slowly, I tried to reschedule myself with speaking skills. I really enjoy attending the Upper House of Parliament. I love being there. I meet different kinds of people and learn a lot of things.

> **I really enjoy attending the Upper House of Parliament.**
> *–Hema Malini*

Karan Johar: I have read recently that you said Dharamji is not enjoying politics. Did he face any problem to cope with?

Hema Malini: Yeah. Basically,

he just wants to act. That was (all there is to) it.

Karan Johar: I can understand his passion.

Hema Malini: Yes.

> **I prefer to explore many things in life...**
>
> *– Hema Malini*

Karan Johar: He is a tremendous actor with huge back up. With accolades from Gen X and his generation.

Hema Malini: Yes.

Karan Johar: Of course, he must have been passionate about films.

Hema Malini: Yes. That is right. I prefer to explore many things in life...

Karan Johar: Yes. But for him, it is just the movies.

Hema Malini: Yes. Just acting.

Karan Johar: Something as a fan: I have grown up watching your films besides Dharamji's. I always wanted to ask you something. I am so glad that I have the opportunity. What was that moment that made you realize he was the man in your life? We have seen so much of your multifaceted romance on celluloid. What was that particular moment that made you decide, 'I want to spend the rest of my life with him?'

Hema Malini: When I saw him for the first time, I never thought he would be my future husband (though) I always yearned for somebody like him.

Karan Johar: OK. So it happened the first time you set your eyes on him?

Hema Malini: Yes.

Karan Johar: So, can we really attribute it to love at first sight?

Hema Malini: No. I would not say that.

Karan Johar: OK.

Hema Malini: I just liked him. He was a handsome man, with the best physique (anyone in) the industry had.

Karan Johar: He was even good looking.

Hema Malini: Indeed, a very good looking man.

Karan Johar: Do you believe him to be the best looking man?

Hema Malini: I had never seen anyone so good looking. Maybe that is why I thought, 'Oh! He's so wonderful looking! I should get someone like him.'

Karan Johar: Alright. Well, then...

Hema Malini: He himself came into my life.

Karan Johar: That is wonderful. And why not? When you look back do you think it has been an amazing relationship, whether onscreen, or off screen, or both?

> **I had never seen anyone so good looking as Dharam-ji.**
> –*Hema Malini*

Hema Malini: Yeah. Initially you dream of so many things. It was nice. It is different today. I am still enjoying everything. Every moment of it.

Karan Johar: Good. That is wonderful. You reigned supreme, simultaneously, of course! Lo! There was this actress with various talents and skills...

Hema Malini: Yes.

Karan Johar: On Indian celluloid. Do you know my next guest?

Hema Malini: Yes, of course I do know her.

Karan Johar: I will introduce her right now.

Hema Malini: Sure.

Karan Johar: While *Dream Girl* Hema Malini-ji was setting silver screens on fire across the length and breadth of the country, the radar was picking up some very unique movements somewhere else. There was a new face in town. Little did anyone know at that time that it was also the genesis of a brave new movement. One that was to revolutionize the way Indian audience perceived their on-screen idols, especially the ladies. Elegant, intelligent, and chic. Indeed, this was a mix of sophistication and bravado that was new, so signature, so fresh, that it was near impossible to define, or slot. And that's how the lady remains to this day.. Indefinable, matchless, untouchable.

It is my immense joy and privilege to present to you the inimitable Zeenat Aman.., the original oomph girl of Hindi cinema, and someone who dared.

To take things to the next level..

ZEENAT AMAN

Zeenat Aman: Thank you, Karan. It is a pleasure to be with you. Thank you.

Hema Malini: Hello!

Zeenat Aman: Hello!

Karan Johar: I recollected how Hema Malini-ji excited me on the show. I don't have any words to explain. I have grown up watching both of your films. It is like a dream come true having you on the show. I hope you are as happy to be on my show.

Zeenat Aman: Karan Johar, I am extremely delighted to be with you. I availed the opportunity to work in the first film made by your dad. It gives me immense pleasure to be a part of *Koffee with Karan Johar (sic)*.

> **It gives me immense pleasure to be a part of *Koffee with Karan Johar(sic)*.**
>
> *–Zeenat Aman*

Karan Johar: Thank you so much. We were just discussing Hema Malini-ji's foray into politics. And of course, you too have campaigned recently for the Indian National Congress.

Zeenat Aman: Yes.

Karan Johar: Of course, we have opposing political parties on the same sofa.

Hema Malini: Yes.

Karan Johar: We have the BJP and the Congress representatives with us.

Hema Malini: We travel at the same time.

Zeenat Aman: Yes. We kept running into each member of parliament in Delhi.. Hugging and being very friendly and warm with each other'c..

Hema Malini: And the moment, we fly in different helicopters. We appear as the people of different hues.

Zeenat Aman: I have not actually joined any political party. But yes, I did campaign for the Congress.

Karan Johar: And no follow-up after that? Why not?

Zeenat Aman: Karan Johar, I'm very clear about my priorities. I have two teenaged children. And my first commitment is towards their upbringing. I really believe if you make a commitment, you must be comfortable enough to follow it through. So, I have not made up my mind to affiliate with the party.

Karan Johar: Al Right. I think to prioritize is very important for everyone. Really!

Zeenat Aman: Well, it has been for me. I am a single parent. So, it really counts.

> I really believe if you make a commitment, you must be comfortable enough to follow it through.
>
> *–Zeenat Aman*

Karan Johar: Yes.

Karan Johar: And has it been difficult to raise two boys on your own?

Zeenat Aman: It has been an adventure *per se*. It has been wonderful.

Karan Johar: OK. This is not the only time that you have crossed the paths of luminance, of course. Indian cinema can vouch for that. (TO HEMA MALINI) There was much talk about you being the reigning number one. (TO ZEENAT AMAN) And you, the glamorous number two. Have you heard the *vox populi*?

Zeenat Aman: Karan Johar, Hema Malini-ji was definitely the reigning queen when I joined the business.

Karan Johar: Yes.

Zeenat Aman: We have worked together.

Karan Johar: Yes. In several films.

Zeenat Aman: Yes. It was always a pleasure to work with her. She has always been wonderful, daring, vibrant and beautiful. Each of us had our own bevy of fans, scores of films and brigade of filmmakers. I do not think anyone wanted anything..

Karan Johar: Yes. Tell me, don't you find much hype and rivalry among our girls (today)? Comparatively, there was so much courtesy, discipline and dignity in your days.

Hema Malini: Yes. We were very friendly.

Karan Johar: Was there any rivalry? Did you feel any such symptom?

Hema Malini: Maybe.. in some insignificant way. However, when we met personally, our bond was so powerful and remarkable. It brings us wonderful memories. We were well supported by our contemporary actresses..... Parveen Babi and Rekha, who have carved the niche by individual efforts. We remain friendly even now when we meet.

Karan Johar: Yes.

Zeenat Aman: Karan Johar, you know Hema Malini-ji and I were slotted for particular roles. Our roles onscreen were well-defined.

Hema Malini-ji got affiliated to extremely classical, traditional and conventional roles befitting Indian women.

Karan Johar: Yes.

Zeenat Aman: I switched over personally to become modern in appearance, action and blend.

> **My bond with Hema Malini was so powerful and remarkable.**
>
> *–Zeenat Aman*

Karan Johar: A western approach of sophistication.

Zeenat Aman: Absolutely. So, we were never slotted for similar roles. We were always cast in very different parts even in the same film. We seldom found any rivalry or competition between us. I don't know who considered herself to be in competition with Hema Malini-ji. When it comes to me, the media spread a rumour of rivalry with Parveen Babi.

Karan Johar: Do you feel that at that time also there was a Zeenat Aman—Parveen Babi rivalry as it is today in the film industry?

Zeenat Aman: I think there was really more of a media hype than what actually happened. Everybody works happily when there is enough work to go around. I do not think we came across any problem.

Karan Johar: OK. Today, you know things are really different.

Hema Malini: Is that so?

Karan Johar: The girls today... ask your daughter. She will tell you about the kind of friendship and related stories which was not there for both of you.

Hema Malini: I believe Esha remains very friendly with many girls of her generation.

> **Hema Malini and me were never slotted for similar roles.**
>
> *–Zeenat Aman*

Karan Johar: Yeah. She is. But she will tell you about the experiences between some other girls. It is not the same any more. You would not find the family bond that used to evaluate fraternal values. Things take their own time and actors compete like robots. The actresses of yesteryear will find it awesome and queer, to recollect.

Hema Malini: Yeah! That's true.

Karan Johar: I think your career graph never spoke of such hitches. It swayed wonderfully for decades. Our cinema took giant steps ahead in anticipation of 3-dimensional approach. Let me analyze your role as sexy, super sexy..

Zeenat Aman: Ouch!

Karan Johar: I mean, we knew. Hema Malini-ji would agree with me.

Hema Malini: Of course.

> Esha remains very friendly with many girls of her generation.
>
> *–Hema Malini*

Karan Johar: There was no one hotter than you on Indian celluloid.

Zeenat Aman: Thank you.

Karan Johar: Lo! The way these girls go on and on through the sizzling skin show, big hype and hoopla for no rhyme or reason. You have done. You have been there. How does it feel?

Zeenat Aman: Well. I have never really thought about it, Karan Johar. I feel good about being appreciated from behind. It really does wonders. It always feels good irrespective of person or organization or any creative person. Am I right?

Hema Malini: That•is right.

Karan Johar: Do you think you were the specific kind of being over-sensational when you were draped in sexy costumes?

Zeenat Aman: Honestly, my mindset was not attuned to what happened in the Indian Cinema at that time. So I could not realize. I have been traversing *a path-breaking situation*.

Karan Johar: Yes.

Zeenat Aman: I just did it.. I was cast in roles like that of *Hare Rama Hare Krishna, Qurbani* and not the least *Satyam Shivam Sundaram*. I was well cast in befitting and unbelievable roles.

Karan Johar: Yes.

Zeenat Aman: Which eventually made waves, one way or the other.

> I was well cast in befitting and unbelievable roles.
>
> *–Zeenat Aman*

Karan Johar: Yes. Well, today you could correlate with wonder girls like Bipasha, Lara, Priyanka. Does it feel good when they appreciate Zeenat Aman? What does that feel like?

Zeenat Aman: Of course, it feels good. It brings back wonderful images.

Karan Johar: Yes. I hope you believe, Oh God! Why are they comparing me with these girls, or to accept it as complement?

Zeenat Aman: I do take it as a compliment. I do. Because, these girls are lovely, tender and do good work with good film makers. Their rapport with changing times is exceptional. So I do take it as a compliment.

Karan Johar: Yes. Wonderful.

Hema Malini: And really lovely figures they have!

> **Everybody is into health and fitness right now.**
> *—Zeenat Aman*

Karan Johar: Yes. Yes. They do..

Hema Malini: That time only Zeenat Aman had. Nobody else.

Zeenat Aman: No, no. Everybody is into health and fitness right now.

Karan Johar: Yes. Hema Malini-ji is right you were the only one who rocked with good gyrations like rock-break dancers.....

Hema Malini: Yes.

Karan Johar: But Hema Malini-ji you were the classical Indian beauty and your roles were completely different during that era.. from Zeenat-ji's kind of roles and story scripts.

Hema Malini: Yes. That's right.

Karan Johar: Absolutely, there were no skin shows. It was like almost everything was covered from head to toe.

Hema Malini: Yes, Right.

Karan Johar: You were extremely particular about such things.

Hema Malini: Very particular.

Karan Johar: And did you ever face a situation where directors tried to make you look a little sexy.

Hema Malini: Yeah. There was one director. I do not want to take his name. I always used to put a pin on my blouse when I was draped in sari. But he insisted that I should remove that pin. I told him in what way it has disturbed you? Just leave it. I do not know why he thought so.. The sequence just called for my fall where he only wanted my sari to unfurl.

Karan Johar: Oh God! My God!

Hema Malini: But I did not let that happen.

Karan Johar: I can really imagine how you must have challenged such sequences. The era has super glamorous flashbacks. That called for Zeenat Aman set of roles and the Parveen Babi kind of glamour. And you did the totally different thing, altogether. So I can imagine there might have been situations where they expected you to almost kind of..

Hema Malini: No. They knew what I was doing or I will be doing. I was doing films like Meera, Razia Sultan, with my body totally covered. So I was extremely comfortable in enacting scenes.

Karan Johar: Yes. Completely. What is your take today when you see the new brand of cinema..? Wherein this new sensuality, sexuality that is paradoxical

Hema Malini: I feel sad looking at these girls. For, they have to expose themselves, whether situation warrants or not.

Karan Johar: Really.

Hema Malini: Yeah. Very, very sorry.

Karan Johar: You feel that it is an absolute requirement.

Hema Malini: It is a requirement. I find how Esha had been struggling... with these ideas.

Karan Johar: OK.

Hema Malini: Though, I do not want her to get exposed.

Karan Johar: Yes.

Hema Malini: So I thought I should bring her up just like me. I mean not to that extent what I was. To some extent... a bit liberal.

Karan Johar: ...the times have changed.

Hema Malini: Yes. It is impossible now.

Karan Johar: Yes, it is not. Whether the predicament disturbs you when you have to see Esha in a sexy costume? Does it bother you as a mother?

Hema Malini: It bothers me. She has got a lovely beautiful figure simultaneously, which is no longer ugly and vulgar. So long as she is not looking bad, I think it will be fine. And she is a very young girl.

> I feel sad looking at today's girls.,
> *–Hema Malini*

Karan Johar: It is a part and parcel of the 2-dimension movies. And the kind of cinema that she's done.. whether it be *Dhoom,* which is aesthetically short..

Hema Malini: Yes.

Karan Johar: In no way..

Karan Johar: The film does not have ugly scenes.

Zeenat Aman: It always makes some difference with whom you work with and who has been presenting it.

Hema Malini: Yeah. The right angle has to be taken on who had been presenting it. .

Karan Johar: Yeah.

Hema Malini: There were some directors of yesteryears who used to keep the camera absolutely in..

> It bothers me if I see Esha in a sexy costume.
> –Hema Malini

Zeenat Aman: Weird angles. Don't we know about that!

Hema Malini: You know who I am talking about.

Zeenat Aman: Absolutely.

Karan Johar: This had happened to you?

Zeenat Aman: Absolutely.

Karan Johar: And where did they put the camera exactly?

Zeenat Aman: I know exactly whom she is talking about!

Karan Johar: So you had to be extremely vigilant about these directors even when you belong to glamorous species often.. You need to be extra cautious about where the director wanted to install the camera.

Hema Malini: One has to be. Today, I think the girls are hardly aware of...

Karan Johar: No. They are not.

Hema Malini: They are not aware. Or they seldom bother about it even after knowing. Where the camera is.

Karan Johar: But you had to be careful as well.

> There were some directors of yesteryears who used to keep the camera absolutely in...!
> –Hema Malini

Zeenat Aman: Well. You had to be aware. I guess.

Karan: OK. During your era, it came to every producer-director-crew that Hema Malini is the Dream Girl . Everyone used to address you with reverence and awe. There was also a section that glorified you as *the ice maiden*.

Journalists were afraid to ask you questions because there was this big wall in between the producer-director. You cultivated such image for yourself or allowed the industry people to secure..

Hema Malini: It was just me. I seldom did anything to create that image.

Karan Johar: Yeah.

Hema Malini: I think I was a little reserved. I never used to talk much to people. May be, I was very shy at that time. Now at least I•am talking to you.

> There was also a section that glorified you as *the ice maiden.*
> –Karan Johar

Karan Johar: You would not have even done that.

Hema Malini: I would have not thought of attending this variety of programme.

Karan Johar: And all the actors were quite afraid also, I believe.

Zeenat Aman: No, no. They had huge crushes on her. I have worked with a co-star. And during the lunch recess, he and the director would just talk about the huge crush they had on

> All the actors used to have huge crushes on Hema Malini.
> –Zeenat Aman

Hema Malini-ji. I do not think she knew about it. Oh my God! Every lunch recess we used to hear about was.. Hema Malini-ji.. Hema Malini-ji..

Hema Malini: Oh God!

Karan Johar: OK. We would like names on this show.

Zeenat Aman: No.

Karan Johar: How can you not name him? I want to know this actor.

Zeenat Aman: I will tell you after the show.

Karan Johar: All right.

Zeenat Aman: She is a married lady now.

Karan Johar: Of course. So we cannot. We cannot do that. Did you feel basically that the actors were little scared of you? And you liked that.

Hema Malini: No. I used to feel why they are not talking to me in fact.

Karan Johar: Really?

Hema Malini: I used to feel rather neglected actually.

Karan Johar: Oh really?

Hema Malini: Yeah.

Karan Johar: And as opposed to that you were very friendly..

Hema Malini: Except Dharam-ji, Shashi Kapoor, Jitendra..

Hema Malini: Others never used to talk much.

Karan Johar: That heroes had and as Hema Malini-ji reported, you were really popular with the media, besides your actors. You were far more friendlier at that time. Was that just you as well.

Zeenat Aman: I think so. I liked to work in an atmosphere of camaraderie you know.. be happy and jolly. And I think most of the people I have worked with are of the same mental horizon. So it was a pleasant working atmosphere.

Karan Johar: Like Hema Malini-ji, of course, who kept controversies at bay, because she never opened herself up to the media. And as opposed to all your controversies, affairs and link ups, the media was always all over the place.

Zeenat Aman: Well. Some were and some were not all over the place.

Karan Johar: Yes, all over the place.

Zeenat Aman: Existent and non-existent ones.

> **They linked me with someone I have never met in my life.**
> *–Zeenat Aman*

Karan Johar: You mean there were made up stories even then?

Zeenat Aman: Absolutely.

Karan Johar: Do you remember a story they made up that was untrue?

Zeenat Aman: Yes. They linked me with someone I have never met in my life. And they carved a page three story on this *persona non-grata.*

Karan Johar: Really! My God! Were there alleged link ups at that time with you, Hema Malini-ji, that got written about, that were completely untrue?

Hema Malini: They were true.

Karan Johar: Only true link ups?

Hema Malini: Yes. They were very nice. I must say.

Karan Johar: Were it so? All right. Hold that thought Hema Malini-ji. Nostalgia finds new meaning. Dharm-ji came from a very conservative family. You still continued to work right after the marriage. I believe that to be an adventure for a woman of your stature.

Hema Malini: Yes. I continued to work. It is good that he did not stop. Neither had he interfered in my work. That was the reason I am able to go ahead in my career. I keep on doing a good lot of things. To say, a lot of creative things! So, it is nice that he does not disturb me.

Karan Johar: So, you enjoy the freedom at will.

Hema Malini: Yes. I enjoy the freedom. He will be there. Any decision we ought to have in family matters, he used to take that. Else, he does not interfere in any of my things.

Karan Johar: What about Esha's career? Any inputs come from there or he steers that away.

Hema Malini: He keeps that away. He was not keen on her coming to films. So, that was the reason. He still feels uncomfortable about her working. She took the decision. I had to support her as a mother.. I have brought her up in a different manner. I have given her the requisite culture for her upright upbringing.

Karan Johar: Of course.

Hema Malini: And she wanted to work in films. She asked me why do you say it is not good for me when papa, and brothers work in films.

Karan Johar: Yes. And what answer could you possibly give?

Hema Malini: He could not answer anything. So, he had to keep quiet. She started working.

Karan Johar: And your boys, madam.. any kind of aspirations they have had to venture into films, any kind of dreams, or are they completely on another track?

Zeenat Aman: My elder son is now on the edge of 18. I think when he was 6 or 7, he took part in his father's film. He played I think Juhi's and Jackie's son. He had a wonderful experience. The memories still linger on him. He has an affiliation definitely towards this business. He studies at the University of Arts in London and is qualifying for his Bachelors Degree in Arts (Film Making).

Karan Johar: Oh wonderful! And what kind of work do you intend to do in cinema? Did you occupy a back seat earlier and desire to exit?

Zeenat Aman: Karan Johar, I took a definite hiatus. I really put what transpired in my personal life. For me, the family means a great bonanza and deal. Moreover, the boys have grown up. Definitely, I think of doing quality-oriented work. You have to discern with the antecedents of good work whether somebody likes or not.

Karan Johar: Yes.

> **Today, I would love to do quality work.**
>
> *–Zeenat Aman*

Zeenat Aman: So I returned to the craft and tried to hone my skills by doing a bit of theatre art. I took part in English stage theatre. And I have done things which rarely take much of the time away from my family. The boys have grown up. I would love to do quality work. I have just done a Malyalam film with an award winning director. I had a stunning experience in speaking Malayalam with perfect intonation of Malbar inhabitants.

Hema Malini: Wow!

Zeenat Aman: It was tough. But, it's fun. It's fun to do different things which give you joy forever..

Karan Johar: That is wonderful. Today, when you look at the roles... that are available in contrast with what Hema Malini-ji took and reached pinnacle of success in *Baghban*. You will find similar roles for actresses of yesteryears.....

Hema Malini: I don't think so. I dreamt of getting signed for many other films after my performance in *Baghban* opposite Amitabh Bachchan.

Karan Johar: Anything came on your way?

Hema Malini: Nothing.

Zeenat Aman: I agree with you. There are very few age specific roles for the era. I have realized ....very few.

Karan Johar: You think after *Baghban*, you got nothing?

Hema Malini: Nothing.

> **I dreamt of getting signed for many other films after my performance in *Baghban* opposite Amitabh Bachchan.**
>
> *–Hema Malini*

Karan Johar: All right. Did you feel the similar pulse?

Hema Malini: People are rather afraid to make films of our age group, since they seldom get feedback or media hype.

Zeenat Aman: The scene in the Western countries is quite opposite where many women-empowerment films get made. The people like actresses like Dan Judy Dange or Meryl Streep or Sigourney Weaver or Diane Keaton. They belong to a peer group of stage actresses. They have excellent role to offer in stage theatre or western films..

> **The scene in the Western countries is quite opposite.**
> *–Zeenat Aman*

Karan Johar: As opposed to today in our cinema?

Zeenat Aman: India had very few such actresses across the country. It would be lovely to enact good roles that are age-specific. Don't you agree?

Hema Malini: Exactly.

Karan Johar: Yes. Why not?

Hema Malini: We can prove it.

Karan Johar: Yes. The romance you depicted with Mr. Bachchan in *Baghban* had mobilized everyone of your age group. My God! They might have imagined, • *'My husband doesn't behave with me like this at home.'*

Hema Malini: I know.

Zeenat Aman: And she looked absolutely lovely in the movie.

Karan Johar: Everyone had their wives complaining to their husband. I have heard it even at the trial show of the film. You don't talk to me like this.

Hema Malini: It has changed lives of many people.

Karan Johar: Indeed it has. It totally has. Of course, the situation in our cinema is quite queer and awesome. The role of such women in the present day cinema is conditioned by age-factor, insecurity and health.

Hema Malini: Somebody might be listening to us right now..

Karan Johar: Today yes. And take note.

Hema Malini: Yes. And take note.

Karan Johar: Look! We have actresses of yesteryears Hema Malini and Zeenat Aman. Why people are not availing them by offering befitting roles to portray their skills and values?

Hema Malini: Exactly!

Zeenat Aman: Absolutely!

Karan Johar: All right. What concept have you observed among the working class? Hema Malini-ji as opposed to what used to happen earlier. Is there anything.. A major difference you noticed in the way the fraternity functions today. As it used to earlier.

Hema Malini: No. I think professionally everything is very perfect. Things are more organized and systemic with stage discipline now

Karan Johar: Today!

Hema Malini: Yes, it was not before.

> **Things are more organized and systemic now.**
> –Hema Malini

Karan Johar: No. That was completely..

Hema Malini: Otherwise I do not notice anything much. I have worked in *Baghban*. The scenes were replete with Amitabh Bachchan. I do not know anything else. I had been working with brigade of new artistes.

Karan Johar: Yeah! All right.

Hema Malini: May be, I will assimilate with the work culture, if I work for the new era.

Karan Johar: What about you? What is..

Zeenat Aman: Karan Johar, I think everything is much larger than it used to be. Everything is done on a bigger scale. There was no cable television. There were no satellite phones. There was no inter or intranet. Added to the scenario, you will fetch fat pay packets. It is more appealing.

Karan Johar: Not so in those days....

Zeenat Aman: Things are done in fabulous and result-oriented manner on a massive scale. Let me deviate even to the event <Miss India>. The Miss India contests have different sort of support. Somebody will describe you about nutrition, hair, skin, poise and conduct. The way you interact or speak or mobilize public opinion is unparallel in the history. Nobody could vent their grievances.. nothing of sorts happened in those days. You carried yourself the way you did. You organized your own clothes with your local tailor. And you went away and did your set of things. And you won or you didn't win. So it was very self-motivated concept whether you liked nor not.

Karan Johar: Yes.

Zeenat Aman: You had the shows screened at the Shanmukhnanda Hall in Mumbai. Now you have it on the scale that you have on a scale that was unthinkable at our time.

Karan Johar: Yes.

Zeenat Aman: So you know, you can compare.. You have been comparing in these shows.

> **Events like Miss India were a very self-motivated concept in those days.**
> –Zeenat Aman

Karan Johar: Of course. And everything else is..

Zeenat Aman: Everything is very large.

Hema Malini: Everything is ready.

Karan Johar: Yes. They are totally pampered.

Hema Malini: Yes.

Karan Johar: Everything is done for them. They just have to come and contribute voluntarily to do their bit. And of course, the times when you were out things were completely different.

Hema Malini: Completely on our own. It is just the parents who are backing you up. That•fs it.

Zeenat Aman: That•fs true.

Karan Johar: You had strong support from your mother, right through.

> **Esha is a girl of today.. she may not like it if her mother walked on to the stage and moved with her everywhere...**
> –Karan Johar

Hema Malini: Yes.

Karan Johar: Esha is a girl of today.. she may not like it if her mother walked on to the stage and moved with her everywhere...

Hema Malini: No she wouldn't... She tells me, please mummy. Don't come.

Karan Johar: I hope you never experienced such position on being heroine. Mummies or elderly people escorted the actresses. Do you agree with the complex scenario?

Zeenat Aman: No.

Karan Johar: You never really had mummy with you ever?

Zeenat Aman: No. I was very close to my mother. But she gave me ample freedom.

Karan Johar: Yes.

Zeenat Aman: To be...

Karan Johar: Yes. Of course. I have read something funny. How Hema Malini-ji hired the services of a teacher to train Esha in Punjabi. Is that true?

Hema Malini: Yeah! That's right. Well, she will be working in a film where she had to speak a lot in Punjabi.

> So, people thought it strange that Dharmendra's daughter did not speak Punjabi.
>
> *–Karan Johar*

Karan Johar: So, people thought it strange that Dharmendra's daughter did not speak Punjabi.

Hema Malini: Yeah! It is really strange! I know. However, the problem with Dharmendra is that he speaks English or Tamil with us.

Karan Johar: He does.

Hema Malini: Only English we speak much.

Karan Johar: Fine, OK.

Hema Malini: Or Hindi. He never speaks to us in Punjabi. I have taught them Tamil very well. Both the girls could speak Tamil without much ado.

Karan Johar: Of course. I have heard them. Esha Deol's training in Punjabi is a very funny thought.

Hema Malini: It sounds funny. It is absolutely true. What to do?

Zeenat Aman: I have a lovely story about Dharam-ji, ok.

Karan Johar: Please tell us.

Zeenat Aman: We worked in the film *Shalimar*.. Yeah...It was the first international crossover debut of its time with Rex Harrison and..

Karan Johar: Yes. Yes. Of course.

Hema Malini: Yeah.

Zeenat Aman: You know. We stayed in the same hotel. And we burnt the midnight oil. All right. We shot the film in two versions. English and Hindi. He burnt the midnight oil with his English dialogue intonation coach. And I did so with Hindi intonation coach.

Karan Johar: Oh God!

Zeenat Aman: And he used to memorize the English verses. And I did all my Hindi dialogues verbatim. Both have the swollen eyes the next morning when we were on the sets. Of course, we had our verses learnt by rote.....

Karan Johar: And you conversed with Dharam-ji in Hindi and English.. and certainly not Tamil?

Hema Malini: A few words I have taught him in Tamil.

> Which Tamil words did you teach Dharam-ji? (KJ) That is something very private.
>
> *–Hema Malini*

Karan Johar: You have taught him?

Hema Malini: Yeah!

Karan Johar: Which word has he learned?

Hema Malini: That is something very private.

Karan Johar: Fine, OK. Indian cinema had another towering personality, called Amitabh Bachchan. You, leading ladies have worked with him. I believe you have done tremendous work. How was your experience today in contrast with yesteryears?

Hema Malini: It remained same for me.

Karan Johar: Really.

Hema Malini: Yeah!

Karan Johar: Did he remain same today?

Hema Malini: Yeah! He was the same. And today also he remained similar.

Karan Johar: All right. Completely. And with you?

Zeenat Aman: Mr. Bachchan has an exceptional sense of humour. He used to have a unique sense of mischief on the sets. He remained always professional, came on time and performed the assigned role with excellence. He remained same when I worked recently in the film *Boom*.

Karan Johar: Yes. *Boom*, of course might have given an unprecedented experience. I am quite sure in every possible manner.

Zeenat Aman: Absolutely!

Karan Johar: When you look back, what do you think about the film?

Zeenat Aman: Yeah! For me, it never proved something unusual. I got a phone call one day. It summoned me to come on the sets. So I was there on the sets the next day. It was something one did for a friend.

Karan Johar: Yes, of course.

Zeenat Aman: It is fun to do it, you know.

Karan Johar: Yes.

Zeenat Aman: But subsequently everybody knew what happened in the film.

Karan Johar: So, Amit-ji was a thorough professional.

Zeenat Aman: Oh Yes!

Karan Johar: And a gentleman in that respect.

Zeenat Aman: Oh Yes!

Karan Johar: Were there any super brat heroes at that time? I mean like someone who was naughty. Like today we have, like everyone. Our heroes are quite, quite entertaining on sets.

Hema Malini: I think it was Shatrughan Sinha.

Karan Johar: He was...May be. That was exceptional and strange. You cannot imagine..

Hema Malini: I mean he used to be very humorous. I will always look forward to working with him.

Karan Johar: Really!

Hema Malini: He used to just make me laugh so much.

> He (Shatrughan Sinha) used to just make me laugh so much.
> *–Hema Malini*

Karan Johar: Really. OK. And what about you?

Zeenat Aman: I thought Shashi-ji was a lot of fun. Shashi Kapoor. He has a great sense of humour. He would always be very witty and funny. And he was very..

Karan Johar: Entertaining. Yes.

Hema Malini: Entertaining. All the time.

Karan Johar: So were there any like super brats in those days as well.

Hema Malini: I don't think I ever came across one.

Karan Johar: No super brat? Were they scared of your debut? Perhaps, you might have never ventured Hema Malini-ji? Maybe you did. Anyone who really kind of..

Zeenat Aman: Super brat!

Karan Johar: I mean naughty one. Naughty heroes.

Zeenat Aman: Naughty, yes! Not super brats.

Karan Johar: And not kind of trying to be kind of over romantic either. Well, of course. All were..

Hema Malini: Well I think the men have to be, isn't it?

Zeenat Aman: Absolutely!

Hema Malini: They have to be..

Zeenat Aman: Absolutely.

Karan Johar: No. But they were.. They were men who said romantic things....

Hema Malini: Yes. Very, very romantic.

Karan Johar: Really! I want to know one hero.

Hema Malini: Yeah! I do not want to say the name of any such actor.

Karan Johar: You don't have to say his name. What about you, Zeenat Aman-ji? You have to mention the names.

Zeenat Aman: No. . I wouldn't want to. I will tell about a wonderful anecdote. Once I was in a makeup room. I got a big cardboard box wrapped up in a ribbon. I unveiled the box and looked in. I found another box within. I found another box on opening the second box. I found a tennis ball in the third box. It carried a small message, *"the ball is in your court"*...

Karan Johar: Who was that person?

Zeenat Aman: That was so sweet! I will always remember it. For, it was so unusual for a seasoned actress.....

Karan Johar: Very innovative! I must say. Absolutely. I am sure the lovely ladies today languish for something similar to happen. I iterate over the fact that men remained men forever in my era. (too complex: suggested – I repeat that men remained..)

Hema Malini: Yes, that's true.

Zeenat Aman: Absolutely!

Karan Johar: We might have many interesting anecdotes in our *Rapid Fire Round.*

Karan Johar: Do you know what it is about?

Zeenat Aman: Absolutely.

Karan Johar: I throw these questions at you. I expect very witty racy answers with pun or fire in them.

Hema Malini: Oh! My God!

Karan Johar: Hema Malini-ji, are you prepared?

Hema Malini: Yeah!

Karan Johar: I will subsequently decide the winner of my *Rapid Fire Round.* And the winner gets the koffee hamper.

Zeenat Aman: The famous koffee hamper?.

Hema Malini: Yeah!

Karan Johar: Yes. This was the koffee hamper your daughter won.

Hema Malini: Yes. She got it. I had the biscuits.

Karan Johar: You had the biscuits. OK. Let me see whether you will get them.

Hema Malini Again. Yeah!

Karan Johar: All right. So I will commence with **Hema** Malini-ji.

Karan Johar: All right.

Hema Malini: Yeah!

Karan Johar: Are you ready?

Hema Malini: Ready.

Karan Johar: All right. The dialogue you were asked to repeat quite often onscreen......

Hema Malini: No!

Karan Johar: All right. After Dharam-ji, the most attractive leading man in Hindi cinema.....

Hema Malini: Aamir Khan.

Karan Johar: Which actor you desire to be reborn to match with your rebirth as an actress par excellence?

Hema Malini: Myself again?

Karan Johar: Which actress will you not like to be reborn as?

Hema Malini: I don't think I would answer.

Karan Johar: OK. One quality that actresses of the present era don't share with actresses of yester years?

Hema Malini: I think the necessity of strict discipline.

Karan Johar: Which young actor should play mythological characters if they were asked to? Whom do you think the best actor to enact the role of Hanuman.....

Hema Malini: Salman.

Karan Johar: All right. Ram and Laxman duo..?

Hema Malini: Ram, I think Shahrukh will be nice. And I cannot think of anybody.

Karan Johar: Who will fit the bill for Laxman? And for Ravan?

Hema Malini: Many would fit the role of a modern day Ravana.

Karan Johar: All right. The best dancer among the current bevy of heroines.....

Hema Malini: Aishwarya dances so well!

Karan Johar: Who could be the eligible would-be groom for your daughter Esha, among the Gen X bachelors......Vivek Oberoi. Abhishekh Bachchan. Tusshar Kapoor or Rahul Gandhi?

Hema Malini: I think Abhishekh.

Karan Johar: OK. He is a good boy. Laloo Prasad Yadav claims to be your fan. How do you react?

Hema Malini: He is my fan. I am his fan. That's it.

Karan Johar: All right. Rank the directors in the order of your preference.....Farhan Akhtar, Aditya Chopra, Ashutosh Gowariker and Sanjay Bhansali.

Hema Malini: Sanjay Bhansali. Then Farhan.

Karan Johar: OK.

Hema Malini: He will be followed by Ashutosh.

Karan Johar: Aditya follows later. OK. The unique quality in Zeenat Aman you desired to possess?

Hema Malini: Her bewitching charm! Her.. beauty blended with poised physique, I wish I should have had.

Zeenat Aman: How sweet! Thank you.

Karan Johar: All right. One thing about Esha, Dharam-ji and you disagree....

Hema Malini: No. She is doing everything fine.

> Many would fit the role of a modern day Ravana.
> *–Hema Malini*

> Avishek Bachchan would be the most eligible groom for Esha.
> *–Hema Malini*

Karan Johar: Oh! You have endorsed her characteristics?

Hema Malini: Yeah! We both agree.

Karan Johar: She is fine. She is perfect. OK. One thing that Esha does that really annoys you....

Hema Malini: Late riser on bed.

Karan Johar: Affix your choices.....do it fast....Shabana Azmi or Jaya Bachchan. Who would make for the better political leader.

Hema Malini: Shabana.

Karan Johar: All right. Dharam-ji as a father or Dharam-ji as a husband. Which real life role does Dharam-ji play better?

Hema Malini: As the responsible father!

> **Basanti is my favorite on-screen character.**
> *—Hema Malini*

Hema Malini: All right.

Karan Johar: Hema Malini as an actor or Hema Malini as a dancer.

Hema Malini: As a dancer!

Karan Johar: Your favourite character *Basanti* or *Sita Geeta?*

Hema Malini: *Basanti.*

Karan Johar: Salman Khan, Aamir Khan, Shahrukh Khan...Rate the best actor in the Khan pedigree.....

Hema Malini: I think all were good in their roles.

Karan Johar: All right. Kajol, Rani Mukherji, Preity Zinta.....Kareena Kapoor, Aishwarya Rai. The dream girl today.

Hema Malini: Aishwarya, straight away.

Karan Johar: She is the dream girl.

Hema Malini: Yes.

Karan Johar: All right. OK. Hema Malini-ji, that was your resultant rapid fire. Thank you so much for answering those questions. Let me revert to Madam Zeenat Aman-ji. Are you ready? All set action...

Zeemat: Absolutely!

Karan Johar: All right. Lovely! A film made portraying your life...what do you think it should be called?

Zeenat Aman: Zeenat Aman!

Karan Johar: Which young actresses would you give the following beauty pageants to? Miss Perfect Ten.

Zeenat Aman: Aishwarya.

Karan Johar: Miss Congeniality?

Zeenat Aman: Rani Mukherjee.

Karan Johar: All right.

Zeenat Aman: She is a very warm and affectionate girl.

> **The Miss Wannabe prize would go to Nakkuja Sherawat.**
> *—Zeenat Aman*

Karan Johar: All right. Lovely!

Karan Johar: Miss Wannabe?

Zeenat Aman: Mallika Sherawat.

Karan Johar: All right. Well done. Miss Oomph!

Zeenat Aman: Sushmita.

Karan Johar: All right. Miss Talented?

Zeenat Aman: It goes to Rani Mukherjee..

Karan Johar: All right. Would you prefer to enact the role of mother or sister onscreen to Dev Anand-ji, if he approaches you with the offer?

Zeenat Aman: You know, I have a great affinity with Dev, Sir. I would accept whatever roles he offers me.

Hema Malini: So sweet!

Zeenat Aman: He is sweet.. He is a sweet and wonderful personality in the industry for ever!

Hema Malini: He is.. Yeah!

Zeenat Aman: Sister, mother, whatever..

Karan Johar: You will do?

Zeenat Aman: Yes, I will.

Karan Johar: OK. The value system of yesteryear actresses missing in the present bevy of actresses. Comment.

Zeenat Aman: Well, I think she (Hema Malini) has put it very well. Discipline. Also dedication.

Karan Johar: All right.

Zeenat Aman: Also the desire to do the best possible that you could.

Karan Johar: The toughest part about being the sex symbol is..

Zeenat Aman: People mistook my screen persona for who I am.. You know, who I am. They blend the two roles. And think that possibly personally I was as sexy as I appeared onscreen. That was not necessarily the case.

Karan Johar: Whom do you shortlist as Zeenat Aman in a movie portraying your autobiography?

Zeenat Aman: I have been told Sushmita will befit my slot.

Karan Johar: Yes.

Zeenat Aman: In some ways.

Karan Johar: Yes. Well, there is..

> **People mistook my screen persona for who I am ...**
> *–Zeenat Aman*

Zeenat Aman: I don't know, Karan Johar. If you happened to be a director, whom would you cast?

Karan Johar: All right. Again the tables turned on me. Well.. I would say Sushmita.

Zeenat Aman: Yes, OK. So, I think we shall agree on that.

Karan Johar: The dialogue you have been asked to say most often onscreen was..

Zeenat Aman: Help me! Help me!

Karan Johar: All right. A quality in Hema Malini-ji, which you wish, you should have possessed....

Zeenat Aman: Hema Malini-ji is eternal (timeless). She, you know, gets on to remain eternal like a *Jin* (Islam) with every year, to blossom as tender bud and lovelier.....

Karan Johar: She is like wine.

Zeenat Aman: Yes. She has great dignity. And honestly, I mean it would be so wonderful if all.. If all women could, you know over the years, be as graceful and as lovely as she is.

> **Hema Malini–ji is like wine. Timeless and eternal.**
> *– KJ in conversation with Zeenat Aman*

Hema Malini: So sweet!

Zeenat Aman: It's a fact to be gauged seriously.

Zeenat Aman: I believe one does not express it, because somebody has these characteristics perpetually.

Karan Johar: Yeah.

Zeenat Aman: What one feels on watching her performance? You know, from a distance..

Karan Johar: I agree.

Hema Malini: So nice.

Karan Johar: All right. Which actor or actress could endorse the following products? Skin fairness cream.

Zeenat Aman: Aishwarya.

Karan Johar: All right. Mosquito repellents.

Zeenat Aman: Oh Gosh, Karan Johar! The way you pull the mosquito out of your hat. Mosquito repellent! Oh Gosh!

Hema Malini: It can be Shakti Kapoor.

Zeenat Aman: Thank you. Shakti Kapoor.

Karan Johar: All right. Well done. Hair dye.

Zeenat Aman: Obviously! Somebody from the senior.. A senior person. And who still looks good. Jitendra.

Karan Johar: All right. The sexiest leading man in India today.

Zeenat Aman: I would say Shahrukh Khan.

Karan Johar: The most attractive leading man you have ever worked with. I would say the brigade of leading men......quickly ....Amitabh Bachchan, Vinod Khanna or Feroz Khan.

Zeenat Aman: Amitabh Bachchan.

Karan Johar: All right. *Qurbani* or *Hare Rama Hare Krishna.*

> **Shahrukh Khan is the sexiest man in India today.**
> *–Zeenat Aman*

Zeenat Aman: *Hare Rama Hare Krishna.* My first film.

Karan Johar: First film! John Abraham, Salman Khan, Akshay Kumar. The best body in the business.

Zeenat Aman: John Abraham.

Karan Johar: Aishwarya, Sushmita, Priyanka. The most deserving beauty queen.

Zeenat Aman: Priyanka.

Karan Johar: Dev Anand or Feroz Khan?

Zeenat Aman: Dev Sir. He is so sweet!

Karan Johar: All right. That was your rapid fire. Very well done! Whom do I give the coffee hamper? I think I will label you for the hamper. I believe you have answered it with more courage. I think Hema Malini-ji also agrees.

Hema Malini: Yes.

Zeenat Aman: Well, she has already had the coffee hamper.

Karan Johar: Yes, she has had one at home. I know she has eaten the cookies already. I believe it will be fair for you to take the cookies back home.

Zeenat Aman: All right. Thank you.

Karan Johar: The coffee hamper goes to Zeenat Aman!

Zeenat Aman: Thank you. Karan Johar. This is the most famous symbol of your show. I am delighted to receive it. Thank you so much. My sons will go euphoric.

Karan Johar: Good! I hope they will enjoy the incident.

Zeenat Aman: They were the reason behind my coming on to the show. Thank you.

Karan Johar: OK. please.

> **The coffee hamper is the most famous symbol of your show.**
> *–Zeenat Aman*

Hema Malini: Oh! There is some more to go.

Karan Johar: Yes. Zeenat Aman wins the Koffee Hamper.

Zeenat Aman: What happened?

Karan Johar: Sorry. Zeenat Aman won the rocking Rapid Fire Round. And takes the Koffee hamper home. All right. Let us go to young boys of Gen Y to find out whom they acknowledge.....Hema Malini or Zeenat Aman? Would you like to see?

> **I have never seen a more beautiful woman (than Hema Malini) in my life.**
> *–Sanjay Dutt*

Hema Malini: Oh yeah! Sure!

Karan Johar: All right. Please watch then.

John Abraham: Hema Malini and Zeenat Aman. Both have made me recollect I should have born in those years. One is so incredibly sensuous. And the other is so incredibly beautiful.

Sanjay Dutt: Hema Malini-ji, I think is *the true beauty* of Indian cinema.

Dino Morea: For me, Hema Malini-ji is a *bubbly, very expressive, bright eyed* actress who completed the full life cycle.

Sanjay Dutt: I have never seen a more beautiful woman in my life. Even till today.

Arjun Rampal: When you say Zeenat Aman, the first thing that comes to my mind is just a complete style icon.

Fardeen Khan: She is every boy's fantasy, I think. I have a picture of her up on the wall. For many, many years.

Dino Morea: When I hear these words - Zeenat Aman, the person who comes to my mind is a beautiful lady walking out of the sea. Looking really nice, looking amazingly hot in *Qurbani*.

Shahid Kapoor: Hema Malini-ji, I think the camera besought her forever. And India delighted in her presence even more.

John Abraham: I probably fit into that category of would-be grooms to marry her. I believe to have married Hema Malini at one point of time. Well, now Esha is my co-star.

Sanjay Dutt: Zeenat Aman, I think is one of the best-looking women we had in our industry. And she is yet so dignified.

Fardeen Khan: Definitely categorised as a quintessential modern Indian woman. One of the first modern Indian who had an international appeal.

Arjun Rampal: Hema Malini-ji as an actress who remains extremely talented and continues to mesmerize. Her comic timing, OK. And that even goes for Zeenat Aman-ji. Her comic timing was splendid. And you don't find that in actresses. Most of them.

John Abraham: *Dream girl* was one movie which I remember I saw as a young lad. And I had been to the theatre in my town called

Dreamland. And I said Wow! This is a dream world. I am watching this *Dream girl* in Dreamland. That was one of my most massive crushes as a child on Hema Malini.

Hema Malini: So sweet!

Shahid Kapoor: I used to love her pairing with Dharam-ji. I thought often that they had a very cute chemistry between them. And they were both really good at comedy.

Dino Morea: What was good about her was actually.. I think that it was just the life that she was brought onscreen. The energy that she had I don't think any actresses could be compared to her.

Arjun Rampal: Hema Malini-ji, even if she did an action sequence. You know that if she would hit a guy, he would really stay down. He would not get up!

Shahid Kapoor: Zeenat Aman was.. She was a diva. She was one of the first divas that the Indian cinema had backed....

Fardeen Khan: She contributed in redefining the Indian actress in a great way.

> **Zeenat Aman was one of the first divas of Indian cinema.**
> *–Shahid Kapoor*

Sanjay Dutt: It was not only that she looked extremely sexy. But the fact that she carried herself in such a way where it did not look vulgar.

Fardeen Khan: She projected the unique female sexuality. Very, very intensely. And in a very, very dignified manner. I mean with extreme dignity onscreen. So it was like cool to be sexy, you know from then on.

Arjun Rampal: Her face was all gone in *Satyam Shivam Sundaram*. You know, just the way she draped her sari, the way she posed for shots, the way she carried her personality into the script and story. One finds seldom the vulgarity which we witness now in this era. But she kept the whole sex appeal quite poised, suave and gentle, at the same time. She was very comfortable with whom she worked and the way she carried herself.

John Abraham: I guess a lot of actresses need to take a leaf out of Zeenat Aman's book. And they should understand how to look so sensuous and so beautiful and at the same time look so classy.

Arjun Rampal: Well, I just want to say that both of you are wonderful women. And thank you for being such strong inspiration to one and all..

Fardeen Khan: I am a huge fan of you in so many ways.

Shahid Kapoor: I wish we had a few heroines like you. I wish I were born twenty five years ago. Unfortunately, I was unlucky!

John Abraham: I would imagine myself as working with you all, putting my spirit back to the time capsule of yesteryears. And I would love to be the quintessential Bollywood hero to both of you.

Sanjay Dutt: Love you madam. And it's an honour for me to speak about you.

John Abraham: I like the new heroines. They are very nice. I really like you so much more. I think you're more special. And so much more beautiful and sensuous.

Zeenat Aman: So sweet!

Karan Johar: Well, we have to clap for these boys.

Hema Malini: Yes. Yes. Yes. Yes.

Zeenat Aman: So sweet!

> **I am a huge fan of both of you in so many ways.**
> –*Fardeen Khan*

Karan Johar: I think it was lovely.

Hema Malini: Oh, lovely!

Zeenat Aman: Oh! They have said wonderful facts.....

Karan Johar: Yeah! How do you feel?

Zeenat Aman: Magnanimous!

Hema Malini: Indeed, unbelievable!

Karan Johar: Well, I want to just say that I want to add to the accolades galore that you have heard and express myself that it was an astounding experience. I have grown up watching both the celebrities. And I cannot tell you how special I have felt to just sit across them today. And I cannot believe that I have put a volley of questions. I mean like it is an out of body experience for me.

Hema Malini: Oh God!

Karan Johar: Thank you so much for sparing your valuable time.. Coming on *Koffee with Karan Johar*. I would like to thank you on behalf of my technical team. It has been an honour, a truly prestigious one.

Hema Malini: I believe so.

Zeenat Aman: Thank you so much.

Hema Malini: Yeah, it has been a pleasure.

Karan Johar: You will find a little cup. I want you to autograph it.

Please remember that this personally autographed mug can be yours only if you take part in the *Koffee Quest Contest*. Fine.

Hema Malini: Fine.

> **Being on Koffee with Karan has been a pleasure.**
>
> *–Hema Malini*

Karan Johar: Any last minute thoughts. Anything you want to say?

Zeenat Aman: We have enjoyed so much being here.

Karan Johar: Do you have anything to say to your daughter who was pensive on your participation in the show?

Hema Malini: I think she will be cool now.

Karan Johar: OK. She will be so. Won't she? Thank you so much. Thank you for singing that. Let us proceed to the coffee wall and place the mug there.

...TURNING TO THE CAMERA:

So that was it.

Dreamgirls Hema Malini and Zeenat Aman.. live, up-close, and personal. A memorable occasion, an evening to cherish forever. Right here on Koffee with Karan, the show that guarantees to scratch under the surface of the stars that light up our lives everyday, every moment. And create a platform where they can share the teasing fantasies, inspired thoughts and priceless wisdom that frame their incredible, thrill-a-minute lives. Today, we brought to you Hema Malini and Zeenat Aman, two personalities who completely rewrote the rules of the glamour game by their originality, pluck and creativity. Two living legends, really, who are as close to our hearts today as they were, many years ago.

But then, such is the magic of superstars.. Such is the power of their larger-than-life worlds:. Such is their enduring charisma. Something you can stay tuned to.. every week, every month.., here with me.

So long.

..Till we meet again, Happy star-gazing..!

● ● ●

23

Amitabh Bachchan &
Shahrukh Khan
The Emperor and The King

He has been a producer, a director, a wannabe costume designer and not the least an awful actor, and spread his wings all over the place on the earth for no rhyme or reason. And thankfully, he is not here tonight on the show. The film fraternity has decided that we have been tortured enough by Karan on the show over the past few months. So, we threw him out. And I am here to do the season finale. So, where is Karan? I have put something in his coffee that he is unaware of.

Ladies and gentlemen, I shall call upon a guest who has been the greatest inspiration for me. I have had the honour of sharing the same cinematic space with him. He had been the living legend for millions around the world. He has been the biggest ever superstar in Hindi cinema. Please welcome Mr. Amitabh Bachchan!

Shahrukh Khan: Good evening, Sir

Amitabh Bachchan: Good to see you.

Shahrukh Khan: It is equally good to see you, Sir. Welcome on the show.

> **Mr. Bachchan has been the biggest ever superstar in Hindi cinema.**
> *–Shahrukh Khan*

Amitabh Bachchan: Thank you so much. And thank God, Karan is not here.

Shahrukh Khan: Yes, we made sure of that, Sir.

Amitabh Bachchan: Thank you so much.

Shahrukh Khan: So, I have the opportunity and if allowed, may I involve myself in some self-indulgence? What did you think of me when you met me for the first time? Perhaps, you don't remember about the incident.

Amitabh Bachchan: No, I do. I ought to make a small request prior to my response.

Shahrukh Khan: Yes, Sir.

Amitabh Bachchan: When were you on my show 'KBC,' remember how kind I was to you?

> **My first impression of you was that you spoke very fast, thought even faster!**
> *–Amitabh Bachchan*

Shahrukh Khan: Yes, Sir.

Amitabh Bachchan: Let us reciprocate that action.

Shahrukh Khan: OK.

Amitabh Bachchan: My first impression of you. You spoke very fast, thought even faster. You had a lot of energy.

Shahrukh Khan: That is about it?

Amitabh Bachchan: Yeah! Nothing more.

THE BACHCHAN TOUCH

Shahrukh Khan: OK. Do you think the films and scripts (with the exception of recent films like *Black*) have provided justice to your talents and acquired skills over the years? You are the most sought after actor in the fraternity based on the knowledge and experience you have acquired. You have proved that you are far above the Indian cinema.

Amitabh Bachchan: Oh, no!

Shahrukh Khan: You do not have to be humble, Sir.

Amitabh Bachchan: No, this is a very loaded question, Shahrukh. I have never looked out for anything in particular. I have always relied on the acumen of my directors and producers. They have been left with sufficient time to create the dialogues and environment. I do not know what is right or wrong for me. I

> As an actor, I do not know what is right or wrong for me.
> –Amitabh Bachchan

have left it to the people like Hrishkesh Mukherjee, Manmohan Desai, Prakash Mehra, Ramesh Sippy, Yash Chopra and everybody else. I take it as a challenge when they design something unique for me. Somebody has thrown the gauntlet and I always try to pick it up and do my best.

Shahrukh Khan: The question that remains for me is more personal as an actor. These will be the nicest moments in life to sit across you and know how to get along with a volley of questions. There are so many personas and kinds of role that could be thought of with you. You have accomplished most of them with finesse. How do you correlate the process of acting and actual actions that you do? What turns you in front of the camera?

Amitabh Bachchan: Actually, this is a very interesting question. Many of us I'm sure, you included, must have wondered. What happens to you when the camera is turned on? I think it is really those magical words when the director says, 'Start! Sound! Camera! Clap! Action!' Later, my conscience responds to present something from within. I am not quite sure why it comes out, which you too could not gauge.

Shahrukh khan: Hey!

Amitabh Bachchan: I believe it is just that moment when you feel that. You just feel for those couple of seconds soon after the camera positions with me. You have to deliver your lines. I don't know what happens. Somehow or the other, something comes out. I do not know why or how does it happen, but it just happens. And I hope for positive development and pray.

> In a shot, I do my lines and hope for positive development and pray!
> –Amitabh Bachchan

Shahrukh Khan: It happens inevitably.

Amitabh Bachchan: Yeah! And people accept it.

Shahrukh Khan: I have not

worked even 1/10th of the volume that you have done. The quality of work you have done is quite incredible. I always find myself losing out on the rawness which I enjoyed as an actor. Some rough edges which were more fun to deal with have been washed away. I have worked with you more than a couple of times, if I count the number of incidences we have been associated with. I have noticed something serene to the craft now. Of course, every actor who works with you could acquire the same opinion. There are so many things that play in your mind as you do some scene. Do you feel that you acquire something unique from the environment, a craft in itself, which blocks developement? I have realized the rawness, the spontaneity, the stuff that used to come out earlier does not happen.

> **I have realized that the rawness, the spontaneity, the stuff that used to come out earlier does not happen.**
> *–Shahrukh Khan*

Amitabh Bachchan: Yeah! Actually, I believe the age factor has a lot to do with it. I do not wish to go on to 63. I am quite sure that when you do, you will realise for yourself that some way you will find yourself a lot more relaxed. You will find a lot more finesse in representing your persona in front of the camera – because this huge burden of stardom will chase you forever; or the responsibility as the leading man. I am no longer so.

Shahrukh Khan: Is that what you think? We still believe you to absolutely lead the fraternity and every film that you do. So long as you are in the film world, we have no problem.

Amitabh Bachchan: You have to shoulder the burden of being the star of the show, the lead man and the risks of other junior actors. There are a lot of expectations, both commercially and creatively. I believe I had to unburden the industry. You have to be very narrow to tread the path. You have to play the lead role dynamically. You have to get rid of the baddie, and get the girl in the end and end up there. When you reach my age and the experience, you have to play more character roles. These little accessories usually disappear, as and when we get experienced.

> **When you reach my age and experience, the absence of additional burden as the lead man will make you more relaxed.**
> *–Amitabh Bachchan:*

Shahrukh Khan: So you have more fun!

Amitabh Bachchan: Yeah, definitely! Because you are playing the character, the absence of additional burden as the lead man will make you more relaxed. I think it has got a lot to do with the fact that you are greatly relaxed. The worries and the anxieties of you as the lead will not be there.

ON PARENTHOOD

Shahrukh Khan: We completely deny the fact that you're not the leading man anymore. We truly believe that every film, every work that you do is led by you. I would revert to that time when you think you were the lead man. This is a personal question regarding the upbringing of my son and daughter. Do you feel you missed out and try to catch up on that?

Amitabh Bachchan: I think you are doing a fantastic job. We were very determined to do well, work hard, and be involved in as many good projects as possible. So invariably, you have ended up doing two to three shifts. So you are out of the house at 6 am when the kids are asleep, and return by 1 or 2 am when they are again in bed. You miss them. There was a very large portion of interaction at this age with my kids that I missed out. And the little that I have seen you interacting with son Aryan and daughter Suhaana, everyone is very complete.

> **There was a very large portion of interaction with my kids that I missed out.**
>
> *–Amitabh Bachchan*

Shahrukh Khan: No, I think times have changed. Things have become a little organised, I guess.

Amitabh Bachchan: I think our working systems seldom change so rapidly. It will be something that comes from within, whether you unburden and relax from your work or opt out to share time with your family. I do feel that a lot of time could have been spent with them.

Shahrukh Khan: But it is good to see that you do it more often now. One could see you with Abhishek. I wish that I grow up and...

Amitabh Bachchan: One could see me with Abhishek because he has been in my profession. He has stepped in my shoes right now. You know he stays next-door.

Shahrukh Khan: You know I would love to continue on this personal

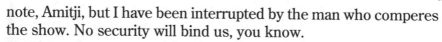

note, Amitji, but I have been interrupted by the man who comperes the show. No security will bind us, you know.

Amitabh Bachchan: Can we get rid of him quietly?

Shahrukh Khan: Ladies and gentlemen! Here is Karan Johar, the man who is to continue to compere the show!

Amitabh Bachchan: Oh! Gosh. Hi, Karan!

Shahrukh Khan: Are you going to touch my feet too?

Karan Johar: No. Thank you. I hope that was not too torturous.

Amitabh Bachchan: Not at all, Karan! He is doing a marvelous job.

Karan Johar: He has been even better than I am.

Amitabh Bachchan: Well, yeah!

Shahrukh Khan: ....which is not a compliment!

Karan Johar: Let me say, Shahrukh! You have asked everything I wanted to. I do not know what I have left, really.

Shahrukh Khan: Why don't you go back?

INITIAL BUMPS

Karan Johar: Shahrukh, I think you have spoken long enough. Both of you have a common factor, which had been the unconventional appeal in terms of film fraternity. I mean, Amit uncle, when you came in there was a lot of opposition to your entry.

Amitabh Bachchan: That is putting the perspective mildly.

Karan Johar: No, you are right. What happened, really?

Amitabh Bachchan: You cannot blame them. Somebody comes off the street without a background. You do not know about his antecedents. You have records of your work nowadays. And people dancing and saying dialogues. It had entered the professional angle. How do you pick somebody just off the street and give him the lead role? I would say that they were kind to me.

Karan Johar: Really, were they?

Amitabh Bachchan: Yeah! But there were few who reacted strongly. I believe that that is a part of the game.

> I do not blame the film industry for opposing my entry as a newcomer. I would say that they were kind to me!
> —Amitabh Bachchan

Karan Johar: All right! What was the strange thing you heard from somebody in terms of criticism?

Amitabh Bachchan: Several things!

Karan Johar: The funniest thing?

Amitabh Bachchan: Too tall. No leading lady would work with me because they were too short.

Shahrukh Khan: I do remember one thing when I saw a shooting event near Bangalore. I was quite surprised. Aruna Irani-ji stood on a box.

Amitabh Bachchan: They continue to stand on boxes even today.

Karan Johar: So, 'too tall' was one of them. No leading lady will work with you was another cause. Any other?

Amitabh Bachchan: 'Just not good enough! Did not have the looks!'

Karan Johar: And in your heart of hearts, did you think, 'I am going to fight.' Or did you say, 'I am going right back and do whatever I was doing before?'

Amitabh Bachchan: No, I did not think about doing something that dramatic.

Karan Johar: You just went with the flow?

Amitabh Bachchan: Yes, I went with the flow. I really never expected to become the leading man. I would have been content with just a passing role or a small one.

Karan Johar: You would have been happy. Oh, yes! Just doing a character role.

Amitabh Bachchan: Oh! yes. That's just what my initial few films were. I was one of the seven roles in *Saat Hindustani.* I was the mute one. Stuff like that. In *Anand,* I was...

Karan Johar: You had the supporting role.

Amitabh Bachchan: Not even supporting. Rajesh Khanna assumed the character role. So, I was very content about my role. Something strange happened in between. I do not know if a lot of people are aware of this. There was a control on how many films an actor could work in as a leading man.

Karan Johar: Oh! Really?

Amitabh Bachchan: Somewhere in the late 60's or early 70's. This was done by the industry. It was an attempt to control actors from working in many projects. The rate stood at six projects per actor. Jitendra was involved in a project called *Pyaar Ki Kahani*. He was asked to step out when he crossed the limit. I stepped in at that time.

> **I was one of the seven roles in *Saat Hindustani* – I was the mute one!**
>
> *–Amitabh Bachchan*

Karan Johar: Oh! Jitendra could not do *Pyaar Ki Kahani*.

Amitabh Bachchan: So, I did not have anything left over.

Karan Johar: So the limit worked, then. It applies to you, Shahrukh. Unconventional looks, long nose, floppy hair as they attribute - 'sexy eyes and tousled hair.'

Shahrukh Khan: OK, but do not rub it in.

Karan Johar: Still, you might have found out that some women considered you sexy even during your television days. You might have faced similar kind of outsider treatment from the film fraternity, and you know nobody from any film family or the background. Did you face it at the initial level?

Shahrukh Khan: Yes. I had done a little bit of theatre where there was nothing as conventional or unconventional approach. You might have learnt that there was nothing right or wrong.

Karan Johar: You just act.

Shahrukh Khan: I know. It seldom made any difference whether it was a dark man, a tall man, a fat man. Everyone ought to enact on the sets. I started doing films when I came to Bombay. I got some critical response initially. I still cannot get the expression on her face out of my mind when the late Divya Bharti met me for the first time.

Karan Johar: How did she react?

Shahrukh Khan: My friend, Sheena Sabin, introduced us. She introduced me as the lead man with whom she was to enact in the films *Dil Ashana Hai* and *Deewana*. She might have walked off. I remember when Juhi was told during *Raju Ban Gaya Gentleman* that I resembled Aamir Khan and was very new to the profession – and then when I met her, her first reaction was 'Eeeks!' She said I was not Aamir Khan when she

> **When I was introduced to Juhi Chawla, her first reaction was 'Eeeks!'**
>
> *–Shahrukh Khan*

was introduced to me. She said I was brown and scruffy with wrong hair. Funniest compliment was by my producer who launched me thankfully – Mr. G.P. Sippy. He said that my hair was like a bear's.

Karan Johar: Is that what G.P. Sippy said?

Shahrukh Khan: He said how can I make a..

Karan Johar: ..film with you if your hair is like a bear. So, it was a similar journey you trod. I think you hailed from the north and remained outsider with a relative unconventional appeal. We have Amitabh Bachchan, the supreme idol whom everybody worships in the fraternity today. In fact, the whole country thinks of you as God, Sir. I mean you know that. And they have rated Shahrukh as the big superstar.

> **Mr. G.P. Sippy said that my hair was like a bear's!**
> *–Shahrukh Khan*

Amitabh Bachchan: Karan, do you want me to leave the show?

Karan Johar: Am I embarrassing you?

Amitabh Bachchan: You are.

Karan Johar: I am just saying what everybody describes you as. Shahrukh is the biggest superstar. It had been turbulent journey for both of you. It is really interesting, I would say. So, you mean to say, 'It is good to be ugly!'

Amitabh Bachchan: It is good to be tall and enact with leading ladies standing on boxes.

Karan Johar: Yeah! It includes your wife!

> **It is good to be tall and enact with leading ladies standing on boxes!**
> *–Amitabh Bachchan*

Amitabh Bachchan: Yeah! She stands on two of them.

Karan Johar: Shahrukh! You have not faced any such problem.

Shahrukh Khan: Yeah! I have not, so far. I mean, height is something I can do a little more with.

THE ENDORSEMENT BANDWAGON

Karan Johar: Another thing a lot of people talk about is both of you sell lot of products – a lot of endorsements.

Shahrukh Khan: Don't be scared, dear! Say it openly. So, what have I sold?

Karan Johar: No. I am not speaking about that. I think all the poor models have vanished. There is no work left for them. Comment, Shahrukh, if the endorsements were thrown at you?

Shahrukh Khan: I think it is a part of the changing times. I also believe it as a fact that the film industry and the people working there are being recognised by the corporate sector, which feels we are good enough to market their product. Maybe, the medium got highlighted at the initial level. You have new vistas and venues now, where

> **Regarding endorsements, Anil Kapoor told me, 'Don't do this, man! It is wrong!'**
> *–Shahrukh Khan*

you are not confined to be mere film actors with the apportioned budget. I personally feel there is nothing wrong in doing it. I believe as one of the first few guys who started enacting in them. I was told by some friends including Anil Kapoor who said, 'Don't do this, man! It is wrong! Don't, you know?'

Karan Johar: Anil Kapoor?

Shahrukh Khan: Yeah! We sell our films. We sell our stories. We sell our dreams. So, if people want us to be attached to their products, it is absolutely all right and fine.

Karan Johar: Your take on this, Sir?

Amitabh Bachchan: My need is more commercial. I started my company as an organization, which was quite unique, the primary investors who injected the core capital seldom had the conventional plant machinery formula to do so as this was sheer entertainment. For the first time, Jaya and I were introduced into the market.

Karan Johar: OK.

Amitabh Bachchan: They put a price tag on us so that the dividend returns to the corpus. The investor often said that there was no plant nor machinery nor real estate to bank upon. How would they get their money back? They told us to perform and earn money from the company. And that is how your investment would come back to you. We were bound to sign the contract that every proceed would reach the company, whether it was TV endorsements, live events, voice over audio discs, etc. So, as a part of the vision of this company, one of the things was...

> **My need to endorse was a more commercial one. Every penny would reach our company.**
> *–Amitabh Bachchan*

Karan Johar: Endorsing.

Amitabh Bachchan: So, I had to do it. That and having done that multiple times, I think I would endorse what Shahrukh said. The times are changing. If a corporation believes an artist is glorifying their products, then why not? They have billions of rupees riding in these corporations. They must have gone through enough research to find whether the formula works out on hiring me or Shahrukh. We knew that such formula does wonders in any business. You work for something that is going to give you the best returns.

Karan Johar: Of course. The customer comes at the other end who buys the products who watches Amitabh Bachchan or Shahrukh Khan as their brand ambassadors.

SHAHRUKH ON AMITABH

Shahrukh Khan: Karan, I have grown up watching Mr. Bachchan and now, I have had the pleasure of meeting him personally and working with him. It is not just his acting that taught me that there are certain other things that Mr. Bachchan has coined.

Karan Johar: Yes.

Shahrukh Khan: It stands for integrity, honesty, and more fun. It stands for entertainment as well as mutual trust. I am not spelling the corporate thought or market research. Other than a young actor observing Mr. Bachchan as the great fun guy, I want to be like him and emulate his performance. He stands for that. I do not think anything is wrong if a product utilizes those qualities. They are not creating those qualities – they already exist. You don't need a big market research to ascertain where Mr Bachchan stands with the product beyond his stature or not. You should buy it and he serves as a wonderful medium. He finishes it in just 30 seconds even as an actor, which is a lot more to us.

Amitabh Bachchan: Thank you so much, Shahrukh.

Karan Johar: The film industry would not be an industry unless it offers kudos to Shahrukh and uncle Amitabh. Shahrukh! Is black your favourite colour?

Shahrukh Khan: Yes.

Karan Johar: You always wear black?

Shahrukh Khan: Always! Dare to wear black.

> **Mr. Bachchan stands for integrity, honesty, and more fun.**
> *–Shahrukh Khan*

Black Beauty

Karan Johar: OK. Black is black. It will remain so. Have you seen the film *Black*?

Shahrukh Khan: Yes, I have.

> The directorial touches in *Black* made me touch Amit-ji's feet. I cried!
> *–Shahrukh Khan*

Karan Johar: What do you think of it?

Shahrukh Khan: I think it is one of the finest movies I have seen in years. The technical aspect of the film has moved me. The directorial touches in the film made me touch Amit-ji's feet. I cried. It was just beautiful to see him enact in the film. Rani's performance was marvelous. Baby Shehnaaz was nice. Everything was beautiful about the film. Amit-ji was absolutely splendid. I really feel Amitji was very emotional about that film.

Karan Johar: I really believe so, too.

Shahrukh Khan: He was wonderful.

Karan Johar: Mr. Bachchan has a huge graph when it comes to his filmography. I think the film *Black* has taken him altogether to another level .Do you attribute a lot to the filmmaker?

Amitabh Bachchan: Entirely everything. It was Sanjay Leela Bansali's concept. The way he has crafted the story and presented the sequence and differentiated the costumes worn by the artistes besides their etiquettes – it was spelendid. A complete creation of his preoccupied mind.

Karan Johar: Yes, it was.

Amitabh Bachchan: But seriously, it pertains to one man's thought – his idea. You made *Kabhi Khushi Kabhi Gham*. You wanted to raise a massive structure, a big house for Yashvardhan.

Karan Johar: In the middle of nowhere! Yeah!

Amitabh Bachchan: Yes. You had everybody dressed up. That was your imagination. You should have the freedom to do so. Director Sanjay Leela Bansali imagined putting a set like this and wove the story around it accordingly.

Karan Johar: And told it beautifully.

> *Black* was a complete creation of Sanjay Leela Bhansali's preoccupied mind.
> *–Amitabh Bachchan*

Amitabh Bachchan: Whatever.

Shahrukh Khan: I think it is one of the finest movies to be made by a director in years.

Amitabh Bachchan: Really!

THE MAGICIAN–SANJAY LEELA BHANSALI

Karan Johar: We should ask him about his thoughts on *Black* and *Devdas*. So, let us call up on Sanjay Leela Bansali. We were telling very beautiful things about *Black*. How does it feel post *Black*, Sanjay?

> **I am a person who disbelieves in myself.**
> –*Sanjay Leela Bhansali*

Sanjay Leela Bhansali: It feels satisfying. A big question haunts me – what next? So, I think post *Black*, my mind is only working on a subconscious level. I am rather confused about doing something better. I do not know.

Karan Johar: All right. Shahrukh said that *Devdas* was his finest work. Mr. Bachchan has gone on record and said that *Black* had been the most satisfying performance. How do you perceive it? Two brilliant actors have held you in high esteem. They rate your film as the magnum opus.

Sanjay Leela Bhansali: I feel I am blessed when the two of you applaud me. I am a person who disbelieves in myself. If they reiterate so, then it is time to believe the statement.

Karan Johar: Otherwise?

Sanjay Leela Bhansali: I would not believe it.

Karan Johar: Shahrukh! Do you have something to tell Sanjay?

Shahrukh Khan: No. Why are you laughing, Sanjay? Sanjay does not believe me. We will write it to you; we will stand on either side of you and yell that it was you who extracted those performances from us. And Amit-ji, I have grown up watching his films. I really felt touched when I saw *his* debut in *Black*. *Devdas* for me remains one of the most satisfactory debuts. So you are quite cool, Sanjay.

Karan Johar: Believe it, Sanjay.

Amitabh Bachchan: I felt very challenged when I was performing.

Karan Johar: You had a repository of work. Was that the tremendous thing that challenged you?

Amitabh Bachchan: Yes. I thought about how a 63-year old was given so much importance in that script.

Karan Johar: Tell me about your experience, Sanjay, about working with both actors, Shahrukh and Mr. Bachchan. I mean,

> **Amitabh Bachchan and Shahrukh Khan will perish if you take acting out of their lives!**
> *– Sanjay Leela Bhansali*

they are from different schools of performance, and yet..

Sanjay Leela Bhansali: They are very similar and intelligent actors. They know their art and love their craft to death. They shall perish if you take acting out of their lives. They have a great sense of humour and are willing to stretch beyond limits. The scripts were very challenging, which worked out. I remember Shahrukh through the climax of *Devdas* resembling absolutely the personality of Devdas, walking like him, even in his day-to-day life. He had become haggard and weak. Amit-ji, I know during the climax gave a shot and told that you were killing me. He would give every bit of himself spontaneously. They are actors who disbelieve in too much discussion. Thank God! I hate discussions beyond a point – on the extent of enacting. It is just about feeling from inside which you have excelled.

Karan Johar: You have hidden something. This will be the right platform to express your feelings. What would you say?

Sanjay Leela Bhansali: I want to thank both the actors. I never rang them to express my heartfelt thanks. Amit-ji has brought me closer to God. Perhaps, God might have come to me through Amit-ji's character in *Black*. I am rather blessed to have worked with him. Thank you so much, Sir.

Amitabh Bachchan: That is very kind.

Sanjay Leela Bhansali: Shahrukh has done one of my most special films. *Devdas* was a tribute to a half consumed alcohol bottle that stayed in my mother's cupboard. It was a tribute to my father. Shahrukh gave a brilliant performance. His performance has brought me closer to him.

> ***Devdas* was a tribute to a half consumed alcohol bottle that stayed in my mother's cupboard – a tribute to my father.**
> *– Sanjay Leela Bhansali*

Shahrukh Khan: This is like closer to God!

Sanjay Leela Bhansali: I really want to thank them as they are special to me.

RAPID FIRE

Karan Johar: Let us have the rocking *Rapid Fire Round.* We have many more questions with more fire. Our hamper has changed – it is the grand finale! The jury for the *Rapid Fire Round* includes renowned directors – the very talented Farah Khan and the super talented. Farhan Akhtar. Welcome, Members of the Jury!

> Amit-ji has brought me closer to God with *Black.*
>
> – *Sanjay Leela Bhansali*

Amitabh Bachchan: I believe them to be respectable as judges.

Karan Johar: Welcome, esteemed jury!

Shahrukh Khan: Welcome, Farah and Farhan!

Karan Johar: Sanjay Leela Bhansali will join you as the third member. Let us know your sentiments.....

Sanjay Leela Bhansali: I should not have been here.

Karan Johar: And you, Farah?

Farah Khan: I want them enact in my next film. I shall be extremely tactful.

Karan Johar: That was nice. And Farhan?

Farah Khan: I also want them in my next film.

Karan Johar: So we have balanced jury. Let us start.

Amitabh Bachchan: May the best man win!

Shahrukh Khan: All the best!

Karan Johar: Amit-ji, Mallika loves the way you run onscreen. What do you love about her?

Amitabh Bachchan: The way she says I run onscreen.

Karan Johar: On a scale of 1-10, how do you rate yourself? (a) as an actor?

> I would rate myself 4/10 as an actor and 11/10 as a father.
>
> –*Amitabh Bachchan*

Amitabh Bachchan: 4

Karan Johar: (b) as a husband?

Amitabh Bachchan: 6

Karan Johar: (c) as a father?

Amitabh Bachchan: 11.

Karan Johar: Your response to the Hollywood highbrows who rate Bollywood movies as 'masala movies.'

Amitabh Bachchan: They will have to eat their words within five years.

> **I am not doing too many films. Pease sign me on!**
> *–Amitabh Bachchan*

Karan Johar: The die-hard fans who are disappointed to see their legend promoting hair oil.

Amitabh Bachchan: It is a very elitist remark.

Karan Johar: You are doing too many films.

Amitabh Bachchan: I am not. Please sign me on.

Karan Johar: One thing about Shahrukh you wish you had?

Amitabh Bachchan: The speed at which his brain works.

Karan Johar: OK!

Amitabh Bachchan: Shahrukh doesn't have my height...

Karan Johar: The most absurd astrological or psychic advice you come across?

Amitabh Bachchan: I should change my surname.

Karan Johar: What does a woman mean when she says – 'I have a headache.'

Amitabh Bachchan: 'I want to go to the hairdresser.'

> **I wish I had the speed at which Shahrukh's brain works!**
> *–Amitabh Bachchan*

Karan Johar: 'We need to talk.'

Amitabh Bachchan: She wants to make a pass.

Karan Johar: 'I am not upset.'

Amitabh Bachchan: You have had it!

Karan Johar: 'It is your decision.'

Amitabh Bachchan: It is not – it is going to be hers.

Karan Johar: The winners of the best under-dressed heroine?

Amitabh Bachchan: Mallika Sherawat.

Karan Johar: The worst hair in a film?

Amitabh Bachchan: Amitabh Bachchan in *Armaan*.

Karan Johar: The best running performance?

Amitabh Bachchan: Myself.

Karan Johar: Your take on the *male item* numbers.

> **The best under-dressed heroine today is Mallika Sherawat!**
> *–Amitabh Bachchan:*

Amitabh Bachchan: About time.

Karan Johar: Monthly award functions.

Amitabh Bachchan: Damn good for TRP's.

Karan Johar: So called Multiplex films.

Amitabh Bachchan: Thing of the future.

Karan Johar: Sting operations.

Amitabh Bachchan: Should be actually 'entrapment.'

> **I would give the title 'Anger Management' to my wife!!**
> *–Amitabh Bachchan*

Karan Johar: A colleague you would gift the title 'Time management – the easy way.'

Amitabh Bachchan: Govinda.

Karan Johar: 'Anger management.'

Amitabh Bachchan: To my wife.

Karan Johar: Paparazzi survival guide – 'How to keep your personal life private'.

Amitabh Bachchan: Sanjay Dutt.

Karan Johar: The giant book of jokes.

Amitabh Bachchan: To myself.

Karan Johar: The one film industry person whose call you always pick up is?

Amitabh Bachchan: Yash Chopra.

Karan Johar: What the world would have been surprised to read about in Jaya aunty's tell-all book about you?

Amitabh Bachchan: 'Hey! He is not such a bad guy!'

Karan Johar: What would you like to change in the Indian film fraternity today?

Amitabh Bachchan: Discipline.

Karan Johar: The best part of being a superstar?

Amitabh Bachchan: Wear the most outrageous clothes and they would say 'it's in!'

Karan Johar: What is the worst part about being a superstar?

Amitabh Bachchan: You know it's not going to last.

> **The best part about being a superstar is that you can wear the most outrageous clothes and they say 'it's in!'**
> *–Amitabh Bachchan*

Karan Johar: Your least favourite Shahrukh film.

Amitabh Bachchan: What was that film where there was a well and people were sitting around it and you come?

Shahrukh Khan: I think that was a Vivek Oberoi film.

Amitabh Bachchan: There was this huge set and a huge wall, kind of. And there were people sitting

around and you were coming down. You wore a hat in the film.

Shahrukh Khan: *English Babu Desi Mem.* Yeah!

Amitabh Bachchan: That's right. Sorry about that.

Karan Johar: A song that best describes you.

Amitabh Bachchan: 'Waqt Ne Kiya Kya Hasi Sitam' from *Kagaaz Ke Phool.*

Karan Johar: All right. If you were a woman, you would be exactly like?

Amitabh Bachchan: Waheeda Rehman.

Karan Johar: What would you like your epitaph to read?

Amitabh Bachchan: 'We realise that he's a good human being.'

Karan Johar: Very quickly then, choices... *Sholay or Black?*

Amitabh Bachchan: *Black.*

Karan Johar: *Main Hoon Na, Dil Chahta hai,* or *Khamoshi* – debut films of the 3 directors who are a part of our jury.

Amitabh Bachchan: *Dil Chahta Hai.* Farhan, please vote for me. Mine is 10.

Karan Johar: Rakhi or Waheeda Rehman?

Amitabh Bachchan: Waheeda Rehman.

Karan Johar: Critical acclaim awards or box office?

Amitabh Bachchan: Box office.

Karan Johar: Lara, Priyanka, Bipasha – who is sexy?

Amitabh Bachchan: Bipasha.

Karan Johar: Vinod Khanna or Shashi Kapoor?

Amitabh Bachchan: Shashi Kapoor.

Karan Johar: Rani in *Black* or Jaya aunty in *Koshish?*

Amitabh Bachchan: Jaya.

Karan Johar: That is the end of the rapid fire.

Amitabh Bachchan: Just making sure that I don't get thrown out or something.

Karan Johar: So judges, have you gone through that and have you made note?

Farhan Akhtar: Absolutely!

Karan Johar: Would you like to say 'well done' to Mr. Bachchan?

Farhan Akhtar: Very well done, actually.

Karan Johar: Shahrukh, are you ready?

Shahrukh Khan: Yes.

Karan Johar: A role of Mr. Bachchan's you wish you had played.

Shahrukh Khan: Don.

Karan Johar: The best choice for *Devdas* after you would have been?

Shahrukh Khan: Sanjay Leela Bansali; before me, too.

Karan Johar: All right, as *Devdas*?

Shahrhukh Khan: Dev Babu.

> **My response to Hollywood highbrows about our 'masala movies' – they are bhaji-pav themselves!**
> – *Shahrukh Khan*

Karan Johar: Your response to the following – Hollywood highbrows who call all Bollywood movies 'masala movies.'

Shahrukh Khan: I think they are bhaji-pav themselves.

Karan Johar: Film critics who say Shahrukh is a star who is learning to act.

Shahrukh Khan: These are the critics who have just learned to write.

Karan Johar: Well done. There was a speculation that you would join the Congress party?

Shahrukh Khan: No. I have already said that the only party I would go to would be dance or a disco party.

Karan Johar: Your take on male item numbers?

Shahrukh Khan: It is fantastic and high time.

Karan Johar: Monthly award ceremonies?

Shahrukh Khan: If I get them, very nice!

Karan Johar: If you don't?

Shahrukh Khan: They should be banned!

Karan Johar: All right!

Shahrukh Khan: Or they should call me to perform and pay me.

Karan Johar: So called multiplex films?

> It is high time for male item numbers and they are fantastic!
> –*Shahrukh Khan*

Shahrukh Khan: I think it is a better name than parallel cinema.

Karan Johar: Sting operations?

Shahrukh Khan: As long as I'm not in them.

Karan Johar: OK. Beauty is all around?

Shahrukh Khan: Absolutely.

Karan Johar: A fan inserted an ad recommending *Black* over mediocre films like *Main Hoon Naa*. As a responsible producer, how do you react?

> *Black* was beautiful, but *Main Hoon Na* has me!
> – *Shahrukh Khan*

Shahrukh Khan: I had inserted the ad myself that *Black* was beautiful, but *Main Hoon Na* has me.

Karan Johar: One thing about Amitabh Bachchan you wish you had.

Shahrukh Khan: Obviously, *Kaun Banega Crorepati*.

Karan Johar: Which trait of yours does Amitabh Bachchan not have?

Shahrukh Khan: A taller wife.

Karan Johar: All right.

Shahrukh Khan: I think that is just about it.

Karan Johar: The most absurd astrological or psychic advice you had?

Shahrukh Khan: Don't be associated with any films.

Karan Johar: A contemporary befitting Hollywood movies. *Last Action Hero*.

Shahrukh Khan: Mr. Jagdish Raj who always comes in last in action.

Karan Johar: *Get Shorty*.

Shahrukh Khan: Rani Mukherjee.

Karan Johar: Woman on the verge of a nervous break down.

Shahrukh Khan: My wife.

> The most absurd astrological or psychic advice I had – 'Don't be associated with any film!'
> –*Shahrukh Khan*

Karan Johar: All right. *Clueless.*

Shahrukh Khan: Karan! Your status as a talk show host!

Karan Johar: Who would be your winners – best performance in politics?

Shahrukh Khan: The voters.

Karan Johar: The most inspired film (Year 2004)?

Shahrukh Khan: *Black.*

> The most boring attempt of a mainstream actor in parallel cinema would be mine with *Paheli.*
> –*Shahrukh Khan*

Karan Johar: The most boring attempt of a mainstream actor in parallel cinema?

Shahrukh Khan: Mine with *Paheli.*

Karan Johar: If a film industry person calls, you pick up as?

Shahrukh Khan: Mahesh Bhatt.

Karan Johar: All right. He always calls. If Gauri decided to write a tell-all book about you, what do you think the world would be surprised to know about you?

Shahrukh Khan: She beats me every Friday!

Karan Johar: If *Dilwale Dulhaniya* were to be remade with a younger cast, whom who you cast?

Shahrukh Khan: I would have to wait to do so.

Karan Johar: The best part of being a superstar?

Shahrukh Khan: Is what Amit-ji said – I can keep wearing the same black suit again and again, and it looks like style!

Karan Johar: The worst part of being a star?

> My advice to Mr. Bachchan – 'I am your father, by relation!'
> –*Shahrukh Khan*

Shahrukh Khan: You cannot pick your nose in public.

Karan Johar: Your advice to Mr. Bachchan, but you failed to say it so far – how would you address it?

Shahrukh Khan: 'I am your father, by relation.'

Karan Johar: One product you would never endorse.

Shahrukh Khan: I would feel shy doing condom or brassiere ads. I would do that if the payback was good, though!

Karan Johar: Your sentiments on your son's favourite film *Koi Mil Gaya.*

Shahrukh Khan: He is pretty young. His interests will improve as he grows up.

> I would even do a condom or brassiere ads if the payback was good!
> –Shahrukh Khan

Karan Johar: What would you like your epitaph to read?

Shahrukh Khan: 'Finally, he is not moving or acting or overacting.'

Karan Johar: Very quickly. Shahid, Vivek, John – who has a better future?

Shahrukh Khan: Whoever does a film with me!

Karan Johar: *Kuch Kuch Hota Hain* or *Dilwale Dulhaniya Le Jayenge?*

Shahrukh Khan: *Dilwale Dulhaniya Le Jayenge.*

Karan Johar: *Main Hoon Na, Swadesh* or *Veera Zaara* – films of the Year 2004. Your favourite?

Shahrukh Khan: *Swadesh.*

Karan Johar: Aziz Mirja or Farah Khan?

Shahrukh Khan: Aziz Mirza.

Karan Johar: Rani or Kajol?

Shahrukh Khan: It is difficult. I like both the Bengali babes.

Karan Johar: Debut films again. *Khamoshi, Dil Chahta Hai,* or *Main Hoon Na?*

Shahrukh Khan: No. *Ab Tak Chhappan.*

Karan Johar: OK. *KBC* or *Koffee with Karan?*

Shahrukh Khan: I want the crores of rupees with coffee.

Karan Johar: All right. Well done. Both of you have performed tremendously well. We have an esteemed jury. I do not know whom to award the hamper to. Please brace yourselves. Farah Khan will stand up and announce the winner.

> The worst part of being a star is that you cannot pick your nose in public!
> –Shahrukh Khan

Farah Khan: After much deliberation and the heart wrenching decision we had to take, I think it is a tie.

Karan Johar: Oh! It's a tie!

Farah Khan: Yeah!

Amitabh Bachchan: You get the bottle; I get that hamper.

Karan Johar: Could you announce the winners?

Farah Khan: The winners are Mr. Amitabh Bachchan and Shahrukh Khan. You have not taken the name of any of their movies.

Shahrukh Khan: I did not take the name of anyone. I was safe.

> I would like my epitaph to read 'Finally, he is not moving or acting or overacting!'
> –*Shahrukh Khan*

Farah Khan: All right.

Shahrukh Khan: Farah! Why does it feel like I have seen you before?

Karan Johar: All right! Applause for the tie, which has happened for the third time! Thank you, jury. I am sure it was a difficult decision.

Farah Khan: Very.

Karan Johar: Thank you for being here, Sanjay. Thank you for being here, Farah. Thank you for being here, Farhan.

Farah Khan: Thank you.

Karan Johar: That was the rocking rapid fire round between the two legends, Amitabh Bachchan and Shahrukh Khan. Of course, we could not arrive at a consensus and nor could the jury. Both have won the round and will share the hamper.

KAJOL

Now, we have someone very special to Shahrukh and someone who has worked with Mr. Bachchan. What an equation! One of my pals and one of the best actresses who started the show with Shahrukh and me. So, the finale will welcome her. Welcome none other than Kajol!

> *Kajol: Karan!* You too look absolutely stunning!
> *Shahrukh Khan:* And stunned!

Kajol: Did you purposely do that?

Shahrukh Khan: No. We were standing for everyone!

Karan Johar: Welcome back!

Kajol: Thank you, Karan.

Karan Johar: How do you feel, Kajol? You look absolutely stunning. Let us compliment you.

Kajol: Karan! You too look absolutely stunning!

Shahrukh Khan: And stunned!

Amitabh Bachchan: I will not comment.

Karan Johar: Why? Don't you think she looks stunning?

Amitabh Bachchan: Yes, she is. Absolutely.

> Kajol was, as usual, very brilliant in *Kabhi Khushi Kabhi Gham.*
> —*Amitabh Bachchan*

Karan Johar: OK. You have worked with Kajol in *Kabhi Khushi Kabhi Gham.* That is the only work you have done with her on celluloid. What was your experience?

Amitabh Bachchan: Well. I have always admired her work. So it will not reflect any difference with Kajol in front of the camera. Obviously, she was as usual, very brilliant in *Kabhi Khushi Kabhi Gham.*

Kajol: And vice-versa.

Amitabh Bachchan: Thank you.

Karan Johar: And you have grown up watching Mr. Bachchan's films.

Kajol: Yes, I have. Totally.

Karan Johar: Do you remember the first moment you met him?

Kajol: Yes, it was on the first day of K3G's set. I had met him earlier as well. I have always respected him immensely on being a fantastic actor. I really admire him for being a great human being. Down here, you have the dignity and courage to face whatever you had and come out being yourself. I really admire that about you. I seriously think that was amazing.

Amitabh Bachchan: Thank you.

Kajol: No, a lot of people have a lot of personal courage.

Karan Johar: Of course, you admire lot of things about Shahrukh.

Kajol: That is right.

Karan Johar: Is there anything you would like to add?

Kajol: I love him to death. He is a sweetheart.

> I really admire Mr. Bachchan for being a great human being.
> —*Kajol*

Karan Johar: I am sure he loves you. He has the same sentiment. She is just coming back with many years into films.

Shahrukh Khan: Yeah!

Karan Johar: Shahrukh, now she has worked with Aamir. How do you feel?

Shahrukh Khan: Well, it is absolutely all right. We should experiment and try different kinds of films as actors. Aamir is a fantastic actor. Kunal is equally a wonderful director. I am sure we shall have some great cinema if these people get together. Do I wish her doing our film together? I have always maintained that one has a little sadness. I am not taking anything away from Rani and Priety for doing the film now, but I do wish she had done the film.

Kajol: I wish I would have.

Shahrukh Khan: Let us cancel that film. Kajol! Will you join this film?

Karan Johar: I remember calling Kajol when I was casting for the film. And Kajol refused for domestic reasons – of course, her daughter.

> I have always admired Kajol for placing your home and your child before anything commercial or professional.
>
> *–Amitabh Bachchan*

Amitabh Bachchan: I really admire this about you. I have always admired you for the quality of placing your home and your child before anything commercial or connected to the profession. I am very pleased; it is a daring act.

Kajol: Thank you.

Amitabh Bachchan: Somebody in your position could have dictated terms, but you choose not to. You always give priority to your child and your family.

Karan Johar: Ajay is a very lucky man!

Amitabh Bachchan: It is a very remarkable thing, indeed!

Karan Johar: You will be back in the movies. Have you taken a career decision to do lots of work? Or is it going to be spacing it out? What will be your move? Everybody wants to know whether you will act in films or return after long break.

Kajol: I do not really know. It will be testing ground for me. I have not weaned nor cut my umbilical cord from my baby. She has weaned herself off me, but not I from her. I am still in the testing stage. Let me see how it works out with this film. I do not want to leave my

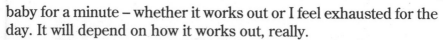

baby for a minute – whether it works out or I feel exhausted for the day. It will depend on how it works out, really.

Karan Johar: OK. We have spoken about the performance of Mr. Bachchan and others in *Black*. I remember the day you saw the premiere, you commented on Rani and Mr. Bachchan. Would you comment on Mr. Bachchan's performance in *Black*? You glorified me today....

Amitabh Bachchan: Are you scaring me?

Kajol: I lied. No, actually it should not be embarrassing. I thought you gave an amazing performance. I thought you did not have much to do. You still have time. You have still so much more to do. But with this role, you have done something fantastic.

Amitabh Bachchan: You have stated that very nicely now.

Karan Johar: Yes.

Kajol: I really thought you were fantastic. I seriously do remember telling so to Karan.

Karan Johar: Yes.

Kajol: I remember telling your son, Abhishek. I could not find proper term in my dictionary to justify it. And I was like, 'What fantastic acting!'

CONCLUSION

Karan Johar: All right. It was wonderful having you here on this segment. Any last words you want to say to Kajol, Shahrukh? We will not see her for a while.

Shahrukh Khan: The next movie will be shot in Juhu, Mumbai, outside Kajol's house, replete with a cradle for Nyasa!

Amitabh Bachchan: I will push Nyasa's cradle!

Amitabh Bachchan: Don't take forever!

Karan Johar: OK. Amit-uncle! You want to say something, Shahrukh?

Shahrukh Khan: Well, nothing really. The next script we have written will be shot in Mumbai at Juhu.

Amitabh Bachchan: In Juhu Parle scheme?

Kajol: Yes. Right outside my house.

Shahrukh Khan: Not only that, sweetheart! We shall have a cradle replete with your baby and Kajol, the character!

Kajol: Is not that sweet?

Shahrukh Khan: So you think that Baby Nyasa will accompany her?

Kajol: Thank you.

Amitabh Bachchan: I will push the cradle.

Shahrukh Khan: Will Amit-ji push the cradle?

Kajol: Amit-ji will push the cradle.

Amitabh Bachchan: Yes, I will!

Karan Johar: OK. Thank you for being here.

Kajol: My pleasure.

Karan Johar: That was Kajol, Shahrukh, and Mr. Amitabh Bachchan all together. Star (channel) will make all its money!

● ● ●

Best of Indian Classics

Rabindranath inherited great mind from his father, Maharshi Devendranath Thakur, a religious reformer who expounded Brahmo Samaj (the Society of Lord Brahma). Rabindranath returned from England without completing studies and started writing poems very early. He captured the rhythm of life from the melody of rain drops, which he composed, developed and researched later. In 1890 his first collection of poems was published, as 'Manasi', which, today critics believe, contained symptoms of his intellectual maturity.

All his life he studied at home, and stopped going to school after seventh standard when he saw class-teachers mercilessly beating students for simple follies. He was naturally learnt. He studied Hindu Scriptures, sciences, and world literatures avidly all his life, but did not take standard university examinations. Despite that, he was the examiner of Calcutta University Bengali Literature answer-scripts, honoured with many honorary doctorates and D Litts., followed by scholars world over in literature and musicology.

He won India's first Nobel Prize in 1913 for 'Gitanjali, Song Offerings', and with the prize money created 'Santiniketan' in Birbhum district of today's West Bengal. Santiniketan translated his vision of education, humanity, rural economy, civil society and research, to disseminate the concept of Visva Bharati, which later became a Central University.

He wrote in all 2,500 lyrics, composed into mellifluous songs which by his nephew Dinendranath Tagore and his first-line disciples, which created a new and universally popular genre in Indian musicology, known as 'Rabindrasangeet'.

Rabindranath Tagore

- Gitanjali
- Gora
- Yogayog
- Aankh Ki Kirkari
- Inside Outside
- Boat Accident
- Choker Bali
- Bau Thakuranir Haat

Diamond Books
X-30, Okhla Industrial Area, Phase-II, New Delhi-110020
Ph.: 41611861, Fax: 41611866, E-mail: sales@dpb.in, Website: www.dpb.in